CROMWELLIAN FOREIGN POLICY

Cromwellian Foreign Policy

Timothy Venning

St. Martin's Press

First published in Great Britain 1995 by
MACMILLAN PRESS LTD
Houndmills, Basingstoke, Hampshire RG21 2XS
and London
Companies and representatives
throughout the world

A catalogue record for this book is available
from the British Library.

ISBN 0–333–63388–1

10	9	8	7	6	5	4	3	2	1
04	03	02	01	00	99	98	97	96	95

Printed and bound in Great Britain by
Antony Rowe Ltd
Chippenham, Wiltshire

First published in the United States of America 1995 by
Scholarly and Reference Division,
ST. MARTIN'S PRESS, INC.,
175 Fifth Avenue,
New York, N.Y. 10010

ISBN 0–312–12499–6

Library of Congress Cataloging-in-Publication Data
Venning, Timothy.
Cromwellian foreign policy / Timothy Venning.
p. cm.
Includes bibliographical references and index.
ISBN 0–312–12499–6
1. Great Britain—Foreign relations—1649–1660. 2. Cromwell,
Oliver, 1599–1658. I. Title.
DA425.V46 1995
327.41—dc20
                                    94–34686
                                        CIP

To my mother

Contents

	Inadequacies of the Expedition	81
	Aftermath of the Design	83
6	**Leda's Mission and the Vaudois Massacre**	**91**
7	**Spain's Breach of Relations with England**	**102**
	Spain's Limited Reaction	104
	The Declaration of War	108
	The French Treaty and its Implications	110
8	**1656 – England Delays an Offensive Alliance with France**	**113**
	First Moves towards Negotiations	113
	Spain's Response: Alliance with Charles II	115
	Lockhart and Lionne	116
	Naval Strategy: A Question of Priorities	118
	The Dispute with Portugal	122
9	**The French Alliance of March 1657**	**125**
	The Preliminaries of the Alliance	125
	The French Treaty and Lockhart's Apologia	130
	The Imperial Election: Plans to Defeat the Habsburg Candidature	133
10	**England, France and Dunkirk, 1657–8**	**137**
	The Removal of Potential Distractions	138
	The Dispute over Mardyke: Anglo-French Mistrust	141
	The Royalist Invasion Threat	143
	The English Offensive	145
	The English in Dunkirk	148
	The Flanders Dilemma	151
11	**Cromwell and the Dutch, 1653–4**	**153**
	The Vermuyden Plan	159
	The Approach to Settlement, Winter 1653–4	161
	The Dutch Treaty	166
	The Crisis over the 'Exclusion Article'	168
12	**The Uneasy Peace: England and the Dutch, 1654–8**	**172**
	Anglo-Dutch Relations, 1654–5	172
	Avoiding the Brink: Veiled Hostility and Sources of Conflict, 1656–7	176

Foreword

This book arose out of my PhD thesis on Cromwell's relations with France and Spain in the period 1653–8, which was prepared under a three-year University of London Postgraduate Studentship at King's College London, and was examined in 1992. The work entailed the detailed examination of the Public Record Office Treaty Papers and diplomatic transcripts, particularly the correspondence between Cardinal Mazarin and his agents in London, extracts from the State Papers Domestic, and the Council of State Order and Committee Books. Other material studied included the correspondence between Condé and his agents in London and other letters (mainly colonial, such as Thomas Povey's papers) at the British Library, records and correspondence preserved at the Bodleian Library, and the letters and agents' reports contained in the vast seven-volume *Thurloe State Papers* published by Thomas Birch in 1742.

My investigation into the work of the Council of State entailed study of the Councillors' dealings with other nations, particularly the Dutch, and, when it was decided to expand my thesis into a full-scale study of Cromwellian diplomacy, extra documents were used from among the Public Record Office diplomatic and colonial records including the invaluable Court and Letter Books of the Levant Company. A full list is included below. Secondary material used has concentrated throughout on the published *Calendar of State Papers Venetian*, containing the reports of the Venetian ambassadors throughout Europe under the Protectorate. This gives a useful picture of how Cromwell was seen by informed observers from one of the most practised group of diplomats in Europe, as well as providing details of current informed – and uninformed – rumour about how Europeans saw this new and menacing figure who had appeared in the diplomatic landscape. A valuable chronological guide to Cromwell's diplomacy was provided by W.C. Abbott's magisterial collection of the *Letters and Speeches of Oliver Cromwell*, which served as an initial framework for the unravelling of events.

This subject would require many years' study of the diplomatic sources on Dutch and Swedish policy towards the Protectorate if these countries were to be treated at the same length as my PhD grant and subsequent work enabled me to deal with Franco-Spanish policy. The Thurloe Papers, however, give a good idea of the English side of affairs, and it is hoped that subsequently my work on the lesser areas of Cromwellian foreign policy can be extended. As it is, the Protector's approach to France and Spain was the most crucial aspect of his diplomacy, on which the regime's survival could depend. The dearth of work on this neglected area of the Protectorate's policies means that any study that deals with the mechanism of policy, and attempts to tie in Cromwell's approach to the different problems which faced him from different states, is breaking new ground. It is to be hoped that this book will serve to give a coherent overall picture of Cromwellian problems and strategy and present new areas for research in years to come.

TIMOTHY VENNING

Preface

Addressing his Council of State during a debate on foreign policy in July 1654, Oliver Cromwell reminded them that 'God has not brought us hither . . . but to consider the work that we do in the world'. Such a statement might seem odd today, and even at the time Royalist propaganda and cynical foreign observers sought to believe that Cromwell was either a hypocrite or a hard-nosed realist masking 'reason of state' behind religious motives. However, there is no reason to doubt that Cromwell was perfectly sincere in trying to seek a Divine purpose to events and to follow whichever path God seemed to be pointing out. Periods of inaction or indecision were followed by zealous, almost manic action throughout his adult career, the latter being justified as fulfilling God's purpose. The crises of the King's execution, the expulsion of the Rump, and the outbreak of war with Spain are three of the most outstanding examples of this – each marked by militant, bombastic language. Cromwell's enemies had to be denounced for moral iniquity, be they the 'Man of Blood' Charles Stuart, the leaders of the Rump or the persecuting Spaniards.

All this has helped to present a picture of Cromwell as a naïve novice in the world of foreign relations, who sought to impose the certainties of his 'Puritan' background and a worldview coloured by the 'Black Legend' of Spanish cruelty on the complexities of European affairs. Indeed, Cromwell's foreign policy is rarely dealt with in biographical studies or works on the political upheavals of the 1640s and 1650s, except as a side issue or an afterthought. There is a large gap in contemporary studies between work by Simon Adams and Kevin Sharpe on policy before 1640 and by Jeremy Black on policy after 1660. Such work as we have on the 1650s has tended to concentrate on the minutiae of Anglo-French policy from 1651 and avoid a wider view. It is my contention that Cromwellian foreign policy has to be seen in its entirety to be properly understood, and that it was both less naïve and more remarkable in its successes than is usually assumed. The Protectorate, after all, was a widely unpopular and grossly overworked regime, hampered by its lack of personnel or support, large and expensive armed forces, and a potential for ideologically based subversion virtually unique among British governments (except Elizabeth I's) before 1793. In a sense, as we shall see, misapprehensions about Cromwell's foreign policy owed much to the lack of parallels by which to judge it before the days of the 'Cold War'. This is not to deny Cromwell's failings as a statesman, or to ignore the opportunities offered to him by the preoccupation with each other of his two great potential rivals, France and Spain. But much was achieved despite lack of experience, time or resources, an achievement owing a good deal to Secretary John Thurloe. It was not luck alone which made the 1650s seem a rare moment of national pride to many observers at the time of the disasters of 1667, when the Dutch towed Charles II's flagship down the Medway.

My thanks are principally due to my parents, Mrs Megan Venning and the late Dr Bryan Venning, for their unfailing help and encouragement over the years. Dr Janina Giejgo, without whose efficient typing the work would have taken many more months, is also thanked for her advice and encouragement. I have also received much useful information on Cromwell over the years from Professor Henry Roseveare of King's College London, formerly my PhD supervisor, and I would like to thank Professor Austin Woolrych and Dr Barry Coward for advice on specific points.

TIMOTHY VENNING

List of Abbreviations

Add.	Additional (Manuscripts)
BL	British Library
CSP Col.	*Calendar of State Papers Colonial 1574–1660*
CSP Clar.	*Calendar of Clarendon State Papers*
CSPD	*Calendar of State Papers Domestic*
CSPV	*Calendar of State Papers Venetian*
DNB	*Dictionary of National Biography*
EHR	*English Historical Review*
HMC	*Historical Manuscripts Commission*
Thurloe	*State Papers of John Thurloe*
TRHS	*Transactions of the Royal Historical Society*

1 Cromwell's Foreign Policy: The Historical Assessment

THE HISTORICAL CONTEXT

Any analysis of seventeenth-century foreign policy must bear in mind its relative importance to the national leadership. The concept of international relations was not highly developed (at least outside Italy), and the English government had only sporadic interest in European power-politics before 1689. Intense diplomatic activity under Elizabeth, when the survival of the regime was at stake, can be contrasted with a more leisurely approach by Charles I after 1628. In any case, the permanent personnel of government was small compared to later centuries and concentrated on those issues which were most important, such as taxation and security. Foreign rulers were only of sustained interest when they were seen as of particular importance to England, as was usually the case with neighbours such as Scotland (until 1603) and France. Foreign policy was pursued at the personal initiative of the monarch, assisted by interested ministers.

Ambitious monarchs had always been interested in showing their importance to their European colleagues, in which diplomatic embassies played an important part for reasons of prestige as much as 'power-politics'. The ideological element to foreign policy only became apparent when the Reformation split Europe into opposing camps and England became involved in their disputes, adding to the contest between Habsburg and Bourbon for dominance in Western Europe. In the 1580s Spanish Habsburg and Counter-Reformationary ambitions coincided, and the threat of religious subversion within England temporarily coincided with political conspiracy. For the first time Protestant England and a major power appeared as ideological enemies, and ministers such as Francis Walsingham could see national survival and obtaining Protestant support on the Continent as linked. The crisis also passed into national folklore, 'Spanish cruelty' being linked in public propaganda with a threat to national survival to heighten xenophobia.

The threat of invasion lapsed, as did the dynastic dilemma, with the accession of James I. Foreign relations only became a major national concern again in the 1620s when the Bohemian crisis seemed to herald a new Catholic offensive and was linked to the personal fate of James's daughter and son-in-law, Elizabeth and Frederick of the Palatinate. On this occasion agitation for European intervention was particularly acute in Parliament, reflecting popular feeling amongst the classes represented there. This could be manipulated by ambitious courtiers against the seeming predominance of the pro-Spanish faction, but was none the less genuine. James regarded attempts in Parliament to force his hand by unauthorised debate and agitation as an assault on the royal prerogative – the first interference in this matter of policy. It was thus the beginning of a conception of foreign policy outside (and even opposed to) that practised by the monarch and an unaccountable group of courtiers. As might be expected, calls in Parliament for a naval war against Spain owed much to nostalgia for the seeming ease – and cheapness – of such attacks under Elizabeth. The crucial point about this reliance on privateering, as with Cromwell's, is that it was a useful alternative to unpopular high taxation.

English involvement in the Thirty Years' War in 1625 was limited and unexpectedly unsuccessful. No notice was taken of calls for a naval war in the West Indies and England became embroiled with France as well as Spain. Buckingham and his successors failed to assist the French Huguenot revolt, which Cromwell later told their representatives he deplored. Peace was duly signed in 1629–30, and both cost and inclination kept Charles I out of European conflicts thereafter. No action was taken to join coalitions against the Habsburgs despite the supposed concern in Whitehall to regain the Palatinate, though such individuals as Sir Thomas Roe and John Dury argued for and built up their own international Protestant links. Men who felt strongly about resistance to international Catholic aggression as well as less scrupulous mercenaries fought as volunteers for the Dutch against the Spanish, among them Cromwell's future Councillor Philip Skippon. The Earl of Warwick, a nobleman who lacked influence among Charles's closest advisers, and some former MPs critical of the King carried on a private war against Spain in the Caribbean through the 'Providence Island Company'.[1] It should be remembered that this was not an 'opposition foreign policy' as such – expeditions and colonising by private initiative had been common since Elizabeth's time and did not imply criticism of the lack of state action.

Warwick, Pym and other opponents of Charles's policies rose to prominence among the Parliamentary leadership, and could be expected to take greater interest in the colonies than the King. Parliament duly set up its own 'Board for the Colonies' in 1644 as part of greater interventionism in many aspects of national life. The Parliamentary triumph provided practical reasons to regard foreign policy as a major concern, the outcome of events in 1642–9 alienating not only Royal partisans but many Parliamentarians. The affront to legality by expelling elected MPs at sword-point and executing the King was compounded in 1653 by Cromwell's removal of the rest of Parliament. The affronts to partisans of legitimate rule provided Cromwell with an all but impossible task in achieving reconciliation. He faced threats from Royalists, Presbyterians, 'Rump' partisans, affronted religious radicals and Levellers throughout his rule, acting singly or in cooperation. This meant that he had to rely heavily on accurate intelligence to an extent not seen since the days of Walsingham's anti-Catholic espionage network. The position of the 'Secretary' was enhanced in both cases.

The current state of Europe was of crucial importance, and the Franco-Spanish War of 1635–59 distracted the two great Catholic powers of Western Europe from aiding Charles II. If the 'Two Crowns' were embroiled with each other neither could risk attacking England, even with Charles resident on their territory (France 1651–4, the Spanish Netherlands 1656–8). Cromwell, unlike Charles I or Charles II, faced such immediate dangers that he could not afford to let the affairs of Europe look after themselves.

In 1660, the republican experiment collapsed and a modified version of the old order was restored, to popular relief, with King, Lords and Commons. Stringent security measures and a paranoid fear of Dissenters revealed the new government's fear of an uprising, but the few dedicated republican zealots at large were no serious military threat. The tendency to let matters drift was partly offset by agitation in Parliament against the proposed division of the United Provinces with Louis XIV in 1674, and ended only with the arrival in power of William of Orange. He was primarily concerned with using England in a coalition against French expansionism, and – like Cromwell – his personal position could be undermined by the state of affairs in Europe.

This said, it is clear that Cromwell's European policy differed from that of his predecessors as did his status. Previous monarchs had not had to rely on military force rather than legitimacy as their ultimate defence. The power of the Army in 1653 necessitated that Cromwell select many of his Councillors from its senior officers, the principal prop of his shaky regime, though in fact they were selected more on the basis of personal/ family relationships and compatibility than power in the Army (hence the exclusion of the powerful but overzealous General Harrison). Accordingly, these men could be expected to reflect the sense of Protestant mission apparent throughout the 'New Model' instead of being a group of personal advisers with diverse ideological standpoints like a sovereign's councillors. Moreover, Cromwell's own complex character possessed a sometimes confused sense of 'mission' that was bound to influence his conception of policy – as seen in his attempts to fit the Spanish War of 1655–8 into the pattern of current Catholic aggression in Europe. In his own words, when considering the 'Western Design': 'We think God has not brought us hither . . . but to consider the work that we do in the world as well as at home.'[2] It will be argued that Cromwell was more of a pragmatist than is sometimes believed, particularly with regard to Spain and the Baltic. He possessed deep-seated prejudices which frequently came out in his pronouncements. These led to a naïvety about such matters as the ease of Caribbean conquest, though lack of adequate information was also a factor. The evidence suggests that Lambert, the pragmatist responsible for the moderate tone of the 'Instrument of Government' after the radical failures of April–December 1653, was much more clear headed.[3]

In the words of Michael Roberts on Cromwell's Baltic policy, the key to a full understanding of the Protectorate's policies to its neighbours is 'not fanaticism but fear'.[4] The position of Cromwell – and the Rump – was similar to that of Elizabeth in that both feared revolt, in Cromwell's case by domestic malcontents, alienated by the nature of his regime, allied to exiled Royalists. Fear of a foreign power intervening centred on France, the Stuarts' closest ally. As Thurloe wrote in his 'Memorandum' of 1661/2, France had to be contained and neutralised – first by aiding her own rebels to weaken her (1651–4) and then by maintaining a friendly relationship to prevent the ultimate danger of a 'general peace' between her and Spain. Spain was less danger as an enemy because of its waning power.[5] The domestic situation in England therefore made the Franco-Spanish War the cornerstone of English policy. Everything else was subordinate to this, and it will be seen that it had an effect on Dutch and Baltic policy in making it essential for England to avoid facing a Dutch – Spanish alliance in 1656–8. Events in Europe were closely interlocked, meaning that Cromwell dared not assist his principal Protestant ally, Sweden, for fear of it leading to a Dutch conflict. Cromwell needed an alliance between Protestants in 1656–8 for strategic as well as ideological reasons, but Charles X's neighbours' fear of Sweden destroyed his efforts.

HISTORIANS' APPROACH TO CROMWELL'S FOREIGN POLICY

Both Protestant ideology and national security were factors in policy-making under the Protectorate, in contrast to the situation under Charles I and Charles II. The existence of Cromwell's own public statements on policy, in letters and in speeches to Parliament, provides extra difficulties in interpreting policy, affording evidence of his strong religious feelings. His obsession with the supposed international Catholic plot against Protestantism was particularly apparent, and thus the question arose as to whether this dominated decision-making. The fact that his principal enemy appeared to be Spain, the focus of the Black Legend myth, seemed to confirm it.

Diplomatic history has necessarily been subject to the opinions of its interpreters with regard to the objectives of policy. Indeed, interpretations of interstate relationships could be projected backwards through history, implying that what was currently a desirable outcome of policy must also have been so in earlier times. The main element of British policy in the

eighteenth and nineteenth centuries was the maintenance of
a 'Great Power' balance among its neighbours, supporting the
weaker against the strong. If it appeared that Cromwell had
not supported the weaker powers in Europe, it followed that
he did not know how to conduct diplomacy in the national
interest. After a glance at the strength of England's neighbours
in the mid-seventeenth century, it was apparent that Spain had
never recovered from the crisis of 1640 and France was ap-
proaching the apogee of dominance that she achieved under
Louis XIV. Hence Cromwell appeared to have chosen the wrong
ally and the wrong enemy. Historians who accepted the need
to keep the Low Countries (the 'Cockpit of Europe') out of
the hands of powers could point to Louis' later aggression and
provide 'evidence' that Cromwell had chosen the wrong ally,
as he had with England's commercial enemies, the Dutch. Thus
it seemed, at first glance, to confirm that Cromwell ignored
commercial considerations in favour of a religious view of the
world, which could appear as an anachronistic survival from
the Wars of Religion in an age of growing nationalism and
commercialism.

Criticism of Cromwell's apparently short-sighted view of
Europe owed a good deal to the advantages of hindsight, at
least with regard to France, which in the 1650s did not appear
to be the threat that it was twenty years later. The most notable
criticism of him on these grounds emerged when Louis XIV
was first becoming a serious threat, for example in Slingsby
Bethell's *The World's Mistake in Oliver Cromwell*.[6] The criticism
was often made by men who were committed radicals and
opposed to the Stuarts but with no love for the Protector who
had 'betrayed' them in the 1650s, and were not likely to be
rebutted by Stuart partisans (as would criticism of Charles II's
partiality for France). The Protector's regime had no obvious
defenders among the polemicists of the next generation. The
correct explanation of his French policy – that he had chosen
France as an ally precisely because she *was* dangerous, and then
only to keep her embroiled with Spain – remained hidden in
Thurloe's papers. Later generations were to point to Edmund
Ludlow's criticism of his former leader – that he had destroyed

the balance of the two crowns of Spain and France . . . and
a foundation was laid for the future greatness of France to

the unspeakable prejudice of all Europe in general and of this nation in particular, whose interest it had been to that time accounted to maintain that equality as near as might be.[7]

They forgot that ex-republicans like Ludlow probably hated him more than many Royalists. Cromwell's few contemporary defenders such as Marvell looked back nostalgically from the days of the Medway disaster to the man who 'made England great and his enemies tremble'.[8] Those who criticised him for ignoring a 'balance' forgot that his regime had other priorities.

A historian writing in the nineteenth century would have less insight about the threat of subversion in the 1650s than one after 1917.[9] Indeed, the whole argument that Cromwell based his attitude towards Spain on ideological hostility – and, conversely, his Dutch policy on natural affinity neglects important factors.[10] It was also easy to put the blame for 'outdated' policies on one man, ignoring the Council. The prominence of Cromwell in national affairs led to a belief that his was the only voice which mattered; he was a convenient scapegoat for the growth of French power or the betrayal of the 'Good Old Cause'. The critics ignored the fact that he could not afford to fight the Dutch in 1654, whereas Charles II did not have to consider a large group of exiles and subversives, expensive armed forces, or French invasion. As the special circumstances of Cromwell's situation when facing Royalists, financial burdens from the armed forces, and France were not repeated, men forgot that the Protector and his advisers had come to power as the leaders of a militantly Protestant army and for reasons of pragmatism as well as natural inclination had had to show hostility to Catholicism. The needs and desires of Cromwell and his advisers were alien to the experience or sympathies of the men who resumed power in 1660. It should be remembered that even Clarendon did not call the Spanish War outdated at the time, writing that 'England will heartily welcome a war against that bloody Popish people'.[11] Parliament's criticisms of the conflict centred on its effects on trade, caused by the rise in piracy and Dutch acquisitions of Spanish trade.[12] In the more secure atmosphere of the restored monarchy it was forgotten that Cromwell was bound to put the interests of financing his armed forces before the mercantile community.

The pursuit of dynastic diplomacy and a 'Great Power' balance was completely alien to the background of rebellion, conspiracy and ideology that underlay Cromwellian diplomacy. Indeed, a state in a parallel situation to the Commonwealth in 1649 – shunned as a nest of ideological regicides – did not emerge until 1793. It appeared, on inspection, that 'old-fashioned' diplomacy in the Middle Ages and the Wars of Religion had been superseded by 'progressive' ideas of national self-interest and commercial gain. Hence Cromwell's Protestant zeal against Spain appeared to be 'outdated'; Dutch merchants should have been England's enemies. This view was taken by the 'Whig' school of history, which tended to consider the worth of past national leaders through their devotion to Parliamentary government and saw everything in the light of its similarity to the ideal of contemporary government. Cromwell had been a military dictator who had more than once coerced Parliament by force. Thus Carlyle and his contemporaries spoke disapprovingly of the Protector's bigoted reaction to his regime's neighbours.[13] They were concerned primarily with Cromwell's career as General and Protector, and necessarily restricted their treatment of diplomacy to the more obvious manifestations of Cromwell's beliefs in his public utterances. Following in Carlyle's footsteps, 'general' historians such as Trevelyan and biographers (as late as Buchan in the 1930s) treated foreign policy as merely an afterthought to a study of Cromwell's military and political career. Thurloe's detailed memorandum of foreign policy, drawn up for his successors in ?1662, had been published as part of Thomas Birch's seven-volume collection of his papers,[14] but the mine of information in this immense work remained largely unsifted.

A reaction was bound to occur against taking all Cromwell's pronouncements as an adequate explanation of his diplomacy. Sufficient study would make it obvious that Cromwell had studied the potential of a Spanish alliance in Europe in 1651–4 when France was feared as a Royalist sanctuary. Similarly, Cromwell showed no enthusiasm for a French alliance until it seemed that France would sign a peace with Spain and free the troops of both sides to aid Charles II. It was also now apparent that Cromwell continued to mistrust both the French and the Dutch. These facts emerged in the major studies of the Civil War and Interregnum undertaken by S.R. Gardiner and of the end of the Protectorate by Firth (commencing where his predecessor had left off).[15] As Firth realised, Cromwell had had 'a constant care for the nation's economic and political interests'.[16] It was still apparent that Protestantism had played a part in Cromwell's thoughts, and religion and nationalism were still regarded as being incompatible aims. Hence, Gardiner believed that Cromwell sought to pursue two 'not always easily reconcilable' aims – the promotion of trade and of Protestantism – using his military power as a means of aggression. The second of these causes gave his aims nobility but led to his worst blunders.[17] Firth admitted that 'he pursued a thoroughly practical national policy, but that he constantly endeavoured to combine with the pursuit of national ends the common interests of Protestantism'.[18]

Some historians took the reaction in favour of Cromwell's pragmatism to extremes and sought to claim that his Protestant zealotry was only a smokescreen to obscure Machiavellian cunning. German historians could see Cromwell as a hard-headed nationalist statesman with certain apparent affinities to Bismarck. Thus at the height of the race for colonies Wolfgang Michael (1907) presented Cromwell as a master of *realpolitik* chiefly desiring the acquisition of more colonies in Spanish America.[19] Other historians were fascinated with Cromwell as the embodiment of military-based national power. Ranke wrote approvingly that his power 'at home was virtually unbounded and abroad was at once grandiose and awe-inspiring. A State power had been created such as the world had seldom witnessed.'[20]

The emergence of historical journals at the turn of the century led to the writing of brief articles on specific, limited aspects of policy. In these circumstances the picture of Cromwell's pragmatic attitude to Europe was reinforced with in-depth studies of the facts behind the rhetoric. Hence the first real studies of the 1655 rebellion and the Protector's attitude to France in 1656 were written by Firth[21] and S.A. Swaine wrote on the occupation of Dunkirk.[22] George L. Beer reassessed Cromwell's attitude to the United Provinces and maintained that 'economic opposition to the Dutch is the fundamental note of Cromwell's policy after the conclusion of the West Indian expedition'.[23] The work of Carlyle, Gardiner and Firth was followed up in the 1930s by W.C. Abbott in his massive four-volume collection of Cromwell's writings and speeches. He followed the prevalent view that the evidence of Cromwell's pragmatism must show that all his statements about the 'Protestant Cause' must be cynical: '[his professions] served merely to conceal, if they did conceal, the worldly motives behind these diplomatic professions'.[24]

Since the last war, historians have sought to elucidate the Protector's motives without the precondition of considering 'religion' and 'nationalism' as mutually exclusive. In particular it has been reaffirmed that Cromwell's beliefs were undoubtedly sincere. In the atmosphere of mistrust, subversion and ideological struggle that has prevailed in this century we can better appreciate the realities of his situation, Christopher Hill's study of *God's Englishman*[25] assisted recognition of the importance of the ideological element in Cromwell's thought and actions. Admittedly it is not sufficient to consider parallels with modern politics; the pitfalls have been shown by misinterpretations of the Levellers. However, we can understand the fears and defensiveness of the Commonwealth better now than was the case before the 'Cold War'.

In this context, Cromwell's pragmatism and ideological beliefs have been studied with a recognition of their interdependence. Robert Paul (1955) reasserted the sincerity of his Protestant convictions in his dealings with the Dutch and Sweden.[26] Other historians have sought to elucidate Cromwell's dealings by a psychological study of his character, which shows that he considered himself a deeply religious man with a sense of mission. If anything he was inclined to be alternately overoptimistic and hesitant rather than severely practical. His limitations are apparent in Hugh Trevor-Roper's account of his dealings with Parliament and his lack of responsibility for the triumph of moderation at the end of 1653.[27] Roger Crabtree argues convincingly that Cromwell's natural desire was often to delay a decision on important matters for as long as possible, and then, when events had pushed him to make a choice, claim that he had been divinely guided.[28] Thus he hesitated over what to do with the King in 1648 and with the Rump in 1653, following this with an outburst of self-righteous zeal. In this manner he delayed a choice between Spain and France for as long as possible.[29]

The complementary nature of practical and religious goals

has been shown in Lamont's work on the nature of the 'Godly Rule' in which Cromwell and his associates professed to believe.[30] In terms of foreign policy, this meant that the defence of the 'godly' nation and its citizens was as morally correct as international Protestant solidarity. Hence Cromwell showed concern for the rights of his citizens abroad, as with his letters to the French and Spanish authorities over outstanding debts and his concern that the Dutch admit responsibility for the Amboyna massacre thirty years after the event. The fact that both France and Spain needed his support against each other enabled a firmer line to be taken over such matters in the 1650s than had previously been the case, irrespective of Cromwell's sense of duty.

The most recent study of the Protector's policy towards France and Spain is Charles Korr's *New Model Foreign Policy*.[31] This concentrates on the minutiae of negotiations, while emphasising the lack of security which led Cromwell to bolster his weak internal position by war and diplomacy. He stresses the similarity between the positions of Cromwell and Mazarin, two 'outsiders' to government. Cromwell 'sought to retain his freedom of action and keep the broadest range of options open to him'.[32] However, not enough is made of the importance of Thurloe or of individual Councillors in decision-making. Indecision over whether to ally with France or Spain was at least partly the result of a split in the Council. Nor, despite the title, is the opportunity taken to assess what was 'New' or 'Model' about foreign policy in 1653–8. Cromwell reacted pragmatically to outside events and was primarily concerned with security, but this was normal practice. Charles I's apparent lack of a policy in the 1630s was primarily due to the lack of a threat to national security, as was Charles II's in the early 1660s. The new element was the difficult domestic situation of the regime without the usual sanction of legitimate monarchical rule. No previous government had depended so much on ultimate military force or had had to pay and occupy such large armed forces.

Cromwell's foreign policy might be more accurately described as the '*New Model's Foreign Policy*'. The armed forces had an implicit veto over such matters as kingship, and Cromwell owed his pre-eminence to being Commander-in-Chief. Officers also sat on the Council of State – though selected as Cromwell's trusted friends rather than *per se* as Army figures. Harrison, an important radical with his own following, had no Council seat or influence after December 1653. Monck, commander in Scotland, did not have a Council seat (probably because he was too busy elsewhere), and the Protector could appoint men such as Fiennes and Wolseley despite military complaints. The need to occupy and finance the armed forces was a crucial reason for the 'Western Design', as is apparent from the Council discussions. They were a constant factor in the formulation of policy in the Protectorate as well as creating some of its most durable problems, among them that civilian alienation which caused much of the trouble with Parliament and provided recruits for Royalist networks. Ultimately, it was their leaders who overthrew the Protectorate once Cromwell was replaced by his son Richard, a man lacking his personal prestige with the armed forces. The New Model thus achieved the final fragmentation of the forces supporting the Commonwealth in 1659 and the Restoration in 1660 – the ultimate defeat for the aims of Cromwell's foreign policy.

2 The Decision-making Process: Council, Secretary and Ambassadors

Before considering Cromwell's policy towards the 'Two Crowns' in detail, it is necessary to investigate the questions as to who made policy decisions and in what manner. English policy had been decided ultimately by the monarch until the triumph of the Parliamentary cause when, after an interval of 'collegiate rule' in 1647–53, Cromwell emerged as the sole dominant figure. His role as head of the Army – the sole remaining 'pressure group' with real power in 1653 – was extended to that of a 'constitutional monarch' by the 'Instrument of Government', though he relied in the last resort upon military force instead of sanctions of law and tradition. However, the constitution as well as prudence required him to take the advice of his Councillors, a body of men from whom the events of 1642–53 excluded most of those accustomed to advise the monarch. The ideological links binding the victorious party in the Civil War meant that at least some of the Council could be expected to have a common religio-political outlook on foreign affairs. Above all, the Head of State himself had emerged from the provincial gentry – an unprecedented occurrence, from which arose his idiosyncratic outlook on foreign affairs. It is clear that the Protector saw his role in a different light from that of the Stuarts. His background and upbringing helps to explain how he saw Spain and Sweden in the light of their international role in the 1620s – in his rhetoric if not in the hard choices of policy. The heightened security problems also meant that there was an enhanced position for the Secretary to the Council, as coordinator of domestic and foreign intelligence.

A BREAK IN CONTINUITY OF PERSONNEL AND POLICIES?

It would be inaccurate to claim that the Civil War saw the usurpation of power by men with an ideological rather than a practical approach to policy. The 'Protestant' approach to European affairs, centred on hostility to the Habsburgs and their allies, had been advocated without much effect by Sir Thomas Roe in the 1620s and 1630s. Noblemen, as well as advisers from the 'gentry', had favoured such an ideological approach under Elizabeth – witness the Earls of Leicester and Huntingdon and the former's nephew, Sir Philip Sidney. The aristocratic courtiers of Charles I were divided into anti-French and anti-Spanish factions. The crucial change was not so much the exclusion of the nobility as the lack of an overriding authority between 1646 and 1660. Nobody possessed either the King's legal powers or the sanction given to him by tradition.

The general tenor of anti-Royalist propaganda has included criticism of the King's alleged willingness to ally with Catholic enemies of the nation. His frantic attempts to bring in an Irish army and his correspondence with hostile European Catholic rulers were notably exposed in the use made of his captured correspondence after Naseby.[1] Cromwell and many others frequently returned to the evils of Popery in their statements in private and in public. Quite apart from the way that Cromwell and his closest allies treated the Irish Catholics as barbarians as well as a genuine threat to national security, hostility to the European Catholic monarchies could be expected through their potential to aid exiled Royalists. The countries most likely to aid them professed the same religion as that which was the target of popular propaganda from the time of Foxe's *Book of Martyrs.*

From January 1649 to April 1653 the primary concern of the Commonwealth was to obtain foreign recognition, but this was not achieved by the time the Rump fell (most notably with France). Cromwell's only major criticism of foreign policy in these years concerned the Dutch War, and it will be seen that although his own policy from 1653 put more emphasis on good-will and Protestant unity it was scarcely more flexible. Similarly, the change in policy towards France and Spain in 1653 was minimal at first, though here Cromwell had had more to do with the formulation of policy in 1651–3. 'Radicalism' was less apparent in public letters and statements of policy under the Rump, though the only obvious example of a 'radical', Protestant threat to the European Catholic monarchies, namely Blake's words at Malaga in 1650,[2] preceded Cromwell's rule. In any case, Blake was expressing a personal preference not serious policy.

The expulsion of the Rump, however, meant the exclusion from power of Vane, Chaloner, Haselrig and other leading figures, for Cromwell's lifetime. The increased Protestant tone of official pronouncements after April 1653 was not backed by the inclusion in official circles of such zealous figures as Thomas Harrison once Cromwell had a full choice of advisers in December. At first, the Councils of State included such figures as well as the men Cromwell himself was to choose that winter; this can be put down to the fact that they were elected by the Army's Council of Officers.[3] Both types sat on the 'Committee for Foreign Affairs'.[4] Indeed, in instances such as the Dutch talks it will become apparent that Cromwell sought to use his lack of control over his colleagues to distance himself from their ideas. This coincided with the final burst of sectarian enthusiasm surrounding the meeting of the 'Assembly of Saints', and ended with its eclipse. Thurloe, a crucial figure in policy, had already become Secretary to the Council and in July took charge of intelligence, retaining both roles throughout the Protectorate.

The major shift in policy arose from the lack of employment or funding for the armed forces at the end of the Dutch War. Cromwell and his advisers had to deal with 160 ships, eighteen regiments of foot and twelve cavalry regiments,[5] a problem which had faced every regime since 1646. Cromwell was if anything in a better position to deal with them than his predecessors, the civilian regimes of 1646–53 having been viewed with mistrust by many officers. Cromwell may well have been more gullible over matters such as Spanish America than men such as Vane, but it should be remembered that Chaloner also had links to the anti-Spanish propagandist Thomas Gage.[6]

There was certainly a degree of continuity to naval policy. Blake was used to 'show the flag' in the Mediterranean by Vane's Navy Board as well as by Cromwell, and the Rump despatched a naval squadron to the Caribbean in the autumn of 1651 (chiefly to deal with Royalists in Barbados). There was continuity also in naval personnel, with the retention of Admiral Penn; at one point the employment of Warwick or Ayescue was considered.[7]

THE COUNCIL AND ITS COMMITTEES

The Council

After the dismissal of the elected Parliament, power rested with the sole remaining body possessing effective power – the Army under its General. The Army duly elected three successive Councils of State consisting of officers and civilians. Power was shared with the new Parliament until it proved irrevocably split and collapsed. The constitution was finally settled in the form of a limited 'monarchy' under the 'Instrument of Government', Great Britain's first written constitution. Cromwell held the historical title of 'Protector' and was in effect chief magistrate at the head of separate legislative and executive bodies – the Parliament and the Council of State. The latter assisted him during the intervals of the former; he was technically constrained to govern Great Britain 'with the advice of the Council' and to control the armed forces 'with the advice and consent' of a majority of them. As far as foreign policy went, he was to 'direct all things concerning the keeping and holding of a good correspondence with foreign kings, princes, and states – with the advice of all'. Questions of war and peace were subject to the 'consent of a majority'.[8]

Cromwell was technically bound to accept advice, but there were no sanctions for the Council to apply if he defied its wishes. In practice it was unlikely that he or they would be prepared to risk such a crisis when their main aim was survival. Tradition favoured the Head of State making his own decisions, and the Council consisted mostly of personal associates of the Protector rather than independent-minded men with strongly held views and their own separate power-bases. Harrison, the only other man with a sufficient body of followers in the Army, was now 'dropped', and none of the Rump leaders was included. In practice the Council did not hold a 'majority' view even on the crucial question of choosing between France and

Spain or delaying a choice for as long as possible. John Lambert led one faction which urged war against France, Sir Gilbert Pickering favoured was with Spain, and Thurloe favoured delay in making a choice. This reinforced Cromwell's own uncertainty. In any case, the Council's primary business was to govern England. Thus the job of dealing with foreign ambassadors would inevitably be delegated to small groups. The probability was that not all Councillors would manifest an equal interest in foreign affairs, and the importance of intelligence gave an advantage to the Secretary who received and sifted it and was thus in a position to give advice from a position of strength. Certain Councillors also had responsibilities outside the Council, for example Fleetwood as 'Lord Deputy' of Ireland (1645–6) and Lambert, Desborough and Skippon as Major-Generals (1655–6).

Opinion is divided on the question of the comparative power of Cromwell and the Councillors. The unprecedented position of the Council as a body with legally defined powers added to the confusion. Its position and power was not made clear in the contemporary *True State of the Case of the Commonwealth* in 1654,[9] and the secrecy in which it operated meant that it was not well known to the public. Cromwell, the only figure of national stature, was inevitably believed to be more powerful than his advisers – and even considered to be an autocrat. A distant relative of his, John Hobart, remarked in Parliament in late 1656:

> It makes me think of the Character given to the Cardinals who were to be of the Pope's Council; they sat in the Council to Assentari [flatter] not Assentiri [approve]. Some want heads, as Skippon, Rous, Pickering, the others want hearts, as that condemned coward Fiennes, Whitelock, Glynn, Wolseley & c., almost all want souls, so that the best quality you shall find in those who usually sit, is that they are the Single Person's confidants and dependants, perfectly awed by him and his 30 000 myrmidons.[10]

Typically, Hobart even got the membership wrong. Closer study of the Council's position and responsibilities reveals that, in the words of George Heath, Lambert's biographer 'great pains were taken to give the impression that the enormous powers of the executive rested solely in the Protector, but close analysis discloses that the Protector was an imposing front man for a powerful Council'.[11]

The most recent study, by Peter Gaunt in 1989,[12] confirms this opinion. Cromwell looked on himself as the 'parish constable' of the nation rather than as a monarch, keeping order and where necessary seeking and accepting advice. He told Parliament on 12 September 1654 that the Council were 'the trustees of the Commonwealth, in all intervals of Parliaments, who have as absolute a negative upon the supreme officer' as did the House.[13] However, this does not alter the argument that because the Council was largely concerned with internal matters their interest in foreign affairs was limited – Thurloe had special advantages as an 'expert'. Foreign ambassadors dealt with the Secretary if they were not considered to be of great importance, for example the envoys of Brandenburg and Venice. Important talks were delegated to a small number of Councillors. Thus from 4/14 April 1654 Cardenas dealt with Lambert, Montague and Pickering, and the French ambassadors Bordeaux and de Baas with Cooper and Strickland.[14] The Swedish talks in 1656 were entrusted to Fiennes, Strickland, Pickering and 'outside expert' Whitelocke who was not on the Council.[15] Thurloe was not even on the Council until the 'reshuffle' of summer 1657, which indicates that this technical position was not the only qualification for influence.

The ultimate power of the Protector is made apparent by the way in which Cromwell launched the 'Western Design' in defiance of Lambert's warnings and no challenge to him emerged when it failed. This might not have been so if the prestigious Lambert had played a more active role. The threat die not materialise and the crisis over the revision of the 'Instrument' in July 1657 ended with Lambert retiring. Thereafter, Cromwell could afford to defy a majority of the Council over his expensive commitments in Flanders. Technically Parliament was granted a veto over appointments and dismissals of the twenty-one Councillors and joint control of proposed shortlists of new Councillors under the 'Humble Petition and Advice' in 1657.[16] However, its infrequent meetings diminished its real power. Aylmer believes that in this last phase of his rule Cromwell settled certain matters of policy with his 'Secretary of State and three or four intimates, some of whom were not even on the Council'.[17] However accurate these reports were, they were undoubtedly in circulation in London in 1658;[18] they seem to refer to two or three of Cromwell's intimate friends whose secret influence is testified to elsewhere without any specific mention of their views. The most obvious are William Pierrepoint, one of Cromwell's close friends who had refused to join the Council but was still influential,[19] and Major-General Goffe.[20] Other influential men who were not Councillors were Bulstrode Whitelocke, a Parliamentarian lawyer who had been Cromwell's trusted choice for ambassador to Sweden and was influential in policy towards that country in 1654–8, and Charles Howard, a junior member of a powerful family whose influence on foreign policy is unlikely to have been great. Parliament served as a sounding-board for Cromwell to make long set-piece speeches extolling his views, achievements and intentions in 1654, 1656 and 1658, but its only involvement appears to have been a committee set up to coordinate European Protestant affairs in 1657 – at the initiative of some Councillors sitting in the House, not back-benchers.[21]

The chief factor behind Cromwell's specific choice of advisers in December 1653 was the current political situation. The resignation of power to him by the moderate majority in the Barebone's Parliament disappointed and alienated one faction led by Harrison. These men, many of them extreme sectarians, joined the leaders of the Rump in political opposition. Accordingly, as Cromwell was seeking trusted and congenial advisers his new Council included three leading 'moderates' from the Parliament – Francis Rous, its 73-year-old Speaker, a veteran Presbyterian writer; the ambitious ex-Royalist Anthony Ashley Cooper (later 1st Earl of Shaftesbury); and 23-year-old Sir Charles Wolseley.[22] The three of them undoubtedly owed their position to their actions in the Parliament, although Rous was a figure of some reputation if not prominence as stepbrother to John Pym and a former member of the Westminster Assembly in 1643. The other Councillors appointed in December 1653 included the following: Cromwell's brother-in-law John Desborough, a senior officer of obscure Fenland origins; Cromwell's son-in-law Charles Fleetwood, a militantly Protestant young officer who was effective ruler of Ireland in 1652–6 and in 1652 had succeeded Henry Ireton as husband to Cromwell's daughter Bridget; the most prominent of the

younger generals, John Lambert; Cromwell's cousin and former
landlord Henry Lawrence; Cromwell's son Richard's father-
in-law Richard Major; Colonel Philip Jones, Steward of the
Protectoral Household; Lord Lisle (Philip Sidney, eldest son
of the Earl of Leicester); Sir Gilbert Pickering; Philip Skippon,
a veteran Parliamentarian officer; Sir Walter Strickland, former
ambassador to the United Provinces; Colonel William Sydenham;
and a young and unknown relative of Pickering's, Colonel
Edward Montague. The Protector duly added three more men
– Colonel Humphrey Mackworth, governor of Shrewsbury (7/
17 February 1654); Nathaniel Fiennes, son of his old colleague
Lord Saye and Sele, but himself most notorious for his surrender of Bristol to Prince Rupert in 1643 (27 April/6 May); and
Edmund Sheffield, Lord Mulgrave (30 June/10 July). Of these
men only Rous and possibly Mackworth were older than Cromwell, most were substantially younger – Wolseley and Montague
were under 30. Within a year the Council was reduced by the
deaths of Mackworth and Major and the resignation of Cooper.

The Protector probably selected four Councillors as trusted
relatives – Desborough, Fleetwood, Lawrence and Major. The
only later addition was to be his son and heir Richard. Lambert, his deputy in the Worcester campaign of 1651, was effectively his closest young protégé, and Wolseley was a personal
intimate with whom he was said to 'lay aside his greatness'.[23]
Army radicals complained that Wolseley had 'done naught for
the cause', though his writings indicate ideological sympathy.
Family influence probably affected the choice of others – the
unknown Montague was brother-in-law to Pickering, who was
himself related to Cromwell's old colleague Lord Saye and
Sele. Fiennes was Saye and Sele's son; Mulgrave was cousin to
Cromwell's former superior, 'Lord General' Thomas Fairfax,
though the wary relations between the two make it uncertain
if that was why he was chosen. Cromwell also used the unknown
Glamorganshire landowner Philip Jones, who had held military
rank and been Governor of Swansea (in 1647) but was more
important as the new Steward of the Protectoral Household.
Having risen from poor origins to become one of the leading
gentry in the county under the new dispensation, Jones was a
man of talent and ambition who was to be accused of using his
influence to build up his estates by dubiously legal methods.
He was to be one of the most active Councillors in matters of

trade, serving on committees and leading the talks for a commercial treaty with the Dutch.[24] Another close colleague of Cromwell's, who was involved with foreign policy, owed his position to earlier promotion and did not serve on the Council – namely his cousin Sir Oliver Fleming, a Hampshire squire and Master of Ceremonies since 1643, who had the official task of receiving ambassadors until the Council's appointment and continued to deal with some (particularly Paulucci) into 1654.[25]

Many of the men with senior political experience were alienated by the end of 1653. The Council did however include experienced diplomats, particularly Sir Walter Strickland, great-nephew to Sir Francis Walsingham. He had been the choice of Parliament to go to the United Provinces to protest at aid to Charles I in 1642 and to consider an alliance with them in 1650; two important and potentially difficult missions. It is also noticeable that the Council included a number of men who had spent time abroad; Lawrence and Fiennes had lived in the United Provinces, Rous had attended Leyden Universiy in 1597, Lord Lisle had travelled to Paris with his father's embassy in 1636, and General Skippon had served as a soldier against Spain in the Low Countries in the 1620s, including the crucial defence of Breda in 1625. Nor were the Councillors devoid of political experience, though none of them had been of first rank until 1653. Mention has already been made of the use which Cooper, Rous and Wolseley had been to the 'moderate' cause in 1653. Pickering, Skippon, Strickland, Rous, Sydenham, Fleetwood, Lisle and Jones had all sat in the Rump with Cromwell without achieving prominence. Skippon, who had commanded the infantry at Naseby in 1645, had been trusted by the authorities with the crucial 'political' appointments of commonder of the trained bands of London during Charles I's advance to Turnham Green in 1642 and military governor of the City in 1648 and 1650. Lisle, though undistinguished in his record, was trusted by Parliament with a one-year post as Lord Lieutenant of Ireland in a vote in January 1646, having previously served there as an officer under his father's Lord Lieutenancy in 1642. Disputes over the terms of his command and the size and nature of his force limited the time he spent in Ireland, but he was regarded as politically reliable if not a first-rate commander. None of the Council had suffered the fate of being 'purged' by the Army except Fiennes. Lisle, Pickering, Mulgrave and Skippon sat on the first Common-wealth Council of State (1649–50); Lisle, Pickering and Skippon on the second (1650–1); Fleetwood, Pickering and Skippon on the third (1651); Pickering, Fleetwood and Lisle on the fourth (1651–2); and Pickering and Strickland on the fifth (1652–3).[26]

Most Councillors were noted for their 'godliness', civilians as well as officers. Rous was a Presbyterian writer of consider-able importance and had sat on the Westminster Assembly in 1643 and the Committee for Propagating the Gospel. Colonel Sydenham, an undistinguished Dorset officer, had a brother, Thomas the physician, who belonged to this group, and pos-sessed strong religious views on the blasphemy of swearing oaths which caused him a crisis of conscience in 1657. Pickering was called by his enemies 'first a Presbyter, then an Independ-ent, afterwards an Anabaptist; a most fiery, furious, implacable man'.[27] Skippon was the author of a number of devotional works; Fiennes had 'improved his disinclination to the Church' in Switzerland; Lawrence was spoken of approvingly by Milton; Fleetwood, a Baptist, believed Cromwell should be 'Head and Protector' of all Protestants.[28]

Most of the Councillors came from a 'provincial' background, and between them they represented almost all England. It undoubtedly helped accurate assessments of the state of feeling in the country to have every area 'represented' on the Council. This is the obvious explanation why Cromwell appointed un-important nonentities like Colonel Mackworth. Thus Cromwell, Lawrence and Desborough 'represented' the Fenland; Skippon, Norfolk; Pickering, Montague and Fleetwood the East Midlands; Lisle, Kent; Major, Hampshire; Sydenham and Cooper, Dorset; Rous, Cornwall; Jones, South Wales; Mackworth, Shropshire; and Mulgrave, Strickland and Lambert, Yorkshire. Geograph-ical representation alone seems to explain Mackworth and Sydenham's choice. Moreover, most of the Council came from that body of Parliamentary gentry active in Parliament which had served the victorious cause in a civilian or military capa-city. Thurloe was the only exception, as the son of an Essex vicar; but he sought to raise his social status with a large new house at Wisbech in the Fens.[29] The fathers of Fleetwood (Sir Miles Fleetwood, Receiver of the Court of Wards) and Wolseley

(Sir Robert Wolseley, Clerk of Patents in Chancery) had served as government officials under Charles I.[30] The Council indeed included four representatives of the nobility. Lord Lisle, alias Philip Sidney (the poet's great-nephew), was the eldest son and heir of Robert Earl of Leicester (d. 1677), who had been entrusted with Charles I's younger children by Parliament. He was renowned for his bad temper and maintained aristocratic cultured tastes, possessing a collection of classical statuary.[31] Lord Mulgrave, a Yorkshire magnate who had refused to serve on the Council of State in 1649 but sat on the Rump, was grandson of a leading backer of the American plantations and married to the daughter of Lionel Cranfield.[32] Fiennes' father was a leader of the 'Providence Island Company' and founder of Sayebrook.[33] Montague came from a cadet branch of the Earls of Manchester.

The most prominent individual on the Council was John Lambert, of Malhamdale in Craven, a popular general twenty years younger than Cromwell, who had risen to prominence as the 'Major-General of the Northern Association' in 1647–8. He made his military reputation in the campaigns of 1650–1, fighting at Worcester and in Scotland. In 1653 he was reckoned the 'general man' and Cromwell's obvious deputy,[34] and in 1654 it was said of him that 'he is now remarkably the army's darling and the only person courted . . . it lies in his power to raise Cromwell higher [as King] or else set up in his place'.[35] The Royalists considered using him to remove Cromwell. Trevor-Roper and other scholars concur that in the period leading to the dismissal of the 1653 Parliament, Lambert not Cromwell appears to have taken the lead in discrediting the radicals,[36] and George Heath maintains that he showed 'great aptitude for political and constitutional leadership' in letting the radicals drive the Parliament into deadlock so he could replace it with a moderate constitution.[37] He was believed to be the main architect of the 'Instrument', and his pragmatic warnings of the follies of Cromwell's American plan were proved right by events. Cromwell was lucky in that Lambert, preoccupied as a Major-General, did not seek to challenge him after the fiasco on Hispaniola. Lambert's potential threat was immense, but he showed loyalty if not political acumen by standing aside from politics after his resignation in July 1657. He showed a heroic lack of realism when he re-emerged into politics in 1659–60, mounting an ill-judged rebellion against the Restoration.

Some commentators have also postulated a 'split' between civilian and military advisers on the Council – the officers were held to be 'radical' and the civilians 'moderate'. The revolt against Richard Cromwell was led by the radical Fleetwood, assisted by Desborough and Sydenham, and was aimed at Thurloe and Jones. The truth is more complex. The moderate, pro-Spanish faction was led by General Lambert; the leader of the anti-Spanish faction was the civilian Pickering. Any definition of a 'military' Councillor must also take into account the fact that many 'civilians' had held military rank during the Civil War, among them Lisle, Jones, Cooper, Major and Fiennes. Cooper had fought as a Royalist colonel in Dorset in 1643–4 before defecting to Parliament. His subsequent activities had included an attempted massacre at Abbotsbury halted by Colonel Sydenham. It is unknown if this incident soured the two men's relations on the Council. Military rank did not imply identification with a 'military' attitude to politics. The Protector's senior military associates had no close personal loyalty to Richard and thought that they had as much right to run affairs in 1659 as men who had not fought for the 'Cause'. The soldiers felt this just as acutely, as is shown by their passivity; the conflict did not however arise until there was a new Protector.

It is instructive to note the attitude of the restored King to the Councillors. Charles II concentrated on tracking down the regicides, who had been excluded from power in 1653, and feared doctrinaires, e.g. Ludlow and Algernon Sidney, and the generals who had led the Army in 1659–60. Hence Fleetwood was fined, Lambert was imprisoned for life, Desborough fled the country before returning in 1666 to be held briefly, and Sydenham and Pickering were excluded from office for life. Thurloe was the only civilian arrested but the Royalists had old grudges against him. Rous, Skippon and Mulgrave were already dead and Sydenham and Lawrence soon died, but the others went unmolested. Cooper and Montague went on to great prominence. Cromwell's advisers, the generals excepted, were mostly considered as less dangerous than the leaders of 1649–53. Even Lambert's harsh treatment resulted from his actions in 1659–60 when he tried to defy the King militarily. He was too dangerous to be let free in the uncertain conditions of the 1660s, though his continued detention when his health declined may indicate personal spite.

It is interesting to note the connections which the Council had with the American colonies. Cromwell himself had allegedly considered emigrating to America with Fiennes' father and Hugh Peter,[38] and from 1644 he sat on the 'Parliamentary Board for American Islands and Plantations'. The Parliamentary admiral, Warwick, patronised the raids of Captain Jackson on the Caribbean, whose success stimulated the Design. The Secretary of the Board was William Jessop, who became assistant secretary to the Council.[39] Desborough must have possessed an interest in the colonies as he was chosen to be the Protector's 'Governor' of the 'Somers Island company', which controlled Bermuda; his brother Samuel had lived in America in the 1630s. Cooper invested in Barbados. The future envoy to the United Provinces, George Downing, had emigrated to New England as a boy and was a cousin of the Winthrops, as was Cromwell's personal steward John Maidstone. Stephen Winthrop returned to England and served as an MP and adviser to the Commonwealth. Edmund Winslow, ex-governor of New Plymouth, was sent on the 'Western Design' as one of Cromwell's five commissioners.[40] Colonel Carter, one of Cromwell's trusted officers on the expedition, had been deputy-governor of Providence.

A number of Councillors also had links with the Protestant 'internationalists' resident in England, principally Hartlib and Haak. Rous had been chairman of the Parliamentary Committee on Universities and had offered to present a scheme based on Hartlib's 'Office of Address' to Parliament in 1648.[41] Hartlib had been resident in England since the 1620s. The veteran Protestant traveller and preacher John Dury had earlier taught at a school which he ran in Sussex.[42] The other Councillor with a marginal connection with his group was Sydenham, whose wife was sister to the wife of the philosopher John Sadler and whose brother Thomas was a member of Hartlib's circle.[43] Hartlib himself had been 'Agent for the Advancement of Learning' since June 1649, but his influence is apparent only on the occasion early in 1656 when Cromwell consulted him over who should be sent as extraordinary ambassador to the German Protestants. He approved of the use first of Ireland and later Jamaica as a refuge for foreign Protestants, but the most

that can be taken for certain is that Hartlib's network of cor-
respondents in Eastern Europe provided Cromwell with most
of his information about the sufferings of the Protestants there.
Hartlib probably instigated the mission of Dury and Pell to the
Swiss in 1543, an initiative reminiscent of Dury's earlier travels
which was independent of Council needs.

Committees and their Work

The Council discussed the major issues involving Spain and
France, but specific negotiations were delegated to groups of
two or three of them (see p. 00). Whitelocke aided three
Councillors in talks with the Swedes over a new commercial
treaty in 1656–7, and proved far more willing regarding accommodation on such matters as wartime contraband than
Strickland (or Thurloe). Thurloe also assisted Wolseley and
Jones over the Dutch 'Maritime Treaty'[44] and reported on
behalf of English negotiators to the Council.[45] This followed
the procedure of 1653 whereby the Council had delegated the
Dutch talks to a six-man group. The other less important
ambassadors had met Thurloe or 'Master of Ceremonies'
Fleming in 1653, and now met Thurloe or sometimes Cromwell
himself.[46] The Council also appointed committees to draw up
State letters to foreign powers. Thus one committee drew up
the letters which were sent out over the Vaudois Massacre, and
another assessed the letters received on the issue although
usually this was left to Thurloe.[47] The wording of instructions
to ambassadors was occasionally delegated to a committee,
though Thurloe sometimes drew them up alone.[48] Letters of
intelligence were addressed to Thurloe and replied to by him,
and in important circumstances such as the threatened abandonment of Mardyke in 1657 Cromwell might write direct.
The only Councillor to write state letters abroad was Lawrence,
its technical head, on the occasion of the official exchange of
letters with New England concerning recognition in January
1654.[49]

Most committees were *ad hoc* bodies set up to deal with one
particular matter, usually a petition from within Great Britain.
Certain long-term committees were set up on important matters, extending their membership to include trusted 'outsiders'.
Thus in 1655 such a body was established to coordinate the

sending of aid to dispossessed Protestants and take charge of a relief fund. The treasurers were the important City financiers Pack and Vyner, and the original members were joined by such men as Montague's father-in-law Crew, Whitelocke, Pierrepoint, St John and Colonel Purefroy.[50] Samuel Moreland, envoy to the Vaudois and the Swiss, was required to report to them on his return in 1657, and in 1658 their responsibilities were extended to include the Poles.[51] Another long-term committee was set up to deal with matters involving trade in July 1655, and included three Councillors (two were added later) and Martin Noell, Maurice Thompson, the ex-Rumper Chaloner, St John, Pack, Andrew Riccard of the Levant Company, Alderman Robert Tichborne, the Treasury Commissioners, and Captain Hatsell who had advised the Western Design.[52] In due course Chaloner was excluded, presumably because of his political opinions, and Richard Cromwell, interested Councillors and merchants from provincial ports were added.[53] Another Council of Trade superseded the original Committee and Whitelocke believed that Cromwell was 'earnestly set upon it'; it was, however, too large a body to be effective.[54]

The other long-term committees were all appointed to deal with matters arising from the supervisory role which the Government needed to take in colonial affairs. Links were limited with the colonies of New England that had always been fairly independent and were not subject to Royalist influence. Only Rhode Island was still dependent enough to proclaim Cromwell as Lord Protector, though he expressed his affinity for the 'godly' New Englanders in his letters to John Cotton.[55] However, in the weaker settlements to the North the territory had been granted to aristocratic proprietors and the Government continued its predecessors' supervisory role. In Acadia, Lord Delatour sought confirmation of his proprietory rights.[56] In Newfoundland, the Kirke family sought the payment of French debts arising out of their occupation of Quebec in 1629.[57] Governor David Kirke, a Royalist, had been arrested and recalled in 1652, and was accused of arresting Tregowrie, head of the Parliamentary commissioners sent to replace him.[58] Following a 1652 Council of State recommendation to abolish the proprietorship, the Council set up a committee to consider the abandonment of the colony[59] and duly approved patents for the new proprietors.[60] Notably, when the Spanish

War affected the fisheries on which Newfoundland relied it was not the Government which promoted a Parliamentary Bill (June 1657), but three Members with some influence in Whitehall – George Downing and the Devon MPs Hatsell (an adviser to the Western Design) and Fowell.[61]

Cromwell lent his support to the plans of New Englanders under Leverett and Sedgewick, in 1653–4, to take advantage of the Dutch War and overrun New Amsterdam.[62] When the Dutch War ended before their departure from New England, they attacked French Acadia instead and took three disputed forts; Cromwell refused to return their conquests as the French demanded. The Council had to deal with petitions for arrears of pay for the expedition for several years.[63]

The situation in the southern proprietory colonies involved the Council because the power struggles in Virginia and Maryland involved 'Royalist' and 'Parliamentary' factions, both of which appealed for recognition of their cause. Parliamentary Commissioners in Maryland had deposed the Royalist patentee, Lord Baltimore, and his governor William Stone, aided by the 'Puritan' faction ruling in Virginia led by Governor Bennett and William Claiborne. However, the Virginians were unpopular, Stone returned to office as candidate of the Baltimore faction, and the issue was finally decided in favour of Bennett's candidate Fuller after a pitched battle (1655). Both factions sought Cromwell's approval for their position in 1656. In January, Cromwell sent Baltimore's appeal to two of the Council of Trade; the matter then went on to the full Council. The 'Plantations Committee' and five Councillors considered Bennett and his ally Matthews' rival petitions, and the Protector's Council considered the matter on 16/26 December 1656. The conflicting petitions were sent on to the Plantations Committee which finally reached a compromise in November 1657.[64]

Less important matters concerning the American colonies were delegated to *ad hoc* committees. Thus on 29 December 1653 Cooper and Strickland were designated as a 'Virginia Committee' to receive the Protectorate's first letters from that state, an appeal to keep Governor Bennett, with Lambert and Wolseley soon joining them and Winslow acting as their specialist adviser.[65] A separate body dealt with the business of the Kirkes and Commissioner Tregowrie.[66] Others considered such matters as letters from Rhode Island, a petition against Governor Osborne of Montserrat for murder, and the improvement of the Barbados plantation.[67] In March 1655, a formal Plantations Committee was created to deal with most matters involving the American mainland.[68] Their duties were to include investigating the improvement of Acadia and Bennett and Claiborne's counterpetition against Baltimore. Separate committees continued to deal with some matters that might have been expected to come within their jurisdiction, for example, confirming the New England Charters and dealing with Bostonian claims against Dutch and Royalist pirates.[69] Virginian complaints that English farmers were growing tobacco in defiance of Acts of Parliament upholding their monopoly were dealt with by the full Council and passed on to the local authorities.[70] Bennett's regime in Virginia was approved in writing by Lawrence on 4 January 1654 on behalf of the full Council,[71] but by 1655 Cromwell had the responsibility for awarding approval to the internally appointed Governor Digges, pending the final settlement of the conflict between the factions.[72] The Council later formally approved him.[73]

The Caribbean colonies were small and isolated positions under alleged threat from Spain, regained by force by the Commonwealth's admiral Ayescue from Lord Willoughby of Parham, Royalist proprietor of Guiana. They remained an object of concern as both investors in England and settlers remained suspect, and Cromwell followed the practice of his predecessors in maintaining Desborough and Colonel Owen Rowe in control of the 'Somers Island Company' which ruled Bermuda. In 1657, the Protector annulled the company elections because of intrigues involving Royalists.[74] In 1658, the elected deputy governor, Sayle, was prevented from taking up his post while his Royalist sympathies were investigated.[75] The Council dealt with appeals from the Company's colonists against the alleged neglect of their masters.[76] The decision to mount the Western Design, an unprecedented example of Government interest, led to the creation of a mixed committee of civilians and officers to collect information and organise the expedition. They considered the state of the islands as well as the plan, despite evident lack of correct knowledge of such matters as the name of the governor of Antigua, 'Rennel' (Keynell).[77] The acquisition of Jamaica led to the superseding of this body by a 'Jamaica Committee' of nine Councillors in September 1655, to which a non-Councillor (Colonel Ingoldsby) was added.[78] They received letters from the commanders and considered all matters pertinent to this essentially military colony, such as arrears owing to the troops, sending out the men's wives, reinforcements, supplies, persuading other colonists to move there, and transporting Irish colonists and other 'delinquents'.[79]

A second committee was set up to supplement the work of this body on 15 July 1656 – the 'Committee for His Highness in Jamaica and the West Indies', variously known as the Americas or West Indies Committee and even in one record as the 'Jamaica' Committee. This consisted of civilians and officers, including Noell, Captains Limbery and Alderne, and Stephen Winthrop. Only in October 1657 did Thurloe and two other Councillors join.[80] They existed in conjunction with the other committee which was called in to advise them on their first day in office, and considered such matters as the transplantation of other islanders from that date and the general safety of the 'Somers Islands'.[81] The Government took greater interest in the security of all the Caribbean now that it was at war, and Colonel Jones held talks with the visiting Governor, Keynell, over granting him aid.[82] The committee seems to have been influenced by current calls for the establishment of an advisory body to supervise trade in the West Indies separate from the general Council of Trade, calls which had come before Charles I's Council as early as 1637.[83] The idea of a 'West Indies' Company never progressed further than an initial proposal by Noell and his associates[84] – an example of Cromwell missing an important opportunity. One of the prime movers of such plans was the merchant Thomas Povey who joined the committee in October 1657 and was seen within a year or two as its effective Chairman.[85] Povey continued putting forward ideas for greater investment in the Caribbean under the restored Rump, maintaining interests in many different aspects of Atlantic and African trade. His letter-book shows the extent of his varied interests,[86] though the Council's papers deal more with security aspects of the situation and the promotion of Jamaica by such means as sending out preachers and Bibles.[87] Noell and Povey together presented specific 'Overtures' to the government for a new Trade/Plantations Committee.[88]

THE SECRETARIES

Thurloe combined the roles of special adviser and receiver of all official intelligence, and thus had more influence than individual Councillors in matters involving national security. Until 1653 the posts of Secretary and chief of intelligence had been divided, Thurloe succeeding Gualter Frost in the first in May 1652 and Captain Bishop in the second in July 1653. Tharloe's position was strengthened by the dearth of experienced men in office after Cromwell's coup. There had been Secretaries since the time of Henry VIII, usually two concurrently, and the position had often been held by men with interest or experience in foreign affairs such as Burleigh, Walsingham, Dudley Carleton and Francis Cottington. After the Restoration the post was to become the office of the men who conducted diplomacy, in due course the Secretaries of State for 'North' and 'South'. However, Thurloe, unlike other Secretaries, was untrammelled by other long-established diplomats or courtiers. Even Walsingham's view of the ideological struggle between Protestant and Catholic was questioned by his sovereign. This was not now the case. The leaders of policy-making in 1649–53 were wholly excluded from power until 1659, and Thurloe was the sole 'expert' in a position of importance to advise the new ruler whose own views on foreign policy were bound to be influenced by his past career as Lord General. The members of Cromwell's Council were neither wholly inexperienced nor ciphers, but none of them except Strickland was trained as a diplomat though Skippon, Lisle, Fiennes and Lawrence had experience of the Continent.

Thurloe's work involved dealing with ambassadors abroad as well as unofficial agents, as the Council did not have the time. They did not have all the relevant facts at their disposal, and in numerous instances committees set up to draft letters, receive important envoys, negotiate on trade, or amend such public documents as the anti-Spanish 'Manifesto' has 'Mr Secretary to assist'.[89] The Secretary drafted the instructions to Penn and Venables, Pell, Lockhart, Morland, Rolt, Jephson, Prideaux and Bradshaw before they left on their missions, though the Council probably read through most of the documents. Significantly, foreign ambassadors reported that Council business ground to a standstill when Thurloe was ill, and without him and Cromwell matters remained undecided for the duration of their absence.[90] Thurloe was not even a Councillor until July 1657, yet his influence was such that after Cromwell's death he and Colonel Jones were seen by the angry officers as the real masters of the country.[91] He was the only 'civilian' the King considered dangerous enough to arrest in 1660. In defence of himself, he drew up his own account of foreign policy during 1653–9 which remains one of our most valuable sources for government policy. It bases its arguments on the perennial fear the English had of France and hence stresses the practical 'security' reasons for Cromwell's choice of enemy, rather than the ideological hatred of Spain which Cromwell expressed. Spain was a weak foe which was less likely to invade than France and the 'radical' opposition to Cromwell were unlikely to seek its aid. Therefore, it was essential to prevent Charles II from gaining French aid; England had nothing to fear from an alliance between him and Spain. The corollary of this fear of France was to keep it weak and divided, first by helping rebels and then by promoting its war with Spain which eventually necessitated accepting an alliance with Cardinal Mazarin.[92]

The tone of Thurloe's statement gives a different picture of diplomacy from his master's statements to Parliament, thus it has been suggested that their views of policy were different. It is true that Cromwell placed an emphasis upon idealistic reasoning which was absent in the dispassionate writings of his Secretary. However, Cromwell was not lacking in pragmatism, and showed no hostility to Spain in Europe until it proved unwilling to finance an alliance. It is too simple to claim that Thurloe the 'realist' restrained Cromwell the idealist. Thurloe's account of policy chooses to include only its strategic reasoning, but Cromwell was just as aware of these factors as his Secretary. Thurloe was writing to justify himself to a Royalist audience who were not interested in ideology or the needs of the Army. It was his business to present himself as favourably to them as possible; he therefore ignored the ideological aspect of policy towards the Dutch. This document is thus inadequate evidence for the existence of a dichotomy between Cromwell and the Secretary.

Other secretaries assisted Thurloe in dealing with Council business, but none had his prominence. Little is known of

Cromwell's personal secretary William Malyn, an Essex man and formerly a Drapers' Company apprentice – 'a truly faceless bureaucrat'[93] – or of Thurloe's deputies Henry Scobell and William Jessop. They do not appear to have had influence on policy, though Jessop had been secretary to the 'Providence Island Company' and the Parliamentary Board for Plantations and provided a personal link with the forerunners of Cromwell's American policy. The 'Latin Secretary' was John Milton of whom Count Bonde jeered: 'there was only one man in the Council capable of putting a few articles in Latin, and he a blind man'.[94] He was responsible for the tone of various state letters, such as those to the French and Dutch rulers on the Vaudois Massacre, and for the 'Manifesto' against Spain in 1655.[95] However, this does not indicate any influence on policy – rather that Cromwell, who used similar rhetoric in addressing Parliament in 1656 and 1658, found his tone congenial. Milton's international prestige coincided with his known expertise in the language of international diplomacy. There is no indication that he ever had practical influence, and he could not even secure the appointment of his protégé Andrew Marvell as his deputy. The man chosen was Philip Meadowe, a Cambridge M.A. recommended by Thurloe who went on to undertake diplomatic missions to Portugal and Sweden. Thurloe's other assistant was another Cambridge graduate, the mathematician Samuel Morland, who had acted as secretary to Whitelocke's embassy and was recommended to Thurloe on his return for his knowledge of Latin. Morland went on to serve Charles II as a hydraulicist after undertaking a mission to the Swiss and the Vaudois for Cromwell and publishing a partisan *History of the Evangelical Churches of the Valleys of Piedmont and . . . the Late Bloody Massacre.* Meadowe retired from active life until 1689.[96]

THE AMBASSADORS

Assessments of the hostile intentions emanating from the French and the Dutch were inevitably influenced by intelligence reports. In France in particular agents played a crucial role in assessing the likelihood of revolt during the years 1651–4 when Cromwell was considering keeping France divided by aiding attacks by Spain and Condé (see Chaper 3). Thus

Cromwell sent out agents to investigate the possibilities of subversion, most notably Colonel Sexby and Russell to Bordeaux in 1652 and Joachim Hane to the French coastal ports in 1653. English agents were supplemented by Huguenots resident in England who went back to their homeland to contact their coreligionists, most notably Jean-Baptiste Stouppe, and British residents abroad such as Colonel Bamfylde in Paris and Pawley in Madrid. Some of these latter had worked for the Royalists – Bamfylde had organised Prince James's escape in 1648 – and their goodwill had to be relied upon. The English agents sent to France often had a personal sense of commitment in support of the men whom they were to assess, for example, Colonel Sexby's support for the 'Ormée' republicans in Bordeaux. Foreign visitors to England reporting on the situation in France were usually Huguenots or Bordellais rebels, with an interest in persuading Cromwell of the safety which England could afford them – for instance, the succession of visitors from Bordeaux in 1652–3. The English agents in Paris were the Huguenot Augier and his nephew Petit (both inherited from the Royalists) who had an interest in denouncing the Cardinal. In the United Provinces, the agent Aitzema opposed de Witt and urged Cromwell to renew the war. All this 'biased' reporting by English agents undoubtedly influenced the view taken in London; Bordeaux claimed that Cromwell learned of the unlikelihood of a Huguenot revolt belatedly and with surprise. However, aid to the rebels was limited and Cromwell made no move until he had sent out spies such as Hane to judge the likelihood of success; he did not repeat Buckingham's mistakes. The sum total of Aitzema's reports did not lead to a new Dutch war.

Agents were in due course supplemented by formal embassies, though unofficial reports from Augier and Bamfylde continued to supplement Lockhart's ambassadorial ones in France. The ambassadors were required to act within the general guidelines laid down by Thurloe; thus Lockhart was to keep in touch with the Huguenots as well as the Court and in the Baltic Rolt and Jephson were to promote Protestant unity and help in mediation.[97] The amount of influence exercised over the actual talks varied, decreasing as the distance from England increased. Thus Lockhart wrote frequently to Thurloe on the state of talks with Mazarin, though precise replies to the Cardinal were left to him. He agreed to the terms of alliance in 1657 on his own initiative due to fear of pressure on Mazarin for peace with Spain. Cromwell was able to send a personal warning to the Cardinal when France was suspected of double-crossing her ally over Mardyke. Meadowe was negotiating at a further distance from England and the process of mediation at Roskilde (1658) was left to his own initiative, though Thurloe regularly corresponded with all the envoys in the Baltic and instructed or rerouted them as necessary.[98] The problem of distance also enabled Meadowe to choose to ignore the attempt to kill him in the interests of achieving a settlement when he visited Portugal (1656), though he was accused of ignoring an insult to national pride (see Chapter 8). William Prideaux's negotiations in Moscow were even less subject to control from London; once he had left there he wrote back to Thurloe without receiving further orders.[99]

The Stuarts had had a wide choice of personnel to head their embassies, and thus selected important noblemen for such prestigious missions as those to Vienna and Paris (the Earls of Arundel and Leicester, respectively, in the 1630s) or professionals whose skill was needed (e.g. Cottington in Spain). They employed quite a few men who made their careers as diplomats, for example Roe and Carleton, but were in no way restricted to them. The events of 1642–53 left Cromwell with a limited choice of personnel and he tended to pick trusted friends for embassies. The earliest of these was Whitelocke, who admitted that his post was due to Cromwell's personal nomination. Most embassies were entrusted to Cromwell's own friends and relations. Thus he entrusted the vital French embassy to the ex-Royalist Scottish Presbyterian William Lockhart, who had just married his niece. Lockhart had lived for years in Holland and Danzig and had served in the French army, so he was not devoid of experience; the French ambassador Bordeaux feared that as a Presbyterian he would be biased in favour of the Huguenots,[100] but he was realistic enough to recognise the dangers of English inflexibility in damaging the Cardinal's reputation. Cromwell chose George Downing, ex-intelligence chief in Scotland, to serve in The Hague. He proved to be as cunning as the States-General and officials with whom he had to deal, and was presumably chosen for his Scottish service and his long residence abroad (albeit in the

Americas). He had also previously shown his hostility to Dutch commercial power when in Parliament.[101] Cromwell sent two inexperienced relatives, Rolt and Jephson, to the Baltic in 1656–7 after considering Whitelocke and Sir Christopher Pack. Jephson had recently been trusted with raising the 'Humble Petition and Advice' in Parliament. The veteran Protestant 'internationalist' John Dury was chosen for the 1654 Swiss embassy, having had the advantage of long experience on such missions in central Europe. The Oxford mathematician John Pell, who had spent nine years teaching in Amsterdam and Breda, accompanied him. The other embassies – Portugal in 1656 and the Baltic in 1657–8 – were of crucial importance to the war effort and went to two Council officials, Moreland and Meadowe.

The Government's cooperation with the City merchant companies has already been noted. The collection of intelligence in the areas they served relied on their agents, copies of whose despatches were retained by Thurloe. Thus the consuls Longland (Leghorn) and Bretton (Smyrna), the Levant Company's representatives in the Mediterranean, acted as the State's eyes and ears there, and Richard Bradshaw represented both the Merchant Adventurers and the State in the Baltic at Hamburg. The latter city, as an object of both Dutch and Swedish ambitions, was of especial importance, as it acted as the chief entrepôt for supplies of grain and naval supplies (timber, hemp, etc.) to England and the United Provinces; hence the Royalist residents' intrigues against Bradshaw were of interest to London. In the Mediterranean, the most crucial post was the Levant Company's residency at Constantinople, which served as an official embassy to the Sultan. The complexities of court life there meant that an 'expert' with local knowledge was important, and when Cromwell obtained power the incumbent was a former Royalist from Essex, Sir Thomas Bendish. In August 1653, Parliament approved the company's proposal to send out Major Richard Lawrence (cousin to Cromwell's own relative Henry Lawrence, future President of the Council of State).[102] Lawrence arrived in Constantinople in February 1654,[103] but Henry Lawrence was warned by a friend that elements in the company opposed to his cousin were already seeking his recall.[104] Bendish, realising his advantages as the incumbent, refused either to leave or to assist Lawrence in taking on his duties.[105] The company spent much of 1654 in negotiations with the former Rump MP Richard Salwey to replace both men, and on 7/17 July a committee reported that Cromwell had warned them that 'the choice of ambassador to Constantinople was in him as Governor of this Nation and he would therefore have the Company submit to his choice'.[106] The company informed Cromwell of Salwey's acceptance on 30 August/9 September.[107] In the following February, however, Salwey changed his mind and the post was offered to the company's William Garway. The dispirited Lawrence, having refused company orders to return until his expenses were paid, obtained the company's agreement to pay through Thurloe's intervention in May 1656, but the money was still outstanding when he gave up and came home in April 1657.[108] Bendish, who was useful in knowing how to deal with the 'Sublime Porte' over such matters as Blake's campaigns, was allowed to stay on, Cromwell in effect accepting defeat.

There was no such trouble over the Muscovy Company's nominee to go to Russia on behalf of the State in 1654. He was William Prideaux (possibly related to the Attorney-General), a merchant who was unsuccessfully to contest the Levant Company's election for consul of the Morea in February 1658.[109] This mission combined the company's request that the chauvinistic Czar Alexis, who had Royalist officers at his court, restore trading privileges withdrawn after the King's execution with Cromwell's desire to inform the Czar of his regime's legitimacy and enquire the reasons for his war with Poland. The Russian mission of 1657 was more crucial, as Alexis was now one of a coalition of Baltic powers seeking to bring down Cromwell's vital ally, Sweden. Accordingly, on 5/15 March the Council determined on a second embassy at the request of George Fleetwood, the Councillor's brother and a long-time employee of Charles X currently negotiating aid for Sweden.[110] The choice of envoy fell on Richard Bradshaw, consul in Hamburg (and cousin of the regicide John Bradshaw).[111] He was very dubious about going, given the Czar's hostility and disdain for normal civilities, and was sent detailed instructions by Thurloe on how to approach the question of mediation between Russia and Sweden.[112] All this planning was useless as he was not let into the country.

3 Cromwell's Approach to the 'Two Crowns', 1651–4

National security determined that the 'Two Crowns' were of more importance to the Protectorate than Sweden or even the Dutch. France was the nearest and strongest power in Western Europe and was also the one with the closest links to the Stuarts. From 1648 the chain of revolts known as the *Frondes* weakened the French government, providing the regency of Anne of Austria with more pressing problems than the regicide heretics across the Channel. France's aristocratic generals, especially Condé, were preoccupied with trying to displace her Italian adviser, Cardinal Mazarin. Cromwell did not take all this as proof that France was permanently weakened, though a better knowledge of French affairs would have suggested the unlikelihood of serious trouble for him during a regency. On the contrary, he feared France's capacity to overcome these problems and sought to prolong them for as long as possible, aided by the coincidence that Protestants and republicans were numbered among the rebels. Spain, France's great European rival, was also seeking to assist the rebels in order to recover the strength which she had lost as a result of French successes in the early 1640s, both in Flanders and the Iberian peninsula. Hence Spain was England's natural ally. It is apparent that both during and after the *Frondes* England's main concern was to distract France's hostility by keeping her embroiled with Spain, although later Spanish hostility to the Western Design provided Cromwell with another reason to encourage the mutual belligerence of Bourbons and Habsburgs.

In the first place, however, we must consider Cromwell's approach to the conflict during the period when there was either rebellion or the imminent threat of it in France. This time, from 1651 to spring 1654, must therefore be considered separately from the rest of Cromwell's dealings with France. It should be remembered that he was not in full charge of policy until April 1653, and less prominent in foreign affairs than

Vane or Chaloner. As Commander-in-Chief he had the major responsibility for defending national security and was in control of the men who would have to carry out the Rump's decisions. Thus he possessed an importance in policy towards the Franco-Spanish conflict which he did not have over the Dutch crisis of 1652, the Navy not being subject to his influence.

The failure of rebellion on the British mainland in 1648 threw the responsibility for restoring the King on to external forces. The regime in Scotland declared in favour of Charles II in return for massive political concessions and was the major external threat until the battle of Worcester. Resistance continued in parts of that country after 1655, but from that date both Ireland and Scotland were effectively neutralised and France became the main Royalist hope and Republican fear. Luckily, however, the European-wide troubles of 1648 had included a dispute between the *Parlement* in Paris and the regency government, which was followed by the *Fronde* of the great nobles. France was neutralised as a threat, and rebellions in the South-West raised the possibility of English aid to the rebels who included Huguenots and republicans, prospective allies. The central interest of the Rump was therefore to keep France weak and disunited, possibly involving aid to potential sympathisers. The counterpart of this was a close relationship with Spain, which had been weakened by rebellion in Catalonia and Portugal and was in desperate need of an ally (even heretics) to counter France. Thus it could not continue to act with the confident arrogance of Olivares, who had not seriously needed English aid in the early years of the Franco-Spanish conflict. Since 1640 the Spanish ambassador in London, Cardenas, had been friendly with the Parliamentary opposition to Charles I on account of the latter's links with the Bourbons.[1] The friendship had been maintained throughout the 1640s while the French were treated with suspicion due to suspected partiality for Charles. Thus, Spain acted with *realpolitik* when, in October 1649, foreign ambassadors were ordered to recognise the regime's legitimacy or leave.[2] Cardenas was the first to recognise the Commonwealth whereas Mazarin's envoy, M. de Croullé, received no such orders and had to leave.[3] Following this the English prepared to send an ambassador to Madrid – Anthony Ascham, ironically a zealous republican author.[4] The prospect of an alliance between the militantly Catholic power and a regime founded on anti-Papist propaganda was foiled by his assassination by Royalists, but good relations continued. Barrière, the representative of the Prince of Condé who had fled to Spain, and two envoys from the French rebels in the South-West (Cugnac and St Thomas) were received in London.[5]

At the same time as this closeness to Spain, Anglo-French relations were deteriorating. Naval clashes and privateering were heightened by commercial jealousy and the willingness of the Paris *Parlement* to stand up to the regency. In the autumn of 1648 the French embargoed English woollens and silks,[6] to which the English replied with a ban on the import of French wines, manufactured woollens and silks.[7] Pressure rose for armed retaliation, though the magnitude of internal affairs and the Dutch negotiations of 1651–2 distracted the Rump. Popular opinion in England was reportedly anti-French[8] with radical Army officers and preachers urging that England's example in revolution be spread abroad.[9] Mazarin, twice in temporary exile, had other preoccupations and his loss of the initiative naturally concentrated English attention on Spain. In these circumstances, his unofficial envoys in London – first Count Grignon, then his secretary Croullé – had no option but to return home and leave the field clear for Cardenas.

Until April 1653 Cromwell was not in command of policy, but he was clearly influential. His differences from the men whom he assisted in 1651–3 over hostility to Spain can be exaggerated; Chaloner for one hated the Spanish empire. Cromwell was wrongly reputed to be a determined republican, who had allegedly said after Dunbar that he would convert all European monarchies into republics. Mazarin was notably disturbed by this.[10] Cromwell was less determined on war against France than Vane.[11]

UNOFFICIAL APPEALS FOR ASSISTANCE FROM FRANCE AND SPAIN, 1651–4

The likeliest choice of target in 1651 was therefore France, as was feared in Paris. Cromwell shared the Army's views on French culpability for the invasion from Scotland, and he half-seriously offered Condé's emissary 40 000 infantry and 12 000 cavalry when he met him after Worcester.[12] In January 1651, Abel Servien warned Mazarin that peace was essential lest English naval power aid rebellion. Accordingly, the Cardinal sought English assistance to relieve the Spanish sieges of Dunkirk and Gravelines. The Cardinal's secret offer of Dunkirk was only an expedient taken out of desperation to avert the humiliation of its fall by offering it on a temporary basis to an ally. However, it became the basis for Cromwell's attempts to demand it from France as a 'pledge' that the terms of an alliance would be carried out faithfully. It would also serve to increase English control of the Channel at this time of dispute with the Dutch and increased French piracy. Cardenas made a rival offer of Calais (provided that England would take it from the French first, which they would not have to do with Dunkirk).[13] Cromwell was enthusiastic about gaining Dunkirk. Colonel Fitzjames, the English envoy to Governor d'Estrades, was apparently acting at his request, although he may well have been acting on an initiative from his colleagues. D'Estrades wrote to Mazarin that Cromwell was their contact in England and would be organising the planned succour to the French garrison.[14] Cromwell was supposed to have been eager enough that when Mazarin hesitated over the expected uproar in France, he proposed that England land troops there and occupy it *de facto* with the Cardinal's secret connivance.[15] In 1656–7, Mazarin was less eager as France could reoccupy Dunkirk without English help. Cromwell refused to accept that and treated Mazarin's efforts to avoid the cession of Dunkirk as evidence of ill-will.

English interest in Dunkirk was lessened by preoccupation with the Dutch War in the summer of 1652 and the Rump decided to prefer aid to Spain in order to weaken France. Blake prevented Admiral Vendôme from sailing a French convoy to Dunkirk (September 5/15 1652). The resulting fury in France ended hopes of an alliance for some time, though Mazarin retained an unofficial ambassador in London (the Sieur de Gentillot). Protestant rebels in south-west France now became the main object of Cromwell's concern. Late in 1651 the rebel governor Count Daugnon of La Rochelle sent an envoy, a burgess called Conan, to seek English military aid for the town in return for its cession. Cromwell apparently studied a map of France and refused.[16] At this time the 'Leveller' Colonel Sexby visited Bordeaux to contact the rebels and became involved with the republican Ormée faction which seized power there.[17] Cromwell's own initiative appears to have been to contact the plotter Cardinal de Retz, an opponent of Mazarin with reputedly republican views, through the medium of a visit to Paris by Vane. De Retz himself wrote that Vane called on him to present a letter, 'importing that the sentiments I had enunciated in my "Defence of Public Liberty" . . . had induced him to enter into the strictest friendship . . . I answered it . . . as became a true Catholic and an honest Frenchman'.[18] This indicates that Cromwell had encouraged him to ally with the Huguenots and France's enemy Spain. It is possible that Cromwell believed from de Retz's works that he was sympathetic to republican ideas and religious toleration to such an extent that he would aid England.

The Huguenots continued to claim that it was England's duty to make up for their failure in 1628; their envoys reminded the Council that 'the churches of these parts have endured very great brunt by the deceitful promises which have been made them by the former supreme powers of Great Britain'.[19] In March 1652, they presented a 'Brief Condition of the Present Condition of Those of the Religion in France and the way to provide for their redressment' to the Council. Apart from the demand for a war of religious liberation, they made two practical proposals: that England continue to bolster their morale by assurances of concern and that a French alliance include written guarantees that all past edicts of toleration be confirmed.[20] These were the policies that Cromwell was to follow towards them once he had decided against war with France, and were to be maintained even during the two countries' military alliance of 1657–8. That indicates Cromwell's genuine concern, though it was also a useful threat to hold over Mazarin.

English policy from 1651 to 1654 remained consistent and pragmatic. Condé claimed Cromwell had promised him 10 000 infantry and 4000 cavalry in 1652 but the only aid received was 1200 Irish mercenaries.[21] In 1653, the rebels were forced on the defensive and the Bordelais rebels considered offering the city to Cromwell. Cardenas continued to recruit Irishmen for the rebel army but they were poor troops and of little real aid.[22] However, in May 1653, an embassy from Bordeaux led by Lenet and Trancas arrived in England to propose transferring its sovereignty; Cromwell supposedly promised 5000 troops and forty ships to break a French naval blackade.[23] It was an indication of his concern but, fortunately, after the rebel leaders had taken an oath on his terms, the Abbé de Cosnac persuaded them to retract it.[24] The possibility remained of an English naval attack but Cromwell was wary, for when the rebels asked for twenty ships and 14 000 men he offered six or eight ships which due to shortage of manpower would have to be manned by Dutch prisoners.[25] The fall of the city ended any such plan.

The continuing Dutch War encouraged Cromwell to pursue a policy of caution, and at the most to offer some small assistance to potential rebels to keep the Court occupied. As Sexby told the Protector on his return, 'it is in your Highness' interests to prevent the making of a general peace'.[26] For this purpose France had to be prevented from obtaining a decisive advantage in the field over Spain, which at this point appeared weaker. Hence Spain should be helped to invade France lest it give up hope and sign peace, freeing French troops to invade England.[27]

Before Cromwell's coup Bordeaux noted the Republic's desire 'to begin a peace with the whole world', officially at any rate.[28] The upheavals of 1653 added to this need which coincided with the failure of the French rebels. Cromwell now sought to lend some troops to Spain for an invasion without any official breach with France, to avoid the expense and enmity of open war. In accordance with this he sent the engineer Joachim Hane to France to examine the state of its coastal defences and the likelihood of revolt, while Conan returned to England to seek aid followed by a Scottish doctor (Dr More) sent by the Huguenots of Nîmes.[29] Condé's agent Barrière persuaded Jean-Baptiste Stouppe, minister to the Huguenot congregation at the Savoy, to go to France as well, as he had more influence with the Government than Hane.[30] Until April 1654 the Dutch War limited the ability to make commitments.

The creation of the Protectorate did not alter Cromwell's attitude to the comparative value of peace with France and Spain. In spring 1654, he consulted the visiting Spanish general Marcin as to whether La Rochelle or Bordeaux was the easier target.[31] There was, however, a new factor to consider – the inclinations of his Council. Cromwell was a 'constitutional monarch' under the 'Instrument of Government' and was technically required to seek his ministers' advice on foreign policy and decide on questions of war or peace by majority vote. The Council was undoubtedly divided between the partisans of France, led by Pickering, and those of Spain, led by Lambert. This division is confirmed by the reports of the Venetian ambassadors, the disputes over policy in April and July when Lambert opposed Cromwell, and a report on the situation by Ellis Leighton unearthed by Gardiner.[32] The latter report also indicates the existence of a third group – those who held that peace with the Dutch, Spain, France and Sweden was essential to preserve the security of the new regime but believed that Cromwell should do all he could to encourage the Franco-Spanish War in order to keep France occupied. They also believed that the Protector should be *Caput et ducem foederis Protestantis*. Leighton names Thurloe as the leader of this faction; his undoubted fear of France is confirmed by his own summary of policy. The Protector's natural instincts in the fact of these divisions was to delay a firm choice as long as possible, though the need to occupy and finance his troops was was such that he had to choose a remunerative target.

Mazarin and Bordeaux currently expected only covert hostility.[33] The Cardinal was concerned enough to send Paul de Castelmore, Baron de Baas, his nephew's fencing tutor, to London in January to supplement Bordeaux's efforts. Baas met Cromwell and Pickering who both refused to discuss specific proposals of alliance,[34] but he was given a Council proposal for the ending of commercial reprisals in return for assurances of Huguenot toleration before he returned to France.[35] This did not rule out simultaneous unofficial aid to Condé. After Baas's departure Thurloe and Cardenas held their first full meeting to discuss an alliance, and Thurloe remarked that France was more vital for English security but Cromwell's natural sympathies were with Spain. He dared not raise the taxes or risk the unrest that open war with France would entail, but if Spain would provide the funds England would send troops to aid attacks by Condé in Flanders and the Pyrenees.[36] No such counter-proposal had been offered to France, indicating that plans to aid Spain were more fully advanced. Cardenas went ahead with plans to raise money on the assumption of success, and Archduke Leopold (Viceroy of the Netherlands) offered him 30–50 000 crowns a month for his allies.[37] The Spanish Council agreed to finance a joint attack by Cromwell and Condé on the French frontiers, as Thurloe had proposed, when they met on 2/12 April.[38]

Two points should however be noted in consideration of this plan. It was to prove difficult for Spain to raise the necessary money without which Cromwell could not lend them an army. Also, English awareness of the weakness of French rebel strength was heightened by reports from France, especially from Hane.[39] Meanwhile, Sexby made his own formal report: a full attack on France would be 'unfeasible and dangerous' as it would require 20 000 foot, 10 000 horse, 100 ships, and two million pounds' expenditure to have a hope of success. This would denude England of troops, aiding the Royalists, and require the raising of new taxes. Therefore, it was simpler and cheaper to seize an 'offshore position' threatening Guienne, such as an island in the Garonne or a port like La Rochelle. This would secure the local customs-receipts and would 'divert your enemies' designs in foreign parts' to regain it. Supposedly this would not entail the open war and resulting French aid to Charles II which would follow a full invasion, though it is likely that France would have been as determined to seek means to occupy Cromwell in his own country as if he had declared open war.[40] The suggestion for the use of a supposedly lucrative offshore base without declaring open war provides an anticipation of the reasoning implicit in the Western Design.

Mazarin was uncertain enough of English goodwill to seek to keep the Dutch War in existence in early 1654, which was reported to Cromwell by Cardenas as an example of French hostility.[41] However, the Spaniards themselves were afraid of the likely consequences of an English–Dutch peace and the opportunities the unoccupied fleet could then seize to attack their dominions.[42] This factor – the wealth of the Indies – was Mazarin's strongest hope of diverting Cromwell from a Spanish alliance.[43]

The Cardinal now upgraded his envoy to the full status of an official ambassador and instructed him to offer full recognition, the essential preliminary to any agreement. His concern is indicated by the reports that he considered sending his close adviser Fouquet to replace Bordeaux.[44] The King, however, did not treat Cromwell as an equal as he had done with the Stuarts, addressing his letter to 'Monsieur le Protecteur' instead of to 'M. mon cousin'. The Council refused to open

Louis' letter as a result.[45] This sensitivity was marked under the Rump as well as Cromwell, though he carried his fear of any underhand contacts by his negotiating partners with the Royalists to extreme lengths (as with the Dutch). Mazarin had indicated that Charles II should leave France to ease the negotiations, but Cromwell was correct to assume that this was only designed as temporary.[46] No formal reply was made to Mazarin's offers of Dunkirk.[47]

SPRING 1654: THE COUNCIL DEBATES ITS CHOICES

Negotiations were formally divided between committees of the Council on 4/14 April. Cooper and Strickland were to negotiate with France and Lambert, Pickering and Montague with Spain.[48] Strickland was believed to be in favour of the French treaty he was negotiating,[49] but Cooper as a representative of the Dorset wool interest would oppose it in order to maintain peace with Spain. Lambert, the most notably pro-Spanish Councillor, was aided by Pickering who favoured France. Thus each negotiating team was divided between supporters and opponents of the relevant talks. Thurloe may still have favoured aid to Condé to keep France occupied; Bordeaux believed he was 'very close' to Cardenas.[50] Bordeaux omits the crucial reason in the English dilemma – the assessment of how best to deal with the French threat to aid Charles II. Some officers undoubtedly favoured Spain for less pragmatic reasons than Lambert. On 15/25 April, an officers' dinner at Henry Cromwell's house discussed policy, and it was said that a Romish cleric would not scruple to break any treaty and England had a moral obligation to the Huguenots.[51]

Baas believed that Cromwell favoured peace but was in a minority in his Council.[52] He apparently spent hours with Lambert defending his views.[53] However, Mazerolles' subsidy showed no signs of materialising and Cardenas' offer of £15 000 per month was rejected as inadequate.[54] Spanish financial weakness added to the risks involved in aiding Condé. The Prince's own capacity for effective action seems to have come under question. It was said that Mazarin's spies had leaked his hopes of aid to Paris and by December the Protector was driven to remark: 'stultus est, et garrulitur, et venditur a suis Cardinali'.[55]

The Council Debate of ?18 April

On a date in mid-April, probably the 18th,[56] the Council debated the factors in favour of three conflicting policies: (i) to attack France; (ii) to attack Spain; (iii) to have peace with both, 'supposing we might have good sums of money from both so to do'. The Dutch peace had been agreed, and it was generally admitted that England's wisest course was to seek to end its isolation and 'render itself agreeable to all the world'.[57] However, the Army needed some occupation and financial rewards to prevent the need to raise unpopular taxes.

Policy (i) was 'apprehended difficult and unprofitable' after Sexby and Hane's reports. 'Latterly France was not so bitter against the Protestants', a recognition that their situation was not so desperate as had been believed in 1651–2. Policy (ii) was more favoured, at least regarding an attack on the West Indies. Thurloe wrote that 'Cromwell was for war, at least in the West Indies, at least unless assurances were given and things well settled for the future'.[58] Events were to show that this settlement was to include 'free trade' in the area, though its unacceptability was not yet known. This plan would be 'the most profitable in the world', more profitable than Sexby's plan or Dunkirk. Some Councillors also remarked upon the Spanish Inquisition. The question of the attack involved whether to 'make a partial work of it this year' or to risk the expense and the manpower of a major assault aimed at securing all the objectives at once. Experts were called in to give evidence on the Spanish defences (Captains Hatsell and Limbery who traded with the Caribbean) and it was decided that the latter was too expensive. Some Councillors preferred to extend the war to an open attack on the Plate Fleet en route to Europe, which would be more remunerative but risk immediate war. However, Cromwell was resolved for the moment only to operate in America, where retaliation for past breaches of peace treaties could be justified. This option would provide financial gain without theoretically involving open war; its legal justification would serve to soften the blow to Lambert's faction.

This plan would involve the setting up of a new colony on a Spanish held island, to which 8–10 000 men a year could be transplanted from Scotland. The easiest way to deal with substantial 'blocs' of resistance was to remove the men in question from their homes, saving the expense of policing and spying on them. Hence a Caribbean island of substantial size would come in more useful than Barbados, where Royalists had previously been sent.

Open war would entail an alliance with France. Pickering's faction put forward the advantages of this; events show that Cromwell tried to avoid taking their advice as long as he could.

(a)   It would fuel the Franco-Spanish War, ensuring that neither power would be free to aid Charles II.

(b)   It would help the Protestant cause by encouraging France to treat the Huguenots well. Friendship with France would do more to ensure that they were well treated than helping unsuccessful revolts. Some Huguenots were now informing the Government that this was the choice of action which they preferred the English to take.[59]

(c)   It would 'discountenance our rebels in Scotland and fugitives'. At this time Middleton and Glencairn were still defying Monck in the Highlands; France was the traditional ally of Scotland.

(d)   France was 'not to be kept from internal divisions and distractions', and would not help the King unless she felt forced to it by English hostility.

(e)   France was the traditional ally of the North German Protestants, who Cromwell desired as allies.

In reply to this, the pro-Spanish faction argued that Spain would cut off trade in reprisal for any attack. Lambert was thus less confident than his master that her war with France would dissuade her from taking a second foe on herself. Cooper, a Dorset MP, would have affirmed the likely effect on the wool trade. Spanish hostility would close the Straits of Gibraltar. Cromwell replied:

(a)   Spain would not dare close the Flemish ports which would be crippled by war with England.

(b)   Other countries would make up the losses, for example Portugal, and France would compensate with Marseilles.

Cromwell seems to have believed that Spain would not dare retaliate for an attack on an island as violently as Lambert believed, though evidence will be presented to show he was quite prepared to attack the mainland too. Ultimately, Thurloe and Pickering's points touched on more dangerous matters than Lambert's. The merchants and wool traders could not overthrow the Protector.

THE RIVAL OFFERS OF MAY–JUNE 1654

The Caribbean plan would take months to prepare. In the meanwhile, the divided state of the Council indicated that delay would be the wiser choice. Most importantly, unlike in 1656 there were no rumours of a Franco-Spanish peace. It was widely believed that Cromwell was making the rivals bid against each other 'to see which of them will offer him the advantage, and he will choose an alliance with that one of them which offers the best conditions.'[60] Lord Lisle was reported to have told Beverning that Cromwell was sure France would not declare war, and English seapower was superior anyway, so he had no intention of signing a French alliance until the time was right.[61] Bordeaux was driven to remark that the delays must indicate that Cromwell either hated France and was planning war or that he proceeded in an entirely different manner from the normal process of diplomacy.[62] Public opinion in France believed the former.[63] The latter was, however, correct. Popular and Army opinion was now significantly held to favour attacking the Indies.[64]

If Cromwell was prepared to wait, the imminence of a French naval expedition to land the Duke of Guise's army in Naples required Mazarin to try to prevent the English fleet from attacking it. It was believed the English would attack the French in Catalonia and Naples.[65] French desperation to prevent this was dutifully reported to Thurloe.[66] This encouraged English intransigence and insistence that the terms of a treaty include the settlement of the debts of Count Cési, ambassador to Constantinople in 1632,[67] and the cession of Dunkirk. Spain offered England French territory (Calais); France had to offer her own (temporarily lost) territory though she could hold the threat of Charles II over Cromwell every time he delayed.[68]

Cromwell presented his terms to Baas on 1/11 May. They were:

1. The expulsion of the Stuarts from France.
2. Cession of Dunkirk as a result of an offensive alliance against Spain.
3. Confirmation of the Huguenots' liberties.
4. Commissioners to be appointed to judge shipping losses, with a French 'advance payment' of £200 000 as the English had suffered most. The Protector continually complained about French piracy to Bordeaux.[69]
5. The pardon of Condé by the King of France: a sop to Cromwell's ally which was negotiable.

The first four points were the basis of the eventual treaty. Baas presented the French terms next day, based on the French need to ensure the Protector's pacific intentions by extending a commercial treaty into a military alliance which would halt his contacts with rebels. This would limit the Protector's future options; a commercial peace would enable him to avoid such a definitive choice. Cromwell's hesitation and Lambert's reputation made such a choice undesirable. However, on this occasion he assured that if Baas was sincere he would 'rush through' a treaty in four days without anyone knowing.[70] This presumably meant that he was prepared to agree without informing the full Council, provided that Baas could supply reasons which seemed to justify it which he could present to them as a *fait accompli*. This did not follow his constitutional requirement to 'take advice' and relied on the Councillors' desire to avoid a crisis. In the event he was not put to this test as Baas refused to proceed until he had consulted the Cardinal, whom he advised to consider postponing the treaty on the grounds that Cromwell's constitution should be confirmed by Parliament.

An equivalent offer was made to Spain without the additional personal advice which Cromwell had given the French. From the timing of events it seems that the Council wanted to make simultaneous offers to both. Cardenas was offered 30 ships, 12 000 infantry and 2000 cavalry in return for £120 000;[71] in reply he offered £200 000 at once with the rest to fellow.[72] Cromwell returned to the French and said he would accept less than the £200 000 'damages' if it could be handed over at once.[73] Bordeaux replied that whether or not France paid England would have to stop commercial reprisals at once, but Pickering assured him that there was no question of a treaty without immediate payment.[74] Next, Cardenas offered to pay £300 000 eventually and two-thirds of it at once, but that was also rejected. Baas suggested that the English attack Spanish America and Pickering replied that the French must cede Dunkirk. If France would pay the £200 000 now Cromwell would 'make a suggestion', but Baas refused this as insufficient.[75]

In this exchange of offers, it is apparent that Spain was required to pay more than France. This is not evidence of bias in favour of France; rather, a French alliance would involve an English attack on the West Indies and in this case England would be able to finance the alliance more easily. The decision being based on a subsidy acted against Spain whose Council of State admitted that they could send little until the Plate Fleet arrived in June.[76] Spain appears barely to have been able to finance her troops that summer, let alone Cromwell. Cromwell was aware of this, in so far as Mazerolles had returned empty-handed from Brussels and he was receiving letters complaining of Spain's inability to pay her Irish mercenaries.[77] A total of £150 000 was owed to Irish officers, as the Protector wrote to Condé.[78] Spain could not pay her own troops; could she pay Cromwell what his troops needed, whatever Cardenas promised?

In this situation, Cromwell was increasingly aware of the unwisdom of allying with Spain, though Council divisions made continued talks essential. Cromwell's last offer to the Spanish was to send thirty (later amended to forty) ships to blockade France – a move which fell short of outright intervention and could be explained as an intensification of the commercial dispute. Cardenas realised that Cromwell was seeking to avoid fully committing himself, and insisted that he declare war as well as with an open manifesto. This was refused on the dubious grounds that England did not declare war by manifesto.[79]

THE 'BAAS AFFAIR'

Indications of English policy by June 1654 were that the 'balancing act' between France and Spain could be upset by a colonial adventure now that Spain had proved herself unable to provide money. However, France's Royalist links could hinder any Anglo-French *rapprochement* should there be any evidence of official French backing for Cromwell's enemies. This fear had lain at the root of hostility to France since 1651. Now France's assistant ambassador in London was to endanger relations by his injudicious interest in Cromwell's opponents in the Army, particularly Harrison – a more serious threat to the Protector than disgruntled aristocrats in Paris.

Cromwell was prepared to delay the French treaty as long as necessary, until his terms were met in full. Moreover, in Paris there was no strong popular or Court feeling in favour of peace with Spain for Mazarin to hold over him as a threat. However, there was considerable annoyance at the continuing English commercial reprisals. Mazarin made little of them,[80] but Count Brienne held that they were almost as bad as an open invasion.[81] Cromwell's contacts with the Huguenots were not really dangerous to France now that the likelihood of an imminent rebellion had passed – indeed, they served to reassure the Protector that no persecution was under way. However, the French government naturally feared that Condé's Huguenot agents would seek to paint as black a picture of the Cardinal as possible and inveigle Cromwell into invasion. In retaliation, Baas sought to investigate the strength of Cromwell's own opponents – particularly the likelihood that General Harrison would revolt. This was apparently intended as a direct reprisal for Cromwell's deviousness in negotiating with the French Court and its enemies at the same time. Mazarin had told his envoys to warn Cromwell of France's potential for disturbing the security of his government, but Baas's practical demonstration of this seems to have been the result of personal pique, a trap into which a professional diplomat would not have fallen.

Unfortunately for Baas, his efforts coincided with the English discovery of the Gerard Plot, the most serious conspiracy since Cromwell had seized power and the first Royalist effort against him since 1651. Thurloe's men had infiltrated the Sealed Knot organisation which planned it and among those arrested were Colonel Fitzjames (ex-envoy to d'Estrades) and Naudin. The indications were that Henrietta Maria and Prince Rupert were implicated, but not necessarily Charles II or Mazarin.[82] Naudin revealed:

> de Baas told me oftentimes that he was . . . truly sent to Your
> Highness for peace, but being afraid that you were not so
> disposed, or at least that you would delay too much that
> work, he thought it very convenient to engineer a division
> in the Army as a way very easy . . . to oblige Your Highness
> to him. He knew Your Highness did practice some designs
> in France by means of the Protestants there.[83]

The threat of a radical mutiny was particularly sensitive after
the disapointment which the 'Instrument of Government'
seemed to be after the hopes of 1653; Harrison was the most
prestigious officer unreconciled with the regime, along with
Colonel Overton. Hence the Government took Baas's plans
very seriously and was encouraged by Cardenas.[84]

Bordeaux professed to believe that Cromwell would realise
that France had no interest in removing him when he thought
about it more calmly, but the Protector was cool towards him
and refused to see Baas.[85] Pressure mounted at Court to regard failure as inevitable and abandon the talks.[86] It is uncertain whether Cromwell deliberately exploited the incident
as an excuse to hold up talks, but if Thurloe did tell Cardenas
that he would receive aid as soon as the Royalists and Scots
had been dealt with he retreated from this offer.[87] A less determined man than Mazarin might have given way to pressure
to recall the negotiators and thus forced Cromwell into alliance with Spain. Instead Mazarin instructed Bordeaux to raise
his offer and stressed again that the West Indies would afford
Cromwell more gain than Guienne: 'nothing will be more
fateful to Cromwell's government than a rupture'.[88] Thurloe
admitted that these were the decisive factors in the situation.

In consideration of the ultimate threat to security, the
meddling of Baas with the Army could not be made the excuse
for a breach. Lambert and others apparently believed
Cardenas's accusations that Baas had acted in concert with the
real intentions of Bordeaux and Mazarin, but Cromwell chose
to restrict his anger to Baas alone.[89] This decision was not
altered by the angry interchange at their last meeting on 12/
22 June, when Baas lost his temper after Cromwell had accused
him of saying that the Protectorate would not last a month,
and of inquiring about Harrison's influence.[90] Baas was given
three days to leave the country and when he had left Cromwell

tried to have him imprisoned.[91] Instead he was given a governorship which fuelled English suspicion as to whether he had acted against his instructions after all. His conduct had shown that this professional soldier, half-brother to the original d'Artagnan, was not the right person to deal with the Protector; his interference with the Army was an adequate excuse to aid Condé had one been sought.

The fact that Baas's indiscretion did not lead to disaster was due to the changed English opinion of Spain's value. Concurrently, Stouppe returned to confirm that a new rebellion in southern France was unlikely.[92] Thus, Cromwell officially assured Mazarin that the blame rested on Baas not his master. Still, he remained suspicious of Mazarin's real inentions and wrote to Barrière, 'I am not a dupe of the Cardinal.'[93]

The 'Baas Affair' is important for what did *not* happen rather than what did, that is, that both participating regimes regarded peace as too important to be risked. Cromwell's pragmatic approach is testimony to the importance of the reports he had received about the unlikelihood of French revolt and about Spanish impecuniosity. However, it was also apparent that there was substantial resentment in France of his manner of proceeding. Cromwell was confident that Mazarin would ignore this, but English behaviour in late 1654 shows that no effort was made to accommodate the Cardinal. Comparisons are appropriate with his behaviour to the Dutch over the 'Seclusion' of the House of Orange from office demanded in that peace treaty – another example of English arrogance.

The weakness of Spain's government, which had led it to seek an alliance, equally impeded it from satisfying Cromwell's requirements. Mazarin knew that he would be ill-advised to accept Cromwell's demands in surrendering French territory to a heretic, but he dared not break off talks even when Baas's indiscretions were detected. The reason for this lies in Mazarin's personal opposition to a peace with Spain, a factor which recurred in 1656 when Cromwell was being equally obstructive and the Cardinal had even sent an envoy to Madrid. Peace with Spain would entail a pardon for Condé – who could then attempt to rebuild a coalition of those of the aristocracy opposed to Mazarin. The Cardinal's grip on the French government was surer without this hazard, even if the Spanish War was offensive to Catholic opinion.

4 The Verge of a Breach with France: July 1654– March 1655

The events of spring 1654 proved a turning-point in Cromwell's relations with France and Spain. Hence, consideration of the coninuing Anglo-French dispute after this date must be dealt with separately. The Baas Affair coincided with the failure of the proposed Spanish subsidy to materialise, which warned England that Spain was not able to finance a continental campaign. Cromwell looked for another target for his restless army; the West Indies would be an easy, rich and justifiable choice. The expedition was not to sail until December and reach its destination until March or April, and it was in Cromwell's interest not to make his intention for a breach with Spain in America (with Europe following) plain for as long as possible. He desired to avoid reassuring France concerning their peace treaty; if Mazarin was certain of that, it would lessen French willingness to sign on terms advantageous to England (e.g. allowing Cromwell to retain Condé's agents in London) and end the English policy of playing off one 'Crown' against the other. Hence Cromwell took a calculated risk that despite French resentment Mazarin needed his goodwill too much to give in to pressure to make peace with Spain. This owed much to 'special circumstances' in France, namely:

(a)   There was no popular outcry for peace as there was to be in 1656–7; reports received in London laid the blame for pressure on Mazarin on opposition among the Court.

(b)   The Cardinal, an Italian outsider who had built up his position *against* rather than on behalf of the nobility, was less vulnerable to Court pressure than another minister.

Even with these advantages, Mazarin was so uncertain of Cromwell's real intentions that he gave passive support to the Royalists in March 1655; Cromwell's obstinacy had its dangers.

INDICATORS OF POLICY, SUMMER 1654

Cromwell continued to meet the envoys of both powers after Baas's departure, but Stouppe's warning of the quiescence of the Huguenots reinforced the decision not to attack Guienne. Bordeaux reported that Cromwell was sending two more Huguenots to investigate the possibilities of aid, but refused to loan any ships to Condé.[1] Cromwell did not rule out a Spanish alliance, but only if Spain would hand over Dunkirk to him as a pledge that they would surrender Calais when it had been captured from the French.[2]

In June, orders were issued to prepare the fleet for action. Six ships were to sail for Newfoundland, twenty-four for the Mediterranean and fourteen for the West Indies.[3] The Mediterranean fleet would necessarily take action against France rather than Spain, as the former's ships were responsible for most of the local piracy. Any attack on the North African ports required the use of Spanish ports, probably in Sicily, as 'refuelling-points'. The attack on the West Indies showed that the Western Design was going ahead, and the small size of the fleet indicated that only a 'partial work of it this summer' was intended. The plan was not a secret; within weeks the Royalists in France heard that all ships would sail against Spain or twenty-two would sail for the West Indies and twenty for France.[4] According to Bordeaux, Condé's agents in London knew of the plan in June and they must have informed Brussels, and thence Madrid.[5] By July the Spanish Council knew of it.[6] Quirini, Venetian ambassador to Spain, noted:

> they have had a discussion in the Council that whereas the Spanish never enjoyed confidential information with the northern nationals and the English from their national habit were devoting their attention to the gains of the sea, they are inclined to suspect that the English have some hankering after the island of Santo Domingo . . . They have decided to send thither the galleons of the Continent charged with orders.[7]

The Spanish suspected what was afoot, but due to the European war they could not afford to withdraw Cardenas and cause Cromwell to ally openly with France. This was what he gambled on, and explains how he could be seen as contemplating sending his ships against Spain in America and France in Europe with no apparent fear of the wrath of either. Moreover, the Protector and Thurloe had given their approval to the intention of the English American expedition, originally aimed at New Amsterdam, to be diverted against French Acadia.[8] Colonial war was thus under way against both powers simultaneously.

Cromwell now proceeded to offer France the counterpart of what he had offered Spain – alliance if a port would be delivered to him as a temporary 'pledge'. In Spain's case, it had been Dunkirk, which was not rightfully their territory anyway: in France's case the latest demand appears to have been for Brest, an integral part of France.[9] France was under intense military pressure during the Spanish siege of Arras. However, the English obstinacy was counter-productive as someone less confident would have realised. Fearing that Cromwell intended to declare war after all when Parliament assembled, the Cardinal renewed pressure on the Huguenots and sought to improve his contacts with the intolerant *dévots* in case he was driven into war with England or even had to flee to Rome.[10]

Two new factors, however, stood in the way of agreement with Spain. The most important was Cromwell's demands for religious toleration for Protestant Englishmen in Spain and free trade with the West Indies. Cromwell has been accused of inflexibility, but it should be remembered that the former demand was one which the Rump had also made and which had been tacitly conceded in the treaties of 1604 and 1630. Toleration had been previously granted to services in private houses 'provided that there is no scandal'. This device was also used in the Anglo-Portuguese treaty of 1654, and it was likely that Cromwell believed that what one Iberian Catholic state had granted the other could do. The cases were not parallel as Portugal was smaller, menaced by Spain and the Dutch and in fear of the English fleet, and even so King John VI feared to ratify this clause for fear of his clergy. Nevertheless, English weakness had encouraged the Spanish authorities to break up a number of 'heretic' English services recently and it was essential to restate the terms of 1630 to prevent repetition of this. The fault was not entirely on Spain's side as Cromwell sought a public admission. The other demand – free trade to Spanish America – was more unacceptable. Such terms of reciprocal free trade were the normal practice in treaties between allies, and the English agreed them with Sweden, the Dutch and Portugal.[11] Spain saw herself as a 'special case' and Cromwell made no exception for her. Ignorance is more likely than malice in his inflexibility, an attitude that he showed equally to France and the Dutch in his negotiations. Ironically, the decline of Spanish shipping meant that in practice the American Viceroyalties perforce accepted visits by 'illegal' English and Dutch interlopers, who were essential to preserve their trade. Madrid usually turned a blind eye to this though English ships were occasionally seized by zealous officials or captains. Cromwell's demand was thus not essential for the welfare of his merchants.

The other aspect of Anglo-Spanish relations to deteriorate that summer was the matter of Spain's debts. Already her inability to pay Condé's Irish mercenaries was known, and the Council were attempting to obtain £3000 arrears of rent owed by Cardenas for his residence.[12] Cromwell sent a complaint to Archduke Leopold at the debts owed to Colonels Luce and Owen for transporting 3000 Irish to Flanders in May 1653 and was also solicited by Christopher Mayo, who had not been paid for shipping 300 Irishmen to Spain in 1652.[13] The Spanish government was notoriously slow, inefficient and bureaucratic, but the Protector desired immediate satisfaction none the less and took delay as a sign of ill-will rather than natural slowness. It would also confirm the impression that Spain could not pay its debtors. Cromwell also sent a 'strong and angry' letter to the King over the claims of the Ricaut family.[14] Cardenas pointed out that the Ricauts had been residents of Antwerp so they were Spanish citizens and that only £1000 was owed, the other £19 000 being questionable.[15] The case was not as straightforward as Cromwell had believed and could be argued as being beyond his jurisdiction, but he did not abandon it. Spanish financial weakness was confirmed when Mazerolles abandoned his hope of aid and left England, remarking in a letter to Condé that Cardenas was effectively penniless.[16]

THE SECOND DEBATE ON POLICY

On 20/30 July there was a further clash in Council between Lambert and Cromwell over the wisdom of the Western Design, recorded in Montague's family papers. The stylised arguments presented here summarise their views rather than record the progress of the debate verbatim. The Protector quoted Spain's obstinacy in the talks as evidence of ill-will: 'They have denied you commerce unless you be of their religion. We cannot suffer our people to go there and be idolaters.' It could be argued that he had not given Cardenas time to moderate his demands, but in fact Spain's refusal to accept the essential English terms was already apparent to Thurloe's agent Pawley.[17] Cromwell gave the following reasons for retaliation in the West Indies:

1. 'Providence seemed to lead us thither, having 160 ships swimming . . . we think it our best consideration to keep up this reputation.' 'Most of Europe our enemies except Holland, and that were well considered also.'

2. 'While considering the two Crowns, and the particular arguments' weight, we found opportunities point this way.' The expedition to Guienne was impractical, Spain was unable to finance war in Europe and refused the terms that were the corollary to this, and the Huguenots were quiescent.

3. It was essential 'not to lay the ships up to the walls'; the same applied to the Army.

4. The factor of cost – 'It was told us that the Design would cost little more than laying by the ships, and that with great profit.' A small outlay would reap large dividends; 'six nimble frigates shall range up and down the Bay of Mexico to get prey'. The fallacy of this hope was proved by the failure of the small fleet operating in the Caribbean to gain much loot in 1656–8.

5. 'To stay from attempting it of superfluity is to put it off for ever, our expenses being such as will in all possibility admit that.' Taxes could not be raised for fear of discontent, and expenditure on the armed forces was unlikely to diminish; the sooner England obtained this new source of income the better. It was hoped that after the first year loot would recoup the early losses. Nothing was said about the expense of building up an adequate colony.

6. 'The good of the design both to the Protestants' cause and to the undertakers.' Apart from the prestige and

money to be acquired, such an attack was in line with the strategy of all opponents of Spanish power in Europe since the 1570s.

Lambert's reply centred upon the risks involved. The work was: (i) 'improbable' to succeed; (ii) 'too far off, having greater concernments at home'; and (iii) 'not likely to advance the Protestants' cause, or to gain riches for us or vent for troublesome people in England, Scotland, or Ireland'. The settlement of Ireland was more crucial to English security and troops there could be moved back home in an emergency; this was impossible from the Caribbean. Cromwell, however, evidently considered that it would be more valuable to use his troops somewhere where there was adequate financial remuneration.

Lambert warned against two factors which Cromwell had neglected and which were to prove serious obstacles. The expedition would be subject to the hazards of tropical disease, and 'New England and the Barbadoes will not flock to you in Hispaniola unless you be settled there in peace'. The lack of the English Americans' expected enthusiasm was to take Cromwell by surprise in 1656–8. He also said that the plan was dubiously legal: 'The case at first wrong stated. The charge not well considered. The regulation of our law and other concernments not well taken care of.' The financial gains and the desire to keep the troops and seamen occupied was no doubt more important to Cromwell and Thurloe than strict legality. The Spanish actions in the area breached the 1630 treaty in that they had been taken against the shipping and colonies of a nation with whom she was at peace, as covered by Articles I and LXXXVIII (see Chapter 7). The Spanish could claim, however, that Providence Island and Tortugas, the two overrun islands, had been occupied by the English since the treaty and the illegal traders were breaking Spanish law. Cromwell was proposing to send a state expedition to retaliate for a few 'minor' breaches of the treaty. He claimed that he was fighting Spain in the West Indies as she had begun the war there,[18] but his reply was disproportionate. Lambert's belief that Protestantism would not receive much help from a few ships in the Caribbean was correct; the crushing victories of the war were won by Stayner and Blake off the Spanish coast, where England could afford to maintain a large enough fleet to take 'Plate' ships. The Caribbean had two advantages which were not mentioned:

1. It would occupy the Army as well as the Navy.
2. Naval war off Europe was remunerative, though the 'six nimble frigates' remark shows Cromwell did not realise this. But this would bring about war, which it was generally believed Hispaniola would not. Cromwell considered this option the following spring; it was the next stage in the escalation of hostilities.

Lambert's most telling remark was of the danger of defeat causing discontent. 'What account whall we give to Parliament for it?' Defeat might also cause mutiny in the Army, though Lambert did not mention this or the likely effect on Cromwell's reputation in Europe. As events showed, after the Hispaniola disaster Cromwell tried to hide the truth from the public by giving out confident statements about success.

It was on this occasion that Cromwell made his famous remark about the importance of moral imperatives in his foreign policy: 'God has not called us hither . . . but to consider the work that we do in the world.'[19] Thurloe admitted: 'Cromwell intended not to meddle with anything in Europe until the Spaniards should begin, unless the Plate Fleet was met with, which was looked on as a lawful prize.'[20] There was nothing legal about this plan; rather, it was a way to finance the Army and help European Protestants in the process. The decision to wait for the Spaniards to begin in Europe implies that Thurloe expected them to do so, though the speed of their reply appears to have surprised the Protector.

DIPLOMATIC DELAY IN EUROPE

The timetable of the expedition involved preparations beginning in August and the fleet sailing in December. In the meantime, talks with France appeared unaffected. Cromwell was confident of Mazarin's need of his goodwill, and the lack of fear of French hostility led to intransigence over Acadia and willingness to let Blake attack French shipping in the Mediterranean. It is questionable how much Cromwell's confidence owed to the cool calculation which appears to have been

Thurloe's forte, and the length of his delaying the French
treaty showed that his confidence bordered on rashness. Certainly, the public impression remained one of a willingness
to treat with either power. Quirini noted why Cardenas continued to treat despite the Design: 'the business will be kept
alive by Spain even if there is no desire to clinch it, at least to
cherish confidential relations over a project of mutual satisfaction and increase the uneasiness and jealousy of France'.[21] The
relief of Arras also made the French less urgent in desiring a
settlement with England, and Bordeaux reckoned that the
Protector was 'still firm to what he pretends, thinking us so
greedy for peace that rather than break we will sign anything'.[22]

Cromwell was primarily concerned during these months
with preparations for and the progress of the first Protectorate
Parliament. Mazarin had earlier feared that the meeting of
Parliament would be the signal for a formal breach with France;
now he believed that if he held up talks for a while the level
of internal dissension would cause Cromwell to seek French
friendship on easier terms.[23] The sitting of Parliament provided new evidence of Cromwell's increasing inclination to
determine his foreign policy by the 'Protestant Cause', though
his truculence towards 'Popery' emerged *after* the Spaniards
had shown themselves unable to finance him and unwilling to
accommodate English demands. Cromwell told Parliament:

> I believe you expect not very much good from any of your
> Catholic neighbours, nor yet they be very willing that you
> should have a good understanding with your Protestant
> friends . . . as a peace with Protestant states has much security
> in it, so it has as much honour and assurance to the Prot-
> estant interest abroad . . . I wish it may be written upon our
> hearts to be zealous.[24]

This was partly designed to justify the Dutch peace, and
Cromwell always believed that Protestant oratory was the way
in which to satisfy Parliaments as well as soldiers. However, it
is likely that the failure of the Spanish talks encouraged him
to believe that he was meant to attack Spanish power. The
corollary was alliance with France, but only when his insistence
on the expulsion of his enemies and a port as a 'pledge' had
been met. The events of 1654–7 show that he would only
proceed with this plan at his own speed.

The English and French talks that autumn centred on the list of Royalists who were considered dangerous enough to be required to leave France. As with the Orangists in Holland, Cromwell sought to minimise what he saw as a threat by extending his demands.[25] He also refused to accept any of the Dutch Provinces other than Holland as commercial mediators as he feared Orangist influence in their decisions.[26] The talks did not prevent further meetings between Habsburg general Montecuculli and members of the Council, probably on the feasibility of an attack in Flanders or (as French rumours still held) Guienne.[27] Talks did not imply a military commitment, but they did imply that that option had not been ruled out. The obstinacy of Cromwell's terms did not help goodwill among Mazarin's advisers, Servien believing that they were 'equally prejudicial to us and favourable to him'.[28]

The strength of Cromwell's position (as he perceived it) was now reflected in his attempt to obtain the right to keep French rebel agents in England after the signature of a treaty. Mutual expulsion of rebels was normal practice. The most he would concede was that the list be kept secret in a private Article. On the other hand, he sought to retain Condé's agents and Huguenot representatives in London, the latter on the not entirely specious grounds that they were coreligionists in danger of persecution in France and whose welfare had to be constantly checked. Mazarin wanted all rebel representatives out of England within three days of a treaty being signed, with no return permissible under any circumstances.[29] As was to become apparent, Cromwell was determined to try to avoid accepting this.

TWO THREATS TO PEACE – ACADIA AND BLAKE

Anglo-French problems were now exacerbated by two new incidents, both of which reflected Cromwell's confidence that France needed his aid against Spain too much to take offence at slights. Without the Franco-Spanish War, such a policy would have been unthinkable. In the first place, the expedition of New England colonists led by Leverett and Sedgewick had taken three disputed French forts in Acadia. This was not a direct instance of Cromwell escalating the Anglo-French commercial dispute into war 'beyond the line', as Thurloe had only sent orders for them to take French shipping.[30] Once the deed was done, Cromwell did not disown the New Englanders for the sake of peace. Instead, he insisted that the conquest be recognised in the peace treaty.[31] This showed a great degree of confidence that Mazarin would not dare to protest. Bordeaux's own interpretation of Cromwell's action in retaining the forts was that he wanted to use them as a bargaining counter to force France to pay the debts which it owed to the Kirke family for their evacuating Quebec in 1632, which had never been paid.[32] It was lucky for the future of the talks that 'the Cardinal cares very little about the loss as it does not affect the King who was content with the acknowledgement of his supremacy and left the direction of everything to the men who founded the colony'.[33] This was a matter of luck for Cromwell rather than of direct and careful calculation. Clearly, the main point of the matter to him was that the conquest was a justifiable retaliation for losses of shipping.

At the same time, maritime reprisals against the French were escalating.[34] This was risky for English hopes of eventual settlement, considering that at the same time no measures were being taken to calm Spanish fears. It is significant that in the autumn a ship was sent from Cadiz to Havana with orders to have the defences of Santo Domingo strengthened.[35] De Haro himself was more suspicious; he told the Venetian ambassador Quirini that it was a good thing that Cromwell was short of money and that 'from now on events might hope that the savage beast would be devoured by itself'[36] – the words of a potential foe who was aware of the fact rather than of a trusting ally. Cardenas's famous remark that Cromwell's demands were 'his master's two eyes' had come to Bordeaux's knowledge that autumn[37] so it cannot be said that he was unaware of Cromwell's inflexibility. Spain could not afford to fight both England and France, particularly when the destination of the Design was still uncertain and the French treaty was unsigned. They feared the potential of the English fleet to cut off their financial supplies from the Indies, a permanent threat to their European armies 'whence they have derived the saying "war with all the world, but peace with England"'.[38]

The second threat to Anglo-French relations, unlike Acadia, was a direct result of English policy. Admiral Blake's fleet left

England for the Mediterranean in October. Its primary intention was to restore the safety of English shipping and the prestige of the English name in the Mediterranean; as French shipping had made most of the recent attacks it was the obvious target for reprisals.[39] The need to sail through the Straits of Gibraltar twice and to use Italian and Sicilian ports to refuel during the voyages to and from the African coast implied that Spanish goodwill was needed. The expedition coincided with the Duke of Guise's French attack on Naples, and accordingly Cardenas tried to persuade Cromwell to order Blake to aid the Spanish defence by attacking the Duke's ships.[40] This was the impression given to observers as Blake sailed into the Mediterranean. In Naples it was officially announced that 'the English have come to fight the force of Guise and because of this His Catholic Majesty has ordered that they should receive the best of treatment at any of the ports they shall enter'.[41] Moreover, two notorious French pirate captains were with the French fleet and it was likely that if he found them Blake would attack whether or not the French government took such action as an act of war. Mazarin himself believed that Blake 'did boast he went to seek the Duke of Guise in order to fight him wheresoever he should meet him'.[42] Other observers noted that the Spanish were more suspicious of Blake than they pretended, but Blake himself admitted when he reached Naples that he intended to capture (or sink) every French ship he met.[43]

Considering that pressure was mounting on Mazarin to withdraw Bordeaux, it was very likely that the outcry caused by the sinking of Guise's fleet would have been irresistible. It was possible that two expeditions of 'reprisal' would outrage the two European Catholic powers simultaneously. In the event, Guise and peace were saved by the length of time which Blake spent sailing to Naples.[44] When Blake arrived, Guise had abandoned his siege of Castellemare, re-embarked his men and returned to Marseilles. The French admiral Nieuchèses, who was sailing his fleet from the Atlantic ports to aid Guise, turned back at Lisbon when he heard of Blake's expedition.[45] The expected battle and the resulting disaster to Cromwell's French policy was avoided, but it was apparent that France could not operate in the Mediterranean until she had peace with England.

RISING FRENCH RESENTMENT

French reaction to Blake's implicit threat to the Naples expedition was such as to reassure the English that they would
not dare retaliate whatever happened, due to their need of
Cromwell's friendship. The Cardinal told Bordeaux to remind
Cromwell of the goodwill which Guise and Nieucheses had
shown,[46] but Court anger was intensified by the incident. Servien
and the Cardinal had interests in French ships which the
English had taken as prizes.[47] In England this danger of French
withdrawal appeared to go unnoticed; Bordeaux reported that
in the streets of London people were saying that 'they would
force France to make peace with a dagger at her throat. They
were certainly not satisfied with specious proposals but would
claim something substantial to satisfy the merchants' claims.'[48]

The danger now arose that pressure would force Mazarin
to recall his ambassador, and Bordeaux was given secret
instructions to ignore such an order as it was only intended as
a sop to Court opinion. Bordeaux's father told him that even
if the Cardinal told him to return he should 'use great delay'
in obeying and and receive ten such orders before he did so.
Mazarin himself briefly favoured a recall after the English had
seized a French salt fleet; the decision to let Bordeaux defy the
order was now taken by Count Brienne. Brienne and Bordeaux's father were agreed that the Articles might be unjust,
particularly in the current refusal to expel Condé's men from
England, but this was 'a matter altogether inconsiderable to
engage us in so great a war'.

Bordeaux's father listed the reasons for France to avoid a
rupture:

(a)   'The power of the Protector'.
(b)   'The power of the Commonwealth [i.e. the Army and
       Navy] and the disposition of the people there against
       France, united in their intentions to make war.'
(c)   The Army had 'nothing more to do than be landed in
       France'.
(d)   'The relations of the body of the Protestant religion in
       the [French] state with them.'
(e)   'The intelligence of the Prince [Condé] and the rebels
       in Guienne with them.'

(f) 'The assistance and union of Spain with them . . . from the very moment of a rupture.' They did not believe that the Western Design meant war.

(g) 'The union of the Hollanders, Sweden, Denmark, with those of the [Protestant] religion that border the North Sea, who, having made a league offensive and defensive, will also become our enemies . . .'[49]

Cromwell's 'Protestant' inclinations did not seem to imply an inevitable league with France to these expert observers, even with the Design under way. Cromwell did nothing to save the talks; Bordeaux himself frequently believed that he had 'wasted my time, my money, and my efforts',[50] but his sense of responsibility kept him at his post, and thus Cromwell and Thurloe's gamble that all his threats were 'hot air' was proved correct. Cromwell was undoubtedly helped by the French misinterpretation of his dispute with Parliament, which they now hoped would make him more reasonable and which encouraged Mazarin to retain his ambassador.[51]

In the New Year the Protector and his Commissioners finally showed signs of genuinely wishing to conclude the treaty, enabling Bordeaux to assure the Cardinal that he had been right to stay in London.[52] An angry letter from the French King calling on his ambassador to leave[53] may finally have persuaded the English to cease prevaricating. Bordeaux was told that certain Councillors were obstructing Cromwell; if this was not just an excuse it may reflect Lambert's faction's determination to see that France should not sign on any easier terms than the equivalent of the terms offered to Spain. Cromwell's refusal to consider a military alliance was a result of the realisation that England should not risk war in Europe until she was ready for it.[54]

FRANCE AND THE ROYALIST REVOLT

The English fleet sailed for the Caribbean on 20/30 December and 25 December/1 January. Their destination was widely reported in England, though the Government sought to persuade observers that it was restricted to a colonial reprisal for past misdeeds and that Spanish propaganda falsely claimed that despite their treaties with England, 'beyond the Line trade and jurisdiction alike are the exclusive prerogative of His Catholic Majesty'.[55] The Spanish were aware of English intentions but 'they say the commerce of the Indies and the traffic of the Northerners in those parts do not amount to a declaration of war'.[56] Spain did not reverse this attitude until Cromwell's 'invincible' soldiers had been defeated and an English war seemed not so dangerous. The English merchants in Spanish ports and at Naples were more concerned than their Government, as they started to close down their businesses and send their possessions out of the Spanish dominions in case of war.[57]

The English government had been facing internal problems since the beginning of 1655 with the dissolution of Parliament, to which was added the resignation of Anthony Ashley Cooper (possibly through discontent at the likely effect of Cromwell's Spanish policy). France had been hoping to take advantage of these problems, and when the expected Royalist rebellion broke out in March they appear to have thought that it was more serious than it appeared. Penruddock's rising was expected to be the beginning of a more widespread revolt[58] and the question arose as to whether it was better to lend some tacit or active help, so that if Charles II was successful he would be indebted to his former allies. A number of port governors took the opportunity to seize English shipping in their harbours to put pressure on Cromwell to satisfy their merchants' and captains' claims. They anticipated official instructions, but Mazarin followed them up by means of a royal order to all port authorities on 7/17 March to seize all English shipping.[59] In the aftermath of the provincial revolts of 1651–3 he could not safely disown such action for fear of seeming unpatriotic. The Penruddock rising was hailed at the French Court as well, providing more evidence for Thurloe of high-up ill-will to his master.[60] Bordeaux did not help matters by putting pressure on Cromwell, announcing that all seized ships and goods would be held until a treaty was signed.[61] It provided every opportunity for harsh English reaction, providing a reminder of the French–Royalist connection which had caused such anger in 1651. Cromwell, however, had the sense to see that a harsh reaction would be unwise.

The revolt provided the worst possible outcome for Mazarin. He had expected a greater challenge to Cromwell and the seizures made Thurloe suspect ouright collusion with Penruddock's plans. Conversely, the lack of any actual French help to the Royalists served to irritate Cromwell without threatening him; if by some mischance he had been over-thrown, Mazarin could not have counted on gratitude from Charles II for genuine assistance. On hearing of the rebels' swift defeat, Mazarin hastily ordered the ships' release and sent assurances of his goodwill.[62] Even so, the English commis-sioners refused to meet Bordeaux until the ships were released and Thurloe told him that 'it was a sign of the little disposition we had to the peace'. There was a quarrel in the Council.[63] Luckily, no action was taken.

The apparently eager French reaction to the possibility of Cromwell's overthrow was potentially more dangerous than the unwise talks between Baas and Harrison. It was fortunate for the Cardinal that two circumstances were different from the previous summer; Spain had proved unable to fund an alliance and the Western Design had set sail to attack Spain's colonies. It was also fortunate that all reports from France in the past two years had indicated the unwisdom of aiding Condé and that there was no current trouble with the Huguenots. Had the Vaudois Massacre, the most shocking evidence for decades of French-inspired persecution, occurred now rather than a month later the results might have been catastropic. As events turned out, English reaction to the seizures is important for what did *not* happen as much as for what did. The French had agreed by now to expel Royalist leaders, whatever the seizure confirmed as to their real opinions.

Cromwell's most significant reaction was to arrange for an expensive and unpopular new tier of government, the much maligned 'Major-Generals'. It did not directly affect foreign policy, except in providing Lambert and several other Coun-cillors with important new duties away from London. Indirectly, however, the effect on local opinion meant that whenever Paliament was summoned again there would be many new grievances to air and less will to fund the State, particularly for an expensive war. This helped to bring about the financial problems of 1656–8, the low-key nature of the Spanish War until adequate finance was provided, and England's need of a substantial French subsidy for a campaign in Flanders. Indirectly, the need to maintain more troops at home prevented sending substantial reinforcements to Jamaica or a substantial number of volunteers to Charles X.

5 The Western Design

The Western Design is crucial to any adequate understanding of Cromwell's foreign policy. It was long regarded as the prime example of his 'outdated' and ideologically based attitude to the Spanish empire, providing a clear parallel with Elizabethan precedents. It could be argued that the Protector was obsessed with attacking Spain in the Americas when his main duty was to thwart French ambitions in Europe, and that nostalgia and religious bigotry made him ignore the current enemy. It should be clear from the foregoing narrative that there were perfectly good financial and military reasons for the expedition. Cromwell had considered a continental war against France in 1651–4 but found both domestic and European circumstances in mid-1654 to be inappropriate. Cromwell's addresses to Parliament in September 1656 and January 1658 should not be taken as sufficient explanation of the whole of his Spanish policy, though they do provide evidence of his latent prejudices. These undoubtedly influenced the Protector's policy in the Caribbean, not least the decision to undertake the expedition with so few and so inadequately trained troops in the first place. The scant preparations show his overconfidence about resistance. Above all, his attitude to the American colonists reveals the extent of his ill-informed naïvety about colonial affairs.

THE BACKGROUND TO THE EXPEDITION

The actions of Cromwell in negotiating with Spain in Europe and attacking her in America have been cited to support a number of theories. It is taken as an example of his alleged deviousness – that he had only negotiated with Cardenas to lull Spain into a sense of security while he was preparing to stab her in the back. In the aftermath of Hispaniola this was the attitude taken by the Spaniards.[1] The expedition appeared to suggest that Cromwell was obsessed with Elizabethan parallels. Whether or not a full war with Spain in Europe was the intention, Cromwell intended to attack them beyond the 'Line'

71

(i.e. in their colonies). Cromwell and Thurloe confirmed that this was the intention when the Design was planned.[2] Hence it was cited as evidence that Cromwell believed in the theory of 'No Peace Beyond the Line'. Cromwell and his adviser Gage both made use of the claims that Spain sometimes used, namely that due to the papal award at Tordesillas (1494) they had exclusive rights to America, and were not bound by treaties signed since then with heretics recognising the latter's possessions.

The Design is inseparable from the internal and international situation in the summer of 1654, as the following points make clear:

1. Some employment was desirable for the armed forces after the conclusion of the Dutch War; the Navy in particular, with its '160 ships swimming'.
2. Financial requirements meant that the target had to be remunerative. New taxes would cause internal discontent. The Spanish empire was reckoned to be rich and easy to attack. Gage's work confirmed this, though it was selective in its evidence.
3. The Design was *not* planned until it had been discovered that the French rebels were unlikely to rise again and that Spain seemed unable to afford the subsidy which Cromwell needed if he was to be her ally in Europe. An attack on France now appeared unlikely; so another target had to be selected.
4. As Thurloe admitted, Spain was not so dangerous as an enemy and could not loan so much support to Charles II should they decide to use him against Cromwell.
5. Spain's entanglement in Europe meant that she was unlikely to be able to afford open war anyway.
6. The divided state of the Council meant that an open was on either France or Spain would alienate a number of Councillors. Cromwell could present the attack to Lambert as a justified response to Spanish colonial aggression, though it was clearly out of proportion to the damage done to the English.
7. It was widely believed that an attack on the Caribbean islands would not bring about war; especially as Spain was weak and embattled enough in Europe already.[3] Cromwell did, however, allow his generals to land on

the mainland if they so desired (see the 'Instructions'); he was therefore not avoiding war at any cost.

All these factors complemented the advantages of damaging Spain's financial viability in Europe. The above reasons for an attack coincided with the traditional way in which the opponents of Spanish imperialism in Europe had previously sought to weaken her. The Dutch had seized Spain's Plate Fleet en route to Europe (1618) and considered raising a revolt in Spanish America by arming Indians and Negroes.[4] The cheapness of the expense, the vast profits to be reaped, and the good to the European Protestants lay behind the encouragement which Parliamentary leaders gave to James I in 1621–4 to attack the same area as Cromwell now chose. Hence Sir John Eliot asked Parliament in March 1624: 'Are we poor? Spain is rich. There are our Indies'.[5] Rudyerd, who was to sit on the Parliamentary Board for the Colonies with Cromwell, proposed to the same Parliament that such an attack be preferred to war in Europe 'by way of diversion to save our charges'.[6] Even in the Elizabethan period, there had been many failures once Spain organised her defences properly, as in 1597, but such strategy was shrouded in nostalgia, memories of its failures being beyond the experience of most people. The drawbacks to continental involvement had been dicovered in the 1620s and criticised in Parliament. Cromwell's delusion of the cheapness and effectiveness of such a plan was not an individual case of 'Elizabethan obsession'; it was a misconception widely shared by men without experience of the restraints of government.

Cromwell's plans suffered from other delusions. Most importantly, his belief that the English traders in the Caribbean needed to receive formal recognition from Madrid ignored their existing position. The Spanish mercantile marine had decreased drastically since 1600, much of the trade between Spain and America falling perforce into the hands of Dutch and English interlopers.[7] All this was still technically illegal, but it was connived at locally as without it the inhabitants would be unable to obtain vital supplies. The Viceroyalites were unable to see that every order was enforced and illegal traders were only harassed on occasion by zealous officials, authorities pursuing private grudges, or individual captains and customs men who wanted to indulge in piracy. The Treaty of Tordesillas was hardly a serious factor, since Spain had previously made treaties with other countries involving recognition of their possessions in America (as with England in 1604 and 1630). It was a rather useful instrument of Protestant propaganda. The recent attacks on English ships and citizens were religiously listed as examples of Popish treachery in the Manifesto of October 1655, but the individuals who had carried out the actions were officers of a ramshackle, inefficient, decentralised regime which had little contact with Madrid. In seeking to achieve official trading rights in the Caribbean, Cromwell did not realise that the English traders were allowed a good deal of trade already by the local authorities and that Spain would never grant this point officially. The Council consulted local traders such as Hatsell and Limbery, and Thurloe's brother-in-law Noell who traded in the region; hence they must have been aware of all the trade that actually occurred. Cromwell, however, insisted on the position being regularised. Control from Madrid was so weak that harassment would have continued anyway. Cromwell's rigid demands only led to a war whch made the merchants' position worse. It is likely that he sincerely believed that his efforts – first excessive demands and then war – were for the ultimate good of his traders, but he showed his total misconception of the attitude to Spanish America adopted by those men who lived and worked in the region.

Cromwell's sending of a state expedition to the colonies was an unprecedented action of governmental interference in local affairs. A fleet had indeed been sent to the West Indies in 1605–2 to deal with the Royalist threat posed by Prince Rupert and Lord Willoughby, but Cromwell was now sending government troops to organise a war on a (friendly) European power's colonies. The militant aggressiveness of the New Model Army indicated that its leaders were likely to pursue an equally aggressive – and Protestant – foreign policy, though their insecurity required them to do so anyway. Cromwell's assumption of power marked the translation into action of two trends of thought and private initiative which had become increasingly apparent among ordinary people and the 'Opposition' to the Stuart Court:

(a)   Anti-Spanish propaganda. This had become popular since the wars with Spain and reflected the militant anti-Catholicism of the period. The Spanish Inquisition formed part of national Protestant demonology, and oppression of the natives had been popular reading among their enemies since the writings of Las Casas were published. The *Tears of the Indians* was regularly reprinted in Protestant states at war with Spain to act as a focus for hatred of the enemy, being translated afresh by Milton's nephew in 1656. This propaganda had revived in England in the 1620s – the formative years of most of the Council – when Spain was seen as the evil force masterminding the Counter-Reformation and trying to turn the Bohemian crisis into a general assault on Protestantism. General paranoia about 'Popery' even among the more educated classes of society is testified to by the successive panics of 1641, 1666 and 1678. This did not prevent good relations between Cardenas and a succession of republican leaders, even Cromwell when he deemed it essential. The Spanish empire was, however, a different matter from Spain itself. The war could be justified to the Army and populace in terms which they would understand, as was proved by the outburst of propaganda which followed the 'Manifesto'. Milton, the most celebrated and skilful author at Cromwell's disposal, published a justificatory *Dialogue containing . . . a Discourse concerning the present Design in the West Indies* in 1655.[8]

(b)   Cromwell's plan was also the logical extension into state policy of the private initiatives taken against Spanish America in the past decades. As early as 1624 a Parliamentary scheme was thought up involving the creation of a 'West Indies Company' to coordinate new Protestant settlements in conjunction with colonial war, and as Spanish indifference to Charles's attempts to have the Palatinate returned by patient diplomacy became apparent this gained some favour at Court. In 1625 Attorney-General Heath warned that England should act openly or secretly to secure her possessions in the region,[9] and in September 1637 the Government considered setting up a company to seize a port in Spanish America and plunder the region by land and by sea.[10] Significantly, the leading backers of this plan were all Protestants without influence with the 'inner circle' around the King, a group of suspected crypto-Catholics. The most notable of them was the veteran diplomat Sir Thomas Roe, whose interest in a European Protestant league (he was a friend of Dury and Hartlib) went hand-in-hand with close interests in America.

Some prominent MPs and Lords who had opposed the King's policies in the 1620s and/or were to do so in 1640, led by Pym, St John, Rudyerd, Warwick, and Lord Saye and Sele, took a course divergent to the Government by launching a private war in the Caribbean. They formed a special company and sent out an expedition to take Providence Island, a small but strategically vital island off what is now Nicaragua, whence they could mke easy pirate raids on the mainland or the Plate galleons leaving Panama for Spain. The strategic position and use of Providence anticipated the use Cromwell intended to make of Hispaniola and did make of Jamaica; the only difference was that Cromwell's attack was on a larger scale.

The English settlements on Providence and Tortugas were clearly pirate bases rather than trading posts and were, moreover, not covered by the treaty of 1630 between England and Spain. Their loss to Spanish assaults in 1635 and 1641 marked the end of a private, unauthorised initiative, so these attacks were not really as indefensible as the loss of English trading vessels to Spanish ships or port authorities. When Cromwell came to commission a list of Spanish misdeeds he made not mention of these distinctions, but chose to regard them all as evidence of Spanish malevolence. The acts of reprisal which followed the loss of Providence consisted of more privateering; in 1641 Warwick commissioned Captain Jackson to raid the American mainland from Caracas to Honduras and in 1642–3 he sailed into the Caribbean and sacked St Iago de la Vega, with little resistance.[11] The policy of pursuing piratical reprisals since official complaints were ineffective was taken over by the Government after the Civil War.

Two further points need to be made. First, Cromwell's expeditionary force was relatively small and consisted of 'second-rate' troops. The successes of Jackson and others would have made Cromwell confident that these forces were adequate. Second, the justification was not that there was 'No Peace Beyond the Line' in any case. Cromwell argued that the point at issue was that whether there was peace there or not in legal terms, the Spaniards were acting as if there were not. According to Venables, Cromwell told him: 'Either there was peace with the Spaniard in the West Indies or there was not. If peace they had violated it, and to seek reparation was just. If we had not peace, there was nothing acted against articles [the Treaty of 1630].'[12] Cromwell's determination to take action can be traced to his general concept of his duties as 'godly' ruler and his aggressive attitude towards all matters of dispute with another Power. This plan was the most notable example of an attitude he expressed equally with the Dutch, the French and the Portuguese.

THE PLANS AGAINST SPANISH AMERICA

There were two main alternatives − to attack an island or to land on the mainland. It had been decided that it was cheaper and more prudent to 'make a partial work of it' at the first attempt, rather than to send a large and expensive army out of the country while the Royalists remained a menace. The success of Providence Island would indicate that the obvious course was to take an island. This was also the wisest choice if it was not intended to drive Spain into open war.

Gage's Plan

The importance of Thomas Gage as Cromwell's main adviser was admitted by contemporaries, for example Whitelocke and Stouppe.[13] He had had the most experience of travel in the Spanish dominions, having resided from 1625 to 1637 as a Catholic priest in Central America before returning to Europe and becoming a Protestant propagandist. He provided supposedly 'expert' knowledge of Spanish weakness, moral turpitude and lack of defence, and it is certain that his zealous optimism of success had considerable effect on Cromwell. Thomas Chaloner had been Gage's patron under the Commonwealth and had written an inflammatory preface to the renegade priest's work, *The English–American His Travels by Land and Sea.*[14] The same ideas were apparent in the 'Vermuyden Plan' which called for a combination of imperialist conquest and missionary work in the Spanish empire.

Gage's arguments usefully combined religion with national interest and could be used in English propaganda. The English had only been deprived of their opportunities in 1492 by 'that narrow-hearted prince' Henry VII refusing patronage to Columbus. Spain claimed that it had saved the Indians from idolatry, war and human sacrifice, but 'they have sacrificed many millions to the idol of their barbarous cruelty'. It was ridiculous to grant the right of conquest of any nation to those who had first 'discovered' it, particularly on the initiative of the Antichrist in Rome. The 'just right and title' belonged to the natives; they could 'legally transfer or communicate it to others . . . [by] their willing and free invitation to protection'. Spain had 'not title but force' and deserved to lose this the way they had gained it. The Dutch had set a precedent of coordinated Protestant colonisation while the English had restricted themselves to 'pursuing a private trade . . . of which we are likely to be deprived'. The existing plantations in the English West Indies meant that 'we have advanced our journey the better part of the way' and were already accustomed to the climate.[15] Gage's warning about climate was repeated by Lambert but ignored by Cromwell.

Early in 1654 Gage drew up a summary of his opinions for Thurloe, entitled *Some Brief and True Observations concerning the West Indies.* He was cautious enough to admit that it was not yet safe to remove substantial forces from England and that enough ships must be left in home waters to 'overpower all enemies abroad and be a safety to . . . trade'. The expedition would, however, undermine Spanish oppression in Europe. God would not put up with sinners for ever, and there were 'no more sinful people than the Spaniards in America, both great and small'. Hispaniola had been the Spaniards' first plantation and hence it would be taken as a bad omen for them if it was lost; it was 'not a quarter of it inhabited and so more easy to take'. Gage also made the most of the implications of Spanish attacks on Providence, Tortugas, St Kitts and shipping in general.[16] Attacking the Spanish colonies was justified as a 'pre-emptive strike'. It appears that Cromwell believed this exaggeration. The Spaniards would not fight back vigorously as they were 'a lazy sinful people, feeding like beasts upon their lusts and upon the fat of the land . . . never trained up to war'.

He also proposed that the English should make use of disaffected Indians, Negroes, Mulattoes and Creoles who all hated their rulers. This tactic had been used on a limited scale by

Drake and Raleigh, but Admiral Brouwer's Dutch fleet had attempted to raise a substantial rebellion in Chile as late as 1632. This would require more effort than Cromwell was prepared to put into the first stage of his plan. Gage did however warn that any attack must be followed up swiftly with reinforcements if Spain was not to have the respite she needed to strengthen her defences after the first attack and prevent further successes.[17] The wisdom of this was proved by the lack of success which Cromwell's limited forces had in 1655–8.

Colonel Modyford's Plan

An alternative to Gage's plan was put forward some time in 1654 by Colonel Thomas Modyford, a former Royalist who owned a plantation in Barbados. His idea owed much to the precedent of Raleigh in that he preferred to consider an expedition to the Orinoco basin with the help of friendly Indians. He urged Cromwell to ignore the islands as the loss of one of them would not seriously damage Spanish power; the only island he considered worth attacking was Havana, the 'backdoor' to the Spanish empire. The difficulties of setting up a new colony on an island were immense as there were copious trees and scrub which would have to be uprooted to build settlements and plant crops; the soil was poor and the time involved in tilling it immense. A descent on the mainland would be easier as there were towns already built, fields tilled and friendly Indians to lend assistance. Jackson's success implied that there would not be much resistance.

Modyford's own preference was for the Orinoco, to the windward of the Spanish empire which meant that it would not be reinforced or attacked except from Europe. It was safe for Caribbean colonists to move there, something they showed great reluctance to do regarding Jamaica. Modyford suggested that Cromwell send 3000 men to Barbados where local reinforcements would double their number; he shared Cromwell's optimism of their willingness to help and of their martial ability. They should then land on Trinidad, expel the Spaniards and abandon the infertile island to the Indians. The English should then overrun the Spanish outpost of San Thome on the Orinoco and proceed westwards and systematically overrun the Venezuelan coast, where Spanish weakness was apparent.

Modyford accurately predicted that a small unsettled island would not attract colonists and might well cause English troops to lose their morale and start to desert.[18]

THE EXPEDITION: THE COUNCIL'S CHOICE OF TARGET

The Council named a committee of officers and civilians in August to superintend preparations for the Design. It included a number with knowledge of the area – Captain Limbery, Vice-Admiral William Goodson (who had visited Cartagena), Noell and Thompson. The other members were the intended commanders, Admiral William Penn and siege expert Colonel Robert Venables; a number of minor naval officers; Andrew Riccard, a prominent merchant; and two less important merchants, Williams and Vincent.[19] Five government commissioners were appointed to command the expedition and to act as supreme commanders of all the English colonies – an unprecedented step of government interference in America which had been recommended by Colonel Modyford to prevent disputes about authority. These were Penn, Venables, Edmund Winslow, the trusted Barbados planter Richard Holdip,[20] and Captain Edward Blagg. The expedition was to consist of 14 warships, 3000 infantry, 100 cavalry and reinforcements from Barbados; more could not be afforded.

In December the preparations were complete and Penn and Venables were issued with their orders. The attack on Spanish possessions was to include all ships found trading with them, which manifestly failed to exclude the Dutch. They were at peace with both England and Spain and, as they did not know of any Anglo-Spanish conflict, had every right to trade with Spanish possessions.

Venables' commission presented the choice of target as flexible. The expedition was 'to gain an interest in that part of the West Indies in the possession of the Spaniard. For affecting whereof we shall not tie you up to a method by any particular instructions but only to communicate to you what has been our consideration.' There were two options:

1.　The islands, in particular Hispaniola or Puerto Rico. 'Many Englishmen will come thither from other parts, and so become magazines of men and provisions for carrying the Design upon the Mainland.' They were 'much to the windward of the rest of the Spanish dominions', and could not be reinforced easily from New Spain. (Modyford's influence is apparent.) Thence the expedition could proceed to take Havana which 'is so considerable, we have thoughts of beginning the attempt on Cuba and still judge it worthy of consideration'. Venables ignored this.

2. The mainland, 'aiming therein chiefly at Cartagena . . . the seat of the intended Design, securing some places by the way thereto that the Spaniards might not be to the windward of us'. This would secure 'houses ready built, a country ready planted, and most people Indians who will submit to you, being but few Spaniards there' – as Modyford had advised. This would enable a close guard to be kept upon Panama.[21]

Modyford had pointed out many of the problems which would be encountered on the islands, and the Government was aware of them. The choice to attack Hispaniola was that of the Commissioners. It should be noted that observers believed an attack on the islands would not mean war, but Cromwell was equally prepared to take the islands or Cartagena; it cannot be said that he would not risk war.

INADEQUACIES OF THE EXPEDITION

Security required that the Government's best troops were retained at home. It was clearly not intended to be more than a 'side-show' to Cromwell's European designs, as is made apparent by the small number and poor quality of the troops who were selected. Men were chosen from standing regiments to form new ones rather than being sent out as existing units who were used to fighting together. Moreover, the men chosen were often the worst soldiers in the regiments whom their officers desired to be rid of. Beggars, deserters, thieves and other riff-raff were gathered off the streets, and were given no adequate training before they sailed due to the need for haste. Experienced troops had enough difficulties in the tropics as was to be shown by future expeditions of regular soldiers. However, the English had not yet had the advantage of experience to warn them of such difficulties, and it should be noted that Cromwell intended seasoned colonists to reinforce them in Barbados. Both Gage and Lambert had warned of the hazards of tropical disease.

The problems which would beset the expedition were apparent before it left England, as Desborough had to be sent down to the fleet to crush incipient mutiny and Venables made protests at the quality of his men before be sailed.[22] Cromwell's choice of Commissioners was also at fault; he made the success of the Design depend on cooperation and tolerance between his commanders, but Admiral Penn was noted for his temper and suspicious nature. Cromwell had already warned him of the need to be less jealous before the fleet sailed.[23]

The inadequacy of Cromwell's assumption of American help was shown at Barbados. The English were not entirely welcome and this cannot be ascribed solely to the remnants of Royalist sympathies. The colonists showed no sense of gratitude for their assistance, but protested at the expedition's arrest of Dutch shipping which had been trading in defiance of the Navigation Act. Planters objected when their servants deserted to join the expedition; these servants formed the bulk of the recruits, as their superiors had no wish to risk their lives for such a hazardous venture. These men were no good as soldiers.[24] The English government also assumed that Barbados wood could be fitted with English pike-heads, which proved not to be the case. The stores sent out from England were inadequate.

The troubles caused by Penn and Butler could have been avoided by better planning, but the Government did not give the Design the thought it needed. Bad luck played a part in the humiliating defeat at Santo Domingo, since the rockiness of the coastline prevented the expedition landing where intended, and when it landed at two different points east and west of the city the width of the River Ozama prevented the two forces linking up. However, the resulting military disaster was clearly the result of human error. The expedition abandoned its plan and sailed to Jamaica, where fortunately the garrisons around the main harbour put up no resistance and fled. Luck thus played a considerable role in this English success, but the capture of one island did not hide the main outcome of the expedition – the first real disaster for Cromwell's armies. This outweighed the capture of Jamaica in the reaction that it had in Europe, unfortunately making Spain confident enough to challenge Cromwell that autumn.

AFTERMATH OF THE DESIGN

In autumn of 1655 the Government set up a specific committee to take charge of Jamaica, resolving to assist the colony by such measures as army reinforcements and persuading other English Caribbean settlers to move there. Already, in July, reinforcements had been sent out before the outcome of the attack on Hispaniola was known. This policy was not reversed when it was realised how limited the success had been, though it appears that the Council were misled by optimistic letters from their commanders to believe that resistance from the remaining Spaniards and Negroes on Jamaica was minimal, when this was not the case.[25] More troops were sent out in October 1655 and October 1656, though many of the latter were drowned en route.[26] The condition of the settlement was in fact extremely precarious, as is apparent from the reports of its commanders back to Thurloe.[27] The losses to tropical disease were severe both among officers and men. There was also trouble among the officers, one of whom was cashiered and a second sent home. The lack of experienced soldiers was reflected in the swift decline in morale, as Sedgewick wrote of them.[28] They were mostly useless at planting, and the necessity to raise crops detracted from their ability to fight the guerillas lurking in the northern mountains and to serve with the fleet as it raided Spanish ports and ships. Sedgewick warned that 'the army can afford no assistance to present prosecution of any Design; it is a mercy if in a capacity to maintain the island'.[29] The colony survived by Spanish weakness rather than its own efforts. By the time Spanish troops landed the position of the colonists had improved under the capable Colonel D'Oyley, and they were routed on 22 June/2 July 1658.[30] After this the remaining Spaniards abandoned serious resistance and the island was clear of them within two years.

The lack of success of the fleet showed up the fallacy of

Cromwell's optimism about the ease with which 'six nimble frigates' could sweep the seas. The weakness of the colony meant less ability to attack Spanish targets, and Cromwell's aim of securing loot could not be met by a force which was too small to attack large towns or the Plate Fleet. Significantly, the latter was not sighted until October 1658 and then by a force which was too small to attack it. Only off Europe could Cromwell afford to concentrate a fleet adequate to attempt this target, and it was in these waters that his admirals achieved the spectacular successes of 1656 and 1657. In the Caribbean, Admiral Goodson attacked Santa Marta in autumn 1655[31] and Rio de la Hacha early in 1656, with small profit.[32] Cromwell thus discovered that the expense of sending his fleet to American waters outweighed the financial advantages, though his limited involvement is an indication of his caution. Caribbean campaigning had been restricted to private endeavour until he resolved to intervene, but in later years it returned to this unofficial involvement as the English colonies became centres of highly remunerative piracy.

Cromwell had shown little concern for that aspect of Gage's plan which involved liberating the Indians. This would take more effort than he was prepared to spend on the Design, particularly once he was at war with Spain. Sedgewick's warning that the English raiders would 'appear a bloody, cruel, and ruinating people' worse than the Spaniards[33] had no effect; London had other priorities. Simon de Casseres, a Portuguese Jew who had sailed with the Design, sent a plan to Thurloe suggesting that the Council should send another force to Chile to assist an Indian rebellion and attack the Spanish treasure ships leaving Acapulco – a repeat of the Dutch attempt of 1632. This offer was ignored.[34]

It can truthfully be said that Cromwell had more urgent priorities in 1656–8 than sending out more troops and ships to the West Indies. He showed no further enthusiasm on those matters concerning which he was offered the help of the mercantile community. Most importantly, the setting up of assorted committees to oversee the West Indies was not followed by the establishment of a formal 'West Indies Company' to channel mercantile funds into the area. In 1656/7, a proposal was submitted to the Council for 'the erecting of a West India Company for the better serving the interests of this

Commonwealth in America', its structure and privileges to be based on that of the East India Company. The principal backers were Martin Noell, Thomas Povey, Lord Willoughby of Parham and William Watts.[35] They requested equal privileges and rights in seizing enemy prizes to the East India Company, together with letters of support to the English governors in the Caribbean and the loan of some ships of war. In return, they proposed to set up new colonies, manage trading ventures and privateering, and bring the Indians to trade with England and become Christians. Their efforts would have the follow benefits: improve the effectiveness of the Jamaican colony (and provide private support for it); increase trade with Spanish subjects to encourage their disloyalty to their masters; induce Spain to make an agreeable peace to save its position in the Caribbean or else make Cromwell's naval war there cheaper to maintain; and use some of the 'young idle Gentry of this nation' who were 'dangerous to the public peace and do things dishonourable to their name and family at home whilst they may find encouragement and delight in foreign action and adventure'.[36] It would thus be useful to distract potential Royalist support, as well as for moral purposes.

Along with this general proposal, Noell and his friends had a specific plan for the next stage of the Western Design. They were prepared, at their own expense, to send a small expedition to Florida and raise the local Indians against Spain, setting up a base to intercept Spanish shipping in the Bahama Channel. This showed strategic thinking – all Spain's galleons would now have to pass close to English positions at Barbados, Jamaica or near Miami. It would 'gain a footing thereby upon some of the most considerable dominions and pretensions of the Spaniard, and endeavour the taking in some eminent forts of his and to erect others to interrupt his trade at sea'. Finally, it would 'settle manage and regulate a trade in and about the Bay of Mexico and the Continent of Florida'.[37] The plan was not taken up but a Floridan chief did later visit London.

One of Cromwell's most serious mistakes was to exaggerate the willingness of colonists already settled in America to aid the Design. The Barbadians in particular were annoyed at English interference with their trade with the Dutch. Their attitude showed that Cromwell's belief that the English colonies were menaced by the Spanish was not shared by the men who were supposedly under threat. Most of the local colonists were peaceful settlers – planters and traders – rather than militant Protestants who would look favourably on war because of the advantages it would offer to their religion. Some of the Caribbean colonists had indeed assisted Prince Rupert and Lord Willoughby, and Royalist intrigues against the Republic's governors (e.g. Searle) were still reported in the mid-1650s.[38] The loyalty of the Caribbean settlers was thus not certain, and in any case it was optimistic to assume that they would leave their existing settlements. Cromwell wrongly supposed that as many of the New World settlers had left England for their consciences' sake, they would be only too willing to assist his Protestant design, as illustrated by the flattering manner in which he frequently addressed the leading 'Saints' in New England.[39] He assumed that these Protestant heroes would be only too glad to uproot themselves and move to his new colony, even though it was a small and unhealthy island still menaced by Spanish and Negro fugitives. Lambert had warned him of the unlikelihood that they would do so, and Modyford had cautioned against the settlement of 'virgin soil' where the colonists would have to plant, clear scrub and build for themselves. Cromwell preferred to believe that the colonists would carry out their Christian duty.

When Jamaica was occupied the Government launched a campaign to encourage settlers and claimed erroneously that all resistance was at an end. It was stressed that the colonists would be 'under the immediate protection of this state and so eased of the danger and charge that other plantations are subject to'.[40] The Western Design itself had been an unprecedented example of state interference. Now the State took a hand in colonisation as well, promoting a specific Protestant venture in the tradition of the 'Providence Island Company' and Warwick's activities on Trinidad. The colonists were to be free from excise for three years and to be under no military obligations except in self-defence; there was to be no rent for seven years and subsequently at 1d per acre. All Protestant adult males were to receive twenty acres and every settler to be awarded English citizenship.[41]

Despite Cromwell's encouragement, the only Caribbean colonists who were inspired to move *en masse* were Governor Stokes and his people from Nevis.[42] They were an unusual case as their island was small and isolated and Jamaica offered them the hope of more security and prosperity, and even so two-thirds of them died after their arrival.[43] The Council ordered the whole of the small colony on Eleuthera in the Bahamas to move, but it appears that most of them returned to Bermuda whence they had come in 1647 rather than obey.[44] Other Governors did not wish to see their revenues denuded by the removal of their subjects, and as such proved as uncooperative as they dared to be; by 1658 only 250 Bermudans had moved to Jamaica.[45] General Brayne warned that 'the interest of the Governors being the inhabitants there, they receiving benefit from them, I fear I shall have little success'.[46]

Cromwell's failure was particularly apparent with regard to the much admired 'Saints' in New England, the people whom he evidently most expected to cooperate with his plan with appropriate zeal. His choice as ambassador to the New Englanders was Vincent Gookin, an American settler resident in England and employed by the Commonwealth who had been involved with the Protestant colonisation plans in Ireland.[47] Cromwell believed the New Englanders should all be willing to move to Jamaica as their own climate was much inferior, an example of his lack of understanding of how serious their own problems would have to become before any colonists considered uprooting themselves;[48] they had 'as clear a call to transport themselves from thence to Jamaica as they had from England to New England'.[49] The official instructions which were sent with Gookin claimed that Cromwell had undertaken the Design out of the 'love, affection, and fellow-feeling' that he had for the colonists, who had been driven out of their own country into the wilderness by Papist persecution; he tactfully said nothing about the more pressing matters of English financial needs and the armed forces.[50] This is a telling argument against any portrayal of him as a calculating and realistic statesman.

The results of Gookin's mission were largely what a more realistic man would have expected, and fulfilled Lambert and Modyford's warnings. When the envoy reached Boston he found that reports spoke of Jamaica's unhealthfulness and the likelihood of Spanish attack – two important reasons why the colonists should stay where they were.[51] His appeal was received and published by the authorities in Massachusetts, Connecticut and New Haven, but the 'best persons' were discouraged by reports of the epidemics on the island and the ministers – the leaders of public opinion – had no incentive to move.[52] Only a few bold persons of minor social standing had little to lose by undertaking such a gamble. Instead of being inspired by his appeal, the colonists were alarmed by the stories which reached New England.[53] A few 'godly discreet persons' agreed to visit Jamaica and see for themselves and reported back that the island was not as ill-favoured as feared, but the colony was too small and undefended to be worth supporting. Gookin only obtained about 300 settlers, mostly people with nothing to lose by the gamble such as 'young persons under family government, many of them females . . . and of low estates'.[54]

One of the Commonwealth's enthusiasms had been for the establishment of an ideal Protestant settlement to be managed by what would now be called 'social engineering'. This idea had been fostered in particular by Samuel Hartlib and his friends, though they had mainly thought in terms of Ireland.[55] Cromwell's support for such an idea is shown by his massive 'clearances' of the Catholic Irish, though this had also involved removing a menace to English security and providing land for his troops. The Protector's desire to settle English Protestants in Jamaica should be seen in this light. For reasons of security the reinforcement troops sent to Jamaica in 1655–7 had to be of a satisfactory standard of efficiency, but this did not exclude a policy of sending men who might cause trouble at home. Lucy Hutchinson maintained that Cromwell used Jamaica as an unofficial means of sending Anabaptist officers into exile.[56] The radicals in the Army in Ireland could still indirectly threaten England and proved a serious problem for the uncongenial Henry Cromwell, the Protector's second son, who ruled the country in 1656–9, but officers in America could not exert any influence on events in the British Isles. The Commonwealth had also used the West Indies as a place of exile for thousands of unwanted Irish and Scottish Royalists; it appears that by 1655 the existing colonies were saturated with them. Jamaica would come in useful if any more were to be exiled.[57] The English agent in Paris, René Augier, presented a plan for transporting European Protestant exiles in need of new homes to Jamaica to the Council in summer 1657,[58] following in the footsteps of Hartlib and others who had planned such a settlement for Ireland. However, the main task of settlement was forced upon various bodies of people regarded as 'social undesirables'. The shortage of women on the island caused Thurloe to ask Lord Broghill for a supply of 'women and maids', though all he was offered was 2–3000 'loose vagabonds'.[59] Early in 1656, 4000 single women, some of them London prostitutes collected in the Tower, were shipped to Jamaica,[60] and the Jamaica Committee was instructed to round up 8000 young Irish men and women.[61] Some young Londoners were taken aboard a ship against their will to 'make up the numbers' in July 1657, and the authorities at the Tower were ordered to prevent this recurring.[62]

The Western Design is the clearest example of the limits to Cromwell's caution. He suffered from a number of serious misconceptions about the situation in America, not least the goodwill of the existing colonists for his plans. His inadequately planned intervention caused more damage by its disruption of trade through a Spanish war than the Spaniards were causing already by occasional harassment, and the colonists did not thank him. The expedition served the interests of the Government rather than those of the local settlers, but there is no need to assume from this that the Protector was insincere in maintaining that he was assisting his countrymen's interests. The Design was marked by the same state interference for its citizens' benefit that marked Cromwell's concern over the debts owing to Englishmen abroad. However, the difference regarding Europe was that Cromwell showed greater caution in 'home waters' and did not intervene on the Continent without near certainty of success and adequate intelligence. The reports received form France in 1653–4 caused him to abandon that plan. His American policy was marked by no such caution. There are, however, three mitigating factors which go some way to explain the mistake, if not to excuse his overconfidence.

1. Accurate intelligence from across the Atlantic was harder to come by than from France and would take longer to collect. Cromwell consulted traders with experience of Hispaniola, and to send his own intelligencers to assess the situation would have required a delay of a year or so.

2. The logistics of campaigning were that Cromwell's troops had to be 'in position' across the Atlantic to take advantage

of the 'dry season'. The months of April–August 1655 were the easiest season for the offensive, assuming that the time taken to collect men and supplies invalidated an attack in midwinter 1654–5. Accordingly, there was considerable haste in the autumn of 1654 to collect troops and supplies in order to ship them in time. An American expedition could not be planned with such leisure as a European one.

3. The expedition was useful to English interests, but it was not as crucial to national survival as the Franco-Spanish conflict. Cromwell had to keep his best troops in England; he could afford to send good regiments to Flanders in 1657 because they could be withdrawn with ease in case of a revolt. The troops sent to America would be useless to national defence and could only be withdrawn at several months' notice. Cromwell could not spare the kind of force that he was to send to Flanders, though he could have sent one or two full regiments with proper officers instead of the sweepings of different regiments. Cromwell had to be cautious when dealing with the invasion of France, but in this less important matter he showed how reckless he could be when there were no such factors to restrain him.

6 Leda's Mission and the Vaudois Massacre

Having discussed the Western Design, it is time to return to the course of relations in Europe and consider the crisis that threatened Cromwell's rapprochement with France when his attack on Spanish territory was already under way. Despite Spain's public fury at Cromwell's 'unexpected treachery', their government was clearly aware of the Design's target since the summer of 1654, although the actual course of the attack was not known until August 1655. Throughout this period Cardenas continued to negotiate and in May 1655 Spain sent the Marquis of Leda to assist him. It was apparent that Cromwell was unlikely to mitigate his harsh demands, the King's 'two eyes', and as Leda did not offer any new terms his mission was not intended to prevent a breach by surrendering to Cromwell's demands. However, France feared for his success despite current events in America. Spain did not retaliate until it was known that Cromwell's expedition had been rebuffed and that his military power was not as great as was feared in 1654.

The summer of 1655 still found both 'Crowns' angling for Cromwell's support, the French despite Acadia and the Spanish despite the Design. A new factor seemed to diminish France's hopes and led to renewed efforts to blacken her reputation on the part of Spain. This was the persecution of Protestants in Savoy, a 'satellite' of France, in which French troops were implicated. It served to counteract Cromwell's earlier claims that France was not so intolerant as Spain and revived the possibility of Huguenot rebellions in southern France. Cromwell seemed to be caught in a dilemma over what action to take, and held up the French treaty while French pressure was brought to bear on the Duke of Savoy to reverse his policy. Moral indignation and confidence of France's need for his goodwill caused the Protector to interfere in this matter; he did not judge Mazarin likely to be angry enough to prefer a rapprochement with Spain to satisfying English demands. Despite the Design he evidently did not consider himself bound to France at this point. Significantly, Spain did not either. As in 1654, the mutual hatred of France and Spain gave Cromwell the luxury of being able to put this new pressure on France at a time when he was instructing Blake to take Spain's Plate Fleet in European waters, an occurrence which Spain could not overlook.

Spain's desire to seek agreement on a military offensive in Flanders shows uncertainty over Cromwell's intentions. Despite the fact that Spain could not find money now any more than in 1654, the old issue of the return of Calais to England was revived. In any case, the Spanish Council of State was a rather cumbersome and slow-thinking body of grandees and bureaucrats, which was not renowned for its flexibility of thought and was not counter-balanced by an adaptable and forceful monarch or chief minister. Accordingly, the idea of reconsidering years of efforts to seek English support against France was not likely to commend itself. Circumstances in the military sphere were not promising enough for Philip IV and de Haro to consider dispensing with potential allies, with Portugal still in revolt and the French in Catalonia. The Spanish government was certainly aware of Cromwell's intentions in America, despite later cries of surprise. According to Quirini, English Catholics had informed Spain of the Design in 1654 and a ship had been sent to warn the authorities on Hispaniola. Cardenas had been 'distressed' at the report but had continued to negotiate.[1] In April 1655, the Royalist Sir Benjamin Wright informed Hyde that Spain had been alarmed over Penn's intentions 'these many months' and many feared for the Plate Fleet.[2] That month Colonel Sexby escaped from custody, fled to Brussels and warned that the fleet had gone to take an island in the West Indies and intercept the Plate Fleet. He unsuccessfully offered to organise mutiny in the English navy in return for £150 000.[3] Spain was thus adequately warned but needed help against France none the less.

The terms of Leda's negotiation did not include anything likely to lure Cromwell into accepting, notably the crucial rights to official English trade in America and toleration of English Protestant services in Spain. These Cardenas had proudly referred to as 'his master's two eyes', and no offer was made on them.[4] As before, the Spanish envoys were only to discuss a military alliance involving payment of a Spanish subsidy and the cession of Calais to England.[5] They considered the chance worth taking at this late stage to avoid an Anglo-French alliance. This decision may well have owed its origin to the misconceptions of Cardenas, who had maintained relations with Parliamentary leaders since 1640 and seems to have underestimated the importance of ideology in English decision-making. He wrongly assumed that Lambert and the merchants had enough influence on the Protector to counterbalance Spain's enemies, since he was still making efforts to use them to put pressure on the Government in the autumn when such hopes were useless. It also appears that de Haro himself was overconfident of Cromwell's goodwill, as even in July 'he cannot digest the idea that England is contemplating a breach with such indignity and has gone so far as to say that Cromwell is his great friend'.[6] When it was finally known that the Design had landed, supposedly on Cuba, Quirini was informed that 'provided they do not attack the ports and fortresses . . . they will pretend that they have no formal war, in conformity with the articles of their ancient confederation'.[7] The turning-point was not the news of the Design but the news of its outcome.

Leda arrived in England with the Marquis of San Steffano, Condé's envoy, and Count Tott (a representative of former Queen Christina, Spain's ally) in May. On 4/14 May Strickland was appointed to take charge of his entertainment and money was set aside for the purpose.[8] San Steffano was to remind Cromwell how weak and exposed French ports were while her troops fought Spain in Flanders, but his bait was not taken.[9] Leda offered Cromwell the chance to take Calais with Spanish aid on 11/21 May, but was told that England demanded the terms of 'trade and toleration' in return.[10] This effectively ended the talks before they had properly commenced and Leda's departure was announced on 4/14 June – two days before the Council had formally refused his offer.[11] The mission had no positive outcome except to prove that Cromwell and Spain's terms were mutually unacceptable but neither preferred open hostilities in Europe yet. Despite this Cardenas remained in London, proof of Spain's unwillingness for a breach while the French treaty remained unsigned. Cromwell made no move to encourage him to leave; Cardenas's presence served a useful purpose in preventing reassurance to the French that their treaty would be signed in due course, however much they procrastinated over the presence of French rebels in London.

While Cardenas remained in London Bordeaux could threaten to leave,[12] but dared not.

In the meantime, Cromwell's secret orders to Blake that spring showed his real attitude to Spain. The Admiral had now completed his mission in the Mediterranean and did not need to use Spanish ports any longer. Cromwell informed him in mid-April that three months' provisions were en route to him; hence he was to cease relying on Spanish ports for his supplies, an indication of impending hostility.[13] Before Leda's arrival in England instructions were sent out telling him to proceed to the Atlantic and await the Plate Fleet. On 3/13 June he received orders to attack all shiping off Spain going to or coming from America.[14] This marked a crucial stage in the escalation of Cromwell's conflict with Spain and showed the falsity of Cardenas's hopes of some agreement even now. There was more justification for action in the colonies, but none whatever for extending the conflict to European waters beyond the help that this would offer to the Design in preventing aid to its enemies. Financial necessity was now obscured by no legal excuses.

It was at this juncture that news reached London of the massacres of Protestant villagers in the Vaudois valleys of Piedmont (part of Savoy) in the first week of April. This no doubt heartened the pro-Spanish faction.[15] The Duke of Savoy, 21-year-old Charles Emmanuel, was a close relative of the Stuarts, and was thus likely to be mistrusted by the English army and its leaders. There have been arguments over the exact extent of the massacres, which occurred when zealous and undisciplined Catholic soldiers evicting Protestant villagers, headed by the Marquis of Pianezza, got out of hand and started killing and robbing their victims. The killing and the accompanying destruction of property was made worse by the coldness of the season (April in the Alps). The scale was small compared with some actions during the Thirty Years' War. Legally speaking, the Duke had the right to restrict the Protestant villagers of the Vaudois cantons to the limits of territory which they had occupied at the time of the last local religious demarcation treaty in 1561 – as the French did not hesitate to point out. It was, however, undeniable that the villagers should have been given more than three days to convert to Catholicism or leave the extra territory they had occupied, as the formal order of

15/25 January set out. The misbehaviour and roughness of the troops had been connived at as a method of providing a warning to other Protestants in Savoy and punishing heretics and potential rebels. It was an early equivalent of the intimidation by 'dragonnade' favoured in France by Louis XIV thirty years later for the same reasons, and France's attitude was ominous. It was totally inadequate for Bordeaux, on Mazarin's orders, to claim blandly that 'the Duke only did what has been done a hundred times to Catholics'.[16]

Reaction across Europe was on a scale which took the authorities in France and Savoy by surprise. Like Cardenas, Mazarin overestimated the pragmatic reactions to be expected from the Protector and his advisers in a situation when religion seemed to be at stake. The same fears which had led to serious concern over the fate of European Protestants at the time of the Battle of the White Mountain (1620) were still operative in England – an example of the strength of the 'Black Legend'. There were two other new factors which posed a particular threat of intervention:

1. The absence of a formal agreement with France which would inhibit intervention against that country or its near ally.
2. Cromwell's concern for the welfare of his citizens was genuine, but also served as a useful excuse for military intervention (or at least diplomatic threats) if that was otherwise desirable. This had been so in particular in the West Indies and lay at the root of the apocryphal claim about his 'civis Romanus sum' boast. The threat of a general massacre of Protestants was sufficient to consider action by Blake's Mediterranean fleet, or some measure of retaliation against the Duke.

The reaction in England was indeed on a parallel with that of the last evidence of a Popish plot, the Irish Catholic massacres of the autumn of 1641. Many of the fervent Protestants who had joined Parliament's army in the years after that incident were still serving, and would have the task of attacking France or Savoy if needed. Popular indignation in London was noted by Evelyn[17] and cannot be ascribed solely to cynical whipping up of hysteria about European Catholics by preachers and Army officers on Government orders. The fasts and charity collections for survivors ordered by the Protector[18] were indeed useful in stimulating a sense of national unity and indignation against the regime's supposed arch-enemies, the potential backers of Charles Stuart. It was after all only a few months since the last Royalist uprising. The indignation was especially apparent in the fleet, where we have evidence of the men's feelings in letters by their officers.[19] The volatility of the Navy had been apparent when a substantial number of men chose to mutiny in favour of the King in 1648, and there was to be more trouble in the following spring. Any diversion of the men's thoughts to a useful channel was therefore to be taken advantage of. Agitation in favour of revenge was to Cromwell's benefit, and the propaganda paper *Mercurius Politicus* expressed the official viewpoint in blaming 'that devilish crew of priests and jesuits'.[20] Councillor Fleetwood saw it as 'a further heaping up of that measure which I am persuaded will hasten the downfall of that interest which is diametrically opposed to that which we call our Lord Jesus' work and design'.[21]

As Spain showed no impending hostility it seemed that England could afford to delay the French treaty while French involvement was investigated. The Council official Samuel Morland was sent to France with letters to deliver to the King en route to Savoy, to assist in a peaceful settlement which was to be based on guarantees of future toleration for the remaining Protestants.[22] The letters to the King, the Duke and to the hoped-for co-mediators, the States-General, were drafted by a Council committee and approved by the full body – an indication of their importance, as such business was usually left to Thurloe.[23] The wording of the letters did not seek to implicate the French in the atrocities, though it was correctly believed that French soldiers had assisted.[24] Cromwell reminded Louis that loyal Protestants were a greater benefit to a Catholic regime than oppressed and disloyal Protestants who would conspire with the government's enemies, citing with approval Henri IV's treatment of the Huguenots, and encouraged him to transmit this advice to the Duke and to continue to carry it out in his own dominions.[25] Full-blown Protestant rhetorical indignation was left to Cromwell's letters to the Dutch and the Swiss for whom it was more appropriate.[26]

The strategic realities of the situation of England necessitated this cautious response to the crisis. Cromwell was in no hurry to conclude the French treaty while Bordeaux remained obstinate about Condé's envoys. He had decided the previous year not to send military aid to the French Huguenots unless they showed no sign of a renewed revolt, implying that he considered it better to encourage toleration by maintaining good relations with Mazarin. The Western Design could not be recalled and Blake had been ordered to attack Spanish shipping in Europe – either of which could lead to war. It was too late to change policies in Europe. The Vaudois were isolated in the Alpine valleys and nothing could be done for them without French cooperation. The only possibility of putting indirect pressure on the Duke was by sending Blake to seize Villefranche, his sole Mediterranean port, as a 'hostage' for his future good behaviour, and to organise an exodus of survivors to new homes in Ireland. It was rumoured that this might happen[27] but Cromwell evidently decided that attacks on Spanish shipping were more important. 'Direct action' was limited to the relief fund to help resettle survivors, an unprecedented example of government concern with the fate of its coreligionists. This method of offering help was the only one which strategic reality and government indebtedness allowed. Cromwell himself subscribed £2000, but what money the State possessed had to be spent on the fleet and arrears of pay for the Army, and so the main burden of the effort fell on voluntary public subscription. As a result the first collection was deemed inadequate and a second one was ordered.[28] Most of the money not sent out at once was put aside for pensions for Protestant refugees but the Government had no scruples about using some of it for the Navy. It could be argued that the armed forces were an arm of militant Protestantism, so this was appropriate.

As the hard-pressed Spanish government dared not recall Cardenas, Cromwell took the opportunity to put pressure on Bordeaux. Thurloe instructed the ambassador that the treaty would not be signed until the Duke of Savoy had come to a satisfactory arrangement with his subjects,[29] and it was feared that England would insist on the Vaudois being included in the final terms.[30] It was generally known that French officers had aided the Savoyards and Cromwell told the Dutch ambassador Nieupoort that he believed this.[31] Louis' official assurance had to be accepted as England could not intervene, but mistrust of France intensified. Pell reported that Mazarin had protested to the Duke not at the scale of the killing but at its timing being embarrassing for France, 'saying it was not altogether unreasonable'.[32] Cromwell's Huguenot intelligencer Augier blamed Mazarin.[33] Mazarin's attempts to persuade Cromwell that the Duke had acted within his legal rights against rebels would appear as evidence that he was seeking to excuse what had happened.

It is instructive to note the attitude taken by the French and Spanish ambassadors. The English insistence on a settlement in Savoy before they would sign baffled Bordeaux, and he took it as a sign that Cromwell was not sincere about peace, whether or not he was swayed by popular resentment of France and believed 'war with France will pass for a war for religion's sake'.[34] In his opinion, 'The zeal of religion is certainly not able to shake the designs of my Lord Protector.'[35] Bordeaux was very concerned when Cardenas put new propositions to Cromwell involving assistance to a possible Protestant revolt in southern France,[36] and Cromwell consulted Stouppe and other Huguenots on the likelihood of this.

Spain's attitude to the crisis shows that they were so much in need of English aid in Europe that this opportunity to achieve success at the eleventh hour could not be overlooked. According to Quirini, de Haro himself was still not convinced that the Design would proceed to attack his master's colonies.[37] Cardenas sought to encourage anti-French feeling with the hope of causing a breach between Cromwell and Mazarin, encouraged by reports that many soldiers in Scotland and Ireland were 'ready to spend their blood to support their brothers' if action was taken against the Duke and his French ally. Bordeaux indeed claimed that Cardenas 'did all he could to stir up the preaching ministers to incense the Government'.[38] At this juncture we have evidence of an unlikely alliance between the ambassador of the 'Catholic King' and radical preachers, albeit only a temporary one based on the current indignation against France. In summer 1655, the preachers' zeal could equally well be turned against Spain or France. The Vaudois Massacre had done much to hinder France's reputation for tolerating Protestants which had been cited in its favour. Bordeaux even feared that Cromwell could use the Vaudois fund to stir up rebellion among the Huguenots in Languedoc.[39]

Cromwell's pressure drove Mazarin to send Servien's brother to conclude an agreement between the Duke and his Protestant subjects. The Western Design was not seen in France as enforcing an Anglo-French treaty or Mazarin would not have bothered; Brienne admitted to Bordeaux that Cromwell's concern alone had caused it.[40] The English did not however trust French assurances, and in August George Downing was sent out to assist Morland and to see that the French mediation was unbiased. With him were sent new letters to Louis XIV reminding him that a just settlement would assure his international reputation as a protector of Protestants like his grandfather and reassure the Huguenots of his goodwill, as would punishment of the officers responsible.[41] Lack of action (against an independent prince and French citizens acting outside their King's authority) would imply that there was no confidence among Protestants in France or abroad in Louis's tolerance. This was as far as Cromwell could go to pressurise him, but when it is remembered that he had just had news of the Hispaniola disaster,[42] it is surprising that he was still concerned with this less important issue.

Downing was accompanied by a secretary, Edward Warcupp, whose diary of the mission provides insights into the current situation in Paris on which he and his master would have reported to the Council. He noted that Mazarin, who especially dreaded Condé and Cardinal de Retz, was most unpopular in Paris and was

> generally hated, spoke[n] ill of by all persons behind his back, not daring to trust himself in his own palace in Paris nor abroad without the King's person for fear of the people ... he is condemned for carrying the King into Flanders to plunder the country at the head of his army and for being an ill minister of state[;] his taxes are great and yet the soldiery is unpaid.[43]

The agreement which the Duke and his subjects reached at Pignerol on 8/18 August seems to have been hastened by the need to settle the matter before Downing and the Dutch mediation mission arrived.[44] The English realised this, and Thurloe received Bordeaux's account of the agreement with 'considerable coldness'.[45] News of the English military disaster did not lead to a moderation of Cromwell's wish for a more satisfactory agreement; an impression of panic would detract from his negotiating position. When Downing called on Mazarin on his way back from Geneva, the Cardinal proposed an offensive alliance based on mutual discussions each winter for a spring campaign and either English concentration in the Caribbean or a joint expedition to Flanders. He would do anything to assist Huguenot toleration 'which might stand with the honour of France', though Cromwell had not shown equal goodwill for the Catholics. An ordinary defensive alliance would 'be no good for either'.[46] Until Spain took action against him, however, Cromwell chose to make no response to this.

The Hispaniola disaster did not alter Cromwell's conern for his coreligionists in southern Europe. Morland was instructed to go to Geneva and complain to the Swiss authorities about their cooperation in the 'destructive' peace of Pignerol which had been brought about by 'the menaces of the French ambassador'. If the Swiss would take the initiative in sending envoys to Turin (capital of Savoy) to renegotiate the terms, Morland was to aid them and 'vigorously prosecute' an amendment. The Swiss were to be told that 'the treaty between His Highness and the King of France is agreed but His Highness will not sign it until he has satisfaction in this business of Piedmont ... he cannot nor will not desert them'.[47] When war had broken out Cromwell continued to show his interest in the region. As late as January 1656 he told Count Bonde that Piedmont was still 'foremost in my thoughts'.[48] Late in 1655 the Catholics in the canton of Schwyz made moves to expel their Protestants. Cromwell's resident ambassador at Geneva, John Pell, informed him of this whereupon he sent a fervent appeal for unity to the Protestant cantons.[49]

The Protector's subsequent efforts on behalf of foreign Protestants extended to the Poles – victims of Catholic reprisals after his ally Charles X's successes. In December 1657, the Council considered a report from the Piedmont Fund committee and ordered Fleetwood, Wolseley, Fiennes, Sydenham and Strickland to draft an appeal to accompany a collection for Poles.[50] On 25 March/4, 'Mr Secretary reports His Highness' approval of the declaration for the distressed Protestant churches in Poland', and twenty exiled Bohemian families were added to the beneficiaries.[51] A formal *Declaration by the Protector for the relief of divers Protestant churches driven out of Poland ...*

followed, blaming 'the persecution of the Jesuits and the House of Austria'. Pack and Vyner were authorised to handle the subsequent national collection which totalled £10 685.[52] A watchful eye was kept on the spending of funds in the Fund Committee accounts – on 1/11 January 1658 'the Committee to meet next Wednesday, and Mr Morland to tell them how the money sent beyond the seas has been disposed of'.[53] Two Council figures – Deputy Secretary Philip Meadowe and adviser Jean-Baptiste Stouppe – produced inflammatory propaganda works inciting hatred of Catholics over the Vaudois Massacre.[54]

7 Spain's Breach of Relations with England

By August 1655 it was apparent that there was to be no Huguenot rising in southern France, and that the French government was (however reluctantly) bringing the Duke of Savoy to an accommodation. In any case, Blake's orders to concentrate against Spain and the limited extent of Savoy's seaboard meant that there was nothing that Cromwell could do without French assistance. News now arrived of the outcome of events in the Caribbean – the worst possible outcome, since the English had suffered a severe defeat but were still in possession of Spanish territory so that the Design could not just be abandoned. As events turned out, once the invincibility of the New Model Army was disproved and Spain chose to recall Cardenas and sequestrate English property. This, however, stopped short of war, and Cardenas exaggerated the strength of domestic pressure on Cromwell to prevent an escalation of the dispute. In 1654, Cromwell had assumed that the Design did not inevitably mean an immediate European war, due to Spain's conflict with France. In the following year Spanish policy-makers, acting chiefly on Cardenas's reports from London, did not think that Cromwell would choose to respond to their retaliation as vigorously as he did.

It is significant that Cardenas did not ask for his recall until the departure of Sedgewick's fleet taking reinforcements to the Caribbean in mid-July, which showed that Cromwell's attack was intended to be followed up.[1] De Haro himself could not believe the reports from Hispaniola at first, or so Quirini was told. One of his principal advisers, the Count of Penoranda, even presented a paper to the Council of State 'defending Cromwell with solid arguments' and arguing against the 'disingenuousness' of war with England.[2] Apart from the threat of England aiding France in the Netherlands, the size of her fleet was much to be feared. The Spanish government was unwilling to go to the trouble of taking counter-measures; the cumbersome and slow-acting nature of official thinking was reinforced by the continued mistakes which Cardenas made in assessing the possibility of agreement with the Protector and in emphasising the opposition to his policy of Lambert and the merchants, both of which Cromwell was able to ignore. A breach with England would bring fifteen years of planning to nothing. As it was, the Royalist observer Wright estimated Spanish weakness as being so severe that war was uncertain even if Penn and Venables had conquered Hispaniola.[3] When the news of the English landing on Hispaniola was confirmed the King complained bitterly to Penoranda 'that his paper was not worth writing'.[4]

The crucial factor in Spain's decision to retaliate was the fact that the seemingly invincible troops of the New Model Army had actually been defeated. The reputation for invincibility won on the battlefields of the British Isles in the past decade had been thrown away. Cromwell's gamble in sending inferior troops who could be spared from England had backfired, for it was not known abroad that these men had been the sweepings of several regiments under second-rate commanders. Accordingly, the disaster served to give Spain the necessary encouragement to attempt to intimidate Cromwell, in a manner which contemporaries compared with their concurrent intimidation of the smaller and weaker republic of Genoa.[5] The withdrawal of Cardenas and the expulsion of English merchants did not amount to a full declaration of war; de Haro and his ministers still feared an Anglo-French alliance too much to precipitate one needlessly when they could take lesser measures. The declaration of war was Cromwell's retaliation to this escalation of the conflict.

The news from Hispaniola was a serious blow to the Protector's prestige as Lambert had earlier warned him would be the result of such a reverse. Initial reports had indicated success on Hispaniola[6] and the disaster was not known until the arrival of a letter from Martin Noell's brother Thomas in Barbados at the end of July.[7] An official report from Venables and Butler followed.[8] The hero of the hour should have been Lambert, who had warned against it,[9] but he did not exploit his opportunity being preoccupied with his duties as a Major-General. That was a bonus for the embattled Protector but a matter of luck rather than of his calculation. It was equally fortunate that the Royalists were quiescent and that popular opposition to the Major-Generals had not yet reached that pitch which it

was to do in the next year. Army resentment of the Protector
was now the only probable way of removing him short of assassination. The purge of the republican officers after the 'Petition
of the Three Colonels' had an unexpected advantage in this
context. Principally, however, Cromwell's chief asset was the
distance from Jamaica to England, which meant that news of
the awful conditions there were slow to reach the home country. Troops involved in the disaster were settled on Jamaica
rather than permitted to return home. Accordingly, it was safe
to order official journalists to concoct falsely optimistic reports
during the three years of struggle which followed, claiming
that all was going well.[10] This had not been the case with
fighting in the British Isles, and would not be so in Flanders.

The effect on Cromwell himself was another factor to be
considered. Military reverses might mean a sign of Divine
displeasure. Significantly, when he first heard of Jamaica's
conquest he was prepared to discuss its return at a meeting
with Cardenas. This indicated loss of nerve. Fortunately, faulty
intelligence (which had led to the ease of the Design being
exaggerated) may now have saved it from being called off
altogether. The first reports indicated that Jamaica had been
taken without resistance,[11] and the strength of the Spanish
forces lurking in the mountains was not realised. It is likely
that had Cromwell known of the strength of resistance he
would have been even more willing to give up Jamaica.
Cardenas did not rule out the possibility of another ambassador
replacing him in due course, showing that he believed that the
situation was not hopeless.[12]

A salient point was raised by Colonel Modyford, who had
specifically emphasised that England's target should not be
an island requiring the effort of planting. He regarded Jamaica
as being in a useful position to attack Spanish shipping, as
Providence had been, but requiring a lot of work and investment to make it fruitful. He 'heartily wished that it might have
been their first attempt, that it might have seemed choice
rather than necessity'.[13]

SPAIN'S LIMITED REACTION

The news of the English defeat emboldened the Council in
Madrid to order Cardenas's return on 21/31 August. He was

to do so whatever Cromwell said, but if he offered to drop the terms of 'trade and toleration' Cardenas should promise an imminent replacement.[14] The Spaniards did not realise Cromwell might feel honour-bound to react violently, despite his lack of ability to finance a war. They, like Cardenas, over-estimated the importance of financial as opposed to ideological factors in his decision-making. It might seem rash to start a war when there was no imminent prospect of funds from Parliament and the Major-Generals had to be financed by the expedient of a special tax on Royalists (being disaffected any-way, their resentment did not matter). In the meantime, the only obvious source of money was the piratical seizure of Spanish treasure by Cromwell's navy, an 'easy option' with a respectable background in Parliamentary thinking as far back as the 1620s. The nature of a conflict was bound to be re-stricted until a satisfatory arrangement about money could be reached with France, and luckily for Cromwell Spain's similar difficulties meant that she was too poor and preoccupied to take the offensive during the time preceding such an agree-ment. Meanwhile, an indication of his renewed resolution was given by his orders to Blake in August to attack the Spanish fleet 'shadowing' him off Cadiz, if he judged this to be op-portune.[15] This order preceded Cardenas's withdrawal or any other Spanish action, and shows that once he had recovered his nerve Cromwell was willing to press ahead with a course of action which might precipitate war in Europe.

The Spanish could not take action in America at once, but as a measure short of declaring war the property of English merchants still remaining in Spain itself was confiscated in September. This amounted to putting on diplomatic pressure rather than opening hostilities, which course the Franco-Spanish war made undesirable. Indeed, it was not carried out with the full rigour of the law, possibly with official connivance.[16]

It should be pointed out that if Cromwell's colonial adventure was of questionable legality, so were Spain's seizures. The English merchants' petition of protest pointed out that the seizures had broken specific Articles of the 1630 treaty: One, Seven, Twenty-Three, and Eighty-Eight.[17] Whatever Cromwell's deviousness in attacking and simultaneously negotiating, the Spanish authorities had now shown no more consideration for strict legality. They were reduced to propagandist claims that England had behaved towards them like 'a wild beast' and that

Cardenas had had to be recalled to save him from the hands of cruel and unscrupulous heretics.[18] In any case, the attempt to put pressure on Cromwell was misjudged. The Rump had been susceptible to City pressure to fight the Dutch, but Cromwell had other priorities.

At first, Cromwell's Council seems to have hoped that the seizures would not be strictly enforced.[19] When they were, this manifest breach of the 1630 treaty was used as the excuse for the declaration of war – a further escalation which Spain does not appear to have expected. Accordingly, Cromwell had worked himself into a state of self-justification and open anger at Spanish 'perfidy' when he received representatives of the merchants on 20/30 September. Dismissing their complaints with the argument that he had given them adequate warning to withdraw their goods, he catalogued a list of Spanish misdeeds. He maintained that 'he had not declared war on Spain [through the Design], the past treaties did not prevent either side from making attacks beyond the Line'. He was not certain of his legal grounds, as Venables' earlier statement makes clear. He sought to avoid charges of 'overreaction' by dwelling on the murder of England's first republican ambassador in Madrid in 1650 when this had not prevented good Anglo-Spanish relations at the time.[20]

Cromwell's reaction was also shown in his explanation of his intentions to the Council. He could have accepted the seizures as the last action of the crisis and not escalated it further, though the earlier orders to Blake to take naval action show that even before the sequestration he was prepared for an action which would have caused war. Now he deliberately sought an immediate conflict. He told his advisers that the Spanish action had been 'too great an insult' to accept tamely and that therefore war was necessary; they should not be too disheartened over Hispaniola as 'even Caesar was not always victorious'. Noticeably, they preferred to put a united front to the nation. Cromwell also chose to be economical with the truth in his official explanations to foreign ambassadors, such as the Brandenburg representative Schlezer whom he told in December: 'Had it been possible to obtain within the period of three years equitable and reasonable terms from the Spaniard, they would not have attacked the King with such great force, though they had always been embroiled with him in conflicts, contests and war.'[21]

The English determination was shown in the new enthusiasm to develop the colony in Jamaica. A Council subcommittee was set up to coordinate policy towards the island, and proceeded to consider the transportation of the Irish and of existing colonists in New England and other Caribbean islands. On 9/ 19 October the Admiralty Commissioners were ordered to prepare a second reinforcement expedition with all possible secrecy.[22] Vincent Gookin was commissioned to sail to New England to collect godly colonists for Jamaica and further the Lord's will by a transfer of pioneers from the supposedly barren continent to the fertile Caribbean where they would be of more use.[23] In the meantime, Penn and Venables were treated as scapegoats for the Hispaniola disaster on their return, the government choosing cynically to ignore its own mistakes. They were both sent to the Tower after reporting to the Council.[24] Neither was re-employed.

The accuracy of Cromwell's judgement of Spain's weakness was shown by the limited nature of their reaction. The Spanish Council of State took no notice of a paper submitted in August by Sir Edward Hyde, who sought to interest them in the Royalist cause as the most effective means of gaining revenge.[25] However, the Spanish government did not sign any treaty with Charles II for six months after the sequestration and even then proved too poor to afford serious support, a fact on which Thurloe based his calculations that they were a less dangerous enemy than France. Accordingly, their first reported plan was to lend secret support to a Royalist rising in Scotland,[26] which Monck's iron control made unrealistic.

It was significant that Cromwell did not immediately rush to sign the French treaty. The Franco-Spanish War gave him the confidence to avoid seeming desperate for an agreement, though this brought about a second outbreak of French seizures of English shipping in an effort to exert pressure. The return of some of the English privateers overpowered by their French captives was refused[27] and at Le Havre Admiral Vendôme refused to return seized ships until a treaty was signed.[28] The admiral, a noble of royal blood and renowned for his independent mind, may have acted on his own initiative as he had during the *Fronde,* but either he or Mazarin decided that the evidence of an Anglo-Spanish breach was sufficient to make a further warning to the Protector timely. Petit protested to the Council and the ships were released. In a similar vein, when the treaty was eventually signed in November the French authorities were most reluctant to implement the commercial clauses granting English merchants freedom from tolls in their provinces.[29] In retaliation Cromwell saw to it that Condé's agent Barrière stayed on in London after the peace – since he might prove useful.

THE DECLARATION OF WAR

In mid-October the Council, unwilling to see Cardenas leave, held three days of 'long and serious debates' on the emergency. It is obvious that Lambert was offering resistance to the breach in relations. The Spanish ambassador himself was confident that Lambert's faction and the influence of the City merchants would cause the Protector to ask him to stay in London, once he had formally announced his departure.[30] Similarly, Cardenas exaggerated the willingness of the Protector to take notice of the merchants, who were no threat to his position. The extent to which his confidence that he understood English politics had been wrong was reflected in his fulminations to other diplomats.[31] He had been aware of the Design and warned Spain well in advance. He was, however, unable to understand the depth of Cromwell's feelings about the justifiability of attacking the Spanish empire in 'peacetime' and to accept that self-interest was not the same under Cromwell as under his predecessors. Equally, his need of aid against France had blinded him to the danger of Cromwell turning on Spain, once he was convinced that the latter could not finance an expedition on the Continent to occupy his troops. Cardenas's failings did not avoid the fact that Cromwell had proceeded in a manner different from norma diplomacy.

The Council decided on 15/25 October that Spain must pay reparations for its action in the West Indies and grant 'trade and toleration' to avoid war, despite protests by Lambert.[32] Cardenas's departure followed, and a Council committee was set up to consider the embargoing of goods and ships belonging to Spaniards in England.[33] This was not likely to have much effect as there were so little of the goods in question. Two days later the 'Manifesto' was ready in Council and referred back to a committee for a few hours to be amended with 'Mr Secretary to assist'. That afternoon it was read out again with one clause omitted, and it was decided to add on the Parliamentary letter of protest at Ascham's murder.[34] It listed all the injustices which Spain had committed in America and elsewhere, their horrible cruelties and persecutions, and the reasonableness of the English cause.[35] The propagandist tone which Milton had used against the Catholic persecutors in his letters and poem on the Vaudois was now specifically concentrated against Spain, making the long series of misunderstandings and practical calculations appear as a natural process based on a moral judgement of Spanish wickedness. This was the biblical tone in which the propagandists of the New Model Army had assailed their Royalist opponents in 1648 and 1651, and which Cromwell used to justify the Spanish war to Parliament. The war was presented both as being 'natural' and as purely 'defensive', which could persuade those who put national interest above the idea of a crusade against the Antichrist.

Despite the official enthusiasm for the conflict, the reality was that neither England nor Spain was in a state to do much in Europe. As late as July 1656 Cromwell told Count Bonde 'they were so hard pressed . . . they would have offered mediation if it had been advantageous'.[36] The financial condition of the country was such that some notable success in seizing Spanish treasure was essential before a major campaign could be mounted. In August 1655, it was estimated that the Navy owed £200 000 to its contractors and that £38 000 was owed for the freight of hired ships.[37] Moreover, on 12/22 October the Admiralty Commissioners reported to Thurloe that £120 000 was owed to Blake's fleet, whose men had been unpaid for twenty months with only £20 000 now available to support them. More than £2000 would have to be found each week to supply the fleet while it was laid up during the winter, and due to the need to spend all the money available on arrears of wages the bills, contracts, and wages for the shipyards had gone unpaid 'which is a great disrepute and prejudicial to the service of the navy'.[38] England could not afford to wage an expensive war, and with the French treaty unsigned it was likely to be many months before a satisfactory offensive alliance could be arranged to make a European land campaign remunerative.

Spain did not show any wish to take offensive action in Europe, and the ease with which some English merchants were allowed to evade the blockade may be an indication that they were still reluctant to proceed to extremes. Thurloe received reports that they were considering a new embassy to London if the English were willing to receive it.[39] At the same time, the reception accorded to the Royalist envoy De Vic by Fuensaldagna, chief minister in Brussels, was cautious in the extreme.[40] Fuensaldagna and Cardenas, encouraged by some Royalists,[41] both made the demand that Charles II become a Catholic as a precondition for aid, showing that they were not yet concerned to use him as an ally except on their own terms. The talks of Fuensaldagna with the Spaniards' other potential ally, Colonel Sexby, had begun in Brussels as early as September.[42] However, it appears that Cardenas played a major role in advising the Council in Madrid over what action to take.[43] His past implied that he was less likely to favour the King, and he appears to have fallen into the trap of exaggerating Sexby's influence. He had exaggerated the Council and City opposition to Cromwell, and his next mistake appears to have been to exaggerate dissidence in the Army and Navy: that Sexby could carry out his rash promises to raise 20 000 men in England and seize a port.[44] In reality the only serious chance of widespread mutiny in the armed forces appears to have been in 1657 when Cromwell was supposed to be taking the Crown and betraying what Army radicals called the 'Good Old Cause'.

THE FRENCH TREATY AND ITS IMPLICATIONS

Peace with France followed the breach with Spain; Cromwell signed the treaty on 26 October/5 November, having tried to avoid making the exclusion of rebels reciprocal until he was forced to abandon his stand by the outbreak of war. The Vaudois crisis had provided one delay, and after the news from Hispaniola was known Bordeaux was told that the Council considered it 'baseness' to conclude the treaty with undue haste because of that rebuff.[45] The English were determined not to sign hurriedly and give the impression of panic.

Reviewing his decision, Cromwell informed Schlezer that France was a preferable ally because of its record in tolerating Protestants: 'although so many hundreds of the reformed religion lived there, they were well-treated and protected, whereas the Spaniards' policies only served to burden their consciences extremely and to exterminate all who professed the Reformed Religion, either overtly by force or by secret machinations'.[46] This view of France cannot have emerged until the summer of 1654, when the unwisdom of aiding an unlikely Huguenot revolt became apparent. Cromwell's hostility to Spain seems to have been stimulated by the coincidence of the renewed persecution of European Protestants and the sequestration.

Thurloe wrote that the main aim of the peace was to force Charles II apart from France – the only country capable of restoring him. It would cause 'perpetual enmity between the King and his cousin's ministers, and force him to depend on Spain'. Even radicals opposed to Cromwell were 'always jealous and afraid of the principles of Spain, and [nobody] had interest there but the Papists'. Thus Sexby could not hope to rally dissidents in the Army and Navy to act on behalf of Cromwell's enemies abroad. The Council was also afraid of the 'great confidence' the French had long had with the Scots, which was suspected to have been behind the war of 1649–51, and the support given to Middleton and Glencairn thereafter. An alliance with France that aimed at offensive action in Europe could not yet be afforded. 'Good correspondence' with Mazarin was safer for the protection of the Huguenots than seeking to stir them to revolt, and France was the traditional ally of the North European Protestants who might suffer renewed attack. However there was as yet 'no prospect and understanding . . . of a conjunction in counsels . . . [it avoided] any obligations . . . to enter into strict leagues offensive and defensive, which do intricate and entangle affairs but are seldom performed or proved of any effect'. The Council chose rather 'that way of a conjunction which is to fix upon a particular design when it has all mutual convenience in it'.[47] English policy was strictly pragmatic; the Protestant–French league would only be formed when it was necessary for national security.

Another reason for Cromwell's friendship with France was postulated by Bishop Burnet, who was not a contemporary but had been informed of these events by Cromwell's former agent Stouppe. According to him, Cromwell feared what might happen if France employed an army of Huguenots to invade England on behalf of the King, as this would counteract the

unpopularity of French Catholics. In the crucial period of 1651–
4 the Huguenots could not have been trusted in this way. No
other evidence of this exists, but it is logical to assume that
France's Protestant subjects could have been courted by the
Commonwealth partly because of their usefulness to the King
if a hostile France sought to invade England.[48]

Despite his recent defeat, the reputation that Cromwell's
army had won was such that Catholics in southern Europe
appear to have genuinely feared that 1656 would see a massive
Protestant naval assault on them. The fear was especially apparent in Italy,[49] showing the positive effects from the naval campaign in 1654–5. Ironically, the prospect of an Anglo-Spanish
war served to delay the Anglo-French alliance, for Mazarin
came under intense pressure not to ally with a heretic. The
papal nuncio and the Venetian ambassador in Paris tried to
warn the Cardinal that Cromwell intended the ruin of the
Catholic faith and that once he was let into Flanders he would
coordinate an assault on the Habsburgs with Sweden.[50] There
was intense opposition to the peace in France, albeit on a popular level which the Cardinal (secure in the Queen Mother's
confidence) could afford to ignore.[51]

The sequestration led to an official attempt through the
'Manifesto' to portray the outcome of the crisis as inevitable,
and to justify the English decision on moral grounds. The
xenophobic Protestant hysteria belied the reality of years of
good relations with Spain due to fear of France. Once rebellion
was ended in France Cromwell considered intervening in
America, but his inclination was not to 'rush' matters in Europe and the Spanish reaction to Hispaniola was evidently an
unwelcome surprise. The 'insult' of sequestration was the final
cause of a European war. Given Cromwell's conception of
Divine planning, it is likely that he saw the Spanish action as
seeming to confirm his latent prejudice against Spanish injustices. It was certainly easier to carry the dispute to the point
of war than to admit that the Protector had miscalculated his
American policy. However, serious financial difficulties impelled
military caution. The events of 1656 were to show that England's strategy was concentrated on naval action to take Spanish
shipping and gain much needed treasure. There was no haste
to conclude an offensive alliance with France until it seemed
that the alternative was a Franco-Spanish peace.

8 1656 – England Delays an Offensive Alliance with France

Sixteen months passed between the outbreak of the Anglo-Spanish War and the offensive alliance with France. The Franco-Spanish War alone had enabled Cromwell to manoeuvre and delay, but the threat of its resolution ended his reluctance. England was cautious of entanglements and would only agree to a joint attack on Flanders on her own terms – the war with Spain enabling her to dictate them. The most essential of these was the cession of Dunkirk, the Royalist presence in Flanders giving it a new importance. In the meantime, financial weakness required that the money not currently obtainable as a subsidy from England's allies, or as taxes on a sullen and resentful people, be raised by attacks on Spanish shipping off her coasts and in the Western Mediterranean. English ships could not protect home waters and take Plate galleons at the same time; Channel shipping suffered and the war became even more unpopular with the mercantile community. France appears to have been more anxious for an English alliance after the reverses it had suffered in the summer and autumn of 1655, culminating in the surrender of Péronne to Spain.[1] However, the English did not sign the alliance until it seemed that France and Spain would come to terms if they did not.

FIRST MOVES TOWARDS NEGOTIATIONS

The English attitude towards Spain was insufficiently belliger-ent for Mazarin to be certain that Cromwell would not aban-don the war if good terms were offered. Bordeaux continued to report rumours of peace talks or unofficial Spanish missions.[2] Mazarin's chief desire was to tie Cromwell down by an offensive alliance – precisely the entanglement which Thurloe feared. Thus Bordeaux was instructed to press for a formal alliance.[3] Mazarin's initial hope was to have Blake's fleet ordered to assist the French in Italy, perhaps by aiding Guise when he returned to Naples or transporting troops from Marseilles to Genoa en route to Milan.[4] This was what the Italians feared and the Pope himself was reported to be 'in great distress of mind'.[5] Catholic pressure on the Cardinal made him change his mind for fear of the effect on his own position, and he excused it on the grounds that 'this would have alarmed the Pope and forced him to cling to the Spaniards'. More immediately important was the ammunition this would have offered his opponents at Court and fanatic *dévots*, among them the exiled but still feared Cardinal de Retz.

Cromwell's new enthusiasm for European Protestant unity was exhibited in other ways. The need for a new embassy to Sweden led to plans to extend this to a mission to Northern European Protestants in general, possibly headed by Bulstrode Whitelocke or Sir Christopher Pack. The former was approached by Sydenham and Fleetwood on Cromwell's behalf. Bishop Burnet was told (by Stouppe?) that Cromwell considered setting up a college to coordinate closer relations between European Protestants and stimulate united action, as a rival to the Pope's college, De Propagatione Fidei.[6] This idea seems to have owed something to Hartlib's schemes for such a Protestant college. Cromwell sent new orders to Pell in Switzerland in February, telling him to go to Zurich to assist in the talks between the Swiss Protestants and Catholics which were to take place there in the wake of the troubles in Schwyz. He was to coordinate his efforts with the French to assist in a just and lasting peace in the Cantons which was 'of so much concernment to the whole Protestant cause'.[7] Cromwell's concern at the Popish menace was also apparent in many of his state letters to the Protestant rulers that spring.[8] Though England was at peace with many countries in Europe she had no formal allies in her war with Spain, and hence efforts to correct this were vital to limit her isolation.

Suspicion hampered the Anglo-French talks in London in the early months of 1656, quite apart from financial difficulties requiring Cromwell to press for a large subsidy. The Protector, confident of Mazarin's need of him and desiring to keep in touch with his coreligionists, kept Barrière in London; in reply France did not immediately expel the Duke of York.[9] Mazarin warned that York would not leave Paris until Barrière left London,[10] and was sufficiently concerned at the latter's presence there to send to London copies of a letter in which he had criticised Cromwell in order to undermine him.[11] In April Cromwell finally expelled Barrière, although it was believed that an Englishman called 'White' or 'Fitts' still represented Spanish interests in London.[12]

French suspicion was also evident when Cromwell finally sent his own ambassador to Paris. Bordeaux was warned that 'Cromwell wants to put him next to the King to encourage him in favour of his co-religionists'.[13] Council opposition to the negotiations was still apparent,[14] although the decision not to send the friendly Pickering, as first reported,[15] in preference to Cromwell's niece's new husband William Lockhart might not reflect this. Bordeaux feared Lockhart as an ex-Royalist and a Presbyterian Scot with affinities to the Huguenots,[16] but his personal link with Cromwell was no doubt why he was trusted. Lockhart's instructions laid emphasis on his maintaining contacts with the Huguenots to ensure good treatment and to report instances of persecution to London; he was to cooperate with other Protestant ambassadors in pursuit of a general alliance and to proceed carefully on arranging a joint campaign in Flanders aimed at Dunkirk. He was to 'insinuate that I have taken France as a friend out of choice not out of necessity'.[17] Principally, the French feared Lockhart's potential to stir up subversion and Mazarin sought to delay his departure to France by insinuating that Royalist exiles there were likely to murder him.[18] Spanish observers hopefully awaited Lockhart's demise as the preliminary to a settlement with England.[19]

SPAIN'S RESPONSE: ALLIANCE WITH CHARLES II

Spain's reaction was as ineffective as Thurloe had reckoned. On 12/22 April 1656 a treaty was signed with Charles II in Brussels, by which Philip IV was to supply 4000 infantry and 200 cavalry if the English Royalists seized a port for them to use. This condition was unlikely to be met, following the penetration of Royalist networks by Thurloe's agents and the comparatively low level of active (as opposed to passive) discontent in England under the Major-Generals. Resentment of government interference and taxes was not sufficient to produce Royalist recruits, even in the last months of 1657 when Thurloe was most afraid of revolt. In any case, the key lay with the loyalty of the Army. The treaty also provided for Charles II to assist Spain to reconquer Portugal and for the return of all English gains in the West Indies since 1630, terms which would confirm resentment of his position as a Popish pensioner among those army radicals most likely to listen to Sexby.[20]

The only real threat from Spain lay in her being able to disentangle herself from the war with France. Ironically, this was assisted by the fact that the head of the French government was a Roman cleric. When the Spanish pensioner Cardinal Barberini encouraged the Pope to mediate,[21] Mazarin turned him down on the grounds that his enemy Cardinal de Retz was being encouraged at the papal court.[22] The other obstacle was the weak position of the Royalist 'court' in Brussels whose relations with the Spanish authorities were uncertain. Father Talbot was collaborating with Cardenas to encourage Charles to become a Catholic, and also persuaded him to place undue reliance on the influence of the Levellers. Cardenas himself was a 'faithful remembrancer' of the slights heaped upon him in London in 1640–1 by the Earl of Bristol, now Charles's representative in Brussels, and persuaded the authorities there to show 'all imaginable prejudice and hatred' to him.[23] As a result, in July, Thurloe's intelligencer at Madrid wrote: 'nor can I perceive of anything of purpose that is done with Charles Stuart; the Spaniards will not conclude anything of concernment until they see if you come to peace this winter'.[24]

LOCKHART AND LIONNE

The Anglo-French offensive alliance was not signed until March 1657. This delay, largely on Cromwell's part, occurred during a period when he lacked constitutional or financial support from Parliament and firm allies on the Continent. He could afford to delay the talks while Mazarin, who had been anxious to hand over Dunkirk to save it from Spain at a time of national collapse, in 1652, but realised there would be more French criticism of such a move now, tried to fob Lockhart off with an offer of the adjoining fort of Mardyke. He was similarly opposed to Cromwell's proposal for a joint naval attack on Italy, fearing for his reputation as chief minister of a Catholic country if he was seen to attack the Pope and his allies in support of heretics, and excused himself on the grounds that his plans were not ready.[25]

At this juncture Catholic pressure on Mazarin redoubled, not only from Rome but from a meeting of the French clergy who 'turn all stones and do what they can to contribute to his ruin'. As a measure of Lockhart's unpopularity in Paris, Mazarin only dared meet him in secret.[26] The English were further alarmed by the arrival in Paris, in April, of the friar Bonifaz on behalf of Spain, though Mazarin assured that he had only listened to him for public consumption.[27] He did, however, send his trusted adviser Hugues de Lionne, effectively deputy foreign minister, to Madrid to find out Spain's peace terms, while assuring Lockhart that 'he knew the King of Spain's demands would be so high that all honest Frenchmen would think it just to continue the war'.[28] Fortunately for Cromwell, Mazarin was able to reject the Spanish terms since they could be presented as unacceptable to the French public. They were:

(a) The return of all French conquests;
(b) French abandonment of the rebels in Catalonia;
(c) Restoration of Lorraine to its Duke;
(d) A full pardon for Condé, with the return of all property and offices.
(e) Peace 'as between a good uncle and nephew', entailing the abandonment of England and Portugal.

Terms (a) and (b) were not difficult given France's poor military position. It was fortunate that Mazarin, who let Condé return in 1659, was not yet fully confident, though Augier and other observers continued to write of his intentions with serious suspicion.[29]

Lionne's failure meant that Cromwell realised that Mazarin had no feasible option to an English alliance for the present. Accordingly, he insisted on the acceptance of his terms – that France pay for an English expeditionary force of 3–4000 men and that Dunkirk be handed over.[30] Lack of Parliamentary finance made the former imperative. The fall of the town of Valenciennes compelled the Cardinal to request emergency military aid,[31] but Lockhart warned him that the suspicious Protector would still only send help against Dunkirk. The seriousness of the French military position made Lockhart urge Cromwell privately to send support lest the Cardinal make peace with Spain in desperation, even on current terms, warning him that it would also encourage the Huguenots who had had 'hard usage' since the meeting of the clergy. Mazarin, obliged to his English ally, would be more useful to them than Mazarin driven by clerical pressure and popular war weariness into peace with Spain.[32] However, Lockhart also had to consider the danger of an English military defeat in Flanders, which could not be covered up so well as one on Hispaniola. If men were killed, 'the clamour which their friends would raise would prove highly disadvantageous to His Highness'.[33] Luckily, the French military position improved.

The Cardinal, recovering his nerve, sought to put the English off Dunkirk.[34] In reply, Lockhart fell back on Cromwell's constitutional position to excuse his inflexibility. The Council had 'offered that [Dunkirk] as their humble opinion to Cromwell, whose goodness seldom suffered him to slight the opinion of so wise and affectionate men'. He had done so over the Western Design, but it is likely that Lockhart was not merely inventing this. After the Hispaniola disaster Cromwell would have been more cautious about rash military expeditions. Opinion in the Council was certainly against the expense of an expedition in 1657. Mazarin was not convinced, and replied angrily that 'he knew very well the Council were not for France and that Spain wanted not his friends there . . . I replied that the Council were neither for France nor Spain but for England'.[35] As Thurloe reckoned, Mazarin had no real choice of an ally.

NAVAL STRATEGY: A QUESTION OF PRIORITIES

The naval campaign of 1656 was essential for England to acquire Spanish treasure to offset government poverty. The size of Spanish convoys meant that only a large fleet could overpower them, so this would have to be done in European waters. Idle seamen were a security risk, as were those short of pay, since many of them had radical sympathies. Charles II was hopeful that the sailors would mutiny and take their ships to Flanders into his service,[36] to repeat the mutiny of 1648. Spain's refusal to open its Flemish ports to such ships, despite Hyde's repeated appeals,[37] hindered this. The Government was, however, discomfited by an incipient mutiny in the fleet in March 1656, apparently organised by the pro-Leveller vice-admiral, John Lawson. Demanding to know the fleet's destination which had been given only to Blake, he either resigned or was dismissed.[38] More worrying was the evidence that certain officers were opposed to war with Spain. Captain Lyons claimed that he was 'not satisfied in the design, neither against whom we should go or where', and Captain Hill claimed that England had started the war and 'his conscience would not suffer him to fight the Spaniards either in the West Indies or Southerly'.[39] Thurloe blamed all this on Spanish intrigues.[40] Moreover, it casts new light on the lack of animosity to Spain among some sections of the supposedly militant fleet.

The concentration of ships away from English waters was dictated by financial imperatives. Flemish, Royalist and Dutch privateers took advantage of the situation and a flood of reports came in from as far afield as the Orkneys.[41] The blockade of Flanders eventually followed on the end of the summer campaign.[42] To make matters worse, the seizure of twenty English ships from a convoy on 30 April/10 May implicated their escort, the Dutch captain, Saloman; a protest was made to Ambassador Nieupoort. Cromwell's order that captured Royalist privateers should be put to the sword as common pirates was largely bluster,[43] given that only a small squadron of ships could be sent to enforce it.[44] As Giavarina believed, the loss did not directly endanger the State;[45] Cromwell's willingness to sacrifice (other people's) ships, however, stored up mercantile resentment for the next Parliament.

One important aspect of naval strategy was the desire for an 'offshore base' (as seen at Rhé and Hispaniola) in the Straits of Gibraltar. A position there would enable a permanent patrol to capture Spanish shipping instead of the English having to retire each winter. Contrary to this, as Montague reported, Cadiz was too strongly defended for a repeat of the raids of 1596 and 1625,[46] so Cromwell urged that Gibraltar be attempted. His phraseology was reminiscent of that in Council debates on the Western Design: 'would it not be both an advantage to our trade and an annoyance to the Spaniards, and enable us without keeping so great a fleet upon that coast, with six nimble frigates lodged there to do the Spaniards more harm than by a fleet?'.[47] It was the logical extension of the Providence Island Company's raiding strategy into European waters. Cromwell asked his admirals to consider landing troops on the isthmus and starving out the town,[48] but they considered Gibraltar too well defended to attempt it.

The failure of the blockade highlighted the problems which beset the fleet. As Meadowe warned, it was only luck that enabled even a large fleet to catch the Plate galleons and thus recoup the expense in men, money and supplies of a blockade.[49] Also, Cromwell was not sufficiently aware that the decline in the Spanish merchant marine meant that most goods entered or left Cadiz on foreign vessels. Montague warned that 'we cannot hinder [this] unless we would fight with all the world'.[50] This was another instance of Cromwell's inadequate intelligence, seen previously with regard to America. Admittedly Spain's Dutch 'carriers' were technically forbidden from supplying 'articles of war' in wartime by their treaty with England, but it was impracticable to stop and search every Dutch ship for contraband. There was already tension between the two powers in the Baltic and a naval clash would only benefit Gamarra, Spain's ambassador at The Hague.

English successes were therefore restricted to the chance of finding the Plate galleons. Cromwell informed his admirals that this was to be central to his strategy.[51] The main hazard was the impossibility of keeping the English fleet in Spanish waters all winter without a local base, which the capture of Gibraltar was intended to solve. In place of Gibraltar, the English negotiated with the authorities in Tetuan, in 1657, for special facilities.[52] It was more by luck than anything else that the fleet achieved a spectacular success when Captain Stayner's squadron found the Plate Fleet on its arrival from the Indies and captured two, sank two, and grounded one galleon (9/19 September). It was estimated that 1 100 000 pieces of eight were lost on the galleons which were sunk and that 2 600 000 pieces of eight were captured with 7–8000 bars of silver. Also taken were a number of important prisoners who confirmed reports of a disastrous earthquake at the Potosi mines which had supposedly cost 50 000 million bars of silver and wrecked production. The effects on Spanish merchants and morale were severe,[53] but the English successes were not extensive enough to ruin Spain's financial viability even after the second blow delivered the following spring by Blake. It cannot be doubted, however, that the lack of finance available to the Spanish armies contributed to their collapse in Flanders, and that the likelihood of their doing so encouraged Mazarin to continue the war in 1657–8 rather than listen to papal peace efforts.

The physical and psychological results of this success were also important to the English. It seemed to prove belatedly that Cromwell's hopes that his frigates could wreak serious damage on the Spaniards in European waters were not as false as his hopes of their doing so in the Caribbean. It served to restore English morale. Propaganda, such as Waller's poem *Of a War with Spain and a Fight at Sea*, served to encourage enthusiasm for the likely attack on Flanders in 1657 and decrease the chances of desertions from the troops which Cromwell's enemies desired. Cromwell told Bordeaux that it proved that God was on his side and that the earthquake at Potosi was Divine wrath against the Spaniards; next year's campaign should be easy now that Spain's resources were so depleted.[54] Unfortunately, the news arrived too late for the opening of Parliament where criticism of the effects of the war could be expected to add to discontent against the Major-Generals. Cromwell chose to defend his Spanish policy by a long, involved, rather incoherent attack rather than making a rational justification, based on moral rather than practical grounds.[55] His rhetorical style owed more to the manner normally used for preaching than to a desire to make a practical statement of policy, and illustrates that lack of understanding of the needs and the likely reaction of a gathering of MPs which characterised his dealings with Parliament. Their protests at the war centred upon the commercial losses.[56] Cromwell's miscalculations of Parliament's attitude to what he saw as the national interest was apparent in his surprise and annoyance at the frequency with which his relations with them broke down – something that better 'packing' with his supporters might have avoided.

THE DISPUTE WITH PORTUGAL

The activities of Cromwell's fleet that summer also included the intimidation of Portugal, whose King had refused to ratify the treaty of 1654. The use of Cromwell's fleet to force the ratification of the treaty centred upon a threat to take the Portuguese Plate Fleet and cut off her links with her Brazilian empire if she did not cooperate. This was especially effective during the current war between Portugal and Spain. Cromwell's threat can be called an early use of 'gunboat diplomacy' which he could practice on the smaller Iberian state with every chance of success. This use of naval power againt a weaker state was not unique to Cromwell, since the weapon of blockade was the ultimate way in which the Rump had intended to enforce its demands on the Dutch, while the Dutch themselves tried to use it against Danzig and Portugal (1657).

The Anglo-Portuguese treaty of 10/20 July had included the two terms which Spain had refused. The English were to have effective freedom of trade (Articles II and III) with the right to export goods to the Portuguese colonies (Article XI), and also gained the liberty to hold Protestant services and possess Protestant books in private houses (Article XIV).[57] This had its impact on the Spanish talks because once one Iberian Catholic power had accepted these terms, it was reasonable for the English to assume that the other would do so if it genuinely desired friendship. Bordeaux believed that Cromwell did not understand the pressure the Portuguese clergy would put on John VI to abrogate Article XIV.[58] On 19/29 August 1655, the King wrote to Cromwell that it was dangerous for him to accept the two disputed clauses.[59] Later he suggested that he could grant the toleration clause if the Pope gave his personal approval, which was necessary in order to stifle clerical protests at its illegality. Cromwell showed no desire to acknowledge John's difficult position and treated the reference to the Pope as an insult.[60]

The break with Spain made Portugal's trade crucial to English commerce and her ports vital to naval strategy. Hence on 19/29 February the Council advised Cromwell to send their Deputy Secretary, Philip Meadowe, to demand immediate ratification of the treaty and a down payment of £50 000 for commercial damages.[61] Meadowe did not achieve success, and when this was reported to the Council the Admirals were ordered to 'take, arrest, and seize upon . . . and detain' the Plate Fleet.[62] Meanwhile, in Lisbon, relatives of Dom Pantaleon de Sa, brother of the Portuguese ambassador, who had been executed in London in 1654, determined on revenge and fired on Meadowe as he was leaving the palace on 1/11 May. He was only hit in the hand so the effects of an assassination on talks were luckily avoided; if he had been killed it is very likely that Blake and Montague would have attacked Portuguese shipping, thus ending the possibility of cooperation against Spain. Fortunately, Meadowe was not as offended as the Admirals and refused to give the King five days to sign and then leave as they advised him. He wrote that a few more days could achieve success which was preferable to adhering rigidly to a deadline.[63] When the fleet arrived at Cascaes Meadowe judged it opportune to demand leave to depart (30 May/9 June); that 'much altered the state of affairs here' and next day the treaty was ratified and the compensation promised.[64]

Blake and Montague were displeased that Meadowe had stayed on in Lisbon after the attack, thouh Meadowe regarded the treaty as more important than standing on his dignity.[65] Montague wrote to him that he 'should have had more thanks at Whitehall had he not concluded it' after such an insult.[66] He would have preferred to intimidate the King: 'You have at this time the Portuguese on his knees, and if we had authority to make demands, we might ask what we could (almost) and he durst not but perform it, or all his country would be in rebellion.'[67] This ignored the loss of goodwill if England enforced its demands and her allies resented her way of doing so. England's need of Portuguese ports was too great to stir up hatred where it could be avoided. Meadowe argued that in any case the Admirals could not be certain of capturing the Plate Fleet.[68] This warning had its implications for the whole basis of Cromwell's naval strategy.

The diplomatic and naval actions of the campaigning season of 1656 showed the limited extent to which both sides pursued the Anglo-Spanish War. Spain had sought to retaliate for Hispaniola by means short of military conflict – something which her entanglement with France made it essential to avoid. However, financial and military constraints also acted upon the English. Apart from the influence retained by Lambert's faction, the state of national finances required that no costly continental entanglements were undertaken until it was certain that France would pay for English assistance and hand over Dunkirk, the latter term being particularly unwelcome to the Cardinal. In any case, as with the French talks of 1654–5, Cromwell was determined to make minimum concessions and believed that he could afford to wait as long as France showed no preference for a peace with Spain. Many officers and men were tied up with operating the governmental experiment of the Major-Generals and could not be spared for duties in Flanders. The absence of Parliament also meant an absence of finance for a campaign until it was recalled. The regime could not afford another disaster to its reputation in Flanders after the events in Hispaniola. Cromwell was assisted by the nature and position of the man currently determining French policy, for Mazarin was in a far less secure position than a crowned monarch to accept the return of the leading disaffected conspirator among the nobility.

9 The French Alliance of March 1657

The Lionne mission provided a clear warning that if the terms were favourable Mazarin might yet be pressurised into peace with Spain. This would invalidate the basis of Cromwell's strategy, enabling Spain to reduce its continental commitments and to assist Charles II. Reports also cast worrying doubt upon Mazarin's commitments to an English alliance, though Lockhart was more optimistic than Augier (who as a Huguenot was inevitably suspicious of the French government) and Colonel Bamfylde. Even so, the fact that Philip IV had insisted on the pardon of Condé blocked a Franco-Spanish peace for the moment. In these circumstances, Cromwell continued to insist on the cession of Dunkirk and Mardyke as an adequate pledge of French goodwill.

THE PRELIMINARIES OF THE ALLIANCE

The English intention was for France to subsidise her troops on the Continent, as discussed in talks with both France and Spain since 1653. The parlous state of the Protectorate's finances and the burden of a large and upopular standing army made this essential. The domestic discontent aroused by the Major-Generals, however, made the task of raising adequate revenue from Parliament more difficult. When Parliament met in September 1656 it showed a greater disposition to obtaining redress for grievances than to meeting the government's financial needs, although objections to military despotism at least distracted attention from the West Indies. On 17/27 October 1656, Colonel Sydenham requested £865 500 for the needs of the Government and its armed forces, while a Parliamentary committee estimated that a full £1 000 000 was in fact required.[1] Luckily, Parliamentary disapproval of the military served to stimulate a desire to provide adequate civilian backing for the Protectorate. On 30 January/9 February, £400 000 was voted in four instalments which were to be raised from 25

March.[2] This was inadequate but sufficient basis to carry on the government.

Cromwell's desire to open up a new field of campaign in Flanders was stimulated by Charles II's presence at Bruges, from where he could send envoys across the Channel from the Flemish ports. However, Thurloe's reckoning that Spain was a less dangerous foe than France remained accurate. One symptom of Spain's inability to assist Cromwell's enemies was the impoverished state of the royal court; in January 1657, Hyde reckoned that his master had only received two months' provisions in nine months.[3] Cardenas claimed that Spain was now refusing to receive envoys from England as proof of its goodwill,[4] but in positive terms the only military aid offered the King was 9000 men from the Duke of Neuberg.[5] Tension between Protestant Royalists and Catholic Spaniards added to distractions. Valuable time was wasted on the proposed conversion of Prince Henry to Catholicism (valuable propaganda for Cromwell), and the Papal Nuncio in Brussels refused to aid Charles unless he became a Catholic.[6] Cardenas continued to rely on the likelihood of a mutiny in England: the only realistic chance of the latter was if Cromwell were to take the crown, a possibility which, significantly, led to Colonel Pride threatening to shoot him. This catalogue of problems was added to by the effective infiltration of the Royalist court in Bruges by Thurloe's agents, who would have learned of any planned crossing of the Channel beforehand. The only advantage the Royalists possessed was the fact that Thurloe's destruction of their earlier networks required them to recruit new supporters as yet undetected. The plans of 1657–8 were no more successful than those of 1655, but the Thurloe correspondence shows that he was seriously worried.

Another propaganda victory was gained for the Protectorate by the desertion of some of the Irish in French service to Charles II, in the autumn of 1656. It seemed to provide the King with men and reveal the weakness of the French army, two factors to Cromwell's disadvantage. However, there was some truth in the French excuse that they had not sought to stop these unreliable and poorly trained men from deserting now rather than await trouble in the following year's campaign.[7] It also served to help English propaganda which was already stressing how much the King was relying on evil Papists.

In September 1656, Cromwell publicised Charles's negotiations with Philip William of Neuberg, who had promised to send 9000 men, in his opening speech to Parliament and Lockhart was confident that the Irish desertions could serve a similar purpose. He wrote to Thurloe that 'all Englishmen who can pretend to the lowest principle of common honesty will abhor a conjunction with so bloody and barbarous a crew'.[8] As Bamfylde gleefully pointed out, 'ten thousand Irish and Papists will contribute much to the preservation of the Protestant religion in England and the liberties and freedom of the nation'.[9] This also served to discourage any French thoughts of backing out of an alliance with Cromwell – or so Mazarin at least pretended, reminding Lockhart that he could be sure of French aid because if Charles II was now restored by Spanish arms, he would be 'a poor prince, obliged to the Spaniards' and a threat to France.[10]

Suspicion of the French was still apparent in England throughout that autumn.[11] Colonel Bamfylde, who was particularly concerned, strongly urged his master to consider a temporary disengagement from the Spanish War. He considered the French alliance 'doubtful' and Spain likely to seek a temporary agreement with England in order to concentrate on affairs in Germany. In his opinion:

> There seldom has been made a peace in Christendom between enemies, that either of them has just cause to break it within a twelve-month . . . If they find it prudent . . . if by a peace Jamaica can be kept and other great advantages gained, which I believe Spain is very apt to agree to . . . is not the total conquest of the Indies much more feasible four or five years hence when your men in Jamaica are more well settled?[12]

This option would have enabled Cromwell to avoid a Flemish expedition and would have freed his troops to send more aid to the Jamaican colony, which was still in an unsettled condition. The expenditure on the Flemish campaign would have been avoided and Spain would have had to call off her privateers and abandon the King. The main reason why this course was not followed can be ascribed not to anti-Spanish hatred but to fear of a 'general peace'.

In these circumstances, events moved slowly towards an

Anglo-French treaty. Spain did nothing serious to halt this. The efforts of their ambassador, Gamarra, to involve the Dutch in the war through their resentment of English 'searches' caused some anxiety, though his memorandum to the States-General in July urging an alliance met with a lukewarm response even from Holland.[13] Spain may, however, have been encouraged to seek accommodation by a report from their agent 'Fitts' in London to Cardenas, saying that the war was 'expensive and dissatisfactory to the generality' and that any 'reasonable overture would be very acceptable'. De Haro told Cardenas to 'entertain the notion with all possible care',[14] but Cardenas argued that 'Charles Stuart's design was in so good a posture that it was fit to expect success; if that answered their hopes a revenge of the injuries received from Cromwell would be more honourable; if that failed then it would be time enough to listen'.[15] The peace effort therefore never received adequate attention, though apparently Cardenas's secretary did visit London that winter.[16] A Spanish overture at the same time as Bamfyde's proposal might have stood some chance, albeit slight, as there was still no progress over the cession of Dunkirk in the Paris talks.

Mazarin sought to remind Cromwell of vague promises which had been made to tolerate Catholics in England in return for toleration of the Huguenots. This served to remind Cromwell of of how irritating the French found Lockhart's constant interference in their internal affairs, but there was a serious point to it as public opinion among devout Frenchmen was aware of the mistreatment of their coreligionists in England, in the same manner as the English were aware of the danger to the Huguenots. Toleration was a sensitive issue with the Army and Parliament, the latter having passed new anti-Catholic measures. As a result, the Protector dared not make any public gesture. He wrote to Mazarin:

> the obligations and many instances of affection which I have received from your Eminence engage me to make suitable return. But though I have set this upon my spirit I may not (shall I tell you I cannot?) at this juncture of time as the face of my affairs stand answer to your call.[17]

Catholic pressure in France was now intensified by the meeting of the clergy, to whom Mazarin had to excuse his failure to make peace with Spain by assuring that Louis XIV's 'sincere and pious endeavours' had been halted by Spain's 'intractable demands' on Condé and Portugal.[18]

French concern at handing over Dunkirk remained an obstacle. Negotiations proceeded slowly during Mazarin's illness in early February and Lockhart reported that he had met General Turenne, Servien and Lionne about Dunkirk, only to find that the former was by no means certain of the practicability of attacking the coast in that campaign. The Cardinal urged Turenne to attempt Durkirk.

> with all the appearance of zeal imaginable . . . Turenne held forth the possibility of it and pressed the ill consequences that would follow upon their failing beside the advantages that would rebound to Spain. It might occasion jealousies and difficulties between England and France; he absolutely refused the command of the army on that account.[19]

Lockhart's attempt to urge the attack on Dunkirk met with no response and he had to agree that Gravelines was easier. At the same time, however, the Papal Nuncio had complained to the Cardinal. Lockhart believed:

> there is really so general inclinations to that peace in all pretend to be good Catholics that Turenne would be much put to it, attacked both with promises and threats . . . these offerings of friendship you are now pleased to make come so very seasonably that were they not in the balance I should be afraid that the scales turn against you and all other Protestants.[20]

There was more danger in the dispute between France and the United Provinces which could have escalated into war and distracted France. Mazarin tried to win Cromwell over with news of how Gamarra was trying to persuade the States-General not to treat Royalist ships as pirates, white Venetian observers reported Gamarra's good reception after Dutch anger at an Anglo-French declaration that Dutch ships would be searched for contraband goods.[21] Lockhart, however, acted as mediator[22] to avoid the unpleasant possibility of England having to choose between France and the Dutch. (If Cromwell chose France,

Dutch shipping could aid Charles II.) Cromwell acted with caution, as also when France sought aid against a threat of invasion from the Holy Roman Empire. Lockhart warned that England feared that the Germans would leave any fighting to them.[23]

THE FRENCH TREATY AND LOCKHART'S APOLOGIA

Mutual desire to avoid a Franco-Spanish peace led Cromwell and Mazarin's representatives to sign the treaty on 3/13 March 1657. To placate French public opinion, Mazarin's heretic alliance was excused by listing 'certain arguments against the Spaniards for their fomenting discord in the Christian world'. The Cardinal had made an offer of peace 'with a love of public tranquillity' but Spain had rejcted it. The alliance would thus force Spain to accept Mazarin's desire for peace on moderate terms and punish their haughty aggression by 're-establishing public peace and tranquillity'. Mazarin, like Cromwell in the 'Manifesto', excused the war as defensive and pretended that Spain had brought it on herself by her iniquities. It was, however, easy to argue that there were better ways of restoring peace and tranquillity by calling a heretic army on to the Continent and ceding French territory to them. The agreement that there should be no peace with Spain for a year without mutual consent satisfied the English fear of a 'general peace' excluding, and aimed against, them, but it had to be put into a secret article. The terms were as follows;

1. Joint attacks by land and sea in April on Dunkirk, Mardyke and Gravelines.
2. France was to provide 20 000 troops for this, England her fleet.
3. England was to provide 6000 men. The French were to pay for the raising and transport of 3000 men and to pay all of them during their service. The original force intended for the campaign had been 3000.
4. England was to garrison Dunkirk and Mardyke, France Gravelines. If Gravelines was taken first the English would hold it as a surety until Dunkirk fell. This showed their mistrust of Mazarin's assurances.

5. Any town under English control was to allow free exercise of the Catholic religion.
6. The Secret Article. There was to be no truce or treaty with Spain for a year except by mutual consent. If the Pope or Venice called a peace conference, English ambassadors were to be invited.[24]

Lockhart wrote to Thurloe explaining defensively why he had signed these terms, 'lest several things in the articles meet with a hard construction'. His main points were:

(a) 'I foresaw there was a necessity of bringing things to a conclusion so as you might have time to take the preparations necessary' for a spring campaign.
(b) 'I had hints given me that the proposition made by the Nuncio about peace with Spain was not so much disrelished as their professions speak it to be.'
(c) 'The advantages arising to His Highness from an interest in the Continent might [i.e. would] overbalance the disadvantage of condescending to some little particulars that they had so tenaciously stuck upon.'
(d) The Catholic toleration clause required that the Catholics bear themselves in a submissive and obedient manner ('nihil adversus regimen qui submissi fuerint molientes'). That left a 'latitude' open to expel troublemakers.

Lockhart reported that he had found Mazarin's negotiators 'much concerned in these expressions in order to the satisfaction of the Clergy and others'. There had been 'so small inclinations for condescending to anything contained in the Secret Article, I was glad to take it on the terms it runs'.[25] The treaty was the best agreement possible. Lockhart, like Meadowe in Portugal in June 1656, considered an acceptable agreement to be of more value than standing on points of honour. The French were now committed to surrender their own territory.

The Anglo-French friendship thus confirmed was recognised on both sides as being the product of necessity rather than genuine goodwill. Both Mazarin and Cromwell desired to continue the Spanish War in the face of opposition from some of their advisers and a substantial body of opinion among their countrymen – the English merchants and the French clerics.

Both preferred to ally with the other rather than abandon their current policy, and each provided enough military aid to enable the other to argue that Spain could now be defeated. The English clearly made the alliance out of necessity. The agreement to hand over Dunkirk would lay Mazarin open to odium and caused an upsurge of hostile propaganda headed by Cardinal de Retz. This seems to have been a more acceptable alternative than giving way to pressure from the *dévots* and enabling Condé to return to revive opposition among the nobility.

The alliance did not end suspicions that Cromwell would find an excuse to evade it if he so desired. Colonel Bamfylde reported that he had had a meeting with a 'person of condition' who believed that England and Spain were treating, putting forward the interesting argument that if Cromwell took the Crown he would no doubt desire to restore peace with Spain to give England a period of tranquillity to recover from the upheaval. In that case: 'The King and Parliament of England would not much scruple for the public utility to retire from that which the Protector had engaged himself to.'[26]

The treaty was extended in a new series of 'Secret Articles' between Lockhart and the French on 29 April/9 May. The main terms were as follows:

1. There was to be no 'union, accord, or engagement' without prior notice with Spain or any other enemy power.
2. One power must aid the other even against its own allies. This provided for English help to France against the Dutch.
3. Each power was to help the other attack any third party which had injured their citizens. This was again aimed at the Dutch whose captains had assisted Spanish privateers against English and French ships.
4. English naval assistance against the United Provinces if and when France attacked them.
5. If more English aid was needed, Cromwell was to supply it and the French to pay his ships for three months.
6. Cromwell was to send 12 000 soldiers to France when needed and was to receive Ostend and Nieupoort when captured. Cromwell must have argued that England had better secure these coastal towns to ensure that the division of the 'spoils' was not totally to France's benefit.

7. Mutual alliance to help Sweden against the threat of an invasion by Denmark (stirred up by the Dutch).
8. Action to prevent a Habsburg succeeding Ferdinand III as Holy Roman Emperor.
9. English naval aid to French expeditions to Catalonia and Naples.[27] The latter was nearly implemented in 1658,[28] Mazarin requesting Lockhart in March that some warships be detached to aid the Chevalier Paul's attack on Naples. However, when the English arrived they found that the expedition had been put off.[29]

THE IMPERIAL ELECTION: PLANS TO DEFEAT THE HABSBURG CANDIDATURE

The Holy Roman Emperor Ferdinand III died on 2/12 April 1657, predeceased by his elder son Ferdinand. The new Emperor had to be at least 18 years old and the next heir was Ferdinand II's second son Leopold (King of Hungary) who was 17. The election was technically open to plans to remove the crown from the possession of the Habsburg dynasty for the first time since 1452, though the inevitable delays would mean that Leopold would be 18 by the time the Electors assembled. The French now raised the possibility of an alternative candidature and Mazarin put forward the idea of Louis XIV seeking election. A more feasible idea was to choose a 'moderate' Catholic prince acceptable to the Protestant electors or a 'moderate' Protestant prince acceptable to enough of the Catholic electors. The main candidate in the latter case was the Elector of Saxony. Cromwell had contacts with a number of the Protestant princes, especially the Landgrave of Hesse-Cassel whom he had praised for his Protestant zeal.[30] In particular, the Elector of Brandenburg's envoy Schlezer was in London.

Cromwell had shown an interest in European Protestantism as early as 1654 when he sent Pell and Dury to Switzerland, conversely he had entertained appeals from Protestant envoys such as the Polish Baron, Zadowski (on behalf of whom an appeal was ordered in summer 1654).[31] His involvement with Germany only became important in 1656 when he needed allies against the threat of Austrian aid to Spain or war in the

Baltic affecting naval supplies. Pragmatism and Protestantism combined to lead the Protector to support the idea of taking the Imperial crown out of the Habsburg dynasty, to distract the Austrian branch from aiding their Spanish cousins. Cromwell and Mazarin's activities should not be judged as hopelessly overoptimistic in view of Leopold's eventual election. Their success was seen as quite possible at the time, for example in Hamburg in April – a war between Catholic and Protestant Electors being the likeliest result.[32] Thurloe later informed the Dutch ambassador Nieupoort that 'The Protector is of the opinion that it would be best if Germany became involved in war, and he would like to see the United Netherlands engaged in this.'[33]

As soon as he heard of Ferdinand III's death, Mazarin became aware of the possibilities and told Lockhart that 'he was anxious to promote the election of anyone not of the House of Austria, and desired His Highness to move the Protestant electors on behalf of any such person as may be agreed upon'.[34] Louis XIV's election was unlikely, but it appears that the English government's agents concentrated on the hopes of the Elector of Saxony. There is thus no serious question of Mazarin duping Cromwell into supporting a hopeless cause. Cromwell took the opportunity of his audience with Schlezer on 14/24 May to denounce Leopold as a Catholic persecutor and to declare that his election would be a blow in favour of the 'Counter-Reformation', presumably due to reports of persecution in Hungary. He asked about the chances of the Elector of Bavaria, the principal Catholic rival to Leopold; which contender Frederick William would support; and what was the attitude and the armed strength of the Elector of Saxony.[35] He assured Bordeaux that although he only knew Brandenburg among the Electors he would do all he could to prevent Leopold's election.[36] In Paris, Lockhart at first supported the efforts being made by Charles X's envoy, Count Tott, to achieve French support for his master, but abandoned his early enthusiasm once he had worked out that five of the eight Electors were Catholic.[37]

In England the election was seen as a secondary matter to the Flemish campaign and the reform of the constitution. Cromwell restricted his involvement to the collection of intelligence on the chances of the most likely contenders – who did not include the King of France. Colonel Bamfylde reported that the likeliest result was that

> France and all the Protestants will endeavour to set up the Duke of Saxony . . . not so much caring whether he has the empire as to bring the election to the determination of the sword . . . Germany is likely to be the scene of the greatest business at this time in Christendom.[38]

Cromwell had enough problems; it was essential that if a war did break out he was not forced by any treaties to intervene in Germany unless he could afford to. Accordingly, Cromwell ignored the attempts of Schlezer to blackmail him into signing a treaty to lend Brandenburg aid if needed in return for the Elector's assistance in the election. Schlezer claimed that if he did not cooperate Frederick William was likely to vote for Leopold and renew his assault on Sweden, but Cromwell replied that unfortunately finance, his expenditure on the Navy and internal matters precluded assistance. The threat was not carried out.[39] Charles Louis of the Palatinate's envoy, von Eilenberg, who was in London to try to have his master's English persion restored, attempted unsuccessfully to interest Cromwell in helping his master's election.[40]

The Diet finally assembled at Frankfurt early in 1658 with England unofficially represented by Colonel Bamfylde. His efforts on behalf of the Protestant cause were less obvious than those of the French mission, but this was inevitable as (unlike Louis) Cromwell had no right to interfere as he had no territory within the Empire. In any case, Cromwell's main mediation efforts at the time were in the business of the Danish–Swedish War which threatened more vital interests in the Baltic. The English could afford to leave the matter of a new 'League' between the German Protestants to their French allies, who had organised such alliances in the 1600s and the 1630s. Cromwell's desire to avoid commitments should be assessed in the light of his current internal difficulties. He did, however, seek to use what influence he had. Thus, once Colonel Jephson had concluded his Baltic mission Thurloe ordered him to Berlin to encourage the Elector of Brandenburg to vote for Saxony. If Leopold was elected, it was essential that he agree in his 'Accession Capitulation' not to give any men or money to Spain, thus neutralising the threat posed to England.[41] Frederick

William assured that he would insist on this matter, though he would only vote for the candidate favoured by the majority, that is, Leopold.[42]

The outcome of the election on 18/28 July saw Leopold elected after prolonged negotiations concerning his 'Capitulation'. The Anglo-French efforts thus failed to prevent his succession but the terms of the 'Capitulation' were according to Thurloe's hopes. The Emperor was not to sand arms, money, soldiers or other commodities to any enemies of France – namely Spain – in return for which France did not oppose Leopold's election. The treaties of Westphalia were to be observed and thus any attack on the German Protestants was ruled out. These terms meant that England need not fear Austrian aid to Spain as long as France was at war with that country – the reason why Cromwell had sought to prevent Leopold's election in the first place. This had been achieved as a result of the efforts of France, Brandenburg and Mainz rather than England – but England benefited all the same. Similarly, the 'League of the Rhine' which the North German Princes formed (14/24 August) and France joined (15/25 August) served to protect the Princes against the Habsburgs and pose a permanent threat to them without embroiling England in any new commitments. England's omission from the League served as a check on Cromwell's expressed intentions to be 'Head and Protector' of the Protestants. France reasserted her traditional role in northern Germany – until the Austrian threat began to appear less dangerous than French pretensions to rule to the Lower Rhine. The 'defeat' was however inevitable, granted that Cromwell's troops were fully occupied with Dunkirk and his financial resources were in a state of collapse. England achieved her main aim of diminishing the threat of help to Spain by the settlement of the German problem in summer 1658, despite her own inability to take a more active role.

10 England, France and Dunkirk, 1657-8

The terms of the Anglo-French alliance provided for the capture of Dunkirk, or of Gravelines as a temporary substitute, during the campaign of 1657. Apart from its importance as a 'pledge' of French goodwill, the port was one of the main bases for the privateers who had been inflicting serious losses on English shipping. Its capture would also serve to prevent the Spaniards from lending troops or ships to the planned Royalist invasion which loomed nearer throughout 1657. The French, however, insisted on capturing all the inland towns guarding its approaches before they would invest it. This delay led to growing English suspicion and a belief that France was using the English expeditionary force to further its own aims in Artois.

England blamed French deviousness for preventing an early attack, but, as Lockhart realised, Cromwell himself was partly to blame. The expedition had been planned during autumn 1656, as is apparent from the discussions of the difficulties involved between Lockhart, Mazarin and Turenne.[1] The commander had already been selected – Sir John Reynolds, Commissary-General of Horse in Ireland, a noted siege expert whose wife was sister to Henry Cromwell's wife.[2] His second-in-command was Sir Thomas Morgan, a veteran of Civil War sieges. However, due to England's suspicion of the French Cromwell did nothing until the treaty was signed. The preparations for the expedition appear to have been hampered by the refusal of some officers to serve in Flanders.[3] The desertions among the soldiers were no doubt mainly due to lack of enthusiasm, as the troops selected were regular regiments unlike the case of the Western Design.[4] The chance of a swift advance passed. St Ghislain was surrendered by the Irish in French service on 23 March/2 April. Dunkirk was reinforced by 2000 Spaniards, and Mazarin informed Cromwell on 18/28 May that their plans had been betrayed and the French were postponing the expedition.[5] Spain's knowledge of the plan was not merely a French excuse as there were sound military reasons against risking a defeat. In any case, French interests were aimed at possession of a 'barrier' of towns in Artois to prevent a repeat of the invasion of 1636. The English saw Mazarin's delay as evidence of his desire to avoid handing over Dunkirk.

THE REMOVAL OF POTENTIAL DISTRACTIONS

The Protector desired to concentrate on Dunkirk but in the summer of 1657 he had a number of distractions. The main difficulty was the stability of his own regime which might have required him to withdraw or curtail his expedition. The 'constitutional crisis' came to a head in the weeks following the French treaty, when the creation of a 'Second House' of Parliament was followed on 31 March/10 April by the Speaker's formal request that Cromwell become King. In the weeks that followed Cromwell's main concern was to assess the potential risks. Significantly, the main supporters of his taking the Crown were men with no military links such as Fiennes and Wolseley, and non-Councillors Charles Howard and Lord Broghill. This one issue might stir up the latent republicanism of army officers and men where all the Leveller conspiracies had failed, and lead those who until now had tolerated the conservatism of the Protectoral institutions to conclude that he was a traitor to the 'Good Old Cause'. It was on this likely reaction that Sexby and Spain depended for the outbreak of the rebellion which must precede any Spanish or Royalist attack, as mutinous soldiers were a more serious threat to the Government than the remnants of the Royalist associations. (Events in 1659 showed the relative importance of these threats to the Protectorate.) If Cromwell took the Crown he could not be sure of avoiding the first serious military dissension since 1649. Until now his prestige had been such that Sexby had to resort to desperate plans to assassinate him.[6] The coronation of 'King Oliver' would give him his only real chance, though it might reconcile moderate Royalists.

The most recent research indicates that Cromwell was not enthusiastic about it – it was only 'a feather in a man's cap'.[7] It appears that his rejection of the Crown on May 8/18 was due to a warning by Lambert, Fleetwood and Desborough that they could not answer for the consequences within the Army.[8] This is probably the most important instance of how Cromwell's interests were ultimately dominated by the need to preserve unity within the Army, which could counter his efforts to civilianise his rule and thus extend the damaging constitutional impasse until his death. As far as foreign policy was concerned, Cromwell's choice avoided the threat of an Army split for his lifetime, and ensured that the discontent over pay in the early months of 1658 was not compounded by an element of ideological controversy. Cromwell could afford to send troops to the Continent in large enough numbers to prove his goodwill to Mazarin and to ensure victory at Dunkirk, which he could not have done had he been afraid of serious trouble at home. The resolution of the crisis in a manner satisfactory to Army feeling also dashed Sexby's hopes.[9] However, it had serious results for internal politics which were ultimately to negate the success of Cromwell's foreign policy in Flanders. Cromwell could hold the 'grandees' in check largely due to his own prestige with them and their lesser officers. However, this was a personal ascendancy, not the ascendancy of Cromwell the Lord Protector. His successor would have no such prestige.

The implications of the refusal of the Crown were serious for Spain, given the failure of Sexby's plans. Cardenas was relying on either a Leveller-led mutiny or peace overtures from Cromwell to end the conflict, and had no strategy to cope with the failure of both possibilities. De Haro, too, did not wish to put it out of his power to treat with England, which infuriated Charles II's new envoy to Madrid, Henry Bennet. In Bennet's opinion, 'the root of all ill is Don Alonso' (Cardenas), on whom de Haro chiefly relied to formulate policy towards England.[10] The chief minister would only promise to send Spanish troops to England 'after being assured that the King was secure of one important port in England, in a province which would enable him to make defensive war under a captain such as Marcin'.[11] The chances of this being secured were extremely unlikely quite apart from Spain being able to get troops across the Channel without interference from Cromwell's fleet.

A second potential crisis within England threatened to distract the Protector from a Flemish campaign in July. The reform of the constitution improved his legal position *vis-à-vis* the Council, ending his requirement to consider majority

opinion on important matters.[12] However, Lambert now refused to take the oath required of all Councillors under the
new constitution based on the 'Humble Petition and Advice'.
He was not usually allied with the men of conscience who
would refuse to take an oath out of principle. However, on this
occasion he took a stand along with one Councillor who probably had a valid objection on the grounds of religious scruples,
Colonel Sydenham. Lambert was the only man in the government to have a military reputation to rival Cromwell's and had
advised against the Western Design and a breach with Spain.
His warnings had been proved correct by events, and it was
lucky for Cromwell that he did not take the opportunity to
remind people of his earlier misgivings or show that speed
of action and political resolution which marked him out in
1653 and again in 1659–60. The objections of Sydenham, and
apparently other councillors also, to the oath on religious
scruples were eventually overcome.[13]

While preparation for the Flemish campaign went ahead,
the English navy made a second attempt on the Spanish Plate
Fleet to bolster morale and finances. The successful arrival of
more silver in Spain that spring would enable Philip IV to pay
his troops for the new campaign. It was also a serious matter
that the Dutch, whose bankers had claims on some of the
money, had sent Admiral de Ruyter to escort the fleet.[14] Anglo-
Dutch tension, particularly over the Baltic, was such that any
naval clash might turn into war. Luckily an outright battle was
avoided when Admiral Blake found the Plate Fleet in the
harbour of Santa Cruz in the Canaries on 17/27 April and
attacked it, sending sixteen loaded ships to the bottom of the
harbour. The attack could be portrayed as another success in
the tradition of Drake; Giavarina reported from London when
the news reached it that 'the victory is here regarded as the
greatest which they have won over the Spaniards since 1588'.[15]
This was of use when seeking to rally patriotic feeling; it was
of more significance that the money on board the sunken
galleons had been lost to the English treasury. Furthermore, the
failure to secure the treasure for Cromwell's weak finances was
compounded by a failure to make an important strategic gain.
Partly due to Blake's terminal ill-health, no troops were landed
on the ill-defended Canaries to establish a base to obstruct
Spanish shipping en route to and from the Americas. Apart

from improving the chances of taking the autumn's Plate Fleet, this permanent English presence would have served a massive blow to Spanish morale in impeding her communications.[16]

The lack of a naval base in the Canaries or at Gibraltar emphasised the importance of a friendly Portugal. Unfortunately, that summer a Spanish land offensive raised the possibility of the loss of that ally. On 30 May/9 June the Spanish took the frontier town of Olivenza and began to press into Portugal, which was feared to be 'greatly weakened'.[17] Concurrently, the Dutch were seeking revenge for Portugal's reconquest in 1654 of territory in Brazil by sending a fleet to Lisbon. The danger arose of coordination between the Dutch and Spain. Gamarra had indeed promised military help for the Dutch, if needed, in their efforts to force Portugal to return the Brazilian colony.[18] Cromwell's suspicions of the Dutch were reinforced by Mazarin, who alleged that the Dutch fleet would compensate for Spain's naval weakness by shutting English merchant shipping out of the Mediterranean.[19] Accordingly, when de Ruyter left port that spring Montague was instructed to confront his fleet in the Downs and delay him from sailing to Portugal for as long as possible. This indirectly rendered great service to the Portuguese.[20] When Bordeaux reminded Cromwell of the threats currently posed to Sweden he argued that defence of Portugal was more important. If Sweden was attacked he would prefer that France assisted it while England concentrated on its beleaguered southern ally – a significant estimation of the comparative value to him of a Protestant and a Catholic king, with the latter coming off best due to his strategic importance.[21] Thurloe later remarked that Sweden could look after itself but Portugal could not, which shows his priorities.[22] Fortunately, the attack on Portugal by Spain did not become serious enough to merit the diversion of forces, though its ambassador Mello requested troops and money that autumn.[23]

THE DISPUTE OVER MARDYKE: ANGLO-FRENCH MISTRUST

The French campaign on the Continent proceeded against Cambrai and Montmedy in the summer of 1657, showing the

French priorities to be other than Dunkirk. Mazarin assured Lockhart that 'Turenne had orders to attempt Dunkirk upon any terms that were possible, but found it wholly impossible at this time'.[24] Lockhart regarded this as an excuse, whatever the strategic importance of securing the inland approaches to Dunkirk first. Control of the Flemish ports was thus vital, as Lockhart recognised: 'If the design [concerning Dunkirk] be prosperous . . . our enemy's design against England this winter will be broken. [If not] . . . I am apprehensive Flanders will contribute even beyond expectation to the transport of Charles Stuart and the rabble he has with him.'[25] Suspicion was exacerbated by new reports of the harassment of Huguenots in Gascony and Piedmont, apparently based upon exaggerated versions of a minor incident at Montauban.[26] It led to a strong protest from Lockhart which did not improve Anglo-French relations.[27]

Cromwell now took a hand to show that his patience was running out. In his irritation he was even prepared to threaten the withdrawal of his troops which would be of great value to Royalist invasion plans.[28] Whether or not as a result of this threat, the inland campaign drew to a close after the fall of Montmedy. Mardyke was besieged, and on 24 September/4 October it surrendered and was handed over to the English. This did not end English suspicion, as the question remained regarding France's willingness – or otherwise – to defend this small and battered fort from counterattack. On 22 October/ 1 November, a Spanish force including Charles II and Caracena launched a night counterattack which was only narrowly beaten off. When Lockhart sought more effective aid for the defenders from the French, Turenne maintained that it would be better to abandon it as it was open to enemy raids, had little strategic value and was costly to defend.[29] The English took this to imply that he would rather the fort was taken by the enemy than help to defend it.

Cromwell warned Bordeaux that if Mazarin insisted he would evacuate Mardyke but he would take it as meaning that France was neither able nor willing to carry out the treaty. Thurloe told Bordeaux that 'the majority of the Council disapproved of the conquest and regarded it as an occasion to drain England of men and money . . . though he himself was as inclined as ever to remain united with France'.[30] Cromwell was no longer required to take his advisers' advice, but despite Lambert's retirement the influence of the 'pro-French' faction was still limited. On 6/16 November Giavarina reported that the Council had been debating all the week whether to keep or abandon Mardyke, and had agreed to the former after a 'long debate'.[31] Thurloe noted: 'Truly the inconvenience we have already found by being put to keep Mardyke without Dunkirk are so many and the charge so insupportable . . . all of which had been avoided . . . had Dunkirk been taken also; the treaty provides that both shall be obtained together.'[32]

As the English were in such difficulties, the question arose as to whether the French had deliberately held up the siege of Dunkirk to weaken their allies. Mazarin admitted that Turenne 'had let slip an advantageous opportunity', blaming his cautious nature.[33] It was customary for the French to withdraw most of their men to winter quarters, but if they did so in Flanders this would mean abandoning the defence of Mardyke to the English. Thurloe warned that it was safer to withdraw the latter rather than see them desert.[34] Accordingly, Mazarin agreed to send some of his personal guards and musketeers to reinforce Mardyke at once and to instruct Turenne to leave troops in the vicinity when he retired into winter quarters.[35] A further setback occurred when Reynolds, the English commander in Flanders, was drowned when returning to England on 4/14 December; next year Lockhart took control of the troops.

THE ROYALIST INVASION THREAT

The Royalist invasion appeared to be the imminent threat to England that winter, while the Spanish retained the ports from which the King could sail. There were formidable difficulties in his path, not least his lack of ships and of organised supporters in a position to seize a port in England. However, Thurloe remained concerned at the threat despite his network of spies. He wrote to Henry Cromwell at the end of October:

> The Cavalier party is exceeding busy and the face of things looks as if they would suddenly break out; I know of some particular persons in England that were engaged that were

never outwardly of their party before . . . it is sure more than ordinary hopes are engaged.[36]

Military rule in the counties and piracy at sea had bred their own threats in 1656–7, as was apparent in Parliament. The gains made at sea by Stayner and Blake had not affected the Government's need of Parliamentary subsidies, which led to more discontent. The number of active conspirators was small and most people would not contemplate active resistance. However, government indebtedness was to lead to new fears of mutinies over pay.

The rumours from England encouraged Spain to belive that revolt was possible, but due to their own weakness they would do nothing until it actually broke out. Bennett feared that while the Spaniards awaited rebellion and the Royalists awaited Spanish help, the King would 'fall between two stools' and nothing would happen.[37] This was what Thurloe relied on and events turned out as Bennet had feared. However, this did not prevent a series of 'invasion scares' in London, particularly in February and March when an invasion was reported to be imminent and people were betting that Charles II would be in England by May.[38] The Government took the threat seriously enough to order all known Catholics and Royalists out of London on 3/13 March and to stage a wave of arrests.

The cost of the war, combined with the end of the hope of obtaining Parliamentary subsidies, posed a more serious threat than popular complaints or hesitant Spanish plans. If the Navy could not be paid the blockades of Flanders and Spain would have to be abandoned, freeing the King to invade and the Plate Fleet to save Spain's financial position. More imminently dangerous was the threat of trouble from unpaid soldiers.[39] The Government had acquired £200 000 for arrears of pay before Parliament was dissolved, but merchants' loss of confidence now posed a threat in that Cromwell had no other source of financial supply. The City refused a loan, so he applied to one of his supporters (probably Vyner) and was believed to have used the £90 000 left in the Vaudois Fund.[40]

THE ENGLISH OFFENSIVE

Cromwell had sought to avoid the possibility of a peace between the 'Two Crowns' throughout the Protectorate; hence his French alliance. The Royalist threat now made it imperative that the offensive proceeded as planned. Cromwell warned his last Parliament, on January 5/15 1658, of the danger which a 'general peace' would propose to England:

> what is there in all the parts of Europe but a consent, a cooperation, at this time and season of all Popish powers to suppress everything that stands in their way? . . . Really, were it not that France is a balance against that party at this time! Should there be a peace made, then England will be the general object of all the fury and wrath of all the enemies of God and religion in the world.[41]

The obvious way to overcome opposition to the expense of the war and to its serious commercial losses was to defend it in moral terms as a patriotic duty. Thus Cromwell repeated his previous arguments:

> You know that your enemies have been accepted as such ever since Queen Elizabeth came to the throne! An avowed designed enemy all along, wanting of no council, wisdom, and prudence to rout you from the face of the Earth, and when public attempts would not do, how have they . . . laid foundations to perplex and trouble our government by taking away the lives of them they judged to be of any use to preserving our peace?[42]

This was a far cry from the unofficial cooperation of 1651–4 and is more reminiscent of the wilder ravings of exponents of the 'Black Legend'. Cromwell had misjudged his audience, and the tone of his speech was designed to rouse a patriotic desire to cooperate with the Government, which did not result.

One part of Cromwell's speech serves to illustrate the whole basis of his foreign policy – the need to avoid complacent isolationism.

> You have counted yourselves happy in being environed with a great ditch from all the worlds outside. Truly you will not be able to keep your ditch nor your shipping unless you

turn your ships and your shipping into troops of horses and companies of foot; and fight to defend yourselves on terra firma![43]

The immediate reference was to the need for defence against the Royalists, but it can be taken to refer in general to Cromwell's belief that he had to pursue an active involvement in Europe to deter and preoccupy aggressors. The threat was to his own regime rather than to the country as a whole. His intention was to make the two seem irretrievably linked; something which MPs were not so sure of.

The 1658 campaign had to proceed despite all England's internal problems, so during the winter plans went ahead. There seem to have been less worries about the French, though Lockhart was so unpopular that he dared not set foot out of doors in Paris.[44] French Catholic opinion resented Parliament's new measures against their coreligionists and in December 1657 Mazarin resumed the protests which he had made about this the previous June.[45] There were disputes in Flanders over France continuing to pay English officers who had left their posts, and over the quality of the remaining English soldiers in the French army.[46] Mazarin remained worried that the occupation of Catholic towns in Flanders by 'heretics' under French auspices would have a bad effect on French public opinion,[47] but he had to rely on Lockhart's assurances. Instead, he tried to divert Cromwell's main interest from Flanders by introducing Lockhart to a Neapolitan exile and protégé of ex-Queen Christina, 'Don Lewis', who 'pretends to be able to put that kingdom into a republic under the protection of any prince he agrees with, and offers it to His Highness'. As a further inducement, Don Lewis claimed to have worked for the papal chamber De Propagatione Fidei and to be able to betray all the papal agents in England. Lockhart refused to have anything more to do with the idea unless he was ordered, as Don Lewis was 'a vain frothy man'.[48]

If Spain was ever to mount an invasion, she would need to use a substantial number of ships and be able to elude or defeat the English blockade. Neither of these was likely. On 27 February/9 March Admiral Goodson resumed his blockade, and the five Dutch vessels which Charles II had hired to transport his men were spotted entering Ostend harbour and attacked. Three vessels were destroyed and the other two blockaded in the harbour, thus ending the Royalists' small hopes of being able to cross the Channel.[49] The Spanish government now put off their intention of aiding the King until winter, effectively ending his hopes because unless the Anglo-French campaign met with disaster Spain would have lost all its invasion ports by then.[50]

The Anglo-French treaty was renewed for another year on 18/28 March, promising an attack on Dunkirk before 10 May (NS) followed by an attack on Gravelines on behalf of the French. When Dunkirk fell Cromwell was to install his own governor and garrison, and if the attack did not take place England was to be reimbursed.[51] There was, however, still some evidence of French disquiet since overtures were made to Giustinian, the Venetian ambassador in Paris, about arranging a peace conference with Spain. He informed Lockhart, who claimed that Cromwell had desired peace also but had been forced to take action by the Pope's plans against him.[52] This probably refers to the Nuncio's mission in winter 1656–7 which brought about the Anglo-French alliance. Lockhart asked for time to consult his masters, later replying that Cromwell desired peace and would be glad of Venice's help if a conference was arranged.[53] His main desire was to avoid being left out of such an event.

The first part of the campaign was to attempt to take Ostend by a surprise assault from the sea, guided by a local traitor called Spintelet. Marshal d'Aumont and Admiral Goodson found that their guide had informed the Spanish garrison and they were driven off with heavy losses.[54] The Spaniards were defeated by the combined armies, Lockhart commanding the English, at the Battle of the Dunes on 4/14 June and ten days later Dunkirk surrendered. Turenne's terms guaranteed the religion, estates, churches, religious houses, relics, privileges and franchises of the townspeople in minute and comprehensive detail.[55] Every effort was thus made to counteract the likely charges of Mazarin's treachery to the True Faith. Lockhart had to accept this, though the 'hand-over' terms included the stipulation that the inhabitants could be expelled if they did not comport themselves obediently.

THE ENGLISH IN DUNKIRK

In his memorandum of 1661/2, Thurloe gave reasons for the importance of Dunkirk to the English.

(a) 'It would oblige France to perform their treaties . . . and in particular that of making no peace but by consent.' The town was a hostage against a 'general peace'.

(b) 'As France would from hence be tender to contract any alliances with others that might be prejudicial to England, so they could not think it safe to undertake any great designs without a perfect understanding with the English . . . because they left a back door behind them in Flanders which might be used for the overthrow of France while they were engaged elsewhere.'

(c) It would serve to reassure the Huguenots of Cromwell's concern and dissuade the French government from persecuting them. Dunkirk could also encourage 'multitudes of people of those parts, suppressed . . . by Spanish severity', to declare their hidden Protestant beliefs and cast off the Catholic 'yoke'. This was the most subversive aspect of Cromwell's armed presence on the Continent; his use of Dunkirk as a rallying point for Protestants and a 'sally port' for further wars was reminiscent of the Swedish use of Stralsund under Gustavus Adolphus. The threat added to the awe and fear in which Catholics held him, which served a useful purpose at a time when his finances were exhausted. Giavarina reckoned in August 1658 that 'the designs of the government are so vast that they aim at taking possession of any part of the world . . . while in the matter of religion they aim at nothing less than infecting the whole Catholic world with Lutheranism'.[56] Steps were certainly taken to encourage the immigration of Protestants; Lockhart proposed a subscription to encourage Flemish Protestants to move in and replace disloyal Catholics.[57]

(d) Cromwell 'being considered as the patron and the protector of Protestant religion, he stood fair for undertaking and prosecuting any design'. This was more wishful thinking in the state of English affairs in summer

1658, but there was potential to use Dunkirk as such
if needed.

(e) 'A bridle upon the Dutch'. The Dutch had shown their
latent ill-will by their secret aid to the Spanish, the
pirates and the King. The Dutch themselves believed
Cromwell had this intention. In Paris, Ambassador
Boreel protested to Giustinian:

> France did not know her own true interests and her
> real enemies . . . to bridle Cromwell it would be
> necessary for the United Provinces to establish neu-
> trality with the other provinces of Flanders . . . having
> remained idle spectators of the affair of Dunkirk to
> their extreme disgust and loss.[58]

(f) It was 'of great importance in point of safety to our
trade which was in all times disturbed and greatly
prejudiced by the Dunkirkers and Ostenders, in whose
hands soever they were'.[59] Cromwell showed his concern over piracy by stressing the importance of this in
a letter to Louis XIV after the capture of the town.[60]

Opinion in France itself was mostly hostile and Giustinian
noted that 'the number of those who deplore the capture is
greater than those who rejoice'.[61] Lockhart wrote that most of
the Court and the Army were 'mad' to see what they called 'un
si bon morceau, or so delicate a bit' pass into their ally's hands.[62]
Opponents of the surrender sought to portray the Cardinal as
Cromwell's dupe, and in particular Cardinal de Retz returned
to the fray with his *Most Humble and Important Remonstrances to
the King concerning the Surrender of the Maritime Towns of Flanders
into the hands of the English.* He accused Mazarin of giving to
Cromwell what he would never have dared demand despite his
military power, and called him 'a monster that Nature never
before produced'.[63] De Retz claimed that an Anglo-Spanish
alliance was not to be feared. Richelieu had used Protestant
allies and Mazarin claimed to be acting in his footsteps, but
Richelieu had never surrendered French territory to heretics.
Mazarin employed Lionne to write an explanation assuring
that France had had no option and claiming:

> it does not belong to us to control the secrets of Providence
> nor to examine too closely why it permits changes which

occur among our neighbours in religion or the state; we are not obliged because of them to break off the commerce and friendship which proximity requires us to maintain.[64]

Mazarin needed to secure the goodwill of England until the threat posed by the New Model Army evaporated in the convulsions of 1659 and Spain simultaneously offered better terms.

The terms offered to the Dunkirkers had been the minimum acceptable to France, but they were queried in London and Cromwell objected to the clergy being allowed to stay without molestation. Lockhart assured him that they had to behave well and that that proviso would give him some latitude: 'not many weeks will pass before they will give . . . [the governor] occasion to turn out a great many of them'.[65] In fact the clergy professed that they were satisfied, though Lockhart had some trouble with his zealous soldiers as

it was openly said that it was fit to pillage the place, and especially the church where there were much riches. Their insolence went to that height that one of them lit his pipe of tobacco at one of the wax lights of the altar where a priest was saying Mass, which occasioned my being sent for in haste.[66]

Lockhart's moderation helped to preserve peace in the town and to reassure Mazarin, who urged him to try to prevent the clerics leaving as the Spaniards wanted them to do so, in order to present them as victims of French-assisted persecution.[67] Some English fanatic pamphleteers urged Cromwell to confiscate all the churches and turn them over to Protestants,[68] but he listened to Lockhart's warnings that it would be unwise to do so. The ambassador, now acting as governor, did not trust either the clergy or the other citizens.[69] However, he believed that the English could only move cautiously with Protestantisation

as Rome was not built in a day, so it will not be pulled down . . . the town not being furnished with anything fit for defence, and two Catholic armies near, I leave it to Your Highness to judge whether it be a seasonable time to turn the inhabitants out of their Parish Church.[70]

Cromwell followed Lockhart's advice and Spanish hopes were disappointed.

One answer was to settle English in Dunkirk and Lockhart promised to aid any whom Thurloe would recommend.[71] He also proposed a subscription for Flemish Protestants to settle there. Ominously, the zealous divine Hugh Peter arrived to encourage the Protestantisation of the town and set up a church in the town hall; Lockhart accused him of meddling.[72] It is probable that the hard-pressed English government had believed since they first showed interest in 1652 that Dunkirk's revenues would be a useful addition to their coffers. They were soon to be disappointed.[73] The garrison was costly – Monck estimated in 1662 that it had cost £60 000 per annum under the Protectorate, while the accounts presented to Parliament in April 1659 showed that £77 366 had already been spent.[74] A total of £21 719/8/4d in revenue was collected in the first year of occupation, but there were two other problems which had not been thought about:

1. The customs officials spoke Dutch, increasing the chances of either muddle or cheating in the accounting.
2. The local countrymen, who were expected to pay taxes and help pay for the cost of the occupation, were too poor to do so or to supply food and fuel.[75]

The primary reason for the acquisition of Dunkirk was in any case strategic. The King had no need of it and it was sold to France in 1662, though its return was the occasion of popular criticism.

THE FLANDERS DILEMMA

The acquisition of Dunkirk was a strain on English resources, but this was only the beginning of a rapid Anglo-French advance in Flanders which was supposed to lead to English possession of Ostend and Nieupoort. The English government had decided to take advantage of French plans to secure as many of the coastal pirate bases as they could: indeed, the only alternative was to see the whole of the area in French hands. However, English financial resources were too meagre to be able to afford a permanent occupation.

In July 1658, an important report on the financial situation was presented to the Council. It asserted that the Parliamentary provision of £240 000 was falling short, in particular due to a deficiency of £200 000 in the Exchequer revenue. The Army was £300 000 in arrears and the Navy £540 000; the militia were owed six months' salary; the Navy needed to find £286 105 to pay men now at sea and £776 531 for next year's pay.[76] Meanwhile Thurloe informed Henry Cromwell: 'We are at that pains for money that we are forced to go a-begging to particular aldermen of London for five or six thousand pounds for Dunkirk. I fear we shall be denied.'[77] In this situation, every advance in Flanders would require more expenditure on the armed forces. The strain on men and resources would threaten a return to the financial crisis and threats of mutiny of winter 1657–8.

The likeliest outcome of the campaign seemed to be a complete French victory. Bergues fell on 29 June/9 July, Dixmunde on 9/19 July, and (following a delay while Louis XIV was ill) Gravelines on 27 August/6 September. On 16/26 July, Mazarin met Lockhart to discuss the capture and transfer of Ostend,[78] and Thurloe later noted in his account of affairs that 'propositions passed betwixt France and England' on the matter.[79] Nothing was said about financial difficulties, showing that Cromwell or – as his health was declining – Thurloe put holding France to its promises above such matters. However, the impending French conquest of Flanders raised another problem: was not French rule of Flanders as dangerous to English interests as that of a hostile Spain?

Cromwell's critics in the next generation, such as Slingsby Bethell and Ludlow, argued that he had paved the way for the French aggression of the late 1660s. The English, however, insisted on occupying invasion ports such as Ostend. Logically, fear of France should have meant a greater willingness to listen to Spanish peace offers in order to halt French conquests. Lockhart was haughtily dismissive of Caracena's envoy Mandossi at the beginning of July,[80] and those rumours which existed of an English consideration of peace were too vague to be of any use. Cromwell obviously trusted France no more than in earlier years but the lack of English plans for a reversal of policy is significant. It was the United Provinces which sought to limit French advances by proposing a Franco-Dutch 'condominium' of the area[81] – a sign of Dutch worries pointing ahead to the 1660s. As events turned out, France only occupied Artois.

11 Cromwell and the Dutch, 1653–4

In the months leading up to and following the outbreak of the Dutch War Cromwell did not bear the primary responsibility for policy. As Commander-in-Chief and an MP he had influence, but not the impact which observers attributed to men such as Sir Henry Vane, Thomas Chaloner, Herbert Morley and Henry Neville. This group was indeed the prime target of politically active members of the Army leadership in 1652–3, for denying military influence, and was the object of Cromwell's tirade on 20 April 1653. His differences with these men were chiefly on matters such as the 'Recruiter' elections to Parliament and its time of dissolution, and it can be seen that their concepts of 'national' interest were not so very different. Chaloner, the dedicatee of the Introduction to Gage's *English-American*,[1] cannot be accused of lack of Protestant zeal, though Cromwell's tone was more inflammatory than Vane's.

There could indeed be no greater example of the stressing of English national rights and mercantile power than the Navigation Act, passed by Parliament on 9/19 October 1651, to prohibit the entry into English territories of goods from America, Africa or Asia, except in vessels owned by citizens of England or its colonies or with crews less than one-half English, or goods from Europe in ships not owned by the nationals of their country of origin. This Act was aimed specifically at stimulating the mercantile marine by undermining the Dutch carrying trade, and is a statement of the primacy of the English 'national interest' over a need to conciliate potential allies comparable with any of Cromwell's nationalistic effusions. The prime movers in this were traditionally Chaloner, whose connection with Gage shows his aggressive nationalism, and Cromwell's cousin St John.

A study of the evolution of English policy towards the Dutch from 1649 to 1653 tends to play down the practical differences between the approach which Cromwell took when he was in charge of policy and that of his predecessors. For one thing, the idea of a close alliance or federation was mentioned by the

Commonwealth's ambassadors to The Hague before the outbreak of war, and did not originate with Vermuyden or other
men who only came to prominence after the fall of the Rump.
The origin of the idea may well have been the close alliance
(for military reasons) of the 1580s, when English generals joined
the Provinces' ruling council to help run campaigns. The
Commonwealth's Council of State evidently had such ideas in
mind when it directed St John and Sir Walter Strickland to
journey to the United Provinces to arrange an alliance in
February 1651. According to their account of the proceedings,
'matters tending to a nearer union' were to have been raised
in their talks with the States-General's representatives in Amsterdam if the opportunity had arisen, 'which the Parliament
had thereupon commanded us to do', and their 'private instructions' from the Council of State on 3/13 May mentioned
'a more strict union than formerly'. These instructions apparently offered to waive a national English prohibition against
aliens holding property in favour of the Dutch, an indication
of mutual rights for each ally's nationals in the other's country
which was revived in 1653.[2]

Again, during talks in March–July 1651 the English appear
to have proceeded on the basis of a closer 'union' than the
Dutch were willing to consider. An alliance was important to
prevent Dutch shipping aiding Charles II's intended invasion
from Scotland, yet the Commonwealth's representatives were
as obstinate over a non-crucial point as Cromwell was to be in
1653–4 over 'Seclusion'. It must be said, however, that a closer
'union' would have a practical import in neutralising the community of Royalist exiles in the United Provinces and their
local Orangist sympathisers, since the inevitable demand that
neither side harbour the other's rebels would lead to some
expulsions. The Dutch preferred to concentrate on an end to
commercial hostility and equal rights for each ally's merchants
in their ally's country, which would be chiefly to their advantage given their larger mercantile marine. Even so, when the
Dutch accepted on 22 April/2 May that each party should
help its ally against the latter's rebels (based on the 1495
alliance between Henry VII and the Archduke Philip, the
Intercursus Magnus), Strickland and St John ignored it. Instead,
they held out for the English right to claim for Dutch-based
Royalist depredations against the property of the infant William

of Orange and his English mother Princess Mary. They pressed their allies as hard as Cromwell was to do with de Witt in 1653–4. National security, as reflected by a public repudiation of the Stuarts' allies, was the crucial factor in both cases; the continuity was illustrated by Strickland's presence on Cromwell's Council. In these circumstances, the Dutch offers to accept equal trading rights in North America and the West Indies and freedom to fish in their waters were ignored, and the English took their leave on 18/28 June.[3]

The murder of the Commonwealth's ambassador Isaac Dorislaus in The Hague by Royalists in May 1649 can be cited as one reason for the ambassadors' suspicion and inflexibility – Strickland had been in the country at the time. Despite the alarm caused by Charles II's invasion, the Commonwealth showed no greater concern for an agreement when Dutch envoys arrived in London in December 1651. They were informed that there was no chance of a revocation of the Navigation Act, their principal grievance, and the English insisted on their right to search Dutch ships for French goods and confiscate any which were found.[4] Early in 1652 the English stated their formal terms: that the Navigation Act be accepted, Dutch participation in the North Sea fisheries restricted, and heavy compensation be paid for English losses in the East Indies. Cromwell insisted on the latter in 1653–4.[5] These were unacceptable, and in May 1652 the escalating naval clashes and English insistence that the Dutch lowered their flags led inevitably to dangerous incidents. Captain Young's encounter with a Dutch convoy off Start Point and a skirmish between Blake and Admiral Tromp off Fairlight a few days later were the first shots of war.[6] Cromwell's captains were to be every bit as aggressive in 1656.

Cromwell's personal disappointment at the conflict is apparent. He assured Adrian van der Pauw, the Pensionary of Holland who was sent as a special envoy to England in June, that the commission which they sat on to investigate the Fairlight incident would not blame Tromp exclusively.[7] He was also among the group who backed the unofficial mission of Balthazar Gerbier – a Dutchman resident in London who had served Buckingham as a designer and diplomatist in the 1620s – to The Hague in August to discuss peace.[8] The radical preacher Hugh Peter sent a private note to the leading Dutch statesman and future ambassador to England, Nieupoort, claiming that Gerbier's backers were Cromwell, Vane, Bulstrode Whitelocke and the MP Denis Bond.[9] Cromwell also backed a petition against the war drawn up at the end of July by the Dutch congregation at the Austin Friars in London at Peter's instigation, telling them 'I do not like the war and I commend your Christian admonition. I will do everything in my power to bring about peace.'[10] However, he did not go as far as Peter who continued his unofficial contacts with the Dutch, encouraged Admiral Sir George Ayescue not to fight them, and was formally reprimanded.[11] The most that can be said is that he was disturbed at the conflict and was glad when peace negotiations commenced It is possible that the way in which men like Chaloner, Vane and Haselrig put commerce above a Protestant alliance increased his disenchantment with them.

Cromwell's first actions towards the Dutch when he took power showed no great change of policy, though he had to take into account the beliefs of political allies in an uncertain domestic situation. On 6/16 May 1653, the new Council of State (chosen by the Army rather than its Commander-in-Chief) rejected the new Grand Pensionary John de Witt's offer of talks in a neutral town, while assuring that those terms of alliance which the Dutch had found offensive in 1651 were not essential for peace.[12] The resultant English naval victory at The Gabbard on 2/12 June led the Dutch to send four envoys – Beverning, van der Perre, Nieupoort and Jongestal – to London to sound out the chances of peace. They did not represent a united front any more than the uneasy coalition of Cromwell's allies in London, Jongestal (representing Friesland) being an avowed Orangist and van der Perre's Zealand also being uncertain in its allegiance. The English did not appreciate the problems which the sympathetic de Witt faced in getting an agreement accepted at home, now or in 1654.

In London, Cromwell faced his own problems with zealots who believed that the Dutch should be forcibly coopted into Protestant aggression against the Papists. Peter informed his hearers at an official sermon in Whitehall that the two nations should unite to drive the Pope from his throne and had to be warned not to have unofficial contacts with the ambassadors.[13] Christopher Feake, one of the popular City preachers, took the 'crusading' view that the war was God's cause and the first step in the conquest of the enemies of the 'godly' cause, having declared in a typical sermon in September 1652:

> Thou gav'st a Cup into the hand of England, and we drank of it. Then thou carried'st it to Scotland and Ireland, and they drank of it. Now thou carried it to Holland, and they are drinking of it. Lord, carry it also to France, to Spain, to Rome, and never let it be out of some or other of their hands.[14]

Feake also declared the sinfulness of a peace which did not coopt the Dutch into the Protestant 'grand design' on the Continent, a campaign of messianic aggression which his Catholic opponents were to suspect Cromwell of as late as 1658.[15]

The Council of State, a body representing disparate supporters of the new regime, appointed a committee of four to negotiate – the former ambassador Sir Walter Strickland, Sir Gilbert Pickering, General Thomas Harrison and Colonel William Sydenham.[16] Only Harrison was not a close ally of Cromwell. Cromwell's brother-in-law Desborough was added on 29 June/9 July, as were others after the Council's enlargement – Pickering's brother-in-law Edward Montague, former Royalist and Rump MP Anthony Ashley Cooper, and Colonels Hollister and Worsley. Cromwell presided as Commander-in-Chief.[17]

The committee met the Dutch envoys first on 29 June/9 July, and subsequently on the 13/23, 15/25 and 21/31 July, and on 25 July/4 August.[18] The affairs of the Nominated Parliament naturally took precedence. Interestingly, we can see a divergence between Cromwell and some other members, probably traceable to the presence of Harrison who was sympathetic to the demands of radical preachers for harsh terms and a full admission of Dutch guilt. When the Council sent the envoys a demand for Tromp's dismissal and admission of his responsibility for a clash off Folkestone before talks began, Cromwell sent Nieupoort a private message dissociating himself and suggesting Tromp's temporary removal as a goodwill gesture. He suggested that the Dutch admit two or three Englishmen to their ruling body and vice versa, as a sign of willingness to proceed on a federal plan.[19] An Englishman (Leicester) had sat on the Dutch ruling council in 1585–8 as military commander, so the idea was not new if circumstances were now different. Nieupoort objected to Fleming that the English negotiators' demands on federation implied that 'they would use us as they do the Scots' in the Union of 1652. Cromwell, moreover, asked the committee to leave his name out of their report to the Council which advised taking this firm line. Clearly, he was in no position to enforce his views on the others, something which could earn him the disapproval of supporters taking the line of Feake and Harrison.

The Dutch proposed a closer form of alliance without going into details (22 July/1 August) and Nieupoort and Jongestal returned to The Hague for further instructions. In these circumstances, the talks were helped by the defeat and death of Tromp in his attempt to break the English blockade (Battle of the Texel) on 31 July/10 August; the Dutch had no option but to stay. In the meantime, Cromwell showed his own ideas in an encounter (accidental or not) with Beverning and van der Perre in St James's Park. Insisting that he spoke 'but as a private man and had not any order thereunto', he assured them that there was no intention to interfere with national sovereignty or privileges and the committee wanted a board of members of both countries to meet to discuss a mutual offensive and defensive alliance without endangering sovereignty. He 'preferred not to answer distinctly' on the mechanics of mutual defence of commerce and on admitting allies to the union. He also tried to insist that the Treaty of Munster (1648) allowed the Dutch to break engagements with other states which might be affected by the union on grounds of national interest. He offered a precedent for the type of federation desired – the Amphictyonic League in ancient Greece,[20] where a board of representatives decided foreign policy on the basis of majority voting without infringing sovereignty. The sources of these points was probably Strickland or Secretary Thurloe. Current interest in ancient precedents for the English Commonwealth was restricted to a group of classical republicans, namely James Harrington and Algernon Sidney, with whom Cromwell had few connections or sympathy.[21]

THE VERMUYDEN PLAN

The most detailed plan for the union was delivered to van der Perre on 23 September/3 October by Sir Cornelius Vermuyden, a long-term Dutch resident in England who was chiefly known for his work in draining the Fens (in which enterprise he would have known Cromwell). He was an engineer rather than a politician, but now sought to unite the two leading Protestant powers and divide trade and colonies in the rest of the world between them – a Protestant version of the papal division of the world into Catholic spheres of influence at Tordesillas in 1494. He had served as an officer in the New Model Army and evidently his plan was in line with the 'radical' wing of government thinking and looked back to the earlier anti-Spanish alliance. Cromwell was sympathetic, though it is unclear if he, Harrison or other figures had authorised Vermuyden to draw up his plans. He instructed van der Perre's son to hold secret talks on this with Dutch ministers in The Hague.

The plan itself proposed:

1. 'That both states do agree a perpetual amity and that they take up arms defensive and offensive jointly against the enemies of both states or one of them; the state of England to bear the two-thirds part and the United Provinces the one-third part thereof.'
2. To maintain an army and
3. A navy for a defensive war, England to bear two-thirds of the naval cost.
4. Alliance with Denmark and Sweden and with those rulers in Germany who did not maintain the Inquisition. France was to be included as long as it did not affect the union and French Protestants were granted liberty of conscience.
5. Englishmen were to have the freedom of the United Provinces like Dutch nationals and to be able to stand for office there (and vice versa).
6. Free commerce for each country's nationals on the other's soil. Equal fishing rights similarly.
7. Free trade and commerce for the nationals of both states in all Europe and Africa, excepting the present Dutch posts in the latter.

8. All trade in Asia, excepting the 'areas bounding the Middle Sea' (the Ottoman Empire and their vassals, the preserve of the Levant Company) was to be restricted to the Dutch, in return for which the English East India Company was to receive an agreed sum. The English would thereby accept the Dutch control of the East Indies which had been asserted, often with force, for the past half-century but close down the East India Company. There is no record of Cromwell or his allies vetoing it on the grounds of this proposal. This is an indication that in the heady atmosphere of 1653 the City was expendable.

9. In return for abandoning the East India Company, England was to have exclusive rights to all the Americas except the Dutch possessions (disputed with Portugal) in Brazil and access to the Venezuelan salt-pans. The Dutch would provide a third of the navy which was to expel the Spaniards (and presumably the Portuguese and French as well). This was the 'pay-off' for abandoning Asia and would enable the English to gain the wealthy Spanish gold-mines. It was only the germ of a plan to divide the world's resources between the leading Protestant powers, but is no less important for that. Despite the unlikelihood of implementation, there were grounds for the fears expressed in France and Spain.[22]

10. The two nations would share the Venezuelan salt-pans, and the English would help expel the Portuguese from Brazil. This would end the current chance of an Anglo-Portuguese rapprochement after John VI had harboured Prince Rupert's ships.

11. Each nation was to provide commissioners for a common Board which was 'to take copies and have knowledge of' all acts of state, resolutions, orders, etc. made by either state. No mention was made of any further powers or of making legislation mutually binding; specific proposals were left to future discussion. This was the joint committee which Cromwell had referred to, and was treated with realistic caution.

12. 'All acts of enmity, whatsoever and wherever dont . . . damages and hostilities on both sides' to be cancelled

out in favour of 'a perpetual bond of amity, love and alliance'.

13. A radical Protestant proposal: to send out missionaries to all peoples 'to inform and enlarge the ways of Jesus Christ'.

Like the Parliamentary leaders in England in the 1620s, Vermuyden assessed the practical usefulness of such a campaign to the power-balance in Europe: 'having lost all America, his sword is as it were taken out of his hand'. He confidently maintained that South America could be overrun in one year 'if secretly' and Brazil in a second 'with no more ships but that England and the United Provinces might easily furnish them, and yet not so many as both now have in use the one against the other'. This would provide 'such a revenue as to discharge all the taxes of the subjects of England' – the lure of decreasing internal opposition to high taxation which was a powerful factor in favour of the Western Design the following year. The whole plan looked forward to the moral and practical usefulness of an imperial Protestant design that was argued in favour of Gage's plan against Spanish America in 1653, with the same overoptimism. Mutual suspicions argued against it being adopted, not least due to the offence to vested interests in the proposals on America and Asia.

THE APPROACH TO SETTLEMENT, WINTER 1653–4

As might have been expected, the Dutch ambassadors preferred to suggest that initial talks dealt with 'just restoration of commerce'. The plan was politely sidelined; it had no chance of passing the Amsterdam merchants even with Cromwell's backing. It is significant regarding Spain's fears of a rapprochement aimed against it that Cardenas was instructed to try to prolong the war.[23]

The States-General resolved on 11/21 October to send Nieupoort and Jongestal back to England for formal talks and accepted an English proposal to exchange prisoners.[24] There was still considerable suspicion in Holland that even the federation scheme was 'only a trick to gain time and strengthen the fleet . . . and to perfect their alliance with Spain and Sweden'.[25] The burgomasters of Amsterdam and the enthusiastic Protestant millenarians in London had little community of ideas. They preferred to tie their opponents down to a 'strict amity and defensive league' first.[26]

After the two ambassadors' return to London, negotiations resumed on 31 October/10 November with the Dutch asking for formal agreement on a commercial peace treaty first and the English asking to see the Dutch proposals on 'religion, union, and confederacy'. Cromwell was notably absent from this meeting, allegedly on the grounds of illness but possibly partly due to awareness of his colleagues' impracticality.[27] He presided as chairman of the English delegation at the conferences on the 17/27 and the 18/28 November, accompanied by five trusted advisers who were soon to be chosen for his own Council (Strickland, Colonels Jones and Sydenham, Lord Lisle, and Cooper), Thurloe and his deputy Jessop, his friend Alderman Robert Tichborne, and only one 'radical' who was to lose all influence after the closure of the Nominated Parliament (Colonel Worsley). He may have been seeking to take a more moderate line on federation by his choice of advisers, and similarly his words showed no explicit demands for a joint governing board. He concentrated on the practical measure of avoiding future disputes between the allies. He called for

a coalition . . . in which all mutual interests of state and the nations would be combined without any distraction in such a way that no differences or misunderstandings could be feared or expected . . . a union, league, and confederation as strong as ever had ben established between two sovereign states'.[28]

Cromwell returned to this theme the following day, 18/28 November, when the Dutch presented their formal reply with a warning about the retention of full sovereignty. He insisted that his aim was 'to find the means of a union that would give security and be permanent and not exist only in appearance and words'. This implied some sort of mechanism for a close alliance without stating it too specifically in case of resistance. Later in the discussion Cromwell became overtly enthusiastic about a Protestant federation again. Risking the alarm of his guests, he expressed the Council of State's hope to achieve a situation where 'the whole sovereignty and government with everything that depended on it would be made common between the two Republics and two nations with the sole exception of the administration of justice according to the municipal laws'. He also expressed his idealism and lack of diplomatic subtlety in an irritable outburst about the Dutch faintheartedness: '[their plans were] a mutilated coalition which appeared to spring from insufficient instructions to conclude anything, and such a proposition could [i.e. should] not be expected from us as we were gentlemen of honour and well-mannered'. He claimed boldly that 'these special words of sovereignty were not so very important'. They were 'only a feather in the hat and that the burden of government was but a bubble'.[29] This rash statement shows the mixture of pragmatism and overoptimistic idealism in Cromwell's approach to foreign policy which was to lead him into trouble on other issues, most notably the Western Design. His lack of understanding of the Dutch point of view was as important as the need to conciliate 'radical' opinion.

The suspicions in the United Provinces which helped to form the ambassadors' unflinching attitude were summed up by Aitzema on 28 October/7 November:

> This state fears not Spain, France, nor the Emperor all joined against them, so England and they have peace. They hope to persuade you in the treaty out of the act of trade [the Navigation Act]; but if you do yield to revoke it, these people will undoubtably engross all the trade of Christendom, and thereby quietly become masters of the sea, and then the English may expect the dregs of their malice . . . They say publicly that the English cozened them at the beginning of this war by surprise; but if now in their necessities they could have a peace, they believe they shall be beforehand in the next war.[30]

The changes in government in England that December acted to consolidate Cromwell's own position. The results for the Dutch talks were threefold:

1. Removal of the most notable adherents of impractical schemes such as federation.

2. Additional internal dissent in the form of the narrowing of support for the new Protector. Another naval campaign against the Dutch would necessitate unpopular taxes.
3. The potential Royalist threat from an Orangist revival in the United Provinces was played up in 1654 (unlike the earlier talks), especially with regard to the 'Exclusion' from office of William of Orange. This demand may have been exacerbated by Cromwell's suspicion of the intentions of the Dutch leadership as manifested by their willingness to side-track the federal scheme.

Cromwell habitually insisted on the full acceptance of his demands by negotiating partners, as has been apparent from the discussion of his policies towards France and Spain. However, the 'Exclusion' demand which featured in the Dutch negotiations added a further hazard to the chances of success, and showed insufficient awareness of the fact that John de Witt's position depended on the exclusion of Orangist influence. De Witt had as much reason as Cromwell to keep William out of office – as the Prince was only 3 years old at the end of 1653, a nominal Stadtholdership of one or more of the Dutch provinces would leave power with the hostile Princess Mary or Orangist nobles. To make matters more complicated, the differing attitudes towards the House of Orange within the United Provinces were reflected by different attitudes among the ambassadors. Van der Perre and Jongestal had Orangist sympathies, reflecting those of their masters in the states of Friesland and Guelderland; the other two represented more commercially dominated provinces sympathetic to the recent struggle of the 'Regent' class of Amsterdam against William II. In public the ambassadors maintained a united front, but de Witt insisted that the relevant article in the treaty on 'Exclusion' be a private one to minimise resentment in the United Provinces.

Cromwell accepted that the article be kept secret,[31] but in return he wanted Frederick III of Denmark to be included in the treaty so that the Dutch could pressurise him to pay compensation for acts of piracy carried out by his subjects on English shipping during the war. The Dutch disagreed with the English over the question of which issues in dispute between England and Denmark were to be comprehended in the treaty, and refused to give way even when Cromwell sent a message offering a compromise (a sign that he could be flexible in a crisis). Beverning, one of the two anti-Orange ambassadors, accepted his offer but the others did not; the fact that Jongestal was the most vociferous suggests that Dutch internal politics were involved. The Dutch nation had a habit of turning to the House of Orange in a military crisis (for example, in the 1580s, the 1620s and 1672). The ambassadors returned home and it was reported that both sides were readying their fleets;[32] the Venetian ambassador in London, Paulucci, believed that the cost of a new campaign was 'inducing a passionate desire for peace in the Protector'.[33]

At the end of January 1654 Beverning, the most sympathetic of the ambassadors, was sent to London as de Witt's personal envoy to continue talks. His return alone made a bad impression in London, and according to Paulucci's informant Cromwell was known to 'resent this delay and could not refrain from saying that the Dutch make a bad return to the friendly and advantageous offers of England'.[34] De Witt assured political rivals that Beverning was only seeking a truce[35] and the ambassadors reassured suspicious delegates to the States-General that the English had moderated their demands for compensation.[36]

Beverning was voted full powers on 9/19 November to negotiate with the English on suh matters as Danish participation in the treaty, and the insulting English reference to the massacre of English merchants at Amboyna in the Spice Islands.[37] Nieupoort and Jongestal returned with formal powers from the States-General on 15/25 February, and were put up with honour at Sir Abraham Williams' house in Palace Yard which was reserved for the Commonwealth's most honoured foreign guests.[38] The six commissioners appointed to negotiate with them reflected Cromwell's personal choice – Strickland, the former ambassador and Dutch expert; 'Lord President' Lawrence, Cromwell's cousin, who had lived in the Provinces; Lord Lisle; Lambert; Sir Gilbert Pickering; and the inexperienced Edward Montague, Pickering's cousin.[39]

One dangerous incident in the Mediterranean at about this time showed the wisdom of reaching an accommodation. Dutch ships had been attacking English ones throughout the war without much hindrance, taking advantage of French hostility to the Commonwealth and lack of an English naval presence.

Cromwell's imminent despatch of Blake to 'show the flag' shows that he was aware of this problem from Christian and Moslem captains alike. A Dutch vessel, the *White Elephant,* seized and plundered an English ship in Leghorn harbour and the Dutch killed local officers sent to investigate by Grand Duke Ferdinand's officials. The Dutch ambassador, Van Der Straten, was arrested to satisfy the 'tremendous outcry' led by local English merchants, and when the news reached London in mid-April a naval expedition to the area was publicly canvassed.[40]

THE DUTCH TREATY

Under the final terms reached in April, a 'true, firm and inevitable peace, more sincere friendship, and nearer Alliance, Union and Confederacy than heretofore' was established (Article I). There were no controversial statements about federal boards of representatives; the Protector needed peace and most of the federal enthusiasts of 1653 had been excluded from his new Council. All acts of hostility were to be forgotten, but there was no mention of any machinery to prevent a recurrence (Article II). Mutual rights for Englishmen and Dutchmen in each other's countries went no further than normal for a close alliance. Each would have to pay the usual tolls for foreigners in passage through the other's territory (Article XII); unarmed traders and groups of up to forty persons could have free passage provided that they kept to the trading laws (Article XVII).

The treaty was said to have been agreed by the two peoples for the 'Defence and Preservation of the Liberties and Freedom' of each (Article V), but the only specific detail involved the practical issue of rebels. No rebels from one side were allowed to reside or hold office in the other's country (Articles VI, IX, XI); this referred to the Royalists (including Princess Mary) in the United Provinces. If a rebel from one country was discovered in the other's territory, he must leave within twenty-eight days of the host country being informed of his presence (Article X). Each power was to aid the other against an attack by the latter's rebels, which particularly implied Dutch help for Cromwell against any French or Spanish attack on behalf of Charles II (Article VII). On the matter of the emotive issue of Amboyna, a face-saving compromise was reached which could enable Cromwell to claim that justice would be done – justice was to be carried out on the perpetrators, 'as the English think fit to style them', assuming they could be caught which was unlikely (Article XXVII). A compromise was reached on the other contentious matter of dipping Dutch ships' flags; they were to do so 'in the former manner', which left latitude for interpretation (Article XIII).

Reason and established practice also determined the other main questions of commercial and other disputes. Damages and restitution were to be granted (chiefly to the English) for a specific list of seizures of ships and other goods during the war (Article XXVIII). A commission of four arbitrators from each side was to assess damages for incidents occurring between 1611 and 1652 (Article XXX); the Swiss were to investigate cases on which they failed to reach agreement. Those who committed future incidents should be dealt with by their own government; if matters had not been dealt with within a year of their occurrence in Europe, America, or Africa or eighteen months in Asia beyond the Cape of Good Hope, the victim's government had three months to achieve satisfaction through an official complaint and could then issue letters of marque (Articles XVI, XXIV). If hostile ships drove one ally's ships into a port owned by the other, they were not to be molested as long as they obeyed regulations (Article XVIII). Neither sailors nor merchants were to go ashore armed to lodging houses, minimising the risk of fights (Article XX). Each power should protect the other's ships if two groups were sailing in the same direction (Article XXI), and intervene should a third power's ships attack their ally's (Article XXII). Up to eight warships belonging to one ally could shelter in the other's ports without permission (Article XXVI); larger groups should seek permission (ditto).

Finally, all Commanders-in-Chief, Admirals, Stadtholders, Chief Governors and Captains-General of the United Provinces were required to swear adherence to the treaty (Article XXXI). These office-holders would be the likely source of a military threat to England should one develop, and were the posts usually held by adult males of the House of Orange at times of national crisis. Cromwell insisted on the 'Exclusion' of William of Orange being written into the treaty, albeit in a

'Secret Article' by which the Estates of Holland and West Friesland (the two most powerful provinces) were required to promise to exclude William from the Stadtholdership and Captain-Generalship.[41] The four arbitrators of commercial losses on each side were duly appointed – Edmund Winslow, James Russell, Jan Beex and William van den Guysen. They reached agreement one day within the deadline set by the treaty, on 31 July/10 August, estimating the English losses in the Sound at £97 973 10s.[42] The eight arbitrators on the pre–1652 losses, mainly in the East Indies, recommended that the English East India Company receive £85 000 for its ships and (agreeing with a preliminary English assessment in 1652) £3615 for Amboyna. Pula Run was to be returned to England.

THE CRISIS OVER THE 'EXCLUSION ARTICLE'

De Witt's regime was as eager for a settlement as Cromwell, but had to proceed carefully to avoid the charge of letting the English dictate their internal affairs over the 'Exclusion Article' – a crisis which Cromwell was prepared to risk. Aitzema reported that the peace was welcomed in the United Provinces.[43] However, the sympathetic Nieupoort and Beverning were the only people except for De Witt to know the full terms of the treaty; de Witt dared not tell Jongestal about the 'Secret Article' lest he leak it to the Orangists to stop ratification. Cromwell did not improve matters by insisting that the States-General pass an Act ratifying the Secret Article within three months or he would not accept the existing agreement, and Nieupoort and Beverning warned De Witt that 'upon this act depends peace or war'.[44] Cromwell could not afford war but he was willing to risk de Witt's possible downfall on his ability to manage the States-General, showing his lack of concern for the state of affairs, there.

The outcome of events was not, however, entirely to de Witt's disadvantage, because the exclusion of William of Orange acted to his own benefit by preventing him from being used as a figurehead by an Orangist revival. He could claim that Cromwell was blackmailing him into accepting the Article as an essential part of the peace treaty and tying it into the Dutch statute-book. Public relief at the end of hostilities could lead to fury should it prove that peace was impossible. At any event, would the majority of members of the States-General be willing to risk this outcome? Whether it was Cromwell alone who was responsible for the crisis, the States-General gave way despite an initial majority of five provinces to two raising objections to the Secret Article, 'being forced to its against their inclinations and out of mere necessity'.[45] Accordingly, they approved the treaty on 24 April/4 May, Cromwell having signed his copy while the outcome of the final vote was still awaited on the 19/29th.[46] Peace was proclaimed on 26 April/6 May.

The crisis continued as de Witt and his allies were accused of a 'sell-out' – something which Cromwell should have realised posed its own threat of a revival in sympathy for his enemies. Peace was not threatened immediately, but even in Holland efforts were made to prevent the signed Article reaching England and Beverning and Nieupoort, worried for their careers, delayed sending it for five weeks.[47] Friesland tried to have the ambassadors' account of their talks sent to them with a view to prosecution, encouraged by threats from Jongestal implicating de Witt.[48] The Province of Zealand tried to pass a vote in the States-General claiming that the treaty broke the articles of confederation of the United Provinces of 1579 by passing an agreement with a foreign power without the consent of the provincial Estates.[49] The Province of Groningen approved a resolution denouncing it as base ingratitude to the House of Orange.[50] The rhetorical indignation did not lead to any serious threat, but Cromwell foolishly became embroiled in it himself when the Estates of Zealand refused to ratify the Article. He needlessly sent them two threatening letters, reminding them of the international Catholic threat (which had nothing whatever to do with the case) and pledging to cancel the treaty if they did not give way.[51] Zealand was rumoured to be so antagonistic to the treaty that civil war was possible between them and Holland – a war in which Cromwell would aid Holland with his fleet.[52]

The representatives of Holland successfully defended the retention of the Dutch ambassadors in England against demands for their recall. They argued that only a resident ambassador could sort out future commercial and naval disputes 'on the spot'; that they could clarify points in the treaty; that they could press for an Anglo-French agreement; and that they could assist Anglo-Dutch talks on commercial losses. These arguments were conclusive, though Beverning was suspended from his post as Treasurer of the United Provinces pending a satisfactory explanation for the Secret Article.[53] However, it laid further grounds for an apprehensive relationship between the two countries. The uneasy peace between England and the Dutch in 1654–8 owed more to mutual unwillingness to renew an expensive and wearisome war than to any feeling of Protestant solidarity.

One side-effect of the Anglo-Dutch peace was the settlement of current English claims against Denmark, arising from the Danish support for the Dutch in 1652–4. Frederick III had seized English shipping in Denmark (and its dependency Norway) at the start of war, and now faced the prospect of English naval reprisals if a settlement was not reached. Both sides asked the Dutch to assist in a settlement, Cromwell himself being most unwilling to risk costly naval expenditure by resorting to a naval blockade, as he was to do against Portugal in 1656. In addition, the importance of free passage of the Sound for naval supplies from the Baltic (timber, tar, hemp, etc.) meant that any unnecessary dispute with Denmark had to be avoided as long as it controlled both sides of the channel. Accordingly, while Cromwell's envoy Bulstrode Whitelocke was putting the finishing touches to a defensive alliance with Sweden, Cromwell received Frederick's ambassador Henry Rosenvinge who was sent to congratulate him on his assumption of power (February 1654). Once his regime was recognised, as with other states, Cromwell could negotiate.

Provision was reached in papers conjoint to the Dutch treaty for the return of all English property confiscated in Denmark since 18/28 May 1652, together with the value of any property sold.[54] The English commissioners (John Edwards and Michael Evans) achieved the return of eighteen of the twenty-two ships involved and the money within the six days' time-limit which they set,[55] and the dispute over the other ships was referred to the Anglo-Dutch commercial claims court at Goldsmiths' Hall, London and then to The Hague.[56]

The main area of commercial conflict between the belligerents had long been the East Indies, the English having a long list of claims against their rivals. According to the treaty, eight commissioners from each country were detailed to investigate these and try to reach a settlement. The English, named on 11/21 May, were William Thompson, Thomas Kendall, William Turner and Admiralty Court judge Dr John Exton.[57] The settlement reached on 30 August/9 September was realistic: the English were to receive £85 000, in two instalments to be handed over by January and March 1655, with £3615 compensation for the victims of Amboyna and the return of Pula Run (not carried out).[58]

In this manner, the urgent necessity of peace with the Dutch was able to include some form of compensation for Dutch aggression in the East Indies during the past forty years – something which no English government had earlier achieved. Cromwell cannot claim sole credit for the achievement which would have been unlikely without the English naval victories of 1653 – a course of action which he had not desired. The outcome was the result of a long process of adjustment between two rival Protestant commercial powers in which dreams of idealistic federations had no rôle. The next few years were to show that even Cromwell could not hope for more than an uneasy 'stand-off' between the two countries.

12 The Uneasy Peace: England and the Dutch, 1654–8

Necessity impelled the maintenance of reasonable relations between the English and Dutch from April 1654. Both parties were financially exhausted and had other priorities – the English with the Franco-Spanish conflict and the Dutch with Charles X of Sweden's efforts to control the Baltic. Once Cromwell had committed his navy to offensives in the Mediterranean and Caribbean late in 1654 there was none to spare to take on the Dutch, even when the latter showed a lack of concern for the niceties of the treaty by supplying military stores to Spain in 1655–8. (To be first to de Witt, he could not control the actions of individual captains.) Cromwell dared not respond aggressively to Dutch blockade-running to Spanish ports lest this play into the hands of his enemies in The Hague, the Orangist faction and exiled Royalists being aided by the Spanish ambassador Stephen de Gamarra. Any renewed dispute could lead to Dutch shipping aiding Charles II, thus making up for the fact that his motley force in Flanders lacked the means to invade.

Cromwell had always maintained his desire for a closer union with the Dutch, as with other Protestant powers. To that extent the limited nature of the Dutch treaty was a 'defeat' for idealism, albeit one imposed by necessity given the Dutch suspicion of federal overtures. It is significant that he did not renew his encouragement of them on such matters thereafter. There were other priorities, though the eclipse of Harrison's radicals in December 1653 and disenchantment over Dutch resistance to 'Exclusion' in 1654 probably helped. The Dutch were omitted from any part in the English agreements with Sweden and Portugal, two states with which they were in dispute and where English help in reaching a settlement would have been very much to their benefit. The Dutch complained about the case of the Anglo-Swedish treaty, where Cromwell would probably not have achieved the good terms obtained for English trade in the Sound if he had insisted that the Dutch be included.[1] Similarly, the tone of his remarks on the peace settlement with the Dutch, in his opening speech to Parliament in September, emphasised the benefits to national security because England needed peace with as many foes as possible to secure peace and calm at home.[2] The tone was attuned to the merchants and country gentlemen who sat in Parliament rather than the enthusiastic officers who had dominated the Council of State in 1653.

One incident in the summer of 1654 showed that Cromwell was careful to avoid fuelling Dutch suspicion even when the rights of his own nationals were at stake. English merchants proposed to force their way up the River Scheldt to break the blockade of Antwerp which the Dutch had maintained since their wars with Spain. Any end to this blockade would threaten the prosperity of Amsterdam. Cromwell did not back up his traders, and when the Dutch appealed to him in July to restrain them they received a sympathetic hearing.[3] The traders' plans were sacrificed to diplomatic necessity. However, Cromwell remained as keen as ever to seek satisfaction for English nationals' demands when there were no complicating factors, as when he demanded justice from the States-General for the heirs of Nicholas Lower in a legal dispute in September.[4]

Dutch distrust had been apparent in the talks during the second half of 1653 and ordinary citizens showed no disposition to trust Cromwell more than any other English ruler. By May 1657 it was reported in The Hague, admittedly by an ever suspicious Aitzema, that 'they hate Cromwell like the plague'.[5] There was no more talk on the English side of goodwill gestures like Vermuyden's scheme to divide the world into commercial 'spheres of interest' and end disputes that way (no doubt to the relief of the East India Company). The East Indies remained one of the major areas of tension, the normal naval clashes in the region being compounded by the question concerning the form of trade to be agreed on there when the East India Company's Charter came up for renewal, Martin Noell and Maurice Thompson favouring a wider subscription.[6] Victory by the 'traditionalist' supporters of a restrictive monopoly was not a foregone conclusion, although here, as with other instances of potential reform such as Chancery, caution eventually prevailed. Freedom of trade for a wider range of subscribers would stimulate investment and shipbuilding, thus endangering the Dutch East India Company's position. On 5/ 15 January 1655, Aitzema assessed the panic which rumours of Noell and Thompson's success in the current debate over the new Charter was causing:

> The merchants of Amsterdam, though the lord Nieupoort writes nothing of it, have advice that the Lord Protector will dissolve the East India Company at London and declare the navigation and commerce to the Indies to be free and open. This doth cause great jealousy at Amsterdam, as a thing that will very much prejudice the East India Company in Holland.[7]

It was also currently rumoured that Cromwell favoured establishing a 'national interest' in India, possibly involving the exchange of an English colony elsewhere for Portuguese Goa in the 1654 treaty.[8]

Luckily for the Dutch, no substance came of these ideas and the East India Company Charter was not altered to any significant degree when it was renewed in 1657.[9] These missed chances indicate conservatism and unwillingness to take risks rather than a desire to avoid offending the Dutch, but the effect was to avoid possible areas of tension in the East. This lack of action, and similarly with any measures to stimulate the building of a merchant navy, illustrated Cromwell's lack of concern for the practical ways of improving national mercantile power. As a result, a serious clash between the two powers was put off for a decade.

Cromwell remained unflinching on matters concerning his nationals' rights. As he was to inform Hamburg over the Hays case in 1656, he considered it 'a chief part of our duty' not to let his subjects appeal in vain for his help.[10] This was particularly evident when his 'Instructions' for the commanders of the Caribbean expedition ordered them to seize, burn, sink and destroy all ships trading with Spanish colonies and to enforce the Navigation Act in taking all ships from European states which traded with English colonies.[11] This ignored the Dutch right under the 1654 treaty to trade with Spain and its colonies, with which England was at peace, besides making it clear that strict legality came before the English colonists' need to obtain goods from all possible national and foreign shipping. Accordingly, Dutch ships which were trading at Barbados were seized by Admiral Penn, and when the news reached Amsterdam Nieupoort was told to protest vigorously.[12] Meanwhile, the English regime was also suspicious of the remaining Orangist influence in the United Provinces, and in March 1655 de Witt had to deny reports that Charles II had entered the country in disguise.[13] A representative of the States-General was said to have met Charles in Cologne,[14] but luckily most English suspicion of foreign support for the Penruddock Revolt was concentrated on France as a result of seizures of their shipping.

The outbreak of the Spanish War caught Cromwell by surprise. Spain's breach of relations was followed by his retaliation with a declaration of war. Financial weakness inhibited both belligerents in Europe, and the most serious threat there was the opening of Flemish ports to Royalist privateers. There was now the threat of Dutch captains with grudges unofficially joinig them.[15] Privateering could serve as a 'safety-valve' for anti-English feeling in the United Provinces, but added to Cromwell's suspicion. However, the financial strain of war with Spain and the need to concentrate the Navy in Spanish waters meant that Cromwell could not afford to take on the Dutch as well, and the need for easy access to the Baltic for naval supplies made it unwise to have outright war with the other naval power in the North Sea.

At this juncture, Charles X's ambitions in Poland in 1655–6 led to a Swedish dispute with the Dutch over the latter's rights at Danzig. The Dutch feared both an Anglo-Swedish naval alliance to exclude them from the Baltic[16] and an Anglo-French alliance against Spain which would divide the Spanish Netherlands and give the Protector the port of Dunkirk.[17] Cromwell personally assured Nieupoort that Sweden dominating the Baltic would be dangerous to all other powers interested in the area, including England, and urged him to encourage his masters in favour of a general alliance of all northern Protestant powers.[18] That prospect would end the danger of an unwelcome dispute in the Baltic when England was heavily engaged elsewhere. Cromwell accordingly made initial soundings among his advisers about a mission to the Protestant powers early in 1656.[19] As with the Anglo-Dutch plans of 1653, practical mistrust between the interested parties made the idea a non-starter.

The Anglo-Spanish War increased the risk of internal pressure forcing de Witt to countenance closer relations with the United Provinces' historic oppressor. This is in itself was testimony to the importance of commercial factors among the Dutch mercantile community: Spain was a good customer and no naval or mercantile competitor. Aitzema reported in November 1655 that Holland had proposed in the States-General that an envoy be sent to Spain.[20] The arrival of this Dutch envoy was reported by Quirini, Venetian ambassador in Madrid, in January 1656[21] and was known in Paris whence Augier could inform Thurloe.[22] Cromwell was furious at this evidence of Dutch duplicity[23] and was encouraged in it by the Swedish ambassador Bonde.[24]

Delays in receiving Nieupoort early in 1656 were due to pressure of business and the illnesses of Cromwell and others rather than ill-will, but the ambassador still complained. However, all talk of a closer alliance was at an end. The outbreak of a naval war with Spain meant strict English naval checks on foreign shipping heading for Spanish ports, raising the risks either of a clash over a Dutch captain objecting to being searched or a refusal to salute the English flag. In these circumstances, a 'maritime treaty' to sort out commercial disputes at sea achieved new urgency. In the meantime, Cromwell delivered a veiled warning to Nieupoort in February.[25] The danger increased, however, as Spain sent a new ambassador to The Hague – Don Stephen de Gamarra – to explore the possibility of an alliance. The Zealanders were especially receptive to his intrigues to undermine the English alliance.[26]

AVOIDING THE BRINK: VEILED HOSTILITY AND SOURCES OF CONFLICT, 1656–7

It was initially intended that the treaty of 1654 be followed by a maritime treaty. Nevertheless, the Council had other priorities in 1654–6, though enough conflicts arose to make the importance of such a move obvious. Nieupoort, now the resident Dutch ambassador, was protesting about English captains' seizures on a regular basis from the autumn of 1654, providing the Council with more work. The most notable instances of those in autumn 1654 were the *Eendracht* (1/11 September) and the *Beehive* (November).[27] A Dutch ship visiting Penryn in Cornwall was robbed.[28] In March 1655 there were more incidents, commencing with the pillaging by Captain Cotterel of a becalmed ship from Edam at Studland Bay in Dorset.[29] English captains seized the *Three Kings* and *St John* which the Admiralty Court allowed to be sold in May.[30]

Each of Nieupoort's protests was dealt with in the same way, being handed over by the Council to a small committee which consulted the Admiralty where necessary and reported back. Thus on 31 March/10 April Fiennes and Strickland reported back on the *Peter* and the *Pigeon*, and the parties in the case of the *Three Kings* were summoned before the Council.[31] On 16/26 May, Desborough, Strickland and Jones made a further report on these ships and the *Oaken Tree*.[32] In due course, Nieupoort protested at Penn's seizures in the West Indies, as on 8/18 August 1655 over the *Charity*.[33] On 18/28 January 1656, Captain Butler, a former Commissioner on the Western Design, reported on the case of the *Seahorse*, a Dutch ship seized at Montserrat, and other seizures in America.[34] Butler also sent a letter to Jessop defending the seizures as covered by the 'Instructions'.[35] Dutch testimonials on the *Seahorse* were referred to Fiennes, Lord Mulgrave, Lisle, Jones and Wolseley, on 2/12 November, and the ship's return was duly ordered.[36]

Interestingly, one of the Dutch complaints referred to the capture of the *Daniel*, in July 1655, for shipping Spanish soldiers to Flanders. Cromwell had not declared war on Spain at that point, so this trans-shipment was technically legal – as Nieupoort pointed out.[37] The English action can be explained by Cromwell's orders to Blake to take shipping in European waters to extend the naval war 'Beyond the Line' closer to home,[38] but was none the less both illegal and contemptuous of his allies who had not been informed. Nieupoort's complaint was referred to Jones and Strickland who reported – in favour of keeping the ship – nine months later.[39] Other complaints included that of 6/16 September over the *Frog* of Zealand, brought into Poole by a privateer, on 5/15 October at the robbing of the *Postillion* of Amsterdam en route from Marseilles, and over the detention of twelve ships in London in November.[40] Decisions usually went against Nieupoort, the exceptions being usually cases of a crop of seizures such as those he listed on 4/14 July 1655.[41]

According to the plan arranged at the time of the treaty, in March 1655 Thurloe submitted a paper to be passed on to the commercial arbitrators concerning mercantile problems that needed to be solved. The Council approved it on 19/29 March[42] and the remaining English 'letters of marque' were suspended in July. The crises in domestic and Anglo-Spanish politics delayed further action until March 1656, when Nieupoort reported to the Council on those trade regulations which his masters wanted to include in any agreement. A negotiating committee was set up – Strickland (the most experienced negotiator), Lisle, Fiennes, Fleetwood (a Baptist, zealous for Protestant unity), Wolseley, Sydenham, Colonel Jones (a hard-headed land-dealer) and Lord Mulgrave.[43] As a goodwill gesture, the Government declared the naturalisation of all Dutch Protestants resident in England – a first step to that 'dual nationality' idea envisaged in the Vermuyden Plan.[44] The talks now got under way and Wolseley reported on Nieupoort's opinion of the initial English proposals on 4/14 April.[45] The Dutch had evidently requested favourable treatment on the matter of what was to be considered contraband and thus prohibited from export to a country with which the English were at war (i.e. Spain). In reply, the Council decided that they could not be offered better terms than those currently being hammered out by Fiennes, Whitelocke and others with the Swedes.[46]

Cromwell remained well disposed towards alliance, without making any serious practical suggestions. As with the construction of the new constitution at the end of 1653, he left details to others. Nieupoort complained of his generalising attitude at audiences: 'I cannot interrupt him when he talks, and he would be very annoyed if I asked him every time interpretations to the point of his general remarks, as I found that he just does not answer questions which he does not wish to.'[47] The mutual suspicions of the two countries were not helped by the inevitable evidence of Dutch captains' 'collusion' with the Spanish and their privateer allies. The most serious instance of this was on 10/20 May 1656 when a Dutch captain called Saloman, escorting an English mercantile convoy in the Channel, allowed its capture by Dunkirk privateers. The Dutch

Admiralty instructed Nieupoort to deny all rumours of collusion[48] and he sought audience to inform the Protector. In retaliation, English searches of Dutch ships in the Downs for 'war materials' (an imprecisely defined commodity) being exported to Spain were stepped up in June and July.[49] The Dutch authorities had told de Ruyter, commanding their fleet in Spanish and Portuguese waters, to avoid Spanish ports but to protect any Dutch ships he found being searched by the English, but he practised restraint. The state of Spanish shipping, however, meant that ports such as Cadiz, under English blockade, relied for most of their imports on Dutch shipping which arrived in such numbers that the Protector's admirals dared not intervene.[50] Quite apart from causing bad feeling, this put the whole blockade at risk and raised the question of what might happen if Dutch warships assisted the Spanish Plate Fleet. If Cromwell could not gain funds from seizure of Spanish treasure, how could he fund the 1657 campaign with Parliament in abeyance and the country restive?

A serious Anglo-Dutch naval clash was avoided, though Blake took some Dutch ships heading for Flanders[51] and in August Dutch ships rescued some of their colleagues when a convoy, including Ostender ships laden with Spanish goods, was stopped by English ships for refusing to lower their flags and escorted into Torbay. The Council protested to Nieupoort at this 'very extraordinary and unusual carriage',[52] and he used it as evidence to urge a quick settlement on 'just and good rules' for both sides to follow in future.[53]

Anxiety continued about a possible Anglo-Dutch rupture throughout the summer, French Ambassador Bordeaux having thought the situation serious enough to offer to mediate even before the Saloman incident.[54] The States-General were alarmed at the content of the current Anglo-Swedish talks, though Cromwell assured Nieupoort that 'he had refused to listen to offers from Sweden . . . if he could not enjoy those advantages together with the Republic'.[55] As he told Bonde, his need for free passage to the Baltic to acquire naval supplies necessitated an even-handed approach between the Dutch and Sweden.[56] The Dutch despatch of a naval squadron to Danzig alarmed the Protector, and led Aitzema to declare: 'Their design is to have all the trade in the East Sea, with the co-operation of Denmark, and this chiefly to the prejudice of Cromwell.'[57]

Similar advice to beware of the Dutch came from the Common-wealth's consul in Leghorn, Longland, who reported Spanish overtures to the States of Holland and a recent Dutch attack on the English at Smyrna, the Levant Company's entrepôt for Anatolia.[58]

In August 1656, Cromwell was concerned enough to send an unofficial ambassador to The Hague, Louis Rosin, with a letter urging the States-General to show caution towards Gamarra's offers of a Spanish alliance. The tone of the letter, probably drafted by John Milton, showed Cromwell's personal concerns rather than making a practical effort to overcome Dutch worries at Charles X's power in the Baltic or English hostility. The recipients were inopportunely reminded that the Dutch and Swedes were the most 'magnanimous and coura-geous defenders of the Protestant faith', and were encouraged to resent the insolence of 'your old enemy and once your domineering tyrant' for seeking alliance against 'your most ancient and faithful friends, England, France, and Sweden'. It showed a fundamental misconception of his audience.[59]

Considering the seriousness of current tension, the Council proceeded on 28 August/7 September to empower its 'mari-time treaty' commissioners to proceed with talks albeit 'in a general way, saving such matters as they shall think fit for the advancement of the Commonwealth and preventing of supplies to enemies in friendly ships'.[60] Courtin, the French ambassador in The Hague, was reliably informed that Cromwell (presum-ably through Rosin) had threatened de Witt with publication of the 'Exclusion Article' if relations did not improve.[61] This would only benefit the Orangists through revealing de Witt's alleged betrayal of national interests in the cause of his polit-ical position and his ally. If true, this shows Cromwell's current anger.

Dutch resistance to English naval searches remained a leading area of tension, and in October the States-General resolved that their captains should make a stand. They were to deny it 'with all civility', and if pressed to 'oppose it and manfully fighting against them, have a care of the country's honour and reputation'.[62] The chief hope of avoiding an incident over clashes lay with the negotiators in London. Nieupoort was able to send an initial draft of a treaty to de Witt in December, but he was not satisfied with the lack of an explicit replacement of the hated Navigation Act.[63] He could not give way on this for fear of Dutch resistance, but a new Act would require Parliamentary approval and Cromwell needed his MPs' goodwill to raise taxes for the 1657 campaign. The 'Council for Trade' showed its opinion, reflecting the majority of merchants' and MPs' priorities, by putting in a Parliamentary Bill to renew the Act in January.[64]

As the threat of a Dutch–Swedish war in the Baltic receded in the winter of 1656–7, tension switched to the Dutch commercial dispute with France and colonial dispute (over Brazil) with Portugal. Both confrontations envisaged two of England's allies at war with one another to Spain's benefit. The Dutch Admiralty were, however, cautious in their December instructions to the departing Admiral de Ruyter, making it plain that he was to forbid the carrying of disputed goods to Spain and instruct captains to strike their flags to the English as required by the treaty.[65] Thurloe warned Nieupoort in February 1657 that

> he had received information that a very secret negotiation between the King of Spain and their High and Mighty Lordships was going on, to form a defensive alliance 'contra quoscunque', that allegedly great advantage had been promised to the Netherlands to that end, and that in exchange for this forty large ships of war would be maintained continuously near the coasts of Spain by this state in order to drive off all who would undertake to disturb free navigation and commerce.[66]

The Spanish lacked shipping and could offer substantial trading advantages, so this was a real threat to Cromwell's navy being able to repeat its stunning success of September 1656 over the Plate Fleet. The probable Anglo-French campaign in the Spanish Netherlands was a stimulus, since the Dutch were alarmed at the possibility of English forces controlling Flemish ports. They may have considered taking over Dunkirk from the weak Spanish forces with the latter's agreement.[67] Cromwell could not call off the Flemish campaign although this might have saved the Dutch alliance, because there were crucial factors of national security involved – principally Charles II's presence in Bruges. The tension led to the Council ordering the seizure of all Spanish goods in Dutch ships in English ports, which contravened the spirit and probably the letter of the treaty.[68]

Two threats of naval clashes arose in the spring of 1657 independently of the Dutch–French and Dutch–Portuguese disputes. In the first place, there was a fishing dispute in the North Sea, about which Nieupoort complained on 25 March/ 4 April in terms reminiscent of similar disputes in English coastal waters in the 1990s. The Dutch fishermen

> not only suffered and sustained great molestation by the English fishermen at sea, being by them driven . . . from their convenient fishing places by reviling, threatening, throwing of stones and discharging of muskets, and cutting and spoiling of their nets and fishing-materils . . . but that moreover some ships of war in the State's immediate service with cannon shot and otherwise have done much wrong and injury to several herring-ships.[69]

The other instance involved the second encounter between the blockading English squadrons and a Spanish treasure fleet. (In contrast to 1656, Parliament had granted taxes so the capture of treasure was not so vital in 1657.) Some Dutch bankers were dependent on the arrival of coins from the Spanish American Empire for the payment of outstanding loans by Spanish customers, without which they might go bankrupt.[70] Accordingly, they had a professional interest in the successful arrival of the spring fleet, as Nieupoort told Thurloe. Luckily, however, the threat of de Ruyter cooperating with the Spanish that spring[71] did not materialise. Part of the treasure aboard the Plate Fleet was landed safely on the Canaries before Admiral Blake arrived, then duly evacuated to Europe on board Dutch ships. This meant that an actual naval clash was avoided.

The danger of a Franco-Dutch war was avoided despite tension in the spring of 1657 and the Dutch belief that Cromwell was supporting France.[72] Lockhart warned Thurloe firmly against taking sides and offered to mediate.[73] Mazarin accepted his offer, and he held exploratory talks with the Cardinal and the Dutch ambassador Boreel which helped to sort out their differences.[74] A formal agreement between France and the United Provinces to prevent further escalation of their commercial disputes was reached in mid-June.[75] This ended the threat of England having to take sides or offend one of its two principal allies, and Anglo-Dutch problems were limited to the continuing attacks on merchant ships. The worst of these was the case of the *Cat* of Hoorn, driven ashore off the Isle of Wight to avoid capture by a French ship. The locals demanded payment for salvage and the crew had to sell 2000 boards of wood, which they had aboard, to find the money. They were then arrested for breaking the trading laws and Nieupoort protested to the Council about it on 30 April/10 May.[76] The case was referred to Fleetwood, Lambert, Lisle, Mulgrave, Pickering, Desborough, Strickland, or any two of them, on 26 May/5 June; a report was made to the Council on 21/31 July.[77]

De Ruyter's campaign to blockade Portugal in the dispute over Brazil that summer raised the new danger of two English allies fighting each other. Moreover, Portugal was essential to the English fleet by providing naval bases for their Spanish blockade. A Dutch attack would aid the Spanish campaign, intentionally or not – and Cromwell was currently letting it be known that he was fed up with Dutch prevarication over war with Spain.[78] Cromwell's Council even requested an approach to Louis XIV for French mediation in the Anglo-Dutch disputes and resolved to stop Dutch ships entering Ostend and Dunkirk (where they could aid Charles II's invasion plans), by force if need be.[79] Gamarra had promised the Dutch asistance in regaining the places in Brazil which they had lost to Portugal in 1654;[80] while Cromwell needed Portugal too badly to take the Dutch side. Thus Admiral Montague shadowed the Dutch fleet in the Channel, and it is probable that his presence there helped to persuade de Ruyter not to risk exploiting Spain's success on land against Portugal.[81] Nieupoort assured Cromwell in October that his masters only intended to pressurise Portugal into paying reparations for its Dutch conquests in Brazil.[82] Thereafter, the threat of a clash between two English allies shifted back to the Baltic.

THE BALTIC, THE EAST INDIES AND DOWNING'S EMBASSY: ANGLO-DUTCH TENSION, 1657–8

It was convenient that the distractions of internal politics in the summer of 1657 served to excuse the lack of progress on a maritime treaty as Nieupoort wanted. Parliament (the chief supporter of the Navigation Act) could not be unnecessarily offended at this crucial juncture. An anonymous MP even reported to Nieupoort that a highly placed opponent of the Dutch, possibly Lambert, had been arguing in favour of war but Cromwell had assured that 'he did not have a high opinion of persons who had such tendencies'.[83] Thurloe told Nieupoort that the Navigation Act could not be cited as a reason for Dutch unwillingness to accept English proposals, since England's other allies did not raise such objections and the Act applied to their shipping too.[84]

The English military presence in Flanders raised the prospect of imminent English control of both sides of the Straits of Dover, a serious threat to Dutch shipping if Cromwell turned hostile. The situation was deliberately exacerbated by the French. Talon, sent to London to coordinate the attack on Dunkirk, told Cromwell that the Dutch intended to assist Spain to retake Mardyke, his first foothold in Flanders,[85] and stories were also spread that the Dutch would help Spain to close the Straits of Gibraltar to English shipping.[86]

The other serious problem arose in the Baltic, where the Dutch were encouraging Frederick III of Denmark to invade Sweden and counter Charles X's recent gains. Thurloe warned Philip Meadowe, ambassador-designate to Denmark, that the two powers were in 'close alliance' and asked him to find out what Dutch aid in men, money and ships was involved.[87] There was concern when eighteen Dutch ships were stationed on the Dogger Bank in case they were to be sent to Denmark, precipitating a new 'Northern War' between Baltic states. Accordingly, on 3/13 October, an order was issued to equip more English ships and Montague (off Flanders) was told to await instructions.[88] Fortunately, the Dutch ships did not sail any further. As with Portugal, the English naval presence was probably decisive.

Thurloe's current opinion was shown in his letter to Henry Cromwell of 20/30 November. The Dutch–Portuguese dispute 'doth much trouble us' and Nieupoort 'seems deaf to anything but their own advantage of trade':

> and truly their carriage in this and the business of Sweden is such as shows no goodwill to this nation or indeed the Protestant cause, however [much] they profess the contrary,

and without [i.e. unless] they do provoke this state beyond measure, little notice will be taken of their injuries but endeavours used to continue in peace with them, it being very dangerous to the whole profession for the Protestants to fall out among themselves.[89]

This summed up English policy towards the Dutch in 1655–8.

Cromwell's uneasiness was reflected in his decision to send his own ambassador to The Hague in December. He could watch the intrigues of Gamarra and the Orangists at close quarters and act as a counter to anti-English pressure on de Witt, in the manner that Lockhart watched the Royalists and supported the Huguenots in Paris. The man chosen, the later notorious George Downing, had not yet acquired that reputation for faithlessness and greed which made him detested in Pepys's time, but had the right background for the difficult assignment as chief of intelligence ('Scoutmaster-General') in Scotland in the early 1650s. He had the appropriate 'godly' credentials to be Cromwell's ambassador to his Protestant ally as a former Massachusetts Bay Colony resident, graduate of Harvard, and chaplain on board English ships in the West Indies. He had also been chaplain to the New Model Army regiment of Colonel John Okey, whom he was to betray to Charles II in the most notorious act of a long and unsavoury career. He had also served Cromwell as his envoy to Mazarin to protest at the Vaudois Massacre in 1655, and it is unlikely to be coincidence that he had complained at Dutch commercial power in Parliament in 1656.

Downing's most immediate duties on his arrival were to lessen the chance of the Dutch turning on Cromwell's other allies. Accordingly, he offered his services as mediator with Portugal, which the States-General accepted on 26 January/5 February 1658.[90] Thurloe advised him that his offer was unnecessary because if the Dutch became embroiled with Portugal they could not fight Sweden at the same time.[91] Portugal was in less danger than at the height of the Spanish offensive in 1657. Charles X now crossed the frozen Sound to invade Denmark in February 1658, raising the danger of Dutch intervention to save Frederick III from humiliation or Swedish closure of the Sound in retaliation. An agreed approach was essential and due to the difficulties of travel or sending instructions in winter much fell to Meadowe, currently in Charles's camp as the representative of his most vociferous (if not so effective) ally. Downing relayed Cromwell's promise to the Dutch that 'he will not desire anything in favour of his subjects unless the same be also agreed unto by this state', on 3/13 February.[92] The practical effort of preventing the peace settlement from causing Dutch anger at Swedish favouritism towards England lay with Meadowe, who wrote that he had caused Charles to moderate the tone of an Article in the peace banning foreign warships from the Sound which 'though directly and immediately aimed against Holland, yet obliquely and remotely reflected upon England'.[93] Frederick, ignoring Dutch ambassador Van Beuningen's advice to resist, surrendered large territories to Charles at Roskilde.

The crisis caused by the Swedish attack thus ended without an Anglo-Dutch conflict, and Beuningen was able to stiffen Frederick against submitting to Swedish pressure on the 'warship clause' by saying that both England and the United Provinces would support him against it.[94] Distrust remained, de Witt snappily telling Downing that Cromwell had caused the crisis by inciting Charles to overturn the balance of power in the Baltic; Downing replied that on the contrary it had been the Dutch who incited Frederick to attack Sweden.[95] In the months that followed Downing did his best to limit the areas of conflict between the Dutch and Sweden. Most notably, he sought to have the Treaty of Elbling ratified, covering Dutch trade with Sweden's Baltic possessions. In August, he brought de Witt and the Swedish ambassador Appelboom together, marvelling at their obstinacy on a few minor issues.[96] This matter was of minor importance compared to the danger of another Sound crisis, the timing of which lay out of the control both of Cromwell and de Witt.

Compared to this problem, other areas of Anglo-Dutch tension were of little moment. Clashes at sea had continued, both nearer home and in the East Indies where a 'collection of divers abuses and indignities' was compiled for delivery by Thurloe to Nieupoort (November 1657).[97] In the East Indies the local Dutch authorities halted English trade with the native ruler of Bantam in the Spice Islands, at which the East India Company delivered a vigorous complaint to Cromwell. Dutch aggression there had been cited by the company leadership throughout the debate over the renewal of their charter in 1654–7 as a strong reason for retaining central control of traders, and now seemed to be justified.

There would be no Anglo-Dutch trust as long as Cromwell's forces were in Flanders. Making use of this, Gamarra tried to bribe the States-General into letting Dutch ships transport Spanish troops to Flanders for the new campaign, offering better conditions of loans of Spanish bullion and salt export concessions at Punta de Araya in Venezuela.[98] Ships which Charles II's agent Culpeper hired to pick up a Royalist invasion force from Ostend were destroyed off the harbour by Admiral Montague. This contravened the treaty, even if it was carried out with permission by individual captains and shipowners. Nieupoort was believed to have met English malcontents.[99]

The siege and conquest of Dunkirk, feared by the Dutch since 1652 as having the potential to turn the Channel into another Sound, proceeded that spring without Dutch intervention as the English fleet lay offshore. The fall of the port in June led to increased fears in the United Provinces, although publicly de Witt accepted the assurances which Cromwell had instructed Downing to make.[100] In private the English attitude was less sympathetic to Dutch fears, particularly when it is considered that in his memorandum on foreign policy in 1661/2 Thurloe wrote that the occupation of the port was intended to be 'a bridle upon the Dutch'.[101] England had other priorities to levying tolls on Dutch shipping in the way that the Dutch had feared Charles X would act if he gained control of both sides of the Sound. The ruinous state of England's finances and desire to avoid unnecessary conflict inhibited any desire on the Commonwealth's part to provoke conflict in the North Sea, popular though this would have been in Parliament. It cannot be argued that the crucial factor was Cromwell's presence, since an even-handed policy continued after his death. In 1659, when war between Charles X and the Dutch threatened again, first Thurloe as Richard Cromwell's chief minister and then the restored Rump (advised by ex-Councillors Fleetwood, Lambert and Desborough) chose to make a joint naval demonstration with the Dutch rather than take the excuse to assist Charles X against them. De Witt's favourable reaction to Mazarin's offer of a joint condominium over the Spanish Netherlands, however, indicates his desire to restrict

English influence. He was afraid that, unlike in 1654, England might want the Scheldt reopened.[102]

The final months of Cromwell's life saw other occasions of tension with the Dutch apart from Dunkirk and the Baltic. News continued to arrive of Dutch misdemeanours in the East Indies, most notably their capture of the *Postillion, Frederick,* and *Francis and John* for trying to trade with blockaded Bantam. The East India Company petitioned Cromwell for their return on 6/16 July.[103] The Dutch replied that the proper course was to lay a claim before their local authorities at Batavia and said that the captains had refused a civil request not to break the blockade.[104] In August the States-General voted to return the ships.[105] The Dutch East India Company tried to ignore their masters and refuse to return the ships, an example of 'grass-roots' hostility to the English among the mercantile community. Downing reported that he and de Witt had nearly come to blows over the issue.[106] Meanwhile, an unfortunate incident might have arisen out of the presence in The Hague of Major Whitford, the Scots Royalist who had murdered Dorislaus in May 1649 and who Downing believed had similar intentions against him. He believed that Cavaliers had been lurking outside his house and reported the matter 'though I doubt very much whether the officers will do their duty'.[107]

Ever since the Spanish War broke out Dutch captains had been taking over the former English trade with Spain, acting as 'middlemen' for those English merchants who wished to carry on such trade through proxies and demanding extortionate terms for so doing (as Parliament was told in a list of complaints in 1659). In May 1658, a series of complaints from English captains referred to the fact that the Dutch

> have lately carried on most of the trade of this nation [and] eat us out of our trade at home and abroad; they refuse to sell us one hog's head of water to refresh us at sea, and call us 'English dogs' . . . They will not sail at us, but shoot at us and by indirect means bring their goods into our ports.[108]

The maritime treaty remained unsettled despite Nieupoort's repeated requests; Cromwell had other priorities even before his final illness intervened. Downing's efforts, as ordered by Thurloe, concentrated on trying to mediate between the Dutch and Portugal.[109]

The Baltic was to be predominant in the final crisis of Anglo-Dutch relations before the Restoration, which began in the final weeks of Cromwell's life with Charles X's new assault on Denmark. The timing of this crisis made it the responsibility of Cromwell's successors. Ironically, therefore, Cromwell had no part in the most important instance of Anglo-Dutch co-operation since the signing of the treaty in April 1654, when the mutual interests of the two nations temporarily overcame that armed 'stand-off' which had persisted throughout the Protectorate and had seen the danger of Dutch assistance to Spain's Plate Fleets or a clash over Portugal. For all Cromwell's protestatios, only an overriding mutual threat such as that to freedom of access to the Baltic in 1658–9 could make them act together. The Vermuyden Plan at least had the merits of seeking to bring an end to the crucial question of colonial competition, even if it offended too many vested interests to have been the basis for serious discussion. Lack of English concern for such an overall scheme of agreement owed something to lack of time as well as lack of concern.

13 Cromwell and the Baltic, 1654–6

Cromwell's relations with Sweden have been particularly open to misinterpretation. An undue reliance on official rhetoric (as illustrated in his letters to Charles X from 1655 to 1658) seemed to show Cromwell as enthusiastic about Charles's role as a Protestant hero like Gustavus Adolphus, as he was in using 'outdated' Elizabethan nostalgia and religious fervour to form his view of Spain. He neglected the national interest in supporting Sweden, an aggressive power which dominated the Baltic to the fear of all its neighbours, without seeming to realise that national advancement and dynastic conflict had as much to do with Charles's campaigns as pure Protestant zeal.[1]

As Cromwell's approach to France and Spain has been reassessed in recent years, so has his Baltic policy. The most notable example of this is the work of Michael Roberts in his article in *Essays on Swedish History*, pointing out the effective limits of Cromwell's aid to Sweden.[2] It cannot be denied that Cromwell expressed approval of Charles in glowing terms, as 'a man ... as good as any these last ages hath brought forth, that hath adventured his all against the Popish interest'.[3] However, in real terms Charles received little support beyond volunteer soldiers and money (although it might have been different if the Spanish War had not imposed limits on Cromwell's ability to follow up his admiring letters). Even in 1655, when England was still at peace, Cromwell ignored an appeal to send 6–8000 troops to Sweden.[4] Professions of support had excellent strategic motives. The threat of the Emperor sending assistance to Spain was a danger to the English war effort, because Cromwell had to centre his strategy on the fairly cheap plan of using his navy to take Spain's treasure galleons en route to Europe. This damaged Spain's ability to pay its troops (or Charles II's army). Thus any assistance to Philip IV negated Cromwell's strategy and any diversion of the Emperor's attention in Europe was advisable. (Jan Casimir of Poland, Charles's principal target in 1655–6, was also pro-Royalist.) Cromwell, like Richelieu in the early 1630s, found it

190

advisable to look for northern European allies against the Habsburgs. Moreover, any chance of an alliance of northern European Protestants would be impossible if the states in question were more interested in watching the ambitions of the Swedish King.

In addition to this, there was the Dutch factor. The English required access to the Baltic for naval stores of wood, tar and hemp, which were vital to the maintenance of a strong fleet even before the outbreak of conflict with Spain. Despite their peace treaty the Dutch, the only potential challenger at sea, were uncertain allies. The commercial classes of Amsterdam were more hostile to Cromwell than de Witt, and a conflict in the Baltic could provide the final blow to Anglo-Dutch relations and push the latter into the arms of Spanish Ambassador Gamarra. Cromwell could neither stand by in case of a Dutch conflict with Sweden (either over the Sound or Danzig) nor exacerbate Dutch suspicions by obtaining preferential commercial aggreements with Sweden.

The Commonwealth of 1649 was faced with the problem of having to obtain admissions of its legality from all states with which it had dealings. Accordingly, envoys had to be sent to or received from each European power to reopen diplomatic relations and demand recognition. Sweden was less important than France, Spain or the United Provinces. Montrose had good relations with Queen Christina and sailed from Gothenburgh in 1650 at the start of his final campaign, but most of his soldiers were emigré Scots and Danes and he had no official support. It was 1652 before the English government, with Cromwell as its Commander-in-Chief, turned to the question of selecting an ambassador for Sweden and considered the merits of MP Richard Salwey.[5] Cromwell had a substantial say in the final choice of Bulstrode Whitelocke, whom he told he had been selected on the grounds of his being a tough and travelled linguist, a man of considerable skill and initiative, and one whom he knew personally to be loyal – the basic grounds for selecting most of Cromwell's ambassadors over the next few years.[6]

By the time Whitelocke arrived in Sweden Cromwell had seized power, but his duties remained to conclude a treaty based upon diplomatic recognition, a defensive alliance and a commercial agreement. The treaty signed early in 1654 centred on these pragmatic priorities and there were no side-issues of a close Protestant alliance, such as had bedevilled the Dutch talks.[7] Cromwell continued to manifest his goodwill towards the northern Protestant states during the following months, most notably offering to mediate in a dispute between Sweden and Bremen in which he had no direct concern.[8] Circumstances were altered by the abdication of Christina on 30 May/9 June, which brought her young and aggressive cousin Charles to the throne. In his first letter to the Protector he professed friendship and goodwill,[9] but in fact he was suspected by a number of observers of being willing to lend aid to or campaign on behalf of Charles II.[10] There was thus some suspicion in London which may have played a part in the Council's refusal to accept an inaccurately addressed letter from the King to the Protector.[11] There was an undercurrent of anxiety in the resultant letter sent to Charles to remind him to ratify his predecessor's agreement to the treaty.[12]

The English Muscovy Company had lost many of its privileges in Russia since 1649, at the instigation of the Czar who had been furious at Charles I's execution.[13] In 1654, they petitioned Cromwell for help and he sent William Prideaux to request the resumption of the privileges and explain his usurpation in terms understandable to the Russians, comparing his appointment to Alexis' father's in 1613.[14] Cromwell did Sweden a service in this embassy, by requesting an explanation for the Russian attack on Charles's current ally Jan Casimir of Poland.[15] This was to Charles's benefit rather than Cromwell's, given English suspicion of the Swedes. Cromwell gave a notably cool reception to Jan Casimir's ambassador de Bye's suggestion of an alliance centred on an English attack on Archangel to punish Russia, reputedly because he was aware of the prominence of Royalist officers at the Polish Court.[16] In a similar manner, Cromwell fought shy of attempts to entangle him in Baltic alliances by his Dutch allies, turning down Nieupoort's suggestion that he join the Dutch in an alliance with Denmark and Brandenburg.[17]

Cromwell took an equally cautious approach to Peter Coyet, who was representing the Swedish King in London until a formal ambassador arrived. Charles wrote to Coyet in May 1655 requesting that he use a new commercial treaty to lure the Protector into an alliance against the Dutch.[18] Meanwhile, he declared war on Poland in June, raising the possibility of the Dutch intervening at sea. Coyet accordingly sought audience with Cromwell as soon as Nieupoort had been received to counteract anything which had been said to Sweden's disadvantage, and subsequently requested a naval alliance for English protection of Swedish shipping during the campaign. Cromwell

> answered as usual, with a great deal of well-wishing as well as with declarations of friendship and gladness, and said that he wishes to mention some special particulars concerning the question of a closer alliance . . . but not just now; he wishes to think it over a bit.[19]

The most he would offer was not to permit the Dutch fleet to attack Sweden[20] and refuse to enter the current alliance being projected between the Dutch and Brandenburg.[21] As in 1657, his assistance to one ally sought to stop short of annoying another. The States-General turned down Elector Frederick William's suggestion of an attack on Sweden, on the grounds that they dared not move without Denmark or the Protector.[22]

The outbreak of conflict between Sweden and Poland required Cromwell to take a closer interest in the region, and he therefore despatched his relative Edward Rolt to Sweden. Rolt, an unknown with no diplomatic experience, was not such a 'high-profile' envoy as Council Deputy Secretary Meadowe was to be in 1657; he was to deliver others' messages rather than act on his own initiative. He was instructed to 'remove any jealousies which you shall observe in the said King' and hinder any Royalist envoys, announcing 'our endeavours for contracting a nearer union and alliance' without going into details.[23]

Charles's ambassador, Count Bonde, arrived in London on 27 July/6 August 1655 to receive an impressive welcome.[24] Cromwell told him at his first audience that he hoped Charles would carry on the policies of Gustavus Adolphus – that is, attack the Catholic states in Germany rather than the all-round promotion of Swedish interests which Gustavus had in fact carried out before his intervention in the Thirty Years' War.[25] He told Bonde that the unfortunate lapse by the Dutch from past opposition to Catholicism meant that he had to consider closer ties with Sweden instead. Bonde inferred that he really wanted Charles to attack the Empire.[26]

In practical terms the Swedes requested an English presence

of twenty ships in the Baltic to 'warn off' the Dutch, in return
for vice versa in the North Sea if necessary. There was no
response. Cromwell gave Bonde the impression that he feared
the Dutch most since 'they are nearest at hand to him' and
believed that they could aid Charles II 'from desperation or
from the danger that they fear in the Baltic'.[27] Accordingly,
Cromwell dared not come down on either side, and talks
continued with both Nieupoort (who tried to undermine
Cromwell's belief in Swedish religious toleration by revealing
details of their strict Calvinist Statute on Religion[28]) and Bonde.
What was needed was some form of initiative to reconcile the
claims of both the Dutch and Sweden in the Baltic. The only
evidence that we have of this lies in a report by Schlezer,
ambassador of Elector Frederick William, that Thurloe suggested to both parties that England might join the alliance
that Nieupoort said the Dutch were constructing with Denmark
and Brandenburg, if Sweden could be persuaded to concentrate her interests against her current enemy Poland. She could
pursue her interests 'as far as the Caspian' in that direction,
that is, against the Ottoman Turks and/or Russia as well, in
return for maintaining the status quo in the West.[29] Apart from
indicating a lack of concern about hostile Russia, it shows that
some practical consideration was taken as to how to avoid the
mutual jealousies of the Baltic powers permanently hindering
any useful Protestant alliance. It was, however, only an idea
and the urgency of the Spanish conflict distracted England
permanently that October. Thereafter, English policy returned
to reacting to an agenda laid down by others; a sign both of
other priorities and of lack of local influence.

EFFECTS OF THE SPANISH WAR: THE 1656 TREATY

The oubreak of the Spanish War saw an outburst of anti-Spanish
propaganda in England. This coincided with a number of signs
of rising religious tension in Europe, chief among them the
emotional shock caused to Protestants by the Vaudois Massacre (to which Cromwell had sought to coordinate response)
and the election of the reputedly persecuting Pope Alexander
VII. Cromwell's need for European allies coincided with the
impression caused by Charles X's invasion of Poland, in fact in

pursuit of a dynastic struggle but seemingly as another Gustavus Adolphus intent on assaulting Catholic powers. The Continent's two foremost aggressive Protestant warrior-statesmen seemed natural allies, Royalist Secretary of State Sir Edward Nicholas writing in September that 'these two will fill Europe with troubles unless prevented'.[30] In Italy, the English consul at Leghorn reported that Cromwell was considered 'an intimate colleague, if not the contriver, of the King of Sweden's expedition to Poland'.[31]

Bonde made use of the English need of allies, and on 23 November/3 December delivered a proposal that Cromwell invade the Spanish Netherlands and thence make his way into Germany to link up with the Swedish army. Cromwell assured that 'he wished in every way possible to help the King' but did not take up the suggestion. Internal problems made a large military commitment abroad undesirable, troops having to maintain the regime of Major-Generals until Parliament met. Moreover, the Swedes did not offer to pay the expeditionary force, something which Mazarin had to do in 1657 to achieve success. In these circumstances, Cromwell fell back on vague expressions of goodwill and trying to bring the Swedes and Dutch together. Nieupoort was reminded of the advantages of a Protestant alliance, and Bonde was reminded of the Dutch concern over their access to Danzig, their 'bread-basket'.[32]

In January 1656, Cromwell made two moves to achieve more allies and satisfy Bonde. It was proposed to send an ambassador to Charles's new base in Poland, accompanied by the City financier Sir Christopher Pack who had been involved in the relief fund for the Vaudois. Whitelocke wrote that on 25 January/4 February 'the Protector sent to me and very earnestly pressed me to undertake the embassy to Sweden, regarding it as a business of the highest honour of the highest concernment to the Protestants' cause'.[33] Whitelocke had however been given adverse advice by the youngest member of the Council:

> Sir Charles Wolseley . . . did not approve of the joining Sir Christopher Pack with me in this embassy, nor the timing of it; for he said he heard the King of Sweden had made an order to desire all foreign public ministers to forbear for a time coming to his camp as he was in the midst of his military affairs.[34]

Whitelocke accordingly advised Cromwell to postpone the embassy and the Council agreed. In March, Cromwell asked John Dury to consider an extraordinary embassy to the German Protestants. Dury advised against it, writing to Hartlib that certain Protestant princes would not unite with an enemy in any circumstances and would only be irritated at Cromwell's interference. He also thought that Hartlib's proposed candidate for the embassy, his colleague Cheney Culpeper, did not possess enough of the requisite qualities (Latin, statesmanship, prudence and discretion).[35] Whitelocke agreed that it would only serve to unite the Catholic princes against it,[36] and on 3/13 March Fleetwood advised him that the mission had been called off. He assured that the lack of serious tension between Sweden and the Dutch made it unnecessary, and Cromwell followed his advice to resort to encouraging correspondence with the Princes instead.[37]

In the other initiative, on 28 January/7 February, the Council at last appointed commissioners to treat with Bonde. They were Whitelocke (the only non-Councillor), Strickland (former ambassador to The Hague), Pickering and Nathaniel Fiennes.[38] They met Thurloe to discuss the Articles which Cromwell desired in the new treaty and presented their initial list to Bonde next day.[39] On 31 January/10 February, talks began with the English trying to have the Dutch included. Bonde resisted fiercely, claiming that he had no authority to include the Dutch and that the Protestant union 'would be a difficult work'. He had no desire to deal with either point in 'this or any other treaty'.[40] The English were faced with an ally more interested in their own advantage. Cromwell desired to use Charles against the Emperor, Charles to split Cromwell from the Dutch.

The main initial debate concerned the terms for the use of one ally's troops in their partner's dominions. There was a danger of English troops or ships in the Baltic becoming involved in a clash with the Dutch and tipping the scales in favour of war, so on 8/18 February the English commissioners desired that such troops were 'not to be employed against the other's friends'. Bonde feared that troops could be employed somewhere inconvenient, such as Cromwell using Swedish troops in Ireland, and Whitelocke and his associates retorted that security 'might be much endangered if a stranger should have the appointment of the places'. They may have had

Swedish treachery in league with Royalists in mind. It was agreed the commander should suggest a destination and if that was inconvenient the host should suggest another, as near as possible. As for ships, Bonde insisted 'on the liberty to employ them against the other's friends if those friends attempted any disturbance of the seas or trade of him that hired them'. The point was left,[41] although Whitelocke had private talks with Fleetwood's brother George, an officer who had emigrated to Sweden and was back in London on Charles's behalf, about raising 2000 volunteers.

One potential threat to a Protestant alliance had been ended in January with Charles's settlement with Frederick William of Brandenburg, the principal potential Dutch ally. The terms he imposed at Konigsberg required Frederick William to pay homage to Charles as rightful King of Poland (overlord of Brandenburg's Prussian lands), hand over half the customs dues of East Prussia and provide military assistance against Jan Casimir. Cromwell was optimistic at the chances of peace arising from this enforced alliance, ignoring that the humiliated Elector was likely to turn on Charles at the first opportunity.[42] Bonde duly encouraged the Protector to think of military aid to Sweden, saying that 'such a design would be of more benefit to the Protector than the sending out of great fleets to the Indies and the coasts of Spain'. Such naval expeditions were, however, the cornerstone of English military strategy. Cromwell's – as opposed to Sweden's – interests were best served by continuing with this. Accordingly he boastfully declared that 'notwithstanding the vast expenses of our fleet at this time, yet a war being begun with Spain it must be maintained . . . the people of England being ever contented to bear the burden of their taxes rather than the injuries and insolencies of their enemies'.[43]

The commercial treaty talks continued on details such as reciprocal customs rates, the restitution of English goods seized in Sweden before the 1654 treaty (and vice versa), and the restrictions on English cloth imports to Danzig which Charles now controlled. Bonde was especially insistent on obtaining better justice for Swedish claims against English privateers from the Court of Admiralty than had been obtained hitherto, while the English (as with the Dutch talks) tried to obtain a ban on the export of Swedish naval supplies – hemp, pitch and tar –

and corn to Spain. Bonde also tried to get the English entrepôt
for Russia shifted from Archangel to Swedish-held Narva on
the Gulf of Bothnia. By 11/21 March the Articles on hiring
soldiers and ships, passports and contraband were 'near agreed',
but those concerning trade and the restitution of seized goods
were deferred. The English showed no hurry to accept their
allies' terms, as with current talks with the Dutch and France,
and Bonde lost his temper badly on 2/12 April when he also
had to contend with a two-hour delay in an audience with the
Protector without reason. Pressure of business was probably to
blame, but Sir Oliver Fleming 'plainly told him [Cromwell]
how unfit it was and ill taken'. Whitelocke also warned the
Protector that 'the King was powerful and successful, that the
Dutch were most for their own interest, and if there be not a
nearer alliance betwixt us and Sweden, probably the Dutch
may step in'.[44]

On 31 March/10 April, they voted that pitch, tar, hemp and
flax must be banned from Sweden's exports to Spain for the
duration of the war. Bonde tried to protest that these 'were
the great commodities of the King of Sweden', whereupon
Thurloe told him smartly that in that case he could surely find
other customers. Fiennes unexpectedly backed Bonde. The
ambassador's assistant Coyet tried to argue that if military
supplies were not to be sent to Spain the English should not
sell cloth that could be used for military uniforms. Fiennes
replied that cloth was not used for offensive purposes, and
Coyet told him that in that case pitch, tar and hemp could be
used for civilian purposes too. Strickland said that guns could
be used to kill birds as well as men but were understood to be
contraband in time of war, and the session ended with a quarrel
over precedents. It was settled with agreement that Charles
should issue a proclamation banning such exports and 'a kind
of undertaking that it should be done'.[45] While the talks
continued the Swedes, through George Fleetwood, were allowed
to recruit volunteers for their campaigns. An initial offer of
4000 men for Sweden was improved to 6000 on 31 March/10
April, provided that the new treaty was agreed.[46] Bonde tried
to get round including the Dutch by claiming that he had
already written to the King saying that he understood Cromwell
was not insisting on their inclusion and that Charles would

take it amiss if the Protector changed his mind. This may have been a deliberate ploy, though Cromwell's words at audiences were frequently vague. The Council took the threat seriously, and advised Cromwell to treat agreement with Sweden as more crucial, 'the Dutch being greatly for their own interest . . . in case there should not be a nearer alliance betwixt us and Sweden, might possibly slip in and make a nearer alliance betwixt themselves and Sweden without taking much care to have us included therein'.[47]

Bonde maintained that Cromwell should supply £200 000 a year to maintain a Swedish army of 30 000 foot and 6000 horse to enforce the Treaty of Osnabruck (1648). The terms were to Sweden's advantage, seeing as the treaty had confirmed their occupation of Pomerania and various North German towns, though some such excuse was necessary not to alarm potential allies that this was unprovoked aggression. Whitelocke retorted that the terms were to Sweden's military benefit and said that it should be aimed more specifically at the Habsburgs. In any case, England could not afford that sum of money. Bonde told him that such a specific Catholic target might frighten off their potential Catholic ally France; imperial breaches of the Treaty of Osnabruck would serve as a rallying point for North German Protestants. The sum of £200 000 would provide 'a good diversion, and trouble the King of Spain more than £2 000 000 a year upon our fleets and sending to Jamaica'. Whitelocke replied that a German war – unlike one aimed at Flanders – would not definitely draw in Spain.

The English commissioners showed signs of not taking a united attitude towards Sweden. Whitelocke was in favour of accommodation on easy terms, fearing the Dutch and grumbling to the other commissioners that it was absurd putting themselves out for them as 'the Dutch had not the like affection to us . . . most of them were our enemies at heart'. Fiennes was 'more inclinable to the particulars of satisfaction' than Thurloe, who was adamant on insisting that England's full terms be met on such matters as contraband.[48]

Replying to Bonde's terms on 21 April/1 May, Cromwell insisted that he could not uphold the Treaty of Osnabruck and ignored encouragement to think that the Emperor should be retaliated against in Germany for sending 10 000 men to

Spain. He expatiated on the need to include other states in the alliance, which Bonde was later told meant the Dutch.[49] He was, however, still unrealistically optimistic in his assessment of the Treaty of Konigsberg between Charles and Frederick William, as he showed the latter's ambassador.[50]

The despatch of a Dutch fleet to the Baltic in pursuance of their dispute with Charles over Danzig brought a threat of war. England was not tied to assisting Sweden and thus causing a Dutch alliance with Spain. Bonde bitterly accused Cromwell over his delay; he blandly assured that he 'had always striven to avoid offending anyone' and had 'taken considerable pains to prevent differences and parting of ways amongst Protestants'. He cited his delay as putting him in an excellent position to mediate but would only promise not to assist any Dutch aggression. It was probably on this occasion that he delivered one of his most important statements on the priority of strategic interests over ideology. English need of naval supplies from the Baltic and recognition of Dutch interests in the corn trade there necessitated neutrality.[51]

The importance of neutrality meant that the Protector held out even when Bonde, like French Ambassador Bordeaux early in 1655, resorted at the end of May to making a final demand for agreement without which he would leave.[52] Bonde, like Bordeaux, had to back down. In the meantime, the Council voted on 9/19 June 'to remind His Highness to speed an ambassador to Sweden'.[53] Cromwell informed Bonde of this and the Ambassador suggested Whitelocke.[54] This was to Sweden's benefit, given Whitelocke's stance at the talks, and the fact that despite his experience he was not chosen may reflect on reports which Fiennes and Strickland made of him. Two other Councillors, Lawrence and Pickering, were also known to prefer the Dutch as allies.[55] Presumably they and Cromwell suspected Whitelocke's partiality for the Swedes.

A straightforward commercial treaty went ahead, without any contentious details of a continental campaign. The result was a victory for English caution, achieved despite the temptation to rush into details of a North German campaign as Charles X desired. The Council may have played an important role here, but Cromwell's own words to Bonde show that he saw the impracticality of accepting any terms which could lead to a clash with the Dutch. The Spanish War was the crucial factor. This is not to deny that Cromwell's approach to the Baltic in 1654–6 had its mistakes, but these were limited to such misconceptions of serious interstate rivalries as his attitude to the Treaty of Konigsberg.

14 Cromwell and the Baltic, 1656–8

BEFORE THE BALTIC CONFLICT, 1656–7

The year between the signing of the Anglo-Swedish Treaty of 1656 and the Danish attack on Sweden saw Cromwell's efforts for a 'Protestant alliance' continue unabated. His financial worries were lessened by Captain Stayner's capture of Spanish Plate Fleet silver in September 1656 and a lesser seizure by Blake in May 1657, while the meeting of his second Parliament increased the chance of legally sanctioned taxation. Meanwhile, the lack of serious Spanish aid to Charles II in Flanders meant that an alliance with France could be delayed until France had agreed to pay the expeditionary force. Thus Cromwell could afford time to look to the prospect of an Anglo-Swedish expedition to northern Germany instead of having to concentrate his efforts on Flanders, though the unsettled condition of England limited effective aid. It remained essential to do nothing which might drive the Dutch into alliance with Spain and negate English naval strategy. Charles X was still occupied in Poland at the time of the treaty, and in June 1656 the Dutch and Danish offer of aid to Jan Casimir raised the danger of his becoming embroiled with them. Cromwell could only watch as the Dutch fleet relieved the Swedish siege of Danzig. Thereafter, Charles's military prospects in Poland declined despite his victory at Warsaw in July. His impending retreat meant that he might turn on the Emperor but a conflict with the Dutch, Danes and Brandenburgers was equally likely.

Bonde's mission to England was completed with the signing of the treaty and on 25 July/4 August he received his farewell audience at Whitehall.[1] Next day he accompanied the Protector to Hampton Court, where he informally encouraged him to beware of the machinations of the Dutch and the Danes. In reply, Cromwell blamed all the problems with the Dutch on the machinations of the Orangists and assured that 'the Protestant cause and its security were the grounds upon which he acted . . . to which he would adhere as long as he had anything to say'.[2] The most support he could offer Bonde was to send 'a stern letter' to the States-General, taken by Louis Rosin, and another to Frederick III of Denmark concerning their enmity towards Sweden. 'It was impossible for him to give the King any real help.'[3] A simultaneous letter was sent to Charles, in which Cromwell covered up his lack of assistance with warnings that a Baltic conflict would be 'fatal to the interests of the Protestant religion' and apocalyptic ravings, probably written by Milton, declaring, 'who is so ignorant as not to know that the counsels of Spain and the Roman pontiff for these two years have filled all these places [Piedmont, Austria, Switzerland] with conflagration, slaughter, and the vexation of the orthodox?'. The Protestants had 'enemies everywhere and to spare, inflamed with inexorable revenge'. The conflict was timed from the massacre of the Vaudois which evidently still made a great impression on the Protector.[4]

Ideological rhetoric was backed up with a farewell present to Bonde worth £1500 which the Council voted on 1/11 August, evidence of his importance.[5] He was presented with a portrait in a gold case, a jewel, four horses, and 100 pieces of cloth, worth another £5000. His own opinion, as he told Whitelocke on 16/26 August, was that 'the Council did not so well relish it [alliance] as the Protector'.[6] In the Baltic, a temporary settlement with the Dutch was reached in which the only English involvement was the implicit threat of Cromwell's fleet assisting either side if the other pushed its advantage too far. The Dutch signed the Treaty of Elbling with Sweden on 1/11 September, whereby the latter guaranteed the neutrality of Danzig in their conflict with Poland and the port gave their Dutch 'protectors' favourable terms in such matters as customs. The Danish offer to assist the Dutch against Sweden arrived too late.[7] It showed the limits of English diplomacy, which was only effective in crises like that of 1658 when they had an armed presence in the area.

Cromwell did his utmost to impress the Swedes with his determination to assist them, holding a military review in London on 6/16 October, which the Venetian ambassador Giavarina reckoned was intended 'to show the strength of his regard for the King of Sweden and show his earnest desire to continue united with him'. One of the regiments present was selected to embark for Sweden.[8] Now that Bonde had left, the

Swedes were represented by George Fleetwood in the matter of recruiting men for the King's cause. Cromwell made no reply to Nieupoort's offer to have England included in the new Dutch–Danish alliance, presumably because it was aimed implicitly against Sweden,[9] and wrote to Frederick III to lecture him on his Protestant duty. The evidence of Popish wickedness as manifested by the Vaudois Massacre was recounted again, and the King was reminded that Denmark and Sweden were 'the chiefest part of our strength, among whom so large a provision of the Protestant strength and puissance lies stored'. A war between them would bring ruin and encourage more persecution, as 'our most embittered enemies seem to have on every side conspired our destruction'.[10] In reality, the conflicts of 1657 and 1658 led to no such Catholic assault.

The talks with France proceeded slowly throughout the latter part of 1656 and were only concluded when a Franco-Spanish peace seemed possible. An English expedition to the Continent was, however, important to distract Spain from lending support to Charles II, now based in Bruges, and while the French treaty hung fire rumours began that Charles X intended to mortgage the Duchy of Bremen to England.[11] The Swedish-occupied duchy could serve as a rallying point for Protestants; any English army on the Continent would be a major psychological threat to the Catholics given Cromwell's reputation (as was to be the case with Dunkirk in 1658). Accordingly, some time late in 1656 or early in 1657, Cromwell raised the possibility of leasing the Duchy through Charles's envoy George Fleetwood. Reminding him of the need to avoid alarming the Dutch, the Protector said that he had thought of the idea for four reasons:

1. 'Not only could the garrisons there be transported elsewhere at His Majesty's orders, but the Protector could reinforce them with money and ships.'
2. 'Such an agreement . . . would rather occupy the Hollanders and would appreciably disturb the extent of their designs against the crown of Sweden.'
3. 'Denmark, because of the danger of an invasion of Jutland, if she should show herself hostile, could be better held in check.'
4. 'Because of the proximity of England, Protestant princes

and estates in Germany would not be a little encouraged to cooperate the more zealously for the common good'.[12]

The plan was a clever compromise between Charles's calls for assistance and Cromwell's desire not to cause Dutch resentment by interfering in the Baltic. It was never made clear what Cromwell intended to do if both France and Sweden agreed to terms for his military intervention, as he could hardly abandon a French military alliance for fear of internal French pressure driving Mazarin into peace with Spain. Such a double commitment would have been dangerously expensive and required a large exodus of troops. It was probably at this time that a 'Proposition in order to a Treaty with Sweden' concerning the rights of the merchants of Bremen under English military occupation was drawn up.[13]

The first months of 1657 saw several diplomatic moves in whic Fleetwood played his part. The Dutch–Danish threat to Sweden now seemed likely to draw in Russia, where Czar Alexis wanted to retake the provinces of Ingria and Carelia on the Gulf of Bothnia (lost in 1617 to Sweden). Accordingly, on 5/15 March the Council decided to send an ambassador to Russia after hearing a report of Thurloe's meeting with George Fleetwood.[14] The Czar had still not restored English trading privileges, but Sweden's plight was clearly the chief reason for the mission which was to be undertaken by Richard Bradshaw, consul at Hamburg.[15] Alexis had invaded Livonia, still a source of dispute between Russia and its neighbours in the 1990s, to besiege Riga, and Bradshaw was instructed to offer mediation and to remind the Czar of the horrors of war between powerful states. He was also to remind him that it was not Charles's policy to force consciences, a reference to the Jesuit-influenced Jan Casimir whose zeal for forced conversions had caused a rebellion in the Ukraine of which Alexis had taken full advantage.[16]

A simultaneous mission was planned to Denmark, the Council deciding on 24 February/6 March to 'advise His Highness to send Philip Meadowe as envoy to Denmark with fit instructions, and the Lord Deputy [Fleetwood, George's brother], Jones, and Strickland with Mr Secretary, to consider what preparations are necessary for his journey'.[17] Meadowe, Thurloe's deputy, was a skilled and pragmatic negotiator who had achieved the ratification of the Portuguese treaty in 1656 despite the provocations of his being wounded by an assassin and Admiral Montague offering to attack the Portuguese treasure fleets in revenge. He was to have a salary of £1000 per annum.[18] His departure was delayed by the pressure of work in London associated with the meeting of Parliament, and was overtaken in May by increasing tension in Germany caused by the death of Emperor Ferdinand III. On 1/11 June Frederick, emboldened by the Dutch alliance and Charles's difficulties in Poland, declared war on Sweden. It is unlikely that Meadowe could have influenced this decision had he been in Copenhagen, but Cromwell clearly put his mission at a lower priority than it deserved.[19]

According to a report sent by George Fleetwood to Charles at the end of March, Cromwell promised to send twenty ships to assist Sweden if necessary on the grounds that the Dutch could not be trusted since their intervention at Danzig. Denmark, moreover, had allowed this Dutch squadron to pass through the Sound, with clearly hostile intent, to Sweden with which she was at peace.[20] The threat of a disputed Imperial election in Germany heightened the possibility of a new Protestant–Catholic dispute over the election of a successor, as Cromwell's agent Colonel Bamfylde warned him.[21] Charles was therefore more likely to abandon his Polish campaign, even before the Danish declaration of war (an annoying distraction for Cromwell's hopes of using the Swedes in Germany). More importance was also given to English relations with Frederick William of Brandenburg, a Protestant Elector who could help to elect a Protestant Emperor such as the Elector of Saxony. In April he had sent a memorandum to his ambassador in England, Schlezer, asking why no moves had been taken to ally with England in the eighteen months he had been in London.[22] Schlezer presented this to Cromwell, mistakenly adding his master's fears of a Russian advance on East Prussia which was supposed to remain secret.[23] Once the news of the Emperor's death reached London Cromwell received Schlezer again, urging the wisdom of taking the Imperial crown away from the Habsburgs who were persecutors with Spanish connections. In return, he assured Schlezer that he had dissuaded the Dutch and the Danes from any action hostile towards Sweden and that he intended doing likewise with the Czar.

The implications of this were that there was no prospect of an anti-Swedish coalition so the Elector would be better employed seeking to elect a Protestant Emperor.[24] The wishful thinking of Cromwell's remarks were shown a mere three weeks later when Denmark invaded Sweden.

CROMWELL AND THE BALTIC CONFLICT, 1657–8

The outbreak of war set at nought all Cromwell's efforts to obtain a united front against the Habsburgs. It showed that the northern powers had other priorities, and that Frederick III was not as concerned with German matters as his illustrious predecessor Christian IV. The coalition against Sweden in 1657–8 looked forward to the events of 1700 rather than back to the 1620s, though on this occasion Russia was weaker and Sweden could resume her career of dominance in the Baltic. Writing in 1661/2, Thurloe had no doubt where the blame lay: '[the Dutch] engaged the King of Denmark contrary to his interests to invade the King of Sweden in his duchy of Bremen'.[25] At the time he was of the same opinion, writing to Henry Cromwell on 28 July/7 August that the conflict had been 'fomented by the Dutch against the Dane, hoping by this means to get the trade and commerce of the East Sea'.[26]

The war with Spain limited Cromwell's ability to react to the crisis, his fleets being committed in the Atlantic, Caribbean and English Channel and his troops now being committed to a campaign in Flanders. Most immediately, he could not despatch troops to Bremen on Charles's behalf; it would have been an excellent opportunity to establish a foothold as Charles could hardly have refused the offer of help and it would have shown his commitment to his all. Troops, however, were needed in London, where the uncertainty over military reaction if Cromwell accepted the Crown was followed by Lambert's resignation. The failure to assist Charles avoided the danger of Frederick III and the Dutch combining to close the Sound to a 'hostile' Cromwell.

Swedish commissioners had arrived in London that spring to negotiate a final settlement of commercial claims arising from the Dutch War. The internal crises meant that the Council delayed appointing commissioners to treat with them, at which they protested on 9/19 June.[27] This was then done.[28] However, no other measures were taken in reaction to the war, not even the limited measure of sending two or three men-of-war to keep an eye on Dutch and Danish warships in the Sound, which was advised by Aitzema.[29] Cromwell was wise to avoid any serious involvement as the Dutch were not yet looking for open involvement in a Baltic conflict. The war was officially condemned in the States-General on 17/27 June, showing that majority opinion favoured caution.[30]

At this juncture there appeared the only evidence of apparent Parliamentary interest in foreign policy. An order was passed on 26 June/6 July recommending Cromwell to form a union of foreign Protestants. The explanation for the initiative, however, lies with the men primarily responsible for it – the Councillors in the House, Fleetwood, Lambert, Jones, Thurloe and Desborough, who presented the order to the Protector.[31] Such a scheme had long been supported by Fleetwood, quite apart from his Swedish links,[32] though Lambert would have supported it for pragmatic rather than ideological reasons. He supported the cloth interests in his native Yorkshire which would be damaged by war in the Baltic.

Cromwell was anxious enough about the threat to Sweden to send a message with Barckmann, the chief Swedish trade negotiator, when he returned home for consultations on 1/11 August. He was given assurances of 'vigorous assistance if Sweden will pay the men promptly as well as give them distinctive treatment'.[33] In tandem with this, the delayed Meadowe mission took place while Cromwell's relative William Jephson was sent to Sweden. Jephson, inexperienced like Rolt, was evidently trusted to deliver important messages and probably owed his choice to recent work in Parliament. He was told in his 'secret instructions' that although no money could be sent to Sweden:

we were not unwilling to ... [give] such assistance as we were able to afford him, and might consist with the other treaties we have with other states and kingdoms. But not finding them [Bonde and George Fleetwood] empowered to treat with us upon the terms of such assistanc ... we were not able to come to any resolutions therein. For in case we should be able to afford either ships or land-soldiers or both, we could not understand from the said persons what places of secure retreat for our men, or secure harbours for our ships, should be put into our power; a thing so just and necessary in itself, and so usual in all like agreements.[34]

Accordingly, if Charles raised the question of Bremen this was to be taken up. Losses could not be hidden as well as they had been in the case of the Western Design. A campaign would have to be properly planned and provided with a base, a pledge of his ally's faithfulness. Cromwell was fearful of the effects of a reverse in Flanders on his situation at home;[35] the same applied to Bremen.

Bremen had a number of advantages. It was only just that Cromwell should have this pledge as the expedition would be 'wholly on account of His Majesty's interests'. Jephson was to 'endeavour to understand His Majesty's mind and intentions in these particulars', and to agree that it should be occupied by infantry, cavalry and ships, and returned when requested once all charges had been paid. He was to obtain information on the condition of the fortresses, their defensibility, and the ability of the inhabitants to pay for their upkeep before he agreed to anything.[36] The occupation of Bremen was thus considered as a serious option at this point, no doubt aided by the slowness of the Anglo-French campaign in Flanders. Bremen – unlike Dunkirk – was already in friendly hands and would not have to be conquered.

While Jephson was despatched to Sweden, Meadowe belatedly went to Denmark to urge Frederick to abandon his plans. He was to remind him that war would be 'of great hazard to the Protestants' cause especially at this time'. Nothing was of more advantage to Philip IV and Leopold, King of Hungary (Ferdinand III's son and heir) and would cause great disturbance to Baltic commerce. Cromwell nevertheless pledged himself to avoid war with Denmark and offered his services in mediation.[37] The ulterior motives do not make Cromwell's professions entirely hypocritical; he was shortly to refuse to dismember Denmark as the basis for the much-needed Swedish military alliance.

This surprising suggestion was made by Charles's special ambassador Baron Friesendorff, who arrived in London on 30 August/9 September with 'particular secrets which he would not trust to letters for fear of their being intercepted'.[38] He was to offer a partition of Denmark, with England acquiring the northern part of Jutland, positions on the Elbe and the Weser, and free access to the Sound via Swedish-occupied Elsinore and Copenhagen. Cromwell could also have East Friesland and as much of Westphalia as he could conquer from the local German rulers; in return Charles would consider an alliance with France and Portugal if Cromwell insisted on an anti-Habsburg campaign. The Dutch could be admitted later.[39] It was probably now that the Swedes relayed an offer of Iceland or Greenland – both Danish possessions.[40] At the very least Charles requested soldiers and ships to relieve the Danish siege of Gothenburg.[41] Cromwell would not trust Charles, quite apart from not having the men, money or inclination for such a large-scale occupation. He informed Friesendorff that 'for himself he desired no foreign conquests, but only desired that he might preserve his position within the Kingdom [England] since he had found that they would not help the English nation' as seen by the Hundred Years' War and Ireland.[42] Accordingly, he offered Friesendorff £30 000 and the right to recruit volunteers in the armed forces, the most which he could afford.[43]

Charles continued to express willingness for a new treaty, as in a paper delivered by Fleetwood and Friesendorff on 10/20 September.[44] The Swedish plans, however, entailed England conquering territory from an enemy rather than being presented with land already in Swedish hands such as Bremen. Disappointment with Sweden thus combined with financial difficulties in making the limited offer of £30 000 difficult to implement.[45] In these circumstances, a friendly ear was turned to Frederick III when he accepted Meadowe's offer of mediation and a formal alliance may have been considered.[46] The King assured that he would only ally with the Habsburgs if he was abandoned by all his coreligionists.[47]

The autumn of 1657 brought two new threats to Baltic peace – Charles' return from Poland and renewed Dutch involvement. Charles turned his attention to Denmark. En route, Jephson met him at Wismar and delivered Cromwell's proposals for assistance based on a lease of Bremen.[48] Charles replied by asking for urgent military assistance against Catholic attack in which he expected Jan Casimir, Alexis and Frederick to assist his enemies.[49] Jephson advised Cromwell overoptimistically that

Charles had so many enemies that he was likely to agree peace with Denmark despite Swedish anger with that country's perfidy.[50] The Council did not press the matter by sending new instructions to Meadowe and Jephson on what terms to offer and how to bring the two sides together. In these circumstances Charles, accepting Friesendorff's rebuff over a partition of Denmark, finally raised the question of Bremen.[51]

The Dutch had intended to coerce Portugal that summer in their dispute over Portuguese Brazil, but had been warned off by the English navy. Now imminent Dutch naval aid to Denmark was threatened, as Thurloe warned Meadowe in his request of 2/12 October to find out what men and money Frederick could expect from the Dutch.[52] Eighteen Dutch ships were off the Dogger Bank, raising the threat of Dutch naval assistance to Denmark and outright war in the Baltic between two English Protestant allies. Accordingly, a message was sent under 'absolute secrecy' to Admiral Montague warning that 'Sweden's affairs are in a most dangerous condition, left alone in the midst of very many powerful enemies'.[53] It is likely that the Dutch decision not to sail to the Sound was at least partly due to his presence. The English fleet served as a deterrent and thus aided Sweden in a less provocative way than the outright naval intervention which Charles wanted.

Charles was able to use Cromwell's failure to pay the promised £30 000 as an excuse for taking little notice of English diplomatic requests, despite Jephson's frantic appeals to Thurloe to send the money.[54] As Jephson realised, 'whatsoever the King shall act . . . that shall seem contrary to the desires or interest of the Protector shall be excused upon that account'.[55] The non-payment of the money was hardly Cromwell's fault, given the current crises in England where there was another breach with Parliament, military mutiny threatening, and Charles II 'at the waterside' expected to invade (using Dutch ships). As Thurloe vainly assured the King via his ambassador, payment was currently impossible and the seamen would have to be paid first.[56]

In December 1657, the States-General voted to promote an end to the Danish – Swedish War on the terms of Bromsebro (1645), which had secured Sweden's possession of the East bank of the Sound without the vast areas of Norway which Charles had since seized.[57] Cromwell could have attempted a joint approach to Sweden with the Dutch, but was preoccupied with internal crises. It is significant, however, that when he told Parliament on 25 January/4 February that Charles was 'a poor prince . . . driven into a corner' he still referred to the necessity to keep the Baltic open – which did not mean concurrence with all this excellent prince's ambitions.[58]

The commercial negotiations in London had also languished although an agreement here would have pleased Charles and was not as dangerous as joining in a partition of Denmark. In February 1658, the finally broke down and on 2/12 February the Swedes announced their departure in a complaining memorandum to the Protector. They protested that they had had to wait until July 1657 for talks to commence on violations of the 1654 treaty and had been held up ever sice by 'daily new and unexpected questions and instances . . . which like a chain to the multiplication of the links and circumnotation of vexations and troubles seemed to be endless'.[59] In reply, on 11/21 March, the English commissioners delivered their own list of complaints, saying that the Swedes had not arrived with the necessary powers and then not turned up by the original date for the talks, had dealt with cases one by one instead of in groups, had relied on Charles's orders rather than accepted international maritime law, and had interpreted how to proceed on damages differently from the way understood in 1654.[60] The English were as tough negotiators with the Swedes as with the similarly stalled Dutch treaty.

ENGLAND AND THE TREATY OF ROSKILDE: RESTRAINING SWEDEN

On 30 January/9 February, Charles took advantage of the ice to cross the frozen Sound and invade the Danish island of Funen. The Danes could not resist his battle-hardened troops as they advanced on Copenhagen, and the ice meant that the Dutch fleet could not intervene. He seemed able to impose what terms he liked, the only restraint possible coming from the local representatives of Denmark's allies – the English would-be mediator Meadowe, the Dutch ambassador Van Beuningen, and the French ambassador Terlon. The interests of England and France lay in using Charles against the Habsburgs, so they coordinated their efforts.

Meadowe pursued his original orders to mediate, and obtained Frederick's permission to join the Danish envoys at Charles's camp at Cogel. He wrote later that he

> began the introduction to a treaty, inviting His Majesty to a peace upon just satisfaction and securities and pressed for a suspension of arms . . . [Next day] the Danish commissioners gave in their project of Articles, the Swedish theirs; both of them monsters, the one 'in defectu' the other 'in excessu'. In fine, the French ambassador and I were forced to draw up a third project to see if we could find the medium.[61]

To exert more pressure, Charles resumed his march on Copenhagen. Meadowe rejected Charles's attempts to acquire the whole of defenceless Norway, 'as giving the Swede the whole and entire possession of the chief materials as masts, deals, pitch, tar, copper, and iron, needful for the arrayal and equippage of our ships, too great a treasure to be entrusted to one hand'.[62] Beuningen counselled Frederick to reject the terms and wait for Dutch help to arrive, but Meadowe's counsels prevailed; however steep the demands, the alternative could lead to an Anglo-Dutch naval clash or England having to show Charles that it put free passage of the Sound above all Cromwell's fine words about being his faithful ally. The States-General reaffirmed their support for the situation at the time of Bromsebro (on the advice of the French).[63]

The final terms reached at Roskilde granted Sweden the province of Scania (the East bank of the Sound), together with parts of Norway's coast north of Gothenburg and the central Norwegian province of Trondheim. Norway was cut in two giving the Swedes access to the Atlantic, thus cancelling out her reliance on a friendly power controlling the Skaggerak for access to the Atlantic. Most of Denmark escaped and she retained equal control of the Sound tolls with Sweden. Neither party could ally itself with its ally's enemies and hostile warships were banned from the Sound. Thus if Sweden was at war with the Dutch, Denmark could not admit Dutch ships to the Sound to assist places like Danzig. However, Meadowe had secured a moderation of this last Article from the Swedes' original intention to ban all foreign warships.[64] Meadowe's sense of his own importance is apparent, but he had done his country a considerable service. His determination was particularly infuriating to Charles, as shown by his attempt to bully Denmark into accepting his original version in June. This showed Meadowe's correct estimation of the worth of his goodwill.[65]

The terms of Roskilde had been moderated, but still left Charles the master of the Baltic and Denmark likely to seek revenge as soon as he was sure of Dutch (and English?) acquiescence. Another coalition against Sweden was a virtual certainty, Charles's overweening strength and ambition meaning that Brandenburg, Poland and Russia might assist his current enemies though with less chance of success than they had in 1700–21. Cromwell misjudged the position in thinking that the Baltic peace would turn the local powers against the Habsburgs.

Two factors can be cited in Cromwell's defence:

1. Meadowe, acting on instructions drawn up in Council, moderated Charles's gains on crucial points. Cromwell rejected all offers of Danish territory.
2. Due to the Spanish War, Cromwell could not afford to send a squadron of ships to the Sound to overawe Sweden in February 1658. This should be borne in mind when remembering the circumstances of 1658 as opposed to the time of the joint Anglo-Dutch naval demonstration against Charles in 1659.

THE LAST MONTHS OF CROMWELL'S RULE: HOPE DEFERRED

The settlement at Roskilde was illusory, due to Charles's restless ambitions as much as Dutch and Danish revanchism. Charles continued to seek English assistance but Meadowe was not fooled. On 28 February/8 March, the day after the signing, the King accepted a goodwill gift of Meadowe's sword and promised to use it against the Habsburgs. Meadowe commented cynically, 'I wish he does not use it against the Elector of Brandenburg.'[66] He also promised to send 3–4000 men to England if a Royalist–Spanish invasion took place.[67]

At this point, Thurloe drew up the 'Heads of a Treaty' for a closer military alliance with Sweden, showing how the English regime wished the alliance to proceed. They are dated 25 March/4 April in the *Thurloe State Papers*. The plan would tie Charles down to an offensive and defensive alliance against 'the Kings of Spain, Hungary [Leopold, Emperor from July] and Poland, the House of Austria, and all others who shall adhere to them or assist them directly or indirectly . . . or shall molest the free navigation and commerce either in the Baltic Sea or the [Atlantic] Ocean'. Sweden would invade the Empire in reprisal for Habsburg violations of the Treaty of Osnabruck, assisted by an unnumbered force of English soldiers raised at Charles's expense. In return, Cromwell would send a fleet against the King of Spain as soon as convenient, attacking his commerce with the West Indies to damage his financial supplies. France, the United Provinces, and such others as should be agreed upon would be invited to join.[68] This would obtain England a firm ally; Charles would be too preoccupied to attack Brandenburg, the Danes or the Dutch. Thurloe's plan also envisaged a warning to Charles that this league was the only way to offset an attack by all his enemies, Protestant and Catholic alike – an exaggeration, but containing some truth. The planned commander for the estimated force of 20 000 allies to be sent into Germany would be the Landgrave William of Hesse-Cassel, the most militant of the Protestant German princes. He was probably the 'Northern prince' to whom Cromwell sent a letter in March commending his zeal for the Protestant cause.[69]

The best practical sign of support which Cromwell could send was the £30 000 owed to Charles, but Meadowe was still pleading in vain for it to Thurloe in June.[70] Some soldiers were sent to Sweden, but they proved to be of poor quality and 'find not things answer promise nor expectation, which makes them mutiny or run away to the dishonour of our nation'.[71]

Ominously for his behaviour towards his Protestant neighbours, in April Charles announced his decision to seek peace with Jan Casimir. Frederick William of Brandenburg had meanwhile signed a treaty with Leopold, in which Poland joined, for an offensive alliance aimed principally at expelling Sweden from Pomerania. This caused concern in London and Meadowe was instructed to go to Charles's peace conference with Poland at Braunsberg.[72] His new instructions for the conference told him to ensure that 'nothing be negotiated between the two said kings to the prejudice and disadvantage of this state, either in honour, trade, or commerce', and to join the party of those seeking to exclude the Habsburgs (Poland's chief ally) from the treaty.[73] Thurloe had underlined one sentence to show its importance: 'everyone who is imprudent and heedless is able to excite quarrels, but very few are those who know how to ally and suppress them'.[74] This was an ironic comment on Charles's own character and applied to his relations with the Dutch and Denmark rather than with Poland.

The Swedes' terms for invading Germany remained unacceptable and Thurloe wrote angrily to Jephson on 26 March/ 5 April:

> His ministers here propound things almost impossible for us to do, namely that His Highness should land an army in Westphalia and pay him a certain amount of money for carrying on his war with the King of Hungary in Germany . . . without being instructed, for aught I can perceive, to agree to anything that hath a reciprocity in it. His Highness is willing to join him in this league against the House of Austria and give him the best assistance he is able, and also to draw in other princes and states of the Protestant party.[75]

The only practical advance was made by Cromwell's ambassador in the United Provinces, George Downing, who averted the danger of a Dutch–Swedish war over ratification of the Treaty of Elbling.

The costly English occupation of Dunkirk prevented any large-scale English assistance to Sweden. In any case, the peaceful settlement of the Imperial election averted the danger of war in Germany, France and Sweden acting as joint guarantors of a local league of Protestant princes excluding Charles's enemy Frederick William. Losing interest in Germany, Charles turned on Denmark again in August. It was clear that he intended to complete the conquest which had been averted by the Treaty of Roskilde, presenting the English regime with an ugly dilemma. Charles showed his obsession with conquest to the real detriment of national interests by stirring up his country's enemies. The scene was set for that choice of outright support or armed restraint of Sweden which Cromwell had narrowly avoided the previous winter, but he died before he had to make the choice. It is probable that he would have sought to protect the freedom of the Sound above good relations with his ally, as his previous utterances on the subject suggest.

If Cromwell had lived another year the pragmatism of his Swedish policy would probably have been much more apparent. Even before the 1658–9 Sound crisis it is apparent that English policy was basically consistent, centring on the need to maintain access to naval supplies and a healthy fear of Dutch–Swedish confrontation. The Spanish War merely exacerbated these factors, while making any large-scale naval demonstration in the Baltic difficult. Cromwell's primary concern was to use Charles X for the benefit of English foreign policy, as Charles's was to obtain another ally against the Dutch and the Danes. This does not excuse Cromwell from a basic misconception of Charles's personality and aims, however limited the results of this were. Charles X, like Gustavus Adolphus and Charles XII, was as much an object of fear to Protestant as to Catholic neighbours. Cromwell sought to recall him to his Protestant duty, relying on an inaccurate assessment of his great predecessor, and seemed unduly surprised at his lack of success.

15 Cromwell and Russia, 1653-8

Commercial, political and military motives coincided and intermingled in Cromwell's approach to the Russian ruler, Czar Alexis. The Russians had always been noted for an inherent xenophobia towards Europeans which broke out at times into acts of overt hostility, and the English merchants' relative immunity from this since relations had been established between the two countries in the 1550s ceased with the execution of Charles I. As a demonstration of his displeasure after the act of regicide (egged on no doubt by certain of his advisers who disliked Protestants), the Czar had expelled the English merchants from Moscow and ended their right to travel around the country from their entrepôt at Archangel, thus placing their efforts to trade under severe disadvantages. In addition, he had decided against recognising the Commonwealth and by 1653 was one of the few European rulers to be still refusing to negotiate with England on terms of equality. He was supposed to be influenced by Royalist officers who had taken up residence at his Court as military advisers (principally to strengthen Russian forces for the war against Poland), although it is now clear that an alleged call by him for an anti-regicide conference to arrange an alliance against England is a Royalist forgery, which in any case was not in existence until later in the decade.[1]

As a remote and relatively weak country Russia did not pose any threat to England and was therefore of no immediate concern to the Rump or to Cromwell, but as part of the Republic's efforts to obtain its recognition throughout Europe it was inevitable that in due course some official effort would be made to reverse the existing Russian position. However, the Czar did not merit enough English concern for the Republic to send an official representative to Moscow, and as the Muscovy Company had adopted the role of intermediary between England and Russia in the past, so now its concern to have its privileges restored meant that the ambassador designate would be one of its own men instead of the choice of the current

English government. Cromwell and his advisers had more important matters of domestic and foreign policy to consider, and their role would inevitably be less important than that of the company who possessed the necessary 'expert knowledge' of Russia. Cromwell, however, even more than his predecessors, showed great concern regarding the satisfaction of all outstanding demands for justice against foreign countries on the part of his own nationals. Moreover, Russia had joined the league of powers against England's new ally Sweden and was seeking to achieve the reconquest of Ingria and Carelia, the provinces at the head of the Gulf of Finland, which Sweden had seized during the 'Time of Troubles' to isolate it from the Baltic. As an enemy of an English ally, Russia was of some concern to Cromwell and his government who were bound to take the opportunity of the Muscovy Company's embassy to encourage a Russian–Swedish peace. It should be remembered, though, that as yet Sweden had not assumed the vital importance as an ally which it was to achieve after the outbreak of the Anglo-Spanish War, so its external problems were not yet of acute concern to the Protector.

At the time of Cromwell's seizure of power the Muscovy Company was deciding to send an envoy to Moscow to solicit the restoration of privileges, and given the factors mentioned above Cromwell was bound to consider their efforts worth supporting though not vital enough to be worth supplementing by his own envoy. Instead, the company's envoy was to be given official instructons by Secretary Thurloe and required to report back to him on his progress – a sign that although the embassy was a company affair the State considered it to be its business as well as the City's. The envoy chosen, William Prideaux, may indeed have been related to the Attorney-General, Edmund Prideaux, and as such chosen partly because he would be acceptable to the Government (much as the men chosen to represent the Levant Company on a similar state-backed mission to the Ottoman Empire, Richard Salwey and Colonel Richard Lawrence, had official connections). However, no formal state instructions to Prideaux have survived and we cannot be entirely certain that he was given any, at least not in the same detail as those issued to his successor Bradshaw in 1657, although his actions in Russia show that he was ordered to supplement his company's commercial demands by trying to obtain recognition of Cromwell's regime and to mention English hopes for peace between Russia and Sweden. The only mention of the Swedish War of which we have a record is Prideaux's question to the Czar at an audience as to whether he could be informed about the 'real motives' of the war,[2] but it is likely that if Alexis had responded well to this overture Prideaux would have gone on to encourage him to make peace. It is clear, however, that he was given orders concerning the need to make Alexis recognise the Protectorate unequivocally, since at his first audience he read out a clear and carefully prepared explanation showing how the new regime had been established with full popular support and how the rest of Europe had accepted the change in government without demur.[3] On 26 May/5 June, a petition of the English merchants trading with Russia was read in Council. It was presumably concerned with the embassy and was referred to Lambert, Cooper, Jones, Montague and Wolseley (the first three of whom were concerned with matters of trade). Cooper read the English translation of the Protector's letter to the Czar, which was approved.[4]

Prideaux informed Thurloe of his departure from Tilbury in a convoy of three Muscovy Company vessels for Archangel on 17/27 July 1654,[5] and arrived in Russia on 20/30 August.[6] The community of English merchants there was evidently apprehensive of its position and glad of the presence of an official representative from London. Prideaux himself was worried enough about official Russian ill-will to inform his 'go-between' with the Governor, the scribe 'Barbraekin', that he would not leave for Moscow until the vessels had finished loading and started their return journey. The merchants considered Prideaux's presence 'very convenient and necessary' as his being there dissuaded the port authorities from imposing any further obstructions on their trade[7] – a sign of the benefit to be gained by both sides from Prideaux's mission which showed official English concern with this recently forgotten outpost of English trade. Prideaux sent the Governor a query about the current restrictions on English trade, requesting the ending of undue delays on export and the right to resume sending English goods further inland from Archangel if they were unsold there.[8] Under the current position, the Russian ban on trade further inland meant that the English would have to accept whatever low price their partners offered for their goods or go home with them unsold, and similarly accept the need to pay whatever extortionate prices the Russians charged them for exports.[9] The Governor replied that the English could still export the same goods as other Europeans and pay the same customs but each group of merchants would have to leave the country at the end of the specific trading-mission for which they had come, although unable to maintain a permanent, manned trading-post with 'stockpiles' of goods at Archangel like other Europeans.[10] The logical end of these restrictions – crippling for English trade – would be the total eclipse of England as a trading-partner in Russia, and the fact that the Governor gave way on these crucial points within a week (subject to Imperial approval of his decision) suggests that he had been ordered to 'try it on' Prideaux and give way if necessary. What is clear is that the Russians would probably have been able to cripple English trade had not an ambassador been sent out from London, and that Prideaux's ability to claim that he spoke for Cromwell as well as the company provided an added impetus to them to give way. Cromwell could not indulge in 'gunboat diplomacy' with Russia to enforce his point as he did with Portugal, but the evidence which Prideaux's mission showed of official government concern was enough to overcome obstacles in the way of trade which the existing 'factory' at Archangel could not do for themselves.

Incidentally, Prideaux's reports to Thurloe show that he was no more impressed with the behaviour of the Russians than Giles Fletcher had been sixty years earlier, and that the English embassy now as then regarded the natives as being little better than savages. He wrote of his first impressions at Archangel that the Russians he had met were 'subtle and crafty, but are very pusillanimous. They are very superstitious and ignorant of learning, and in part are held so by the Prince . . . 'Tis said the men are very addicted [to] . . . the abominable vice of Sodomy and in those vices [are] not inferior to the Turks and Italians.'[11]

Arriving in Moscow on 5 February 1655 (OS) after a journey lasting a month, Prideaux was immediately required to commence impressing on the Russians that the Commonwealth must not be treated as in any way inferior to other European states – an attitude which ran considerable risks of leading to disaster and even his own detention, given the notorious lack of Russian respect for such niceties of Western behaviour as diplomatic immunity. The 'chancellor' sent to inform Prideaux that 'I could not be received in the same manner as the ministers of kings and great princes', and when an audience was agreed upon at an hour's notice it was suddenly cancelled without reason. Prideaux was told that the letter which Cromwell's government had sent with him to be presented to the Czar did not include all his titles and was unacceptable. These minor procedural wrangles and rudenesses to ambassadors were normal practice in Russia and Prideaux was calm enough to take them in his stride. This was rewarded when the planned audience took place on 16 February, a day late, and the Czar received him in the company of his advisers 'Morosene' (i.e. his brother-in-law Boris Morozov) and 'Elya Danelovitch' (his father-in-law Ilya Miloslavsky). After Cromwell's official letter had been presented the Czar explained that commissioners had been appointed to hear Prideaux's business. There had been concern over what title Alexis would use for Cromwell, technically neither a King nor a Prince and hence likely to be regarded as undeserving of full honours. Alexis 'asked after the good health of the Protector, using this word in Russian, "how is the good health of Oliver *Utaditela* (that is to say sole communicator or director)'.

In his formal reply, Prideaux informed the Czar of the past events in England and their justification, with a warning that the end of monarchy had by no means diminished England's power or prestige and hence Cromwell's ambassador would not accept inferior treatment. This message was presumably agreed by the Council in advance on Thurloe's recommendation, though there is no record of it. 'The great Council of the land hath changed the government of State, elected and established the most excellent and most prudent Protector,' he explained. This was not strictly correct, but was designed to give an impression of the legality of the new regime in terms acceptable to a Czar whose own throne rested on his father's election by the *Zemsky Sobor* of 1613. The Muscovy Company had presumably informed Thurloe of this episode in Russian history to point out the parallel between Cromwell and the Romanovs, both of the new regimes being 'parvenues' touchy about their rights. The usurpation was excused on the grounds of 'the many and great abuses perpetrated in England in the last king's reign, without hope of redress so that for remedy and prevenion of further damage to the public weal' he had been replaced. This change had been based on 'the unanimous consent of all degrees and conditions of persons' to a new 'perfect and solid government', which moreover all the principal powers of Europe had accepted. Cromwell had 'composed those differences between it [England] and the lords States General of the United Provinces, renewed alliance with the crown of Sweden and the kings of France and Spain, with many other princes, potentates, and republics of Christendom that by their ambassadors, agents, and ministers have sent to congratulate his Highness for his assumption of his pre-eminent dignity, to procure his amity and friendship, and some of them his protection'. In 1649 Alexis could have claimed that he was in tune with most of Europe in deploring regicide, but now it was made clear that he was out of touch with common opinion among his neighbours and trading partners. He was, however, flattered that Cromwell 'hath in the midst of these affairs been mindful of your Imperial Majesty for the goodwill borne to your Imperial person and the ancient good intelligence and correspondency betwixt your Majesty's renowned predecessors of famous memory, your Imperial self, and our nation'. The stress on 'nation' added to the argument that the Russians had long dealt with the English, who as a people had rejected the Stuarts; the Royalists were thus isolated exiles who were representatives of nobody. Accordingly, the message concluded, Cromwell desired that the privileges granted to 'a particular company of our merchants' be restored.[12]

The business of the mission was discussed when Prideaux met the 'chancellor' on 6/16 March. He relayed the Protector and Council's 'wonder' at the English being restricted to Archangel, 'who were the first to introduce the commerce to this country and had continued it so many years to the weal and great benefit of this empire'. The other Europeans now had an unjust advantage as they 'were modern to these parts'; if any specific misdeeds of individual Englishmen had annoyed Alexis, they should be enumerated and justice would be done. Prideaux also warned that he expected the Czar to rise from his throne to greet him at his audience, as occurred for other European ambassadors. The usual honours were granted to English ambassadors elsewhere, and 'His Highness reasonably cannot expect less from his Imperial Majesty as heretofore . . . I did not advance this as a complaint but as an advertisement'. A protest was made at the Russian insistence that no swords be worn at audiences, as they were the norm at 'the greatest courts in Christendom . . . such actions are accounted very ill in princes' courts . . . such persons as have been sent by these emperors into England have found a clean contrary courtesy and civility'.[13] This attitude of Prideaux's is to be compared with the warnings given by Cromwell's representatives to the first Venetian envoy to enter republican England in 1652 and to France's ambassador, Bordeaux, over how to address his King's letters to the Protector in 1654. However, a show of confidence did no harm in seeking to impress the Czar that Cromwell would stand no nonsense and that his wishes should be met. Prideaux also enquired about the 'real motives' for the war which Alexis had now mounted against Poland, his supposed ally against Cromwell's new ally Sweden. Alexis's aggression could be taken to mean a closer relationship with Sweden, whose new monarch Charles X was not yet treated by Cromwell with terms of effusive friendship (significantly, this arose from his need of an ally against Spain and the Empire later in 1655), but was perceived to be young, restless and determined on aggression. In fact the Russian–Swedish War arose almost entirely from a desire to regain territory ceded at the humiliating Treaty of Stolbovo in 1619 after the final failure of the Poles' attempt to conquer Russia, but it might, for all Prideaux knew, presage a new attitude to Sweden as well as Poland and affect English naval interests in the Baltic.[14]

At the Imperial audience on 11/21 March, Alexis's attitude to Prideaux showed that his protests had had some effect. He 'moved up a little from his throne and said that I should remember him to *Utaditela*, to whom he wished good health', while his attendants removed their hats 'which ceremony for certain would not have been done had I not made the discourse above mentioned to the Chancellor'.[15] This concluded his dealings with the Czar, but there were still some frustrations ahead akin to those suffered frequently by seventeenth-century ambassadors to Muscovy. He was refused permission to leave as soon as possible for Riga, capital of Livonia, though this was no doubt primarily due to the fact that he would have to traverse the war zone and the suspicious Russians feared what

he might report of their activities to their enemies. He warned
the court the 'his Highness cannot take well my detention',
but in a letter to Thurloe he feared that he might have to stay
in Moscow for four or five months (the duration of the fighting
season). He also blamed the efforts of Royalist exiles serving
at the Russian court, who may have been responsible for Alexis's
apparent belief in the truth of stories about 'some alteration
in the affairs of England'.[16] Possibly the Royalists had got wind
of Penruddock's rebellion. Some of Prideaux's Russian servants
were arrested, at which he protested, and there were indications that the presence of guards around his residence to
'protect' him and the absence of the Swedish ambassador who
had been expected to visit him were not entirely coincidental.
Prideaux saw through the Russian excuses as intended to
'colour their incivility',[17] and also blamed the Patriarch for being
'extremely . . . averse to all strangers, but more to our nation
than any other'.[18] However, in describing the latter as an old
man and an ignorant peasant's son Prideaux was clearly showing
that he had confused the current incumbent, the youngish
and dynamic Nikon, with the previous Patriarch (Joseph) who
had died a few years earlier. He was on more sure ground in
suspecting his interpreter Hebden, a man long resident in
Russia, of being 'more Russian then English in affections'.[19]

The chancellor's reply arrived on 22 June/2 July. It named
a few specific misdeeds by the English, in particular the fact
that some roguish merchants had used the names of men
empowered to trade by Czar Michael as a cover when undertaking secret trading and exporting goods without paying
customs duties. Various debts also remained unpaid.[20] It was
clear, however, that these complaints were in the nature of
excuses, and Prideaux laid the blame on Alexis' encouragement
by exiled English and Scottish officers that 'Charles Stuart may
come to the crown of England and His Imperial Majesty receive
damage for his correspondence with His Highness'.[21] He replied that despite promises nothing had been done about lifting
the restrictions, and warned that he had heard about the
chancellor telling the arrested Russian servants that their crime
was serving Cromwell's ambassador.[22] He wrote angrily to
Thurloe that the Czar, 'formerly of a good natural disposition,
has been corrupted by his education and is now much given
to avarice, cruelty, self-wilfulness, and esteeming much more

of himself than is in him'. His father-in-law Miloslavsky was 'of
base and mean heart, averse to strangers and particularly the
English', and the ministers were 'generally much hated by the
generalty of the people of all conditions, by whom much evil
was spoken of them' – remarks with much truth in them, given
the recent (1648) disturbances against the misrule of Morozov,
but principally inspired by frustrated dislike.[23]

No further contact with the Czar's court followed and
Prideaux was no doubt glad to leave Moscow unmolested. The
Czar was obviously awaiting news of events in England and
would not yet believe that Cromwell's regime was permanent,
but at least he had been forced to take notice of the Republic
and had condescended to receive a regicide ambassador. The
English were to remain restricted to Archangel, a measure
whereby other countres' ambassadors concurred with the Czar's
Royalist advisers for reasons of commercial jealousy. However,
Alexis was to be reconsidered by the Protectorate once the
outbreak of the Swedish–Polish War in 1656 gave the Baltic
region a new importance which was intensified by Spain's
hostility.

The danger to Sweden from a coalition of the United Provinces, Brandenburg, Poland and Denmark in 1656–7 could
also be hazardous for English naval supplies in the Baltic. Given
the war with Spain, England was in greater need of the usual
supplies than before, in addition to which the defeat of Charles
X might lead the Dutch (formal allies but commercial rivals)
to control the Baltic and ban English shipping. The threat of
commercial hostility stimulating a Dutch–Spanish alliance was
also present, apart from the fact that if Charles X could be
encouraged to invade the Empire it would distract Ferdinand
III from sending money or men to aid the impoverished and
ineffective Spanish war effort. Undoubtedly Cromwell was concerned at the threat to the current Protestant champion in the
Baltic, the heir of Gustavus Adolphus, from a Catholic-inspired
coalition, but he was equally concerned for his own interests,
in protecting his supplies and in staging a 'diversion' from the
main theatre of the Anglo-Spanish War. Accordingly, a new
diplomatic offensive began, with the enthusiastic Protector even
considering sending out the financier Sir Christopher Pack
as a roving ambassador to the north German Protestants to
forge a coalition against the Emperor.[24] Councillor Fleetwood's

brother George, an officer in the Swedish service, was able to assure his masters that Cromwell would send twenty ships to the Baltic if needed (February 1657),[25] and rumours reached France of a loan of 200 000 crowns to Sweden.[26] Debating the crisis on 5/15 March 1657, the English Council decided to send an ambassador to Moscow to assess Alexis' attitude to Sweden, which had occupied Ingria and Carelia in order to cut Russia off from the Baltic in the 'Time of Troubles' and was now the subject of a Russian attack while she was preoccupied elsewhere. This decision was apparently the result of a meeting between Thurloe and George Fleetwood, currently in London on his master's behalf.[27] A week later the envoy was announced as Richard Bradshaw, the Republic's consul in Hamburg where the intrigues by Royalist residents had ensured that only a trusted and competent envoy would be chosen to occupy that difficult post.[28] (He was also a cousin of the president of the court which had tried the late King.) He was no fool and was thus unwilling to take on this perilous journey to a Royalist-infested court. He informed Thurloe when he received his letter that the choice 'put me into a straight between the danger of such an employment and my duty to obey. If that great prince had owned [recognised] our state or made any overture to the intended mediation, I need not then to question my welcome . . . it's to be doubted he will slight the mediation.' He would have preferred to hear the Czar's acceptance of his mission before he set out, fearing the effect on Cromwell's reputation in Moscow, if, like Prideaux, he had to suffer 'the affronts put upon me by [my] state's own [Royalist] subjects'.[29]

Bradshaw, however, finally accepted the duty of going to Moscow on 12/22 May and asked that the distinguished Scottish traveller and thinker John Dury, formerly resident in Prussia and Cromwell's ambassador to the Swiss, be allowed to accompany him.[30] In his instructions he was told to assure Alexis of Cromwell's 'particular affection towards him and the nation with whom the English were the first that ever traded him from this part of the world by the Northern [White] Sea'. Cromwell would be very content if Alexis would mediate between his belligerent neighbours Sweden, Denmark and Poland and 'thereby stop the effusion of blood and the miseries which do inevitably ensue upon war between so great and powerful princes'. He was not asked directly to initiate any mediation on Cromwell's behalf (which he might well have refused to do), but Thurloe wrote that Bradshaw was to say instead that Cromwell had heard that overtures to peace were under way and offer England's services in 'so good a work'. In particular, Bradshaw was to stress that peace would ensure 'great trade and riches' to Russia by the reopening of Sweden's ports on the Baltic to Russian trade, providing easier routes to the West than Archangel. He was to remind the Orthodox ruler of the fact that it was no desire of the Protestant Charles X 'to force consciences, as is that of the Polonian King, which if it [Catholicism] get footing in his dominion by Polish Jesuits, will not fail to work alterations'.[31] Jesuit missionary work had done much to inflame the Orthodox Ukrainians, whose resentment had caused a rebellion against Poland in 1648–54 of which the Czar had made full use in his efforts to win back the Ukraine for Russia. Thurloe was evidently aware of this, probably through the contacts of Dury and his friend and fellow-thinker Samuel Hartlib with the Polish Protestant community at Lieszno in the western Ukraine, led by the educationalist Jan Comenius. Indeed, the Protectorate was shortly to receive Polish Protestant refugees (persecuted by the Polish King for alleged collaboration with Charles X during his invasion of Poland) in England.[32] Bradshaw was to go to Swedish-held Riga and proceed to further without a safe-conduct to Moscow; if he did not get one, he was to do his best by correspondence with the ambassadors there. He was in any case to repeat Prideaux's protests about the Czar's withdrawal of English privileges and seek their restoration.[33]

Arriving in Riga on 29 May/8 June, Bradshaw sent an envoy on to Moscow and settled down to await his safe-conduct. The inhabitants reminded him of the 'great miseries and calamities' their city had suffered by the recent invasion of the savage Muscovites.[34] In July a Russian envoy came to meet him at Mitau, but claimed that Cromwell's letter to the Czar was improperly addressed (a usual excuse for delays) and demanded an account of his entourage and a copy of his credentials. Bradshaw was affronted by the accompanying letter from the Russian chancellor, which 'dealt most uncivilly with me after their rude and proud manner', and asked permission to send a letter directly to the Czar as he believed him to be more inclined to peace with Sweden than his councillors. He gloomily believed that 'such a beginning promises no better issue to the negotiation', and privately considered Alexis' grandiose titles 'arrogant if not blasphemous'.[35] A messenger duly left for Moscow, but the governor of the nearest Russian border-post insisted on replacing him en route with one of his own men lest he had the plague[36] and Bradshaw dared not proceed himself without a minister, interpreter or doctor, whatever the urgency of his mission.[37] In December, Bradshaw was still awaiting a reply from Moscow, the Duke of Courland having assured him that one could have been sent in half the time had the Czar considered the matter important. The excuse might have been the fault in Alexis' titles as listed in Bradshaw's credentials, or so the Livonian administration told the frustrated ambassador.[38] He assured Thurloe in February 1658 that, given the chance, 'nothing shall be wanting on my part . . . that the mediation may yet take effect for . . . the advantage of the Protestant cause',[39] but the matter was out of his hands. Sweden had now invaded Denmark and Bradshaw reckoned that Alexis was awaiting the outcome of Charles X's campaign, in the expectation that he would be defeated and Russia would have no more need to fear a Swedish attack (or to desire mediation).[40] The Swedes, however, crossed the Baltic ice and marched on Copenhagen and Bradshaw was accordingly sent permission to proceed to Moscow.[41] In the meantime, Cromwell's other Baltic envoy Philip Meadowe, in the Swedish camp in Denmark, was doing his best to mollify the terms which Charles was seeking to impose on Denmark, and Bradshaw's mission was increasingly peripheral to the English attempts to safeguard her position in the Baltic. Charles's stunning victory also diminished the threat he faced from Poland and Brandenburg, while the Dutch (encouraged by an English fleet watching their own as they considered sending aid to Denmark) backed away from conflict.[42] Bradshaw had still received no formal word from Moscow, as opposed to provincial officials on the Livonian border, and therefore decided to call off his mission. By 28 February/8 March he was back in Konigsberg in Prussia, writing that he considered success impossible so he was returning to Hamburg to look after his neglected consulate.[43] Thurloe did not pursue the matter.

16 Cromwell, the City and Trade: Venice and the Turks

The Protectorate is generally regarded as a return to cautious pragmatism after the heady days of the 'saintly' experiment which had followed the dissolution of the Rump. The failure of General Harrison's alternative to rule by the Commons, namely rule by a nominated assembly of Saints who were supposed to be prime exemplars of godliness, had failed as Lambert and his supporters had predicted. Instead, a form of 'limited' monarchy was set up under Britain's first written constitution. A return to the nearest possible equivalent of the good old Elizabethan constitution was accompanied by a general desire for a return to other old values, such as law and order and low taxation, after the upheavals of the 1640s. That this could not be established was due to a variety of reasons, not least the power and opinions of the Army on which (instead of on precedent) the power of the Lord Protector ultimately rested. After the recent crises Cromwell sought a return to peace, conciliation and order in civil affairs, and even his foreign policy (which provided a use for his restless armed forces) was curtailed throughout his rule by the restraints imposed by finance.

Buttressing the established order of society naturally included the promotion of trade and mercantile prosperity, although close links with the City leadership were inhibited by Cromwell's sense of priorities (e.g. war with a continental Catholic power), his position as a military 'dictator' which inhibited trust, and expectations that his regime might well fall to one of the many Royalist or republican plots against it. It might well be worthless to invest heavily in a man who could be assassinated or deposed and who, moreover, was notoriously hard-pressed to pay his debts. The Army and Navy swallowed up a vast proportion of the regime's annual income, which Parliament was able to curtail drastically in 1654 by the expedient of asserting its right to control ordinary and extraordinary taxation.[1] At the height of Cromwell's military reputation abroad, in 1657–8, he was refused loans by the majority in the City and had to pay his army in Flanders through subsidies from his unwilling French ally.

Apart from this lack of confidence, Cromwell's links with the City were limited to a few personnel with personal connections, such as his Secretary of State Thurloe's brother-in-law Martin Noell and the latter's friend Thomas Povey, Alderman Robert Tichborne, Sir Thomas Vyner the goldsmith, and Sir Christopher Pack. Accordingly, little notice was taken of some suggestions which might have drastically improved prosperity, such as Lambe's proposal for a national bank and Captain Limbery's for a system of maritime insurance.[2] The main initiative which Cromwell took was the formation of the Committee (or Council) for Trade, on 12/22 July 1655. The members consisted of the four Treasury commissioners; Maurice Thompson; Martin Noell, Thurloe's brother-in-law; Lord Chief Justice Oliver St John; Councillors Philip Jones, Sir Gilbert Pickering and Sir Charles Wolseley; Thomas Chaloner, a former leader of the Rump (later excluded); Lord Mayor Sir Christopher Pack; Alderman Riccard; Captain Henry Hatsell (a leading Cromwellian from Plymouth); Denis Bond (a leading merchant, from Dorchester); George Foxcroft; Sir Henry Blunt; Sir Job Harvey (excluded); and Mr Upton.

The principal concern of the Protectorate was national security, and for this accurate and comprehensive intelligence was essential. As a result, the position of English mercantile consuls in the Mediterranean was important in providing information for Secretary Thurloe, who could rely on the trading companies' representatives instead of paying his own agent. The Levant Company was particularly important, having acted effectively as the Government's local delegates in political as well as commercial matters since the first mission to the Ottoman court in 1583. As a result the Government and the company cooperated (sometimes uneasily) over the question of an English representative at Constantinople, as has been discussed earlier. Significantly, it was the company's representative in Constantinople in 1653, Sir Thomas Bendish (a suspected Royalist), who got the better of the new emissary Major Richard Lawrence and was eventually allowed to keep his post. Meanwhile, the Secretary and his employers continued to rely on the intelligence submitted to them by the mercantile consuls in Mediterranean ports, men such as Richard Aldworth at Marseilles, Longland at Leghorn, and Bretton at Smyrna, whose reports appear in the Thurloe Papers throughout the period.

The restoration of national prestige after the Government's recent neglect of English interest was a concern both of the Rump and of the Protector. In practical terms, 'showing the flag' by English warships in the Mediterranean served to decrease the risk of piracy and other acts of disrespect both by Christian and Turkish shipping. The commercial disputes with France since 1647 had resulted in frequent attacks on mercantile ships in the Mediterranean, a problem exacerbated by Dutch attacks during the war of 1652–4. Hostility towards the Commonwealth by some English residents in ports such as Leghorn was complemented by a lack of fear of English reprisals by such rulers as Grand Duke Ferdinand of Tuscany, the latter having done nothing to assist vice-admirals Badiley and Appleton during or after their defeat by a Dutch squadron in 1652,[3] and having allowed the Dutch *White Elephant* to plunder an English ship in Leghorn harbour early in 1654. The 'Barbary' pirates of Algiers and Tunis, always a menace to Christian shipping, had not been chastened by an English expedition since Mansell's in 1621, Blake having failed to intimidate Algiers into releasing any prisoners in 1651, although captives in Algiers had been ransomed and a promise of no future enslavements obtained by a Parliamentary ambassador, Edmund Casson, in 1646.[4] Indeed, the only English governmental expedition into the Mediterranean in recent years had been Penn and Blake's unsuccessful search for Prince Rupert's Royalist fleet in the summer of 1651, an expedition which had taken a number of French prizes and obtained the release of the arrested English consul at Tunis, Boothouse.[5] Some such expedition to overawe actual and potential enemies was advisable after the Government's lack of interest in the Mediterranean during the Dutch War, and this in turn provided another reason why Cromwell should continue friendly relations with Spain while France remained hostile.

The part Blake's expedition played in English relations with France and Spain has already been discussed. His fleet was intended to take French shipping in pursuit of mercantile reprisals, and it was fortunate that he missed the Duke of

Guise's expedition to Naples. He duly reprovisioned at Leghorn on 21/31 December, and despite reports in London did not demand financial compensation from the Grand Duke.[6] Spanish ports in Sicily were important to his other target, a demonstration of strength against North African pirate bases. Tunis was a particular target after Boothouse's treatment. His exact orders are not known but the general tenor is clear from his actions; Cromwell's cousin Sir Oliver Fleming, Master of Ceremonies, assured the Venetian ambassador Paulucci that he was 'to take a high tone and use force if his demands are refused'.[7] His expedition coincided with the expected despatch of shipping by the North African powers to assist their Ottoman overlords' siege of Candia, the last important Venetian stronghold on Crete. The Venetians had been pressing for English naval assistance and the admiral's presence in Italian waters provided an opportunity to carry out such an action. His correspondence shows that in January, while refuelling at Leghorn, his intention was to attack either Tunis or Tripoli and that he looked to Providence as well as instructions to provide him with a target.[8] Once he heard a rumour that Barbary shipping was gathering to assist the Ottomans, in Crete, he decided to aid them.[9]

Unfortunately for Venice, the report proved false. Instead, Blake arrived off Tunis on 8/18 February to demand the release of some sailors captured on board the *Princess*, got nowhere, and prospected the chances of attacking Porto Farina before withdrawing to Cagliari (Sardinia) to reprovision.[10] On 4/14 April he managed to destroy nine Turkish ships at Porto Farina and overwhelm the defenders' guns on shore,[11] a substantial military achievement, but the practical result for English captives was nil as the Dey, secure in Tunis, still refused to negotiate.[12] Blake had no option but to leave. The English behaviour made no concessions to the fact that the authorities in Tunis had some justice for their recent behaviour, following the action of a Captain Mitchell in 1651 of selling some Tunisian passengers on his ship as slaves to the Knights of St John on Malta.[13]

On Blake's arrival at Algiers, the Dey duly renewed Casson's treaty on 2/12 May and allowed the English to redeem their own captives and some Dutchmen who swam out to their ships.[14] However, the admiral's success probably owed as much to the reasonable relationship between Algiers and London as to his armed presence. Relations were so good that in 1657 Cromwell received the first Algerian ambassador,[15] though the English Consul Browne was subsequently arrested for smuggling an escaped slave out of the city of Alglers.[16] Contrary to current reports, Blake did not sail on to Tripoli to intimidate the other semi-independent Turkish Dey. That task was left to Admiral Stokes who concluded a treaty with Tripoli on 8/18 February 1658. He managed to ransom seventy-two captives for a little over 11 000 dollars – and wrote that he believed Blake had been tricked into paying too much at Algiers.[17]

The Levant Company, far from approving Blake's actions, was alarmed in case of repercussions from Constantinople on the trade there. (The burnt ships at Porto Farino had belonged to the Sultan.) On 15/25 May 1655, their company court discussed whether it would be better to petition Cromwell that Blake sail to the Dardanelles and explain his actions from a position of strength, or to send an explanatory letter with Cromwell's new ambassador. They decided to wait for more news. They also petitioned Cromwell to keep Blake in the Mediterranean 'that the French with other nations as well as the Turks may be awed and withhold from further violence or injuries'.[18] The crisis passed without incident, though there was a rumour at one point that the Sultan had executed Bendish and some merchants.[19] The company remained opposed to any naval action against the Turks throughout the Protectorate, and the Venetian ambassadors were accordingly heartened at any evidence of company resentment against the Turks as with the seizure of the *Resolution* en route to Smyrna in the spring of 1657.[20] The company's influence at Whitehall owed much to the role of Andrew Riccard, one of the Protectorate's chief supporters in the City, who was elected annual governor of the company successively in January 1655, February 1656 and February 1658.[21]

Despite the importance of the company, Venetian ambassadors continued to solicit the Commonwealth's aid, with ships or men, for six years following the arrival of Lorenzo Paulucci as an informal envoy from Paris in April 1652. Once the inevitable hurdle of Venetian recognition of the Commonwealth had been surmounted, he began a series of meetings with Fleming and others regarding the hire of mercenaries (who

were also currently being supplied to the rebels at Bordeaux).
Cromwell restricted his own involvement to polite effusions of
approval for the Venetian cause at audiences. He told Paulucci
at their first meeting in January 1654:

> We had long considered the most Serene Republic the strong
> bulwark against the most potent enemy of the Christian faith.
> The state might rely on his doing all he possibly could in
> her defence, when she stood a solitary champion against the
> Turks and their impious projects. If he had the power he
> would exert himself in so just a cause.[22]

The key phrase here was 'if he had the power'. Other matters
had priority, quite apart from Levant Company influence –
though a hostile Ottoman reaction to Porto Farino could have
provided the stimulus to react. Paulucci was reduced to noting
hopeful signs of sympathy from Cromwell, as at his audience
in early August when he assured that 'the obstinate war waged
with the Turk for ten years invited some generous resolve from
him to put a limit to Ottoman aggression'.[23] Fleming, his interpreter for these audiences, claimed that the Council 'have
often referred to the importance of Candia and the iniquity to
Christendom should it fall under the Ottoman yoke'. However, Cromwell 'is really thwarted by the merchants concerned
in the Levant trade'.[24] Venice, however, was hopeful enough
to upgrade its representation, Giovanni Sagredo arriving from
Paris as full ambassador in September 1655.

Anglo-Ottoman relations were normally cordial, and in the
spring of 1655 it was believed that a Turkish envoy sent to
France to hire ships for the besiegers of Candia could call in
London. Paulucci promised his masters that he would protest
if the man arrived, though he was hindered as 'affairs here
find themselves condemned to exercise extraordinary patience
and have to apply to a single ... Secretary of State, most difficult of access and with scant knowledge of foreign affairs like
most members of this government'.[25] The report proved false.
Nevertheless, there was the insult of the Turks, desperate for
shipping to oppose the Venetian fleet, impressing English ships
and sailors into their service. Cromwell was firm on this point,
assuring the new Venetian ambassador, Francisco Giavarina,
on the return of the *Gran Principe* (an English ship in Turkish
service captured by Venice in June 1655) that English ships

did not fight for the Turks with his 'intention' or his 'consent'.[26] He wrote to Bendish on 19/29 October 1655 telling him that such action could cause 'the utter subverting of all trade and commerce' (by Venetian reprisals). Bendish was to inform the Sultan of this, 'who we are confident will in no wise interpret this in any ill part not only in regard of the reason of the thing but more especially if he considers the Moderation and Equanimity with which we have always governed our affairs in relation to Him'.[27]

The years 1656–7 saw several significant Venetian victories in their naval war to defend Candia, their supremacy at sea encouraging beliefs that the Ottomans' wrath was not to be feared. Most notably, Lorenzo Marcello's victory in the Dardanelles in June 1656 led to Giavarina using it as propaganda for English intervention in his subsequent audience with Cromwell. The Protector expressed 'great delight' and 'spoke highly of the Senate and such heroic and extraordinary actions', but 'as things are now constituted he must regretfully allow his goodwill to serve instead of the deeds that are desirable'. He also promised to punish the captain of the *Gran Principe*.[28] This polite approval for Venice's successes cost nothing, risked nothing, and was maintained throughout the Protectorate, similar sentiments being expressed after Lazzaro Mocenigo breached the Dardanelles and approached Constantinople (the furthest Christian naval advance since the city's fall in 1453) the following year. On this occasion (23 November/2 December 1657) Cromwell claimed that he 'heard the news with peculiar satisfaction' and assured that the English ship captured fighting for the Turks had not done so on his orders.[29]

Bendish's protests to the Sultan partly concerned the seizures of English ships by individual Turkish and Tripolitan captains – the only incidents which could have caused a repeat of Blake's reprisals (assuming that England could spare ships from the squadron off Spain). The most notorious incident had been the Tripolitans' seizure and sale of the Levant Company's *Resolution*, and Bendish 'took a high tone against the Barbary corsairs to whom orders have been sent directing them to make restitution'.[30] Cromwell sent a letter to the Sultan, dated 11/21 August, complaining at 'so barbarous an act'.[31]

At the November audience, Cromwell assured Giavarina that a squadron would soon arrive in the Mediterranean 'to abate

the pride of the Corsairs', and if the *Resolution* incident was
not solved

> active hostilities would be begun against the Tripolitans, as
> the merchants here desire, who would be glad to see the
> destruction not only of Tripoli but of Algiers, Tunis, and
> other places on the Barbary Coast, if this would not irritate
> the Grand Turk and break the peace with the Porte. . . . Your
> Excellencies [the Senate] would understand the loss this
> nation would suffer, which has such treasures scattered about
> the chief places of the Turkish empire, if he sent ships
> directly against the Ottomans. It would be followed by the
> confiscation and spoiling of all the precious capital, the
> impoverishment of the English dwelling in those parts, and
> the total ruin of the numerous families which are supported
> by that trade.[32]

In due course Admiral Stokes took a squadron to Tripoli to
ransom captives.

Cromwell continued to press matters on individual cases,
such as the imprisonment of Captain Galilee, an Englishman
captured by the Turks in Venetian service who was owed back-
pay by his employers.[33] Conversely, Cromwell was equally
concerned to see that justice was done to the Turks where they
had grounds for legitimate complaint. In the most serious
incident, reported by Longland to Thurloe on 12/22 January
1657, Captain William Ell (or Ellis) was commissioned to carry
some of the Sultan's provisions (valued at 70–80 000 crowns)
from Alexandria to Smyrna but took them to Leghorn and
sold them there for his own benefit. Longland warned of 'the
great danger that hangs over our nation here',[34] if the Turks
instituted reprisals, and the Grand Duke's authorities were
asked to make an enquiry. Finally, in November Ell and his
ship were seized.[35]

17 The Financial Aspects of Foreign Policy

The principal aim of any government must be to survive, but it cannot do that without avoiding bankruptcy. In this respect, the antiquated financial structure for raising the English government's revenue presented it with an especial problem concerning enforcement of its orders, hampered as it was by its lack of a central tax-collecting service and its reliance on the cooperation of the local gentry, whose intention was naturally to fulfil their obligations as sketchily as possible. Any contemporary government was hampered by similar problems of local autonomy, and they were to remain so until the rise of the modern state – hence the relatively small size of European standing armies and bureaucracies. The English government, however, was more dependent on the cooperation of the representatives of the local community (in Parliament) for the legalisation of methods of revenue as well as its collection. Hence the problems of central government finance even under the parsimonious Elizabeth, the ruinous effect of higher Court expenditure under James I, and the problems which beset Charles I when he endeavoured to raise revenue without Parliament. No English monarch could afford the munificence of the Court grandeur of their continental contemporaries, as the state of their palaces bore witness. Extraordinary expenditure – principally on war – was crippling to any regime, as shown by Elizabeth's refusal to take on commitments in the Netherlands for as long as possible and the ruin which forced Charles to recall Parliament when faced with a Scottish revolt. The Parliamentary leadership in 1642–6 had offset this problem by the expedient of raising revenue through local committees for what the men responsible accepted as a just cause, but it is noticeable that as soon as the menace of conquest by Charles's alleged army of Papists was over local complaints redoubled. The local resistance to any form or size of taxation which was seen as new, unnecessary or imposed without consent is proven by the extent of the rebellions of 1648, in which former Parliamentarian sympathisers made common cause with the defeated Royalists against the power of London.[1] The Parliamentarians could also raise money by enforced exaction upon 'malignants' by fines and the selling of their estates, but this could not be more than a temporary expedient – neither could the sale of Charles's palaces and art collections.

Cromwell inherited the Parliamentarians' two new expedients in raising revenue. However, the defeat of Charles II and the Scots in 1651 ended the visible emergency which had caused many to accept the recent years' unpopular taxes. Thereafter external danger was not seen as acute, and resistance to high taxes would return as it did after the end of an external threat in 1646–7. Moreover, local gentry would not see the need for the maintenance of a large army, not understanding (or understanding only too well) that it was the sole source of Cromwell's power once he had expelled the Rump. The local gentry leadership in Parliament in 1647–8 had then been notable for their refusal (not solely for religious reasons) to fund a large, Independent-dominated Army. These men maintained their local power-base independently of Parliament or the leadership of the Protectorate, as is shown by their reappearance and reiterated attacks on the Army in the Cromwellian Parliaments. In any case, after Cromwell's unashamedly brutal dismissal of the remnants of the elected Commons in 1653 he had made many permanent enemies among those devotees of 'legitimism' who would seek to resist a government which, for the first time in known history, relied on naked force. The importance of a legitimate regime as a focus for national unity and a symbol of stability is emphasised by the quasi-royal nature of the settlement imposed under the 'Humble Petition and Advice', with its monarchical trappings for the Lord Protector and the readiness with which former MPs in 1659–60 turned to the popularly discredited Rump. Cromwell's own lieutenants, such as Lambert and Fleetwood, could think of nothing better than to attempt to use the legitimate Parliament, and innovators such as Harrington were a tiny minority.[2] After the Penruddock revolt Cromwell's use of the Major-Generals was perceived as a blunder in imposing military rule on the provinces, and provided an exaggerated but symbolic series of legends about the arrogance and uncouthness of the military bumpkins and fanatics raised up to rule over the natural leaders of provincial Englishmen.[3]

Cromwell's problems were accentuated by this mistake, which as an example of his political naïvety is comparable with his inability to manage the elections to his Parliaments[4] and his belief that the New England colonists would flock to Jamaica. It is obvious that the thought processes of 'God's Englishman' and the country squires of his Parliaments were on different levels, as is illustrated by his (somewhat despairing) harangues to them on what he conceived as the national priorities in God's design.

Despite these fundamental problems, it can be argued that Cromwell had some advantages over his Royal predecessors, if not over the collective leadership of the Rump. His practical experience in the fields of warfare and administration meant that he was likely to take a more realistic attitude to problems than a Prince brought up in the comparatively rarefied atmosphere of a Court, though his military skills did not mean that he would be any less dependent on skilled administrators and his past career had alienated a substantial body of the latter. As an administrator he was inferior to Vane and as a politician he was inferior to Haselrig. All the Republican regimes, however, were closer to the leadership of the City of London than the Stuarts had been, though the purges of 1648 and 1653 distanced Cromwell from most of the country gentry who bore the burden of collecting and paying the main taxes. The potential accordingly existed for the adoption of money-raising schemes in collaboration with the City that might have offset the impossibility of raising the county assessments to pay for the Army. The most forward-looking English financial thinkers were certainly aware at that time of the potential of such schemes that could make England rival its commercial competitors in the United Provinces. These men included a close adviser of the Protectoral government, Captain Limbery of Plymouth, who in 1654 had acted as an adviser to the Western Design and two or three years later put forward a scheme for a form of national maritime insurance, 'to the greater encouragement of merchants in their navigations and carrying on of trade with honour and safety to this nation'.[5] Thomas Mun had proposed the free export of bullion to stimulate trade.[6] Henry Robinson, in *England's Safety in Treasure's Increase* (1641), had called for low export duties to provide encouragement for trade and the building of shipping – which would have duly provided more ships to be impressed to serve in the nation's defence, enabling the government to rely less on the ships built in the expensive and corruption-riddled dockyards.[7]

The fact that these and similar propositions were not attempted for another half-century was the fault of Cromwell, who lacked imagination in this as in other matters and could not see the usefulness of innovation. He was not a mercantile expert himself, but was further hampered by the fact that his government was made up of a mixture of officers and civilians associated through ideological sympathy, personal friendship or ambition, who conceived of economic matters as not deserving any degree of priority (when they understood such matters at all). It was at a disadvantage compared with the civilian leadership of the Rump, men who had declared war on their Dutch commercial rivals despite ideological/religious sympathy, whereas Cromwell had then preferred peace or impractical schemes for political union. It can be argued that Cromwell's attitude to trade matters was further illustrated by his reported readiness to sacrifice the Navigation Act early in 1656 to secure Dutch support against Spain, though in fact a section of the mercantile community had also opposed the Act.[8]

Whatever Cromwell's attitude to the City and economic schemes, it is undeniable that a substantial section of the City (probably the majority) never conceived of him except as the military dictator who had expelled the Rump. Those who were not alienated then, moreover, had to steel themselves to ally with a man who had overthrown the legitimate government and whose own security in power was uncertain. It was ominous that Cromwell, alienated from his Parliaments and for a time relying on a military oligarchy to which no King had ever resorted, did not dare to take the crown in 1657 and faced repeated plots, rumours of plots and foreign invasion. He faced a continuous 'crisis of confidence' which became no less acute as his regime became more established. The unwillingness of most City merchants to lend him money early in 1658[9] is shocking evidence of a continued lack of business confidence such as had never affected the established Parliament. The Protector's unfriendly reception in the City on his way to a banquet at Grocer's Hall on 8/18 February 1654 can be seen as the norm rather than an exception, and this lack of confidence would naturally be reflected in Cromwell being less willing to listen to commercial proposals.

It is significant that he even ignored the proposals of Richard Wylde in 1653 that he plan for a national interest in India, which could be potentially lucrative.[10] Such proposals, moreover, were mostly aimed at producing greater national prosperity in the long term. Commercial prosperity would indeed improve the revenues from the customs and excise, but he showed no significant interest in this form of income and the long-established tradition of farming revenue collection out to groups of trusted commissioners was not altered in favour of any new method of greater efficiency. As a military ruler still perturbed by the Royalists, whose plans were the principal concern of his chief adviser Thurloe, Cromwell can be forgiven for seeing the merchants as people of subordinate importance to the crucial problems of the country. It was the gentry who dominated Parliament, who would either pay or evade the most important source of revenue (the assessment), and might provide recruits for a foreign invasion. Accordingly, the English government might take a different attitude to economic proposals from the ruling oligarchy of the United Provinces but it had different priorities. The Dutch Grand Pensionary Jan de Witt was surrounded by a relatively united class of mercantile nobility, centred on Amsterdam, which despite its conflicting ambitions was united in considering commercial interests as of great priority, and which was usually able to enforce its will on a numerically fairly small class of discontented provincial landowners. The Protectoral regime lacked both this broad base and its commercial connection, drawing most of its revenue from the gentry besides relying on an unprecedently large Army with disaffected officers and a tradition of political involvement.

Cromwell was not without his mercantile connections, though it is significant that these (like his military associates) were centred upon a group of personal associates with family connections. Most notable among them was Thurloe's brother-in-law, Martin Noell, and other members included John Ireton (brother of General Henry Ireton, Cromwell's late son-in-law) and a personal friend, Robert Tichborne. It is a measure of Noell's solitary eminence that he held so many of the government's farms for customs and excise, as well as heading their list of contractors to supply Jamaica. The other chief advisers of the government included Thomas Povey, one of the City merchants most involved with plans for the expansion of English interests both in the Caribbean and in Africa. It was he who made the initial suggestion for what was to become the 'Jamaica Committee', in his *Essay or Overture for the Regulating His Highness's Affairs in the West Indies* (undated, but probably 1655). Giving the matter careful consideration, he advised the establishment of a council of a 'competent number of persons of good reputations, prudent and well skilled in their professions and qualifications' – preferably one serving West Indies merchant, one retired merchant, one well-experienced seaman, one citizen of 'general repartee and conversation', one gentleman learned in languages and the civil law, 'one that understands well our municipal Laws' and constitution, and a secretary. These men would consider the improvement and extension of the plantations, reducing all the colonies to a more uniform way of government, maintain correspondence and intelligence with the colonies without bothering the Council, give 'all possible encouragement and advantage' for adventurers and merchants, and consider shutting out foreigners from the colonial trade 'by making them not necessary to it, and drawing it wholly and with satisfaction to all parties into our ports here' to improve our stock of bullion and trade.[11]

Apart from this, which was taken up but not used to its full effectiveness as Povey had hoped, most of the merchants' advice to Cromwell was in fact ignored. Most importantly, nothing was made of the proposal of Noell, Povey, Captain William Watts, Lord Willoughby of Parham and others to set up a 'West Indies Company' to further the Caribbean trade and act as a focus for investment in the manner of the East India Company – something which their initial petition made clear that they were willing to 'adventure at their own charge'.[12] Their main plan submitted to the Council pointed out that they would be able to use a charter giving them similar incentives to the East India Company, to collect providers of shipping and goods, persuade Spain's American subjects from their loyalties, assist Jamaica, convert the Indians to Christianity, increase bullion and exports, and even use 'some of the young idle gentry of this nation' who were 'dangerous to the public peace and do things dishonourable to their name and family at home whilst they may find encouragement and delight in foreign action and adventure'.[13] Cromwell neglected even this list of financial, political and moral reasons for such concerted action, despite the cost of his current establishment in Jamaica (see Chapter 5). Another proposal not followed through was the same adventurers' design for a private expedition to 'gain a footing upon some of the most considerable dominions and pretensions of the Spaniard', by establishing trading and military links with the independent Indian Chief in Florida,[14] for which Noell, Povey and their associates wanted another charter to place them on a comparable footing with the Bermudas (Somers Islands) Company. Cromwell did, however, receive a Floridan chief in London.[15] His excuse for ignoring these cheap and useful plans to assist his Caribbean war, as relayed by Noell to General Brayne in Jamaica in April 1657, was that he was 'diverted by affairs of the highest magnitude'.[16] This does not excuse his complete unwillingness to follow up such plans at any time during his Protectorate, which clearly resulted from a different sense of priorities.

When we glance at Cromwell's attitude to other companies and mercantile plans, it is clear that his lack of interest or initiative in these matters was total. The Dutch peace of 1654 did indeed avenge the East India Company's recent losses, obtaining compensation for incidents as far distant in time as Amboyna. However, once the Dutch compensation money reached England Cromwell promptly seized £50 000 to pay his pressing debts, irrespective of the inevitable resentment.[17] Similarly, when the company's charter came up for renewal in 1654 a chance arose to widen its membership, or even open the East India trade altogether, and thus stimulate investment and shipping. Schemes to do this were submitted by several groups of merchants, including Noell and Maurice Thompson, though the company submitted its own furious defence of its privileges with dire warnings about the effects of anarchy.[18] Richard Wylde even tried to bribe Thurloe with an offer of a pension for him and a diamond for his wife in return for securing his post in the company in any eventuality.[19] It was reported that the threat of free East India trade was especially menacing to the Dutch, who could be dealt a major blow without Cromwell having to resort to war at a time when he could not afford it.[20] The company's charter was renewed without major changes in 1657, thus providing evidence of the power of those who feared the effects of innovation on Cromwell's thoughts. It is clear that while Cromwell was not sufficiently aware of the advantages of innovation no other Councillor was prepared to champion them either, not even Thurloe. Lambert, despite his warnings about the danger of a Spanish war to the mercantile community, did nothing practical to oppose Cromwell on this matter, or to offer support for compensatory schemes to divert City interests elsewhere.[21]

Before dealing with the central question of government finance, it is advisable to consider one of the chief charges against Cromwell – his neglect of commercial interests in declaring war on Spain. It is hoped that the preceding narrative has made it clear that Cromwell's military and political priorities led to conflict with Spain irrespective of any alleged 'outdated' prejudices, and that the outbreak of war in Europe was an unwelcome shock. The damage to shipping in the Channel in 1656–8 was not strictly the work of an enfeebled Spain, which had to hire Dutch shipping to transport the intended Royalist invasion fleet, but of Flemish privateers who were duly hampered by the occupation of Dunkirk. The effects of war with France would have been just as bad, in unleashing the notorious privateers of Brest and St Malo who were wreaking havoc on English shipping in the situation of undeclared war in 1651–4. The fault partially lay with Cromwell for not stimulating the building of English ships to assist his hard-pressed fleet, but that situation was principally the result of years of low government expenditure dating from the 1620s. Cromwell's rule saw pirates boasting in 1656 that 'while the Lord Protector is fetching gold from the West Indies we will fetch his coals from Newcastle'.[22] His fleet was, however, absent on campaign at the time, and had the ships been in port there would have been greater danger of a mutiny by untrustworthy officers such as Lawson. At the time of comparable humiliation in the 1630s (by the Algerine corsairs), Charles I had been at peace with no such extenuating circumstances. It should be pointed out that the shipbuilding programme of the 1640s and 1650s was the most extensive for many years, providing ships such as the *Naseby* and *Marston Moor* which could stand up to encounters with the greatest Dutch admirals. Moreover, it is inaccurate to claim that the Spanish War entirely ruined sections of the mercantile community. Most merchants were able to transfer goods destined for Spain to ships under 'flags of convenience' with Dutch masters and crews, albeit at considerable cost. This practice was openly carried on by the English consul in Leghorn, Longland, who admitted it to Thurloe,[23] and was confessed to Parliament in a mercantile petition of 15/25 February 1659.[24] Some goods otherwise destined for Spain could be diverted to Portugal, which conversely was able to supply some of the English needs in wine and wool.[25] The depression of 1659–60 cannot be blamed entirely on the Spanish War, though this undoubtedly affected confidence. Prices of food were rising and those of goods for sale falling in 1657–9,[26] but the minting of new coins from Stayner's Spanish bullion in 1657 may even have delayed the effects of the slump. The worst of the depression undoubtedly resulted from the political uncertainty following Cromwell's death. Povey blamed his losses on the 'last year of violence and mutation' with its 'so great a confusion and improbability of settlement' in a letter of 29 October/8 November 1659.[27]

The central problem of deficiency in tax-raised finance was made much more acute by the needs of Cromwell's Army. Thus, it can be claimed that it was the events of 1648–53 which doomed Cromwell's government to financial disaster, given that the revenues raised by the assessment could not be increased drastically for fear of rebellion. The existing taxes were indeed collected fairly efficiently under the Commonwealth; the receiver-general of Middlesex reckoned that out of £176 000 due to be collected in 1651–9 only £3000 was not obtained.[28] The assessment was, however, collected and used locally without passing through the Exchequer, apart from the political problems in obtaining a higher rate from Parliament to meet the needs of any emergency. Cromwell was faced with a near impossible problem in raising comparable sums from other sources which were subject to closer governmental control, even before the 1654 Parliament (badly managed by his supporters) created another problem by asserting its constitutional right to control all sources of ordinary and extraordinary revenue. The only way to evade this would have been to provide major stimuli for the City to invest more in the national economy, principally by assisting trade and hence improving the customs revenues. As it was, the evidence above concerning the East India and putative West Indies Companies illustrates Cromwell's inability to think so flexibly. Instead, the customs continued to be rented out to annual commissioners and subject to their vagaries and dishonesties in collection, while the constitutional struggle against paying 'illegal' duties continued to undermine payment (as illustrated by George Cony's challenge to them). In 1655, the committee for the 'preservation of the customs' was revived, but one of its members (Colonel Harvey) was soon in the Tower for embezzlement.[29] Eventually, in 1657, Parliament approved a committee to farm the customs in return for £800 000 per annum, a body headed by the ubiquitous Martin Noell.[30] The excise duties were mostly farmed out to a series of commissioners under the supervision of Treasury commissioners, with Noell again playing a central role. Other sources of income were mostly static and incapable of substantial improvement, such as the income from delinquents' lands, probate of wills, the Post Office (currently farmed by Thurloe), fines for alienations, and the duty on coal. The only major source of extra revenue was the sale of prize goods seized during wartime, which naturally offered occasional windfalls but no steady revenue. Thus in 1652–4 the Dutch War brought in goods worth £208 658; only £2900 came in during 1655–6, in peacetime; Stayner's action gained the government £249 599 in 1656–7; and only £3770 came in from Spanish prizes in 1657–8.[31]

A total estimate of government revenue was provided by a Parliamentary subcommittee in December 1654:

Excise and customs	–	£800 000
Assessment: England	–	£1 108 000
Assessment: Scotland and Ireland	–	£120 000 each
Post Office	–	£10 000
Probate of wills	–	£8000
Exchequer revenues	–	£20 000
Delinquents' estates	–	£70 000
Fines from alienations	–	£20 000
Revenues from Jersey and Guernsey	–	£2000[32]

In addition, it was later added that £10 000 per annum came from government mines, £2000 from tin, £9000 from Royal revenue in Scotland, and £1250 from palaces.[33] Portugal provided an additional windfall of £48 058 compensation in July

1656,[34] and in 1657–8 a tax on new buildings in London was farmed out to a group of financiers (including Ireton, Vyner and Pack) in return for special loans.[35]

Cromwell's regime had the added problem of a standing army as well as the traditional deficiencies of Stuart revenue raising. However, he had one substantial advantage not enjoyed by any continental government except the Dutch – the absence of most of the usual obligations for expenditure of a crowned monarch. Any European ruler was expected to spend a substantial part of his revenue on Court expenditure, displays and palaces, and though the Catholic monarchies were more prone to this even Protestant rulers such as Christian IV of Denmark had not been exempt. The wise policy of reduced Court extravagance under Elizabeth had been much criticised, while the European-influenced grandiose ideas of Prince Henry and Charles I were regarded as natural and fitting by many observers.[36] Cromwell was at least saved this problem, though the power of the public's expectations of its ruler played a part in his retention of the palaces of Whitehall, Hampton Court, Greenwich, and Somerset House. The investigating Parliamentary subcommittee estimated the cost of these palaces in December 1654 at £1254 13 4d per annum.[37] The entire civil establishment, including the Ordnance Office, was estimated to cost £200 992,[38] of which Thurloe's reputedly costly spy system in fact only cost some £2999 in the year April 1656–April 1657.[39] The charts of official expenditure throughout the Protectorate show the disproportionate amount spent on the armed forces, which equalled any continental drain on a monarchy from palace-building and entertainments:

	Total:	Army:	Navy:
1654	£2 877 079	£1 566 705	£1 059 832
1655	£2 327 512	£1 508 000	£569 512
1656	£2 067 357	£1 057 819	£768 538
1657	£2 878 174	£1 900 489	£742 034
1658	£2 197 985	£1 346 706	£599 108[40]

The subcommittee in December 1654 estimated the cost of 15 cavalry regiments at £2377 13 4d with extra costs at £463 645; the cost of 18 regiments of foot at £1538 2 6d with extra costs at £35 921 5 2d; and the charges of 35 ships, 500 seamen, weapons, gunpowder and victuals for the fleet at £269 750.[41] Hence the revenue for 1654 amounted to approximately

£1 586 175 and the expenditure to £2 877 079; a deficit amounting to approximately one year's taxes. France was three years' taxes in arrears, but the regime did not face comparable problems of legitimacy and mutiny after 1656 despite its unpopular Spanish War and the exiled Condé. Hence Cromwell's necessity to reduce his armed forces and find some lucrative 'vent' for them overseas at his allies' expense, which in turn led to Spain's refusal to find a crippling sum of money to satisfy him and his turning towards France. The problem was worsened by Cromwell and Thurloe's inability to manage the Parliament of 1654, though gentry resistance to any high taxes except in cases of extreme emergency (e.g. 1643–5) was a perennial problem. The Parliamentary subcommittee which investigated the revenue in September–December 1654 was headed by an old opponent, Colonel Birch, and reasserted the Commons' cherished right to control revenue by extending it to all forms of ordinary and extraordinary revenue. Another annoying proviso in their report insisted that part of the revenue be raised by the duty on French wines (an estimated £150 000) which could not be acquired until peace was signed with France, and more was to be acquired by selling various delinquents' lands in the government's possession. A quarter of the excise should be set aside to meet some of the Commonwealth's debts, irrespective of other priorities. In all, the armed forces were to receive £1 210 000 and the civil establishment £200 000, a proposal which Councillor Montague tried unsuccessfully to raise to an overall total of £2 250 000.[42] Cromwell duly had to try to make economies after his dismissal of the refractory Commons and managed to dismiss 10 000 soldiers without causing mutinies. It was, however, just as well that this crisis preceded the breach with Spain and the efforts of Sexby to revive Leveller conspiracy on the King's behalf, or the trouble might have been worse. As it was, the shortage of soldiers did nothing to help the provision of adequate forces for the Western Design, which due to the shortage of disciplined men to defend England was provided with riff-raff. Financial problems hence indirectly helped the defeat on Hispaniola and Spain's willingness to break off relations with England, precipitating war.

Cromwell's use of the Major-Generals worsened opposition among the classes which were chiefly represented in Parliament, precipitating more resistance to taxation in the Parliament

called in the autumn of 1656. Even the pro-Cromwellian
faction which organised the 'Humble Petition and Advice'
found it prudent to restrict their offer of an annual revenue
to £1 300 000 which Cromwell managed to increase by a further £600 000. An additional assessment was imposed to raise
£215 000 in three months as a result of the emergency incurred
by the Spanish War, a new excise book was imposed, and a
special tax raised more money from new buildings in London.
Despite this, in his speech of 20/30 January 1658 Cromwell
admitted that the Army was in arrears by £300 000 and the
Navy by £540 000, while the (less important) militia was owed
six months' pay.[43] Cromwell could not help his military costs,
given the fragile nature of his regime and the threat of invasion.
He did, however, dare to take one initial step to 'civilian rule',
a drastic reduction of his forces which were down to 36 000 by
1658. It is questionable whether sufficient numbers of important
people would have ever forgiven him for his past actions in
1648–9 and 1653 or overcome their long-term resistance to
taxation, even had he taken the throne in 1657. The outbreak
of war in 1655 intensified the vicious circle of opposition, taxation and military rule. By early 1658 he faced virtual bankruptcy,
even with French fear of Spain meaning that Mazarin was forced
to fund the Flanders campaign.

Given the almost insuperable problems which he faced,
Cromwell's unwillingness to consider measures to stimulate
trade revenues or commercial confidence only made a difficult
situation worse. As we have seen, his government was not devoid
of links with the City or awareness of its problems, though
Cromwell preferred raising money by semi-legalised piracy in
the Caribbean to economic schemes such as those used in
Amsterdam. Undoubtedly his Parliaments' niggardliness was
heightened by the continuing memories of how both Kings
and Cromwell had misused the Commons in past decades,
which led to a desire to use the powerful lever of finance
against the executive power. Financial security, hampered by
traditions of local autonomy, fell victim to the struggle between
legislative and executive branches of the British constitution
as established by the 'Instrument of Government'. The only
ultimate answer to this was that close alliance of personnel between the two which would end with the head of the Executive
leading the Government via (or from) the legislature.

Conclusion

As seen by observers such as Giavarina, Cromwell's acquisition of Dunkirk marked the emergence of a new threat to Catholicism comparable to that of Gustavus Adolphus. Cromwell's achievements were also admired with nostalgia in the mid-1660s when compared with the current string of disasters. In reality his government was virtually bankrupt and was hard pressed to pay the troops who were supposed to carry out his designs. Behind this façade of success lay a Government that had seen off the Royalist threat but had many other problems left to trouble it, not least that of its own supporters. Despite the restoration of a semi-monarchical government in successive stages in 1653 and 1657, it was a regime ultimately depending on its armed forces among whom were men whose affection for some form of republic was only held in check by the reputation of the Protector. Once he was gone, they soon showed that their loyalty had been to the man rather than to the institution which he and his civilian advisers had built up around him. The Protectorate collapsed in eight months, though admittedly Richard Cromwell's deposition was the work of a small group of Cromwell's senior officers (led by Fleetwood and Desborough) rather than of the bulk of the Army. Attempts to patch up a new republican constitution were ruined by internecine disputes among officers and restored Rumpers alike, and the only solution proved to be the return of the King. Charles II was back in London within two years of the fall of Dunkirk.

The clue to the dichotomy between the regime's apparent military strength and its real weakness lies in the very nature of that strength. Cromwell's success owed much to his unique position, but the very existence of large armed forces imposed its own constraints. An active foreign policy had to be pursued to make use of them, and money had to be found to finance them to decrease his reliance on unpopular taxes which could increase internal dissension. The riches of Spanish America thus had advantages apart from the moral imperative (misjudged, as it happened) to intervene. His financial weakness also served to make Spain an unwise ally on the Continent in

251

1654; his auction of his services between France and Spain was the result of necessity not arrogance. This problem coincided with the crucial requirement to keep the Franco-Spanish War alive, impelling, first, offers to both sides in 1654, then peace and talks on an alliance with France when Spain reacted strongly to the Western Design, and finally in 1657 the alliance with France.

Pragmatism governed Cromwell's relations with the 'Two Crowns', with efforts to weaken an implicitly pro-Royalist France in 1651–4 and to bind it to England as an ally against Spain (on English terms, and with alliance subject to an English timetable) thereafter. Similarly, once the more idealistic approach to the Dutch had proved a failure, Cromwell's primary aim was to prevent commercial disputes or Orangist influence pushing her into alliance with a hostile Spain – something which would tip the scales against England in the conflict by making up for Spain's financial and naval weakness. The necessity not to antagonise the Dutch dominated Cromwell's approach to Sweden, negating the effects of his admiration for Charles X. This does not, however, clear him of a lack of awareness of the self-serving nature of Charles's ambitions against Protestant as well as Catholic neighbours, a naïvity which was also apparent in his overconfidant approach to the Spanish Empire or (initially) to alliance with the Dutch. Cromwell, unlike Lambert and Thurloe, possessed a degree of miscalculating idealism which most notably led to disaster in the Caribbean. His misunderstandings of the need to assist local traders and of the nature of past Spanish attacks undoubtably shows his latent prejudices arising from the 'Black Legend' and a degree of overconfidance which Lambert did not share. Cromwell's willingness to use the mutual need of his services by France and Spain was apparent in his strictness on either party meeting his full terms in 1654–5, though Council divisions played a part here, and in the possibility of Blake attacking French ships while Penn and Venables attacked Spanish colonies. The 'gunboat diplomacy' against Portugal and the rigid insistence on 'Exclusion' of William of Orange were other instances of an inflexibility which could have been counterproductive had England's position in the European conflicts of the mid-1650s not been so strong.

The mutual antagonism of France and Spain gave Cromwell

the opportunity to raise English prestige in Europe to a new height by August 1658, despite his internal difficulties. Conversely, the antagonism between Charles X and his rivals around the Baltic prevented any serious possibility of England being able to unite the 'northern powers' in a manner which was conducive to the dreams of Protestant 'internationalists' but more practically would serve to threaten Spain's Imperial allies. The Protector's achievement owed much to external circumstances, but would have been impossible without the unprecedented size and sense of purpose within the English armed forces. The achievement was that of Cromwell himself rather than that of the New Model Army (and Navy), but events in 1659–60 were to show that the edifice and reputation which he had created were his alone. Men like Thurloe had played a crucial role in his success, but the ultimate purposes of Cromwellian foreign policy – the regime's survival and national advancement – were impossible without the presence of Oliver Cromwell.

Notes

1 Cromwell's Foreign Policy: The Historical Assessment

1. 'Spain or the Netherlands? The Dilemmas of Early Stuart Foreign Policy', in Howard Tomlinson (ed.), *Before the English Civil War*, pp. 79–101.
2. *Clarke Papers*, vol. 3, pp. 207–8.
3. See discussion in Chapter 5.
4. Michael Roberts, 'Cromwell and the Baltic', in his *Essays on Swedish History*, p. 174.
5. Thurloe made it clear to Clarendon that he regarded this as the crucial reason why England preferred France to Spain. See the 'Memorandum' in *State Papers of John Thurloe* (subsequently referred to as *Thurloe*), vol. 1, pp. 759–63.
6. *Harleian Miscellany*, vol. 1, pp. 287–9.
7. Edmund Ludlow, *Memoirs*, vol. 2, p. 3.
8. *Poems and Letters of Andrew Marvell*, vol. 1, p. 212. In a similar vein, Pepys noted nostalgia for Cromwell's successes after the disasters of the Second Dutch War; *Diary* (ed. Latham and Matthews, Cambridge University Press, 9 vols), vol. 8, p. 332 (12 July 1667). Foreign powers held a similar view of the strengths of Cromwell and Charles II; Burnet records that when the Dutch refused to return fugitives to England in 1672 the King complained that they had done so for Cromwell. Their envoy retorted: 'Ha! Sir, that was a different matter. Cromwell was a great man and made himself feared by land and sea' (*History of my own Time*, vol. 1, p. 145n).
9. In a way, Cromwell's policies could never be adequately appreciated until the commentators were sufficiently aware of his special problems, for which a parallel case was an advantage.
10. This mistake is based on a misinterpretation of Cromwell and Thurloe's priorities, and overemphasis on public statements.
11. *Thurloe*, vol. 4, p. 188.
12. See speeches in the 1659 Parliament, e.g. by Sergeant Maynard (*Diary of Thomas Burton*, vol. 3, p. 461).
13. Thomas Carlyle, *Letters and Speeches of Oliver Cromwell* (ed. S.C. Lomas), 1857 edition.
14. Birch's edition of Thurloe's papers had been published in 1742, but the first scholar to make systematic use of them was S.R. Gardiner.
15. S.R. Gardiner, *History of Commonwealth and Protectorate*; Sir Charles Firth, *The Last Years of the Protectorate*.
16. Firth, *Last Years*, vol. 1, p. 340.
17. S.R. Gardiner, *Cromwell's Place in History: Six Lectures Delivered to the University of Oxford*, p. 201.
18. Firth's review of Wolfgang Michael's biography of Cromwell, *EHR*, XXV (1910), p. 776.

19. Wolfgang Michael, *Oliver Cromwell.*
20. Leopold von Ranke, *Englische Geschichte* (Berlin, 1859–68), III, p. 396.
21. Firth, 'Cromwell and the Insurrection of 1655', *EHR,* III (1898), pp. 313–50; 'Cromwell's Instructions to Lockhart 1656', *EHR*, XXI (1906), pp. 742–6; 'Royalist and Cromwellian Armies in Flanders, 1657–61', *TRHS,* XVII (1903), pp. 69–110.
22. S.A. Swaine, 'The English Acquisition and Loss of Dunkirk', *TRHS,* I (1884), pp. 93–118.
23. George L. Beer, 'Cromwell's Policy in its Economic Aspects', *Political Science Quarterly,* XVI (1901), pp. 582–611.
24. W.C. Abbott, *Writings and Speeches of Oliver Cromwell,* vol. 4, p. 48.
25. Christopher Hill, *God's Englishman: Oliver Cromwell and the English Revolution.*
26. Robert Paul, *The Lord Protector: Religion and Politics in the Life of Oliver Cromwell.*
27. Hugh Trevor-Roper, 'Oliver Cromwell and his Parliaments', in ibid., *Religion, the Reformation, and Social Change,* pp. 345–92.
28. Roger Crabtree, 'The Idea of a Protestant Foreign Policy', in Ivan Roots (ed.), *Cromwell: A Profile,* pp. 160–89.
29. See Chapters 3 and 4.
30. William M. Lamont, *Godly Rule: Politics and Religion, 1603–60,* pp. 136–8.
31. Charles P. Korr, *Cromwell and the New Model Foreign Policy: England's Policy Towards France, 1649–58.*
32. Ibid., conclusion, pp. 196–211.

2 The Decision-making Process: Council, Secretary and Ambassadors

1. *The King's Cabinet Opened,* see Gardiner, *History of the Great Civil War,* vol. ii, p. 258.
2. Basadonna to Senate, 8 February 1651 (NS), *CSPV 1647–52,* p. 169.
3. List of the 'Rump's' Sixth Council of State, *CSPD 1652–3,* p. xli.
4. List of the 'Committee of Foreign Affairs' in 1653, *CSPD 1653–4,* p. 53.
5. For the size of the armed forces as of December 1654, see BL Add. Mss 2884.
6. See Chapter 5.
7. Giavarina, 24 August 1657 (NS), *CSPV 1657–9,* pp. 101–4.
8. Whitelocke, *Memorials of English Affairs,* pp. 56–70. The effectiveness of the 'Instrument' was limited by the absence of sanctions to enforce compliance on Cromwell.
9. BL Thomason Mss E 728 (5), pp. 21–46.
10. Bodleian, Tanner Mss 52, f. 159v.
11. George D. Heath III, 'Cromwell and Lambert 1653–7', in Ivan Roots (ed.), *Cromwell: A Profile,* pp. 72–90.
12. Peter Gaunt, 'The Single Person's Confidants and Dependants: Oliver Cromwell and his Protectoral Councillors', in *Historical Journal,* XXXII (1989), pp. 537–60.

13. W.C. Abbott, *Writings and Speeches of Oliver Cromwell*, vol. 3, p. 455.
14. Negotiations were regularised on 4/14 April by the appointment of separate committees to deal with Cardenas and Bordeaux, *CSPD 1654*, p. 73.
15. Whitelocke, *Memorials of English Affairs*, p. 222.
16. Firth, *Last Years*, vol. 2, pp. 7–9.
17. G.E. Aylmer, *The State's Servants: The Civil Service of the English Republic, 1649–1660*, p. 47.
18. Brodrick to Hyde, 2 March 1658 (NS), *CSPClar*, vol. 4, p. 9. According to this report matters of importance were dealt with by Fleetwood, Desborough, Whalley, Goffe and Thurloe, and the trivia by Broghill, Wolseley and Pickering. The pre-eminence of Thurloe in foreign affairs in certain, but the Protector's most trusted officers (e.g. Goffe) were probably restricted to security matters; apart from Fleetwood, none of them seem to have been interested in foreign affairs.
19. *Thurloe*, 1, pp. 754–5; Whitelocke, *Memorials of English Affairs*, vol. 4, p. 289 on Pierrepoint's influence in 1657.
20. *Harleian Miscellany*, vol. 3, p. 483.
21. Parliamentary Committee appointed 26 June/6 July 1657; Lambert, Jones, Fleetwood, Desborough, Thurloe; to consider reunion of Protestant churches. Lambert resisted the efforts of the other officers for this; Firth, *Last Years*, vol. 1, p. 340, and G.H. Turnbull, *Dury, Hartlib, and Comenius: Gleanings from Hartlib's Papers*, p. 285.
22. A. Woolrych, *Commonwealth to Protectorate*, p. 381.
23. *Harleian Miscellany*, vol. 3, p. 477.
24. See Roy Sherwood, *The Court of Oliver Cromwell*, pp. 142–6 on Jones's position as Comptroller of the Protectoral Household.
25. See Chapter 16 on Fleming's meetings with Paulucci; also Chapter 2, n. 48.
26. Blair Worden, *The Rump Parliament, 1649–1653*, pp. 389–91 for the lists of attendance at Westminster of Cromwell's Councillors and other MPs. Lists of the Councils of State 1649–53 in *CSPD*: 1st Council (1649–50), *CSPD 1649–50*, pp. lxxiv–lxxxv; 2nd Council, *CSPD 1650*, pp. xl–xli; 3rd Council, *CSPD 1651*, p. xxxv; 4th Council, *CSPD 1651–2*, p. xlvi; 5th Council, *CSPD 1652–3*, p. xxiii.
27. See Pickering's entry in the *DNB*, vol. 45, p. 242. He was also cousin to the poet Dryden.
28. *DNB* Skippon, vol. 52, pp. 353–6. *DNB* Lawrence, vol. 22, pp. 256–8. *DNB* Fiennes, vol. 18, pp. 430–2. Fleetwood (*DNB*, vol. 19, pp. 261–3) asserted after the Vaudois Massacre that 'His Highness was particularly raised up for such a day as this, to be a shelter to poor persecuted Protestants in foreign parts', Fleetwood to Thurloe 23 May/2 June 1655, *Thurloe*, vol. 2, p. 468.
29. *Victoria County History: Cambridge and Isle of Ely* (ed. R.B. Pugh), vol. 4, p. 254.
30. G.E. Aylmer, *The King's Servants: The Civil Service of Charles I, 1625–42* (Routledge & Kegan Paul, 1961): for Wolseley's father Sir Robert Wolseley, Clerk of Patents in Chancery, pp. 303–4. For Fleetwood's father Sir Miles Fleetwood, Receiver of the Court of Wards, pp. 357, 361.

31. See *DNB* on Lisle (Philip Sidney), vol. 52, pp. 234–6. See also *HMC, 77th Report: De L'Isle Papers (Penshurst)*, vol. 6, pp. 502–3 on Lisle's residence at Sheen, Surrey, with its Classical statuary. For Sidney's bastards, see Alymer, *State's Servants*, p. 399.
32. *DNB* Mulgrave, as 'Edmund Sheffield', vol. 18, pp. 12–13. Mulgrave's son John became Earl of Buckingham and built the original Buckingham Palace. For other sources on the background of the Councillors, see *DNB* on Wolseley (62, pp. 320–3); Rous (49, pp. 316–17); Sydenham (55, p. 246); Jones (30, pp. 151–3); Desborough (14, pp. 403–5); Strickland (55, pp. 54–5).
33. *DNB* on William Fiennes, Viscount Saye and Sele, vol. 18, pp. 433–6.
34. Lord Hatton to Hyde, 13/23 May 1653; *CSPClar*, vol. 3.
35. Carte, *Original Letters*, vol. 2, pp. 89–90.
36. Hugh Trevor-Roper, 'Cromwell and his Parliaments', in ibid., *Religion, Reformation, and Social Change*.
37. Roots, *Cromwell: A Profile*, pp. 72–90.
38. Christopher Hill, *God's Englishman*, pp. 166–8. Abbott (vol. 1, p. 73) discounts this.
39. Aylmer, *State's Servants*, pp. 234–8.
40. *DNB*, vol. 21, pp. 672–4.
41. Charles Webster, *The Great Instauration: Science, Medicine and Social Reform, 1626–60*, pp. 72–3.
42. Ibid., pp. 72–3, 67–9.
43. Webster, *The Great Instauration*, p. 73, n. 140.
44. Whitelocke, *Memorials of English Affairs*, vol. 4 (1853), pp. 221 ff; *Thurloe*, vol. vi, p. 477.
45. See entries in the Council 'Court Books' (SP, 25). In particular, Thurloe took the lead in the approach to the Swedish talks in spring 1656: SP, 25/54 (27 March/6 April 1656), Thurloe insisted that the negotiators be instructed to insert a provision for banning the export of 'articles useful in war' as contraband as in the Dutch treaty; SP, 25/55 (1/11 May), Thurloe reported on behalf of the negotiators; SP, 25/55 (1/11 May), Thurloe also reported on behalf of the Dutch Maritime Treaty team. The impression given is that the Secretary acted as general coordinator of the Government's approach to the terms of these talks; due to his position, he was involved with *all* talks and could make comparisons between them.
46. The most fully documented, e.g. of the process of English talks with a 'minor' power is that of Venice. In this case, Ambassador Paulucci's negotiations before the advent of the Protectorate were conducted with the 'Master of Ceremonies' Sir Oliver Fleming, who had held this position throughout the Republic but was retained by Cromwell, whose cousin he was. Fleming was ex-ambassador to Savoy and thus aware of European politics. See Paulucci's despatches of 20 September 1653 (NS), *CSPV 1653–4*, p. 126, and 5 December (NS), ibid., pp. 152–3. Under the Protectorate, Thurloe normally dealt with the Venetian envoys, e.g. Paulucci's despatch of 13 September 1654 (NS). Each new ambassador would have an audience with the Protector; e.g. Paulucci (31 January 1654, NS, *CSPV 1653–4*, p. 177), Sagredo (12 November 1655, *CSPV 1655–6*, pp. 135–7), Giavarina (21 July 1656, NS, ibid., pp.

243–4). Cromwell would normally receive an ambassador on other occasions where there was something important to discuss, e.g. Paulucci on 31 July 1654, NS (*CSPV 1653–4*, p. 232). Thurloe would receive him if Cromwell was busy or indisposed, e.g. he met Giavarina 30 July/ 9 August 1658 (*CSPV 1657–9*, pp. 229–30).

47. Examples of letters drawn up or amended by committee: letters to New England confirming the existing regimes were approved and amended by the Council after report by Lord Lisle, 9/19 March 1654 (*CSPCol, 1574–1650*, p. 414); 17/27 May 1655 Thurloe, Fiennes, Strickland and Pickering to draft letters urging action over the Vaudois Massacre; 8/18 January 1657 Fiennes, Lisle and Lambert to consider a letter which Giavarina wants sent to Bendish (SP 25/77). A committee also amended the 'Manifesto' against Spain, October 1655 (*CSPD 1655*, pp. 399–400).

48. Those 'Instructions' which we can identify are Thurloe's work, e.g. Lockhart's orders April 1656 (*EHR*, XXII, 1906, pp. 743–6), Jephson's orders April 1658 (Thurloe, vol. 7, p. 63). It is likely that all the instructions were drawn up in detail by him, under the general supervision of Cromwell and the Council who approved their contents. The Council's deliberations were restricted to general matters of policy, e.g. the two debates on the Western Design and the order to Fiennes, Fleetwood, Desborough, Strickland, Rous and Thurloe on 14/24 July 1657 to consider what to do about the Danish threat to Sweden (SP 25/77).

49. Lawrence's letter to Virginia, 4/14 January 1654; *CSPCol*, p. 412.

50. The list of the original 'Vaudois Committee' of June 1655 and its additions of January 1656 and November 1657 are in SP 25/126.

51. 27 June/7 July 1657 Lambert reports to the Council on Moreland's speech to the committee; SP 25/77. 24 December/3 January 1657/8 the committee reports to the Council on a draft declaration for a collection for Polish exiles, *CSPD 1657–8*, p. 229. The Polish exiles' agents requested £100 to pay for some Bibles, 6/16 July 1658, *CSPD 1657–8*, p. 89.

52. *CSPD 1655*, p. 240.

53. *CSPD 1655–6*, pp. 1–2.

54. Whitelocke, *Memorials*, vol. 4, p. 216.

55. See *Massachusetts Historical Collection*, 4th Series, vol. 7, pp. 462–4.

56. Approval of Lord Delatour's petition, 29 May/8 June 1656, *CSPCol*, p. 441.

57. *CSPCol*, p. 416 (14/24 April 1654).

58. Ibid., p. 416 (24 April/4 May). Both petitions were sent to Jones, Mackworth, Cooper and Wolseley on 8/18 May (ibid., p. 416).

59. 27 November/7 December 1656, Lambert, Wolseley, Fiennes and Mulgrave to consider abandonment of Newfoundland, ibid., p. 452.

60. 29 May/8 June 1656, patents granted to St Stephen, Crowne and Temple (ibid., p. 441). In April 1657 a naval convoy was ordered to escort Temple to his colony (ibid., p. 456).

61. *Acts and Ordinances of the Interregnum*, vol. ii, pp. 1099–1100.

62. 8/18 February 1654, Cromwell to Sedgewick and Leverett and Thurloe's orders to the Governors, *Thurloe*, vol. 1, pp. 771–2.

63. 1656: 15/25 July, Leverett's arrears considered (*CSPCol*, p. 445); 18/ 28 November, Leverett complains and Council recommends payment of £4482 3 1½d (ibid., p. 450). 1657: 22 September/2 October, Leverett complains at non-payment (p. 459); 17/27 December, Desborough, Sydenham and Wolseley to consider (p. 461).
64. For an account of the dispute between Baltimore and his enemies, see Charles M. Andrewes, *The Colonial Period of American History: The Settlements*, vol. 2, pp. 315–22.
65. December, 1653, 'Virginia Committee' created: Cooper and Strickland; later Lambert and Wolseley added, *CSPCol*, p. 412.
66. 31 March/10 April, Kirke's petitions, 24 April/4 May, Tregowrie petition, ibid., p. 415; 8/18 May, Jones, Mackworth, Cooper and Wolseley to consider the petitions, ibid., p. 416.
67. Rhode Island petition to Cooper, Lisle, Montague and Wolseley, 15/ 25 February 1654, ibid., p. 414; 14/24 January, Richard and other traders to Barbados request a new commission of government loyalists to run Barbados, ibid., p. 413; 6/16 December 1654, petition of Samuel Waad of Topsham over shooting of his son at Montserrat by Governor Osborne, ibid., p. 419; 29 January/8 February, to Desborough, Mulgrave, Montague and Pickering, ibid., p. 421; 20 February/1 March, Council endorses report and orders Searle of Barbados to investigate, ibid., p. 421.
68. 2/12 March 1655, creation of 'Plantations Committee': Lambert, Lisle, Mulgrave, Fiennes, Pickering, Wolseley, Desborough, SP 25/122 (Council Committee Book).
69. 29 February/10 March 1656, business of the New England Charters to Sydenham, Desborough, Wolseley, Lisle, Skippon, *CSPCol*, p. 437. 29 May/8 June 1655, Boston piracy complaint to Mulgrave, Wolseley, Fiennes, Montague; 26 June/5 July, Wolseley and Montague report (ibid., p. 426).
70. Virginia petitions Council against illegal planting of English tobacco in Gloucestershire, 6/16 July 1654, *CSPCol*, p. 417. Virginia's complaints considered in Council, 6/16 March, ibid., p. 422; 24 March/ 3 April, ibid., p. 423; 27 April/7 May, ibid., p. 423. Council approves order to local authorities to uproot the plants and quell disturbances, 27 April/7 May, ibid., p. 423 and SP 25/75. 14/24 June 1655 order to local authorities to quell disturbances, SP 25/75.
71. *CSPCol*, p. 413.
72. 18/28 December 1657, Cromwell approves Digges, *CSPCol*, p. 461.
73. 18/28 December 1657, Jamaica Committee approves Digges and Council follows suit, ibid., p. 461.
74. 30 April/10 May 1657, order to suspend 'Somers Island Company' elections, ibid., p. 456. Desborough was succeeded as Governor in 1655 by John Oxenbridge.
75. 7/17 September 1658, Bermudans petition against Sayle, ibid., p. 468. 14/24 September 1658, Noell, Sydenham, Bridge and Mills agree on behalf of the 'Americas Committee'; 23 September/3 October, Desborough and Jones recommend sending him with a warning, ibid., pp. 468–9.

76. 23 March/2 April 1658 petition; 25 March/4 April to Desborough, Fiennes, Fleetwood, Richard Cromwell, Jones, Mulgrave, Wolseley, *CSPCol*, p. 463.
77. *Thurloe*, vol. 2, pp. 542–3.
78. 'Jamaica Committee' listed 26 September/6 October 1655 – Fiennes, Lambert, Lisle, Jones, Sydenham, Desborough, Strickland, Montague, Wolseley, *CSPCol*, p. 430. Pickering added 11/21 September 1656, CSPCol, p. 440.
79. Committee considers sending out wives, 19/29 December 1655, *CSPCol*, p. 434. Committee considers reinforcements (600 men and 4 months' provisions), 11/21 April 1656, ibid., p. 438. Committee considers supplies, 8/18 May 1656, ibid., p. 440. Committee considers pay, 8/18 May, ibid., p. 440, 15/25 May. Committee considers Lambert's report on the tools needed on Jamaica (e.g. 2000 spades, 2000 hatchets, 40 000 nails) and to treat with Noell or whomever they think fit, 19/ 29 June; *Council Committee Book*. Committee considers other colonists to be removed to Jamaica: Long Island, 19/29 August, *CSPCol*, p. 446; America, 13/23 November, ibid., p. 450; Eleuthera, 23 December/2 January 1656/7, ibid., p. 453. Committee considers sending out Irish, 3/13 October 1655, ibid., p. 431, 1000 youths and 1000 girls; also 30 November/10 December 1655, ibid., p. 433.
80. 'Americas Committee' created 15/25 July 1656, *CSPCol*, p. 445. Original members, Limbery, Colonel White, Tobias Bridge, Alderne, Noell, John Thompson, Salmon, Talbot, Mills and Stephen Winthrop. Pickering added 13/23 September, ibid., p. 448.
81. 'Committee for Jamaica to call to advise the Committee appointed this day to whom the management of His Highness' affairs in the West Indies is referred', 15/25 July, *Council Committee Book*. Committee considers American transplantation, 13/23 November, 1656, *CSPCol*, p. 450. Committee considers Nevis removal, 26 September/6 October, ibid., p. 448. Committee considers the safety of the Somers Islands, 13/23 September, ibid., p. 448. Report of this issued, 7/17 October; recommends: (a) patent granted for owners, the current regime for the moment; (b) commission for the Somers Island Company, with Desborough as Governor and Colonel Rowe as deputy governor, ibid., p. 449.
82. The Council's dealings with the visiting Colonel Keynell in 1656; 3/ 13? April, Keynell presents proposals, ibid., p. 439; 15/25 May, Keynell petition to Council for Trade, ibid., p. 440. 1/11 July Keynell presents his requests to Council; for (i) free customs for Antigua, (ii) 500 soldiers, or (iii) servants and negroes, ibid., p. 443. 3/13 July, Keynell meets Colonel Jones on his proposals on customs, ibid., pp. 443–4. 15/25 July, Keynell meets Colonel Jones on his proposals on customs, ibid., pp. 443–4. 15/25 July, Keynell urges haste as he has nearly ruined himself supplying Antigua's defence requirements until now and is in London at his own expense, ibid., p. 445. 6/16 August, Cromwell issues his commission as governor to Keynell, BL Egerton Mss 2395, f. 68. Keynell also required an amount of public arms and ammunition from the Tower (warrant issued, 24 July/3 August, *CSPCol*, p. 448).

Notes

83. Charles I's Council had considered a 'West Indies Company' in 1637, see *CSPCol*, p. 257, 'Propositions for a West Indies Company'. This paper's strategy foreshadowed Cromwell's: 'some fit port in the Indies should be seized for a safe retreat, and the opportunity to invade by land and make prizes at sea'. The Committee the King was urged to appoint would have included Roe, whose idea it may have been.
84. BL Egerton Mss 2095, ff. 87–8.
85. *DNB* Povey, vol. 14, pp. 235–6.
86. Povey's 'Letter-Book'; BL Add. Mss 11 411. He was particularly interested in the Surinam colony founded by the imprisoned Royalist commander Lord Willoughby of Parham, and may have speeded Willoughby's release to go to Surinam (*CSPCol*, p. 461, 26 November/6 December 1657). Povey's brother William was Provost-Marshal at Barbados.
87. 9/19 June 1655, 2000 Bibles to be sent to the West Indies, ibid., p. 426. 29 September/9 October 1657, the Americas Company to consider the lack of ministers on Jamaica, ibid., p. 459.
88. BL Egerton Mss 2095, ff. 56–7, 89–113, 202–37.
89. 'Mr Secretary to assist' the Committee drawing up the 'Manifesto', *CSPD 1655*, p. 399.
90. For reports of the chaos and delays that ensued when Thurloe was ill, see Giavarina's report of 10 March 1656 (NS), *CSPV 1655–6*, p. 187; and 1 March 1658 (NS), *CSPV 1657–9*.
91. See Thurloe's entry in the *DNB*, 56, pp. 431–2.
92. *Thurloe*, vol. 1, pp. 759–63.
93. Aylmer, *The State's Servants*, pp. 264–5.
94. BL Add. Mss 38 100, f. 367.
95. Masson, *Life of Milton*, vol. 5, p. 398. The 'Manifesto' is referred to as Milton's in *CSPD 1655*, p. 397.
96. *DNB* Morland, 13, pp. 965–70. *DNB* Meadowe, 14, pp. 192–4.
97. For Lockhart's instructions, see *EHR*, XXI (1906), pp. 743–6. Cromwell's instructions to Jephson, 22 August/1 September, 1657, *Thurloe*, vol. 6, pp. 478–9.
98. For example, Thurloe to Jephson on Cromwell's attitude to a league with Sweden, 26 March/5 April 1658, *Thurloe*, vol. 7, p. 727; and Thurloe's orders to Jephson on the mission to Brandenburg, 9/19 April 1658, ibid., p. 63.
99. Prideaux's letters to Thurloe; e.g. *Thurloe*, vol. 2, pp. 558, 597, 607–8; vol. 3, pp. 173, 187, 255–7, 575–7. Cromwell was evidently his main proposer.
100. Bordeaux to Brienne 8 May 1656 (NS), PRO SP 31/3/99.
101. Burton, *Diary*, vol. 1, p. 181.
102. Turkey papers (SP 105/17), entry for 16 August 1653.
103. Turkey papers (SP 97/17, f. 119), 10/20 February, Lawrence announces his arrival.
104. Ibid., f. 121, Hagen to Lord President Lawrence, March 1654.
105. Levant Company Committee Book (SP 105/151), entry for 19/29 June notes Bendish's refusal, as a result of which another petition was being sent to Cromwell for Salwey's appointment.

106. Levant Company Court Book (SP 101/151), entry for 7/17 July 1654.
107. Letter book (SP 105/112), entry for 30 August/9 September 1654.
108. See the Levant Company's 'Letter-Book' and 'Court Book' for 1654–6: SP 105/112, 151.
109. Levant Company's Court Book, 6 February 1658.
110. *CSPD 1656–7*, p. 304.
111. Ibid., p. 110.
112. *Thurloe*, vol. 6, p. 278.

3 Cromwell's Approach to the 'Two Crowns', 1651–4

1. A.J. Loomie, 'Alonso de Cardenas and the Long Parliament, 1640–8', *EHR*, XCVII, 1982, pp. 289–307.
2. *CSPV 1647–52*, p. 126.
3. France was hindered by Mazarin's need not to offend leading nobles by appeasing regicides; Spain had more freedom of manoeuvre.
4. He had written *A Discourse wherein is examined what is practically lawful during the confusions and revolutions of Government* (London, 1648).
5. *Weekly Intelligencer*, 20–27 April 1652.
6. *Articles proposées et arrestées en la chambre S. Louis par les deputez des quatre compagnies*, Paris 1648, article 22.
7. *Commons Journals*, vol. 6, pp. 284–5.
8. Croullé to Mazarin, 26 September and 7 November 1650; PRO SP 31/3/90.
9. Grignon to Brienne and Mazarin, 15 February 1649; PRO SP 31/3/89.
10. Mazarin to Le Tellier, 13 October 1650, *Lettres de Cardinal Mazarin* (ed. Chéruel), vol. 3, p. 865.
11. French Intelligence quoted in Philip Knatchel, *England and the Fronde*, pp. 271–2.
12. Morosini to Senate, 14/24 October 1651, *CSPV 1647–52*, p. 202.
13. Cardenas to Madrid, 13/23 April 1652, Simancas Mss 2569; PRO SP 94/43.
14. D'Estrades to Mazarin, 15/25 February 1652; quoted in *EHR*, XI (1896), pp. 482–9. Paulucci also believed that Cromwell was in overall charge of the Dunkirk business; see his despatch to Morosini, 28 April/8 May: 'General Cromwell is the one who has the first word and the last for all necessary decisions' (*CSPV 1647–52*, p. 231). Mazarin's advisers were currently warning him that an English alliance was essential to offset Spain's advantage in the war, even if Dunkirk had to be sacrificed: see anonymous memorandum 'Avis touchant les affaires d'Angleterre' (3/13 and 14/24 February 1651, PRO SP 31/3/90). Mazarin's envoy to London the Sieur de Gentillot, claimed that Dunkirk was the one means to avert an Anglo-Spanish alliance; see his despatch to Servien, 13/23 February 1652 (PRO SP 31/3/90).
15. J. Jusserand, *Angleterre: Recueil des Institutions* (Archives du Minisère des Affaires Etrangères, Paris), vol. 1, p. 134.
16. Cardenas to Philip IV, 8/18 November 1651, Simancas Mss 2034, PRO SP 94/43.
17. Knatchel, *England and the Fronde*, pp. 198–200.

18. Violet Rowe, *Sir Henry Vane the Younger: A Study in Political and Administrative History*, pp. 247 ff.
19. *The Journal of Joachim Hane* was edited by Sir Charles Firth and published in 1895–6.
20. BL Add. Mss 29 546, f. 89; 32 093, f. 281.
21. Knatchel, *England and the Fronde*, pp. 198–200.
22. Bordeaux to Brienne, 13/23 June 1653, PRO SP 31/3/91.
23. Theodorus to Conway, 19/29 May 1653, *CSPD 1652–3*, p. 340.
24. Abbé de Cosnac, *Memoires*, vol. 1, pp. 66–9.
25. Bordeaux to Brienne, 7/17 and 11/21 August 1653, PRO SP 31/3/91.
26. Sexby's memorandum, in *Clarke Papers*, vol. 3. Paulucci informed Sagredo, ambassador in Paris, that 'the government favours Condé rather than the Court party' and 'would seek to foment civil strife': 30 July/9 August, *CSPV 1653–4*, p. 130.
27. Sexby's memorandum, as above.
28. Bordeaux to Brienne, 28 February/10 March 1653, PRO SP 31/3/90.
29. Bordeaux to Brienne, 4/14 November 1653, and Bordeaux to Mazarin, 1/11 December 1653, PRO SP 31/3/91.
30. Barriere to Condé, 5/15 December 1653, BL Add. Mss 35 252.
31. Bordeaux to Brienne, 26 December 1653/5 January 1654 and 16/26 January, PRO SP 31/3/92.
32. Quote from Vatican Archives to Gardiner, *History of Commonwealth and Protectorate*, vol. 3, pp. 119–20.
33. Sagredo to Senate, 7/17 February 1654, *CSPV 1653–4*, p. 183. See Bordeaux to Brienne, 8/18 and 19/29 January and 13/23 March 1654, PRO SP 31/3/92 and 31/3/93; see also Bordeaux to Brienne, 22 March/2 April and 26 March/6 April, PRO SP 31/3/94 and White to Servien, 27 March/7 April, ibid.
34. Baas to Mazarin, 15/25 January, PRO SP 31/3/92.
35. Bordeaux to Brienne, 26 January/5 February, PRO SP 31/3/93.
36. Cardenas to Philip IV, 3/13 March 1654, quoted in Guizot, *History of Oliver Cromwell*, vol. 2, pp. 380–3.
37. Leopold, governor of the Netherlands, to Philip IV, 11/21 March, ibid. Leopold may have been assisted by his captain of the guard, Don Francisco Villaquirean, who was in London to congratulate Cromwell on his accession (*Thurloe*, vol. 2, p. 69).
38. Guizot, *History of Oliver Cromwell*, vol. 2, pp. 380–3.
39. Hane's letters of ?15/25 October and 5/15 November 1653; *Thurloe*, vol. 2, pp. 553, 578.
40. *Clarke Papers*, vol. 3, pp. 197–202.
41. Quirini (Madrid) to Senate, 22 February/4 March 1654, *CSPV 1653–4*, pp. 179–80.
42. Quirini to Senate, as n. 45.
43. Bordeaux had been pointing this out since his arrival.
44. *Thurloe*, vol. 2, p. 61.
45. Hyde to Wentworth, 10/20 March 1654, *CSPClar*, vol. 2, p. 325.
46. Sagredo to Senate, 21 February/3 March 1654, *CSPV*, p. 190.
47. Paulucci to Senate, 24 March/3 April 1654, *CSPV*, p. 197. Bordeaux believed that aid to Condé depended on Mazerolles' successful return with the proposed subsidy; Bordeaux to Brienne, 10/20 March 1654,

PRO SP 31/3/93, p. 94. He still believed that Cromwell 'will have some connection with our enemies', Bordeaux to Brienne, 13/23 March 1654, PRO SP 31/3/93.

48. *CSPD 1654*, p. 73.
49. Mazarin to Baas, 29 March/8 April 1654, PRO SP 31/3/94. Mazarin recommends the use of Sir Gilbert Pickering as a useful supporter.
50. Bordeaux to Brienne, 10/20 April, ibid. Baas singled out Lambert as the enemy of France (Baas to Mazarin, 21, 24 and 27 April, ibid.). Bordeaux believed Thurloe was also hostile (to Brienne, 13 April, ibid.).
51. De Patt to Mazarin, 17/27 April, in Guizot, *History of Oliver Cromwell*, Appendix 8, no. 3.
52. Baas to Mazarin, 11/21 April, PRO SP 31/3/94.
53. Baas to Mazarin, 14/24 April, ibid.
54. Barrière to Condé, 7/17 April, BL Add. Mss 35252.
55. Burnet, *History of my own Times*, vol. 1, p. 134.
56. Unpublished thesis by J.F. Battick, 'Cromwell's Navy and the Foreign Policy of the Protectorate, 1653–8', Boston, 1967.
57. Bordeaux to Brienne, 25 December 1653, PRO SP 31/3/92.
58. Venables' 'Narrative of the Caribbean expedition', chapter 3 in *Harleian Miscellany*, vol. 3, p. 513.
59. *Clarke Papers*, vol. 3, pp. 203–6.
60. Mazarin to Bordeaux, 3 May (NS), PRO SP 31/3/94.
61. Bordeaux to Brienne, 14 May, ibid., 31/3/94.
62. Bordeaux to Brienne, 2 May (31/3/94).
63. French Intelligence, 5/15 May, *Thurloe*, vol. 2, p. 262. Petit informed Thurloe that Mazarin had informed the Duke d'Arpajon that an English invasion was planned on behalf of the Huguenots; letter of 12/22 April 1654, *Thurloe*, vol. 2, p. 246. The Huguenots were optimistic of the new respect with which they were being treated by the French government lest they revolt. Petit informed Thurloe that 'all these favours came, after God, from my Lord Protector for whose prosperity . . . [they] had cause to make continual prayer'. However, they now counted a peace treaty, with 'some clause to be put therein for them in general . . . desiring not that the business should come to extremities', better than a war. They also feared lest Mazarin fall and a less tolerant minister come to power (*Thurloe*, vol. 2, p. 262).
64. Barrière to Condé, 1 June (NS), BL Add. Mss 35252.
65. Sagredo to Senate, 3 March and 5 May 1654, *CSPV 1653–4*, pp. 187–8, 208–9. Spain hoped that this would be the case, Sagredo, 18 August, ibid., p. 248. See also Bordeaux senior to his son the ambassador, 26 May, *Thurloe*, vol. 2, p. 283.
66. French Intelligence, undated, *Thurloe*, vol. 2, p. 275.
67. Bordeaux to Brienne, 2 April 1654, PRO SP 31/3/94.
68. For example, Mazarin's instructions to Baas of 27 March imply that he should use this weapon, ibid., 31/3/93.
69. Bordeaux to Brienne and Baas to Mazarin, 14 May 1654, ibid., 31/3/94.
70. Baas to Mazarin, 14 May 1654, as above.

71. Gardiner, *History of the Commonwealth and Protectorate*, vol. 3.
72. Barrière to Condé, 15 May, BL Add. Mss 35252.
73. Bordeaux to Mazarin, 11 May 1654, PRO SP 31/3/94.
74. As n. 72.
75. Baas to Mazarin, 21 May 1654, PRO SP 31/3/94.
76. Guizot, *History of Oliver Cromwell*, vol. 2, pp. 385–8. Mazerolles agreed: 'the Spanish ambassador has not got a sou', Mazerolles to Condé, 14 July 1654, BL Add. Mss 35252.
77. Colonel Walters wrote to the Council over money owing for his shipping of 10,000 Irishmen for Spain in 1652–3, Bodleian Lib., Rawlinson Mss A261, ff. 13–13v. Colonels Luce and Owens also complained, and Cromwell wrote to Leopold on their behalf on 4/14 August, Rawlinson Mss A261, ff. 12v–13. Baas wrote that Cromwell had been informed of the poor pay Condé's men received and was very surprised, Baas to Mazarin, 25 June (PRO SP 31/3/95).
78. *Thurloe*, vol. 2, pp. 308–9.
79. Barrière to Condé, 20 May, BL Add. Mss 35252.
80. Paulucci, 29 May, *CSPV 1653–4*, p. 216.
81. Brienne to Bordeaux, undated, PRO SP 31/3/95.
82. *Thurloe*, vol. 2, p. 398. On 27 June Bordeaux reported that Cromwell's agents in France had informed him of French culpability, PRO SP 31/3/95.
83. Naudin's confession, *Thurloe*, vol. 2, p. 412.
84. Pickering informed Baas of this; Baas to Mazarin, 8 June, also Brienne to Bordeaux, 19 June, PRO SP 31/3/95.
85. Baas to Mazarin, 8 June; Bordeaux to Brienne, 15 June, ibid.
86. Louis XIV to Bordeaux and Baas, 17 June, ibid.
87. Mazarin to Bordeaux, 17 June, ibid.
88. Ibid.
89. Bordeaux to Mazarin, 15 and 27 June, ibid.
90. Baas to Mazarin, 25 June, ibid. In fact Whitelocke (*Journal of the Swedish Embassy*, vol. 2, p. 73) says the alliance was Queen Christina's idea.
91. Bordeaux to Mazarin, 14 July, PRO SP 31/3/95.
92. Bordeaux to Brienne, 23 July; *Thurloe*, vol. 2, p. 447 and PRO SP 31/3/95.
93. Cromwell to Marcille, 10/20 June, Abbott, *Writings and Speeches of Oliver Cromwell*, vol. 3, pp. 324, 5; Cromwell to Louis XIV and Mazarin, 29 June/9 July, Bodlelan Lib. Rawlinson Mss A261, ff. 10v–11. Thurloe was currently gloomy about the treaty, writing to Pell on 14/24 July that 'little is to be expected' as Mazarin was obstinate over granting toleration to the Huguenots; quoted in Vaughan, *Cromwell*, vol. 1, pp. 25–6.

4 The Verge of a Breach with France: July 1654–March 1655

1. Barrière to Condé, 17 July (NS), BL Add. Mss 35252.
2. Barrière to Condé, 26 June (NS), ibid.
3. *CSPD 1654*, p. 201.
4. Intelligence to Hyde, 29/30 June 1654, *CSPClar*, vol. 3, p. 379.

5.   Bordeaux to Mazarin, 25 June (NS), PRO SP 31/3/95.
6.   *Thurloe*, vol. 2, p. 414.
7.   Quirini to Senate, 29 July (NS), *CSPV 1653–4*, p. 241.
8.   Abbott, *Writings and Speeches of Oliver Cromwell*, vol. 3, pp. 85–8.
9.   Bordeaux to Brienne, 22 June/2 July, PRO SP 31/3/95.
10. Petit to Thurloe, 15/25 July, *Thurloe*, vol. 2, p. 458.
11. 'Free trade' appeared in the treaties as follows: French Treaty, Article IV (SP 103/12); Swedish Treaty 1654, Articles III and X (SP 108/56); Dutch Treaty, Articles XII and XVII (SP 103/56); Portuguese Treaty, Articles II and III (SP 103/57). Particular care was taken to recover the goods of Englishmen who died abroad, a point which had been subject to abuse when foreign governments knew there was no strong regime in England to take such matters up.
12. Cromwell, more inexperienced than Charles's advisers some of whom had been to Spain (e.g. Cottington and Endymion Porter), did not know or take account of traditional dilatoriness.
13. Rawlinson Mss A261, ff. 7v–8v; 13–13v.
14. *CSPD 1654*, p. 236, and Paulucci's despatch of 25 July (NS), *CSPV 1653–4*, pp. 238–9.
15. Cardenas to Thurloe, 15/25 July, *Thurloe*, vol. 2, p. 461.
16. Mazerolles to Condé, 24 July (NS), BL Add. Mss 35252.
17. Pawley to Thurloe, unknown date, *Thurloe*, vol. 2, pp. 338–40.
18. *Thurloe*, vol. 1, pp. 759–63.
19. *Clarke Papers*, vol. 3, pp. 207–8.
20. As n. 18.
21. Quirini to Senate, 2 September, as above.
22. Bordeaux to Chanut, ambassador at The Hague, 8/18 August, *Thurloe*, vol. 2, pp. 549–50.
23. Petit to Thurloe, 15/25 July, *Thurloe*, vol. 2, p. 458.
24. Cromwell's address to Parliament, 4/14 September, Abbott, *Writings and Speeches*, vol. 3, pp. 434–43.
25. Bordeaux to Mazarin, 1 October and 19 October (NS), PRO SP 31/3/95.
26. Servien insisted that Holland not Hamburg mediate, Servien to Bordeaux, 24 September (NS), ibid.
27. Bordeaux to Mazarin, 22 October (NS), and to Brienne, 26 October (NS), ibid.; and *Thurloe*, vol. 2, p. 360.
28. Servien to Bordeaux, 24 September (NS), as n. 26.
29. Mazarin to Bordeaux, 27 October (NS), ibid.
30. Leverett to Cromwell, 5/15 September, *Thurloe*, vol. 2, p. 584.
31. Bordeaux to Brienne, 26 October (NS), PRO SP 31/3/96.
32. Bordeaux to Brienne, 26 October (NS), as n. 31.
33. Sagredo to Senate, 1 December (NS), *CSPV*, pp. 282–3.
34. Paulucci to Senate, 26 October (NS), ibid., p. 271.
35. Quirini to Senate, 7 October (NS), ibid., p. 266. De Haro was not persuaded and still thought that Cromwell intended to use the fleet against the Orangists in the United Provinces, Quirini, 14 October (NS), ibid., p. 268.
36. Quirini to Senate, 11 November (NS), ibid., p. 276.

37. Bordeaux to Brienne, 10 October (NS), PRO SP 31/3/96.
38. Quirini to Senate, 7 October (NS), *CSPV 1653–4*, p. 266.
39. See the 'Instructions' to the commanders, Chapter 5. Paulucci (letter of 14 November (NS), *CSPV*, p. 277) reported that in London it was expected that Blake would 'give the salute with shotted guns' to the French fleet.
40. Paulucci to Senate, 14 August (NS), *CSPV*, pp. 193–5.
41. Rosso, Venetian ambassador to Naples, 8 December (NS), ibid., p. 285.
42. Mazarin to Bordeaux, 2 January 1655 (NS), *Thurloe*, vol. 3, p. 41.
43. Sarotti, Venetian ambassador to Tuscany, 2 January 1655 (NS), reports that Leghorn believed Blake's intentions to be against France (*CSPV 1655–6*, p. 3). The Viceroyalty in Naples agreed or so the Governor publicly declared, Rosso, 29 December (NS), *CSPV 1653–4*, p. 293. Cardenas declared that he had an understanding with Cromwell on what Blake was to do, Cardenas to Philip IV, 4 January 1655 (NS), PRO SP 94/43; Paulucci to Senate, 6 December 1654 (NS), *CSPV*, p. 283.
44. Longland to Thurloe, 8/18 December, *Thurloe*, vol. 3, p. 12.
45. Sarotti, 12 December (NS), *CSPV 1653–4*, p. 285; Sagredo, 12 January 1655 (NS), *CSPV 1655–6*, p. 6.
46. As n. 42.
47. Anon. to Bordeaux, 3 March (NS), *Thurloe*, vol. 2, p. 163. Implied in Bordeaux's letter to Mazarin of 31 December (NS), PRO SP 31/3/96. Servien told Sagredo that 'not to meet aggression with aggression was a sort of maritime servitude', Sagredo to Senate, 15 December 1654 (NS), *CSPV 1653–4*, p. 287. In fact French privateers were taking increased action without waiting for official sanction.
48. Paulucci to Senate, 16 January (NS), *CSPV 1655–6*, p. 79.
49. Bordeaux senior to Bordeaux, 5 December 1654 (NS), *Thurloe*, vol. 2, p. 738.
50. Bordeaux to Count Charost, governor of Calais, 21 December 1654 (NS), *Thurloe*, vol. 3, p. 18.
51. See n. 47.
52. Bordeaux was temporarily encouraged by Cromwell's willingness to settle, Bordeaux to Brienne, 19 December (NS), PRO SP 31/3/96. He was soon disillusioned, *Thurloe*, vol. 3, p. 135.
53. Louis XIV issued a formal order to Bordeaux to depart on 8/18 December 1654 (BL Add. Mss 4156, f. 103) which was not put into effect. To this was now added a French Council of State order of early February 'to conclude the treaty or come back, that they might see whether they had peace or war' (*Severus Proculus*, 5/15 February).
54. Bordeaux informed Brienne on 22 March (NS) that 'I will suddenly put an end to my negotiation unless some sudden accident happen that I cannot foresee', but must have had second thoughts (PRO SP 31/3/97). For Cromwell's statement that it was the Councillors who were adamant on Acadia, see Bordeaux to Brienne, 18 February (NS), ibid.
55. Paulucci to Senate, 14 February (NS), *CSPV 1655–6*, pp. 19–20.

56. Quirini to Senate, 13 March (NS), *CSPV*, p. 30.
57. Rosso, 9 March (NS), ibid., p. 29.
58. Sagredo, 13 April (NS), ibid., p. 45.
59. *Thurloe*, vol. 3, p. 198.
60. *Mercurius Politicus*, 29 March–5 April (OS).
61. Bordeaux to Mazarin, 15 April (NS), PRO SP 31/3/97.
62. Thurloe to Pell, 6/16 April, quoted in Vaughan, *Cromwell*, vol. 1, p. 64.
63. As n. 61.

5 The Western Design

1. Sagredo, 20 October 1655 (NS), *CSPV 1655–6*, pp. 128–9.
2. *Thurloe*, vol. 1, pp. 759–63, and *Harleian Miscellany*, vol. 3, p. 513.
3. For example, Quirini, 17 June 1655 (NS), *CSPV*, p. 55; and also James Wilson's letter of intelligence from Madrid to Thurloe, *Thurloe*, vol. 3, pp. 389–90.
4. Examples of Dutch actions in the same manner as Cromwell's attack are legion, see Geoffrey Parker's article, 'The Dutch Revolt and the Polarization of International Politics', in Parker and Smith (eds), *The General Crisis of the Seventeenth Century* (Routledge & Kegan Paul, 1978). The most notable examples were the attacks on South America, e.g. the attack on Callao in 1624 and Brouwer's expedition to Chile in 1645. The Dutch were more interested in stirring up the Indians against Spain than the English usually were, e.g. Van Spilzbergen's plan for a revolt in Chile in 1614. There was a precedent for a large-scale continental campaign against a rival imperial power in South America, namely the Dutch attempt to wrest Brazil away from Spanish-occupied Portugal in 1630–45. Significantly, the main exponent of a South American campaign in 1655–6 was the Portuguese Jew, Simon de Casseres (see n. 34).
5. Robert E. Ruigh, *The Parliament of 1624: Politics and Foreign Policy*, quotes Eliot's speech of 19 March 1624 (OS), p. 220. Incidentally, Eliot was father-in-law to Nathaniel Fiennes, Cromwell's Councillor.
6. Rudyerd's speech of 1 March 1624 (NS), ibid., pp. 177–9. These bellicose sentiments about Spain and what to do with her empire were not confined to 'Parliamentary opposition' leaders; they were shared by Sir Francis Bacon.
7. P. Chaunu, *Seville et l'Atlantique* (Paris, 1959), vol. 3.
8. See William Maltby, *The Black Legend in England: The Development of Anti-Spanish Sentiment, 1558–1660*, and Benjamin Keen, 'The Black Legend Revisited', in *Hispanic American Review*, XLIX (1969), pp. 703–19.
9. *CSPCol 1574–1660*, p. 73.
10. Ibid., p. 257.
11. C.M. Andrewes, *British Committees, Commissions, and Councils of Trade and Navigation*, vol. 1, p. 50.
12. Venables, 'Narrative' ('A Brief and Perfect Journal'), in *Harleian Miscellany*, vol. 3, p. 513.

13. Whitelocke, *Memorials*, vol. 4, p. 189 (March 1655). According to Burnet, who had most of his relevant information from Stouppe, 'Spain would never admit of a peace with England between the tropics; so he [Cromwell] was in a state of war with them in those parts, even before he declared war in Europe'; Gage told him that once Hispaniola and Cuba were conquered the rest would follow (*History of my own Times*, vol. 1, pp. 134–6.)

14. Thomas Gage, *The English–American His Travails: or a new survey of the West Indies* (ed. A. Newton).

15. Ibid., preface, p. 2.

16. Gage's *Brief and True Observations*, Thurloe, vol. 3, p. 59–61.

17. Ibid.

18. Ibid., p. 62.

19. Ibid., vol. ii, pp. 542–3.

20. Noell's brother Thomas was his agent in Barbados, and was confirmed as Provost-General by Cromwell. Povey's brother was Provost-Marshal, Anthony Ashley Cooper had invested in Barbados, and Maurice Thompson had interests there since he had introduced the first African slaves in the 1620s. The area was also familiar to George Downing, ambassador to Savoy in 1655, and to the preacher John Oxenbridge (Skippon's brother-in-law).

21. *Thurloe*, vol. 2, pp. 28–9.

22. Paulucci reported the anger in the fleet (23 November (NS), *CSPV 1653–4*, pp. 143–4) and Desborough's visit (ibid., 1 December (NS), p. 146), Desborough's reports on the situation are in *Thurloe*, vol. 3, pp. 3 and 7. Volunteers were unlikely for the tropics, see 'F.B.' to Sir J. Barrington, 14/24 July 1655, *Historical Mss Commission Report*, vol. 7, p. 571. Venables objected to the haste with which his troops were despatched: 'Narrative' 6, in *Harleian Miscellany*, vol. 3, p. 513. He described his recruits as 'hectors, knights of the blade, common cheats, cutpurses, and such like lewd persons' ('Narrative' 33). Venables was evidently aware of the dangers involved in the insufficiency of his troops, but he could not have made much protest at the time; the fact that he took his wife ('Memorial of Elizabeth Venables', *Chetham Society Miscellany* iv, pp. 9–28) indicates that he was as confident of the lack of resistance as Cromwell. It is clear, however, from his performance at Hispaniola that he was not lacking in military abilities, and was unjustly treated by Cromwell on his return. Penn was a more proper scapegoat.

23. Cromwell to Penn, 20/30 December 1654, *Historical Mss Commission Report*, vol. 13, app. ii, no. 8.

24. Venables, *Narrative*, pp. 30, 40. See also Winslow to Thurloe, 16/26 March, *Thurloe*, vol. 3, pp. 249–52.

25. This was implied in Cromwell's proclamation encouraging settlement.

26. On 19/29 October 1655 the Council ordered a further eight ships to be sent to Barbados (*CSPD 1655*, p. 610). A further reinforcement, led by Colonel Brayne, was ordered in April 1656; see *CSPCol*, pp. 438–40. Many of them were in fact drowned en route off Ireland, Henry Cromwell to Thurloe, 7/17 November 1656, *Thurloe*, vol. 5, p. 570. It

is noticeable that the Government was now taking more care over the quality of troops and officers sent out. There were no more blunders like the choice of Captain Butler.

27. For example, Sedgewick to Thurloe, 5/15 November 1655, *Thurloe*, vol. 4, pp. 151–5; Goodson and Sedgewick to Thurloe, 24 January/3 February 1656, ibid., p. 454; Goodson and Sedgewick to Thurloe, 12/22 March 1656, ibid., pp. 601–2. D'Oyley to Thurloe, 12/22 March 1656, (pp. 602–3), 18/28 April (p. 711), 6/16 October (*Thurloe*, vol. 6, p. 476). Brayne to Thurloe, 12/22 March 1657, *Thuloe*, vol. 6, p. 110.

28. Sedgewick to Thurloe, 5/15 November 1655, *Thurloe*, vol. 4, pp. 151–5. Colonel Holdip's cashiering is reported in Goodson's letter to Thurloe of 25 June/5 July 1656, ibid., vol. 5, p. 151.

29. Sedgewick to Thurloe, 12/22 March 1656, ibid., vol. 4, pp. 601–2.

30. D'Oyley to Thurloe, 18/28 July 1658, ibid., vol. 7, pp. 260–2.

31. Goodson to the Council, 7/17 November 1655, ibid., vol. 4, p. 159.

32. Goodson to the Council, 7/17 January 1656, ibid., vol. 5, p. 96.

33. Sedgewick to Thurloe, 18/28 April 1656, ibid., vol. 5, p. 711.

34. Simon de Casseres to Thurloe, undated, ibid., vol. 4, pp. 62–3.

35. BL Egerton Mss 1095, f. 109.

36. Ibid., ff. 87–8.

37. Ibid., f. 110.

38. For example, Secretary (Thomas) Noell's letter to Thurloe of 20/30 March 1655 denying Royalist intrigues in the militia, *CSPClar*, vol. 3, p. 13.

39. For example, Cromwell to Cotton, *Massachusetts Historical Collection, 4th Series*, VII, pp. 462–4.

40. Council's Proclamation on settlement of Jamaica, c. 10/20 October 1655, *CSPCol 1675–6*, p. 97.

41. Ibid.

42. Stokes to Cromwell, 29 May/8 June 1656, *Thurloe*, vol. 5, pp. 565–6. The Council ordered the Commander-in-Chief on Jamaica to send them ships for free transport as they requested, *CSPCol*, p. 453 (23 December/2 January 1656–7).

43. Brayne to Thurloe, 12/22 March 1657, *Thurloe*, vol. 6, pp. 110–11.

44. See Paulucci's report of 6/16 December 1654, *CSPV 1653–4*, p. 284.

45. D'Oyley to Thurloe, 27 February/9 March 1658, *Thurloe*, vol. 6, pp. 723–4.

46. Brayne to Thurloe, 12/22 March 1657, as n. 51.

47. *DNB* Gookin, vol. 8, pp. 154–5.

48. Cromwell to Searle, October 1655, *Thurloe*, vol. 4, p. 130.

49. As quoted in Leverett to Endicott, 20/30 December 1656, Hutchinson, *History*, 1936, vol. 1, pp. 163–4. Interestingly, Lord Saye and Sele had also believed that the New England colonies were only a stopping place for godly colonists, who should move on to the Caribbean when they acquired state backing. Letter to John Winthrop of 9 July 1640, quoted in Karen Kuppermann, 'Errand to the Indies: Puritan colonization from Providence Island through the Western Design', in *William and Mary Quarterly*, XLV (1988), pp. 70–99.

50. Gookin's instructions, 26 September/6 October 1655, Penn, *Memorials*, vol. 2, p. 585.
51. Gookin to Thurloe, 24 January/3 February 1656, *Thurloe*, vol. 4, p. 449.
52. Gookin to Thurloe, 10/20 May and 24 June/3 July 1656, ibid., vol. 5, p. 6 and 147–8.
53. Gookin to Thurloe, 8/18 September 1656, ibid., vol. 5, pp. 509–10.
54. As n. 49.
55. Hartlib's epistle dedicatory to Bate's *Ireland's Natural History*, London, 1645.
56. In fact there was a republican mutiny against D'Oyley's proposal to return to Charles II's allegiance in 1661, and two officers were shot. BL Add. Mss 11411, f. 9.
57. BL Add. Mss 11411, f. 9.
58. Augier to the Council, 25 July/4 August 1657, *CSPCol*, p. 456. The idea was submitted to a Council Committee on 20/30 October (ibid., p. 460) and nothing more was heard of it.
59. Broghill to Thurloe, 18/28 September 1655, *CSPD 1655–6*, p. 196.
60. Ross to Nicholas, 11/21 February 1656, ibid.
61. On 14/24 August 1656 the Council issued an order to apprehend 'lewd and dangerous persons, rogues, vagrants, and other idle persons' for removal to Jamaica, *CSPCol*, p. 456.
62. 6/16 August 1656, Council to Sir John Berksted, *CSPCol*, p. 456.

6 Leda's Mission and the Vaudois Massacre

1. Quirini, 27 February and 20 March 1655 (*CSPV 1655–6*, pp. 24 and 55–6). Paulucci reported that Cardenas was distressed but continued to negotiate, 8 March (pp. 27–9).
2. Wright to Thurloe, 20 April 1655, *Thurloe*, vol. 3, pp. 366–7.
3. Sexby to de Haro, May 1655, *CSPClar*, vol. 3, p. 41.
4. Paulucci, 30 May and 5 June 1655, *CSPV*, pp. 60 and 62–3.
5. Mazarin to Bordeaux, 25 May, PRO 31/3/98. Bordeaux to his father, 24 May, *Thurloe*, vol. 3, p. 437. Paulucci, 14 June, *CSPV*, pp. 65–6.
6. Quirini, 3 July, ibid., p. 74.
7. Quirini, 12 June, ibid., p. 65.
8. Council Order Book (SP 25/75), entries for 4/14 May and 24 May/3 June.
9. Paulucci, 18 May, *CSPV*, pp. 54–6.
10. Paulucci, 30 May, ibid., pp. 59–60.
11. Paulucci, 14 June, ibid., pp. 65–7; this was expected by Bordeaux (Bordeaux to Brienne, 27 May, PRO 31/3/98).
12. Bordeaux to Mazarin, 20 May, PRO 31/3/98.
13. *Thurloe*, vol. 3, p. 541.
14. Ibid., p. 611.
15. Letters of intelligence received by Council, 17/27 May, *CSPD 1655*, p. 165. Fiennes reports on draft of letters on the crisis, 23 May/1 June, SP 25/55 (Council Order Book).

16. See Gardiner, *History of the Commonwealth and Protectorate*, vol. 4, pp. 180–6.
17. Evelyn, *Diary*, ed. de Beer, p. 359 (12 and 24 June OS). See also Whitelocke, *Memorials*, vol. 4, p. 203, and Paulucci, 28 June, *CSPV*, p. 71.
18. Collection ordered, 23 May/2 June, *CSPD 1655*, pp. 182–3. Fast ordered, 30 May/9 June, *CSPClar*, vol. 3, p. 45. Second collection ordered, 12/22 July, ibid., p. 45.
19. *CSPD 1655*, pp. 184–5; Hatsell to Blackborne, 26 May (OS), Bourne and Foster to Blackborne, 28 May (OS).
20. *Mercurius Politicus*, 10/20 May.
21. Fleetwood to Thurloe, 23 May/2 June, *Thurloe*, vol. 3, p. 468.
22. Abbott, *Writings and Speeches*, vol. 3, pp. 726–7.
23. Fiennes reported to the full Council on the drafts of letters, 23 May/ 1 June, SP 25/55 (Council Order Book).
24. The French soldiers were actually in Savoy en route to assist their King's cousin and ally against Spain in Italy, as they had for each campaign during the Franco-Spanish War.
25. Cromwell to Louis XIV, 25 May/4 June, Abbott, *Writings and Speeches*, vol. 3, pp. 726–7.
26. Cromwell to the Swiss Cantons, 25 May/4 June, Symmons, *Milton*, vol. 6, pp. 385–6.
27. Paulucci, 4 July, *CSPV 1655–6*, pp. 75–6.
28. *Perfect Diurnal*, 16/26 July, *Clarke Papers*, vol. 3, p. 45.
29. Thurloe informed Bordeaux of the likely insistence on a Vaudois settlement preceding the treaty in early June, Bordeaux to Mazarin, 3 June, Bordeaux to Brienne, 5 June, PRO SP 31/3/98. Bordeaux refused Cromwell's attempt to put the Vaudois settlements into the French treaty at the end of July (Bordeaux to Brienne, 29 July, ibid.).
30. Bordeaux to Brienne, 5 August, ibid.
31. Nieupoort to Ruysch, 8/18 June, *Thurloe*, vol. 3, pp. 527–8. For popular hatred of Catholics, see Bordeaux to Mazarin, 10 June, PRO SP 31/3/98. Had the Vaudois Massacre occurred in 1651–4, instead of happening *after* the attack on Hispaniola, it would very likely have pushed England over the brink into war with France.
32. Pell to Thurloe, 3 June, *Lansdowne Mss* 745, f. 95b.
33. Bordeaux to his father, 28 June, *Thurloe*, vol. 3, p. 558.
34. Bordeaux to Mazarin, 19 June, PRO SP 31/3/98.
35. Bordeaux to Brienne, 13 June, *Thurloe*, vol. 3, p. 470.
36. Reports of rebellion in Languedoc were noted in Bordeaux's letter to his father of 28 June (ibid., p. 558). Cromwell asked for the opinion of Stouppe (Bordeaux to Brienne, 15 July, PRO SP 31/3/98) and foreign Protestants, presumably the Huguenot congregation at the Savoy who had sent Dr More to France in 1653 (Bordeaux to Mazarin, 23 July, ibid.). Mazarin thought it worth his while to bribe Stouppe to assure Cromwell that the trouble in Languedoc was over (Bordeaux to Brienne, 1 July, ibid.). The main responsibility for the stories of revolt circulating in London was believed to be Barrière (Bordeaux to Brienne, 5 August, ibid.).
37. Quirini, 3 July, *CSPV 1655–6*, pp. 74–5.

38. Bordeaux to Lionne, 21/31 July, *Thurloe*, vol. 3, p. 680. See also Bordeaux to Brienne, 3 June, ibid., vol. 2, p. 470.
39. See n. 36.
40. Brienne to Bordeaux, 3 September, ibid., vol. 3, p. 731. Servien to Bordeaux, 21 August, ibid., vol. 3, p. 706.
41. Cromwell to Louis XIV and to Mazarin, 31 July/10 August, *Archives du Ministère des Affaires Etrangères*, vol. 66, pp. 98–9v.
42. Thomas Noell's letter of 5/15 June announcing the disaster (*Thurloe*, vol. 3, p. 514) was known in London by the time Paulucci wrote his despatch of 8 August (*CSPV*, p. 91).
43. Bodleian Lib., Tanner Mss 52, ff. 121–2.
44. English belief that Mazarin pressurised the Duke to reach a quick agreement with the Vaudois before Downing interfered is implied in the instructions later sent to Pell, Abbott, *Writings and Speeches*, vol. 4, pp. 104–5. Mazarin's pressure on Savoy is revealed in Le Tellier and Brienne's letters to Ambassador Servien of 23 and 25 May/2 and 4 June, *Archives des Affaires Etrangères* ('Savoie'), vol. 49, ff. 299, 301.
45. Bordeaux to Mazarin, 10 September, PRO SP 31/3/98.
46. Bordeaux to Brienne, 12 and 26 August, 2 September, 14 October, ibid. Cromwell was believed to be awaiting Downing's report on Pignerol, Bordeaux to Brienne, 9 September, ibid. For Downing's report of 4 September, see *Thurloe*, vol. 3, p. 734.
47. Thurloe to Pell, 10/20 September, quoted in Vaughan, *Cromwell*, vol. 1, pp. 260–1.
48. Carlbom, *Karl X*, pp. 55–6.
49. Masson, *Milton*, vol. 5, p. 245; Symmons, *Milton*, vol. 4, pp. 394–5.
50. *CSPD 1657–8*, pp. 229–30.
51. Ibid., p. 344.
52. *Mercurius Politicus*, 25 March–1 April (OS).
53. Council Order Book (SP 25/78a), entry for 1/11 January, 1658.
54. Philip Meadowe, *History of the Evangelical Churches of the Valleys of Piedmont and . . . the Late Bloody Massacre*; Jean-Baptiste Stouppe, *A Collection of several papers sent to His Highness concerning the bloody and barbarous massacres in Piedmont*.

7 Spain's Breach of Relations with England

1. Quirini, 24 July, *CSPV 1655–6*, p. 84.
2. Quirini, 7 July, ibid., pp. 81–2.
3. Quirini, 17 July, as n. 2.
4. Quirini, 7 August, *CSPV*, p. 90.
5. Sagredo, 12 November, *CSPV*, pp. 135–7.
6. On June 27–8 (OS), two reports arrived supposing the fall of Santo Domingo, *Thurloe*, vol. 3, pp. 558–9, 566–7. This would have increased Cromwell's confidence in pressurising the French over a Vaudois settlement, and made the news of disaster even more shocking.
7. Bordeaux knew of the disaster by 26 July/6 August (letter of that date to Brienne, PRO SP 31/3/98), and Paulucci by 29 July/8 August (*CSPV*, p. 91).

8. Butler and Venables to Cromwell, 4/13 June, *Thurloe*, vol. 3, pp. 509–11.
9. Bordeaux to Mazarin, 5 August, PRO SP 31/3/98.
10. See the 'Proclamation' on settlement, *c.* 10/22 October 1655, where the enemy was reported hiding and resistance effectively over when it continued for four more years. To be fair to the Council, they may well have been misled by Butler and Venables' account of the victory; it was not known when they wrote that Y Sassi would carry on fighting. However, there is no such excuse for later attempts to hide the truth, e.g. a report in *Public Intelligence* of 6–13 July 1657 (OS) that 'all things go well and our troops are in perfect health'.
11. See the 'Proclamation' of *c.* 10/20 October.
12. Gardiner, *History of the Commonwealth and Protectorate*, vol. 4, p. 169. Sagredo heard in October that the English would give up the Caribbean War if Jamaica was lost, *CSPV*, p. 125. In April 1656 it was said that Jamaica would have to be abandoned if the English did not capture that year's Plate Fleet to finance the war, Bordeaux to Mazarin, 17 April, PRO SP 31/3/99.
13. Modyford to Thurloe, 20/30 June, *Thurloe*, vol. 3, p. 565.
14. Quoted in Guizot, *Cromwell*, vol. 2, p. 548.
15. Cromwell to Blake, 13/23 September, *Thurloe*, vol. 3, p. 734.
16. Sagredo, 25 November, ibid., pp. 142–3.
17. Bordeaux to Brienne, 30 September, PRO SP 31/3/98; *Thurloe*, vol. 4, pp. 44–5.
18. Quirini, 11 September, *CSPV*, pp. 108–9.
19. Sagredo, 8 October, ibid., pp. 119–20.
20. The formal committee consisted of Lambert, Lisle, Fiennes, Strickland, Sydenham, Desborough, Montague and Wolseley (Committee Book PRO).
21. *Urkunden u. Actenstuhe...*, pp. 728–30, quoted in Abbott, *Writings and Speeches*, vol. 4, pp. 43–4.
22. *CSPD 1655*, p. 610.
23. *CSPCol*, pp. 429, 434.
24. A committee was set up to consider the Design – headed by its chief critic, Lambert – on 12/22 September, and received Penn's report eight days later, *CSPCol*, p. 428. Penn and Venables were arrested on the latter's arrival in London, 20/30 September, ibid., p. 429.
25. Hyde to de Haro, 31 August 1655, PRO SP 94/43, f. 132.
26. Quirini, 3 July, *CSPV*, pp. 74–5.
27. Bordeaux to Brienne, 22 September, *Thurloe*, vol. 4, p. 27.
28. Bordeaux to Mazarin, 10 September, PRO SP 31/3/98.
29. Lockhart to Thurloe, 9 June 1656, *Thurloe*, vol. 5, pp. 75–6.
30. Bordeaux to Mazarin, 30 September (PRO SP 31/3/98) and Cardenas to Philip IV, 8 November (Guizot, *Cromwell*, vol. 2, pp. 454–5).
31. Sagredo, 29 October, *CSPV*, pp. 128–9.
32. Gardiner, *History of the Commonwealth and Protectorate*, vol. 4, p. 171.
33. Desborough, Lisle, Mulgrave and Strickland were the committee.
34. *CSPD 1655*, pp. 397, 399, 400.
35. *Public Intelligence*, 27 October/6 November.

36. Carlbom, *Karl X*, pp. 111–12.
37. Carte, *Original Letters*, vol. 74, f. 29.
38. Admiralty Commissioners' report of 12/22 October 1655, in *Thurloe*, vol. 4, pp. 79–80.
39. Intelligence to Thurloe, 11 November, from Brussels (ibid., p. 443), 18 December, from Brussels (ibid., p. 298), and 17 December, from Madrid (ibid., p. 292).
40. Hyde to de Vic, 14 and 17 December, *CSPClar*, vol. 3, p. 71.
41. Father Talbot to the King, 24 December, ibid., p. 75. See also Talbot's letters reporting the Pope's insistence on Charles making an open declaration on Catholic toleration, or becoming one himself, in return for aid; something which he supported. For example, Talbot to Ormonde, 31 July, ibid., p. 151, to Hyde, 13 August, p. 60. Hyde distrusted Talbot, see ibid., p. 86.
42. Richard Talbot to Ormonde, 7 January, ibid., pp. 84–5, and Dillon to Ormonde, 7 January, p. 86.
43. See *CSPClar*, vol. 3, pp. 70–5.
44. Talbot to the King, 9 December 1655, *CSPClar*, vol. 3, p. 70. These terms were revealed to Thurloe by his spy in Cologne, Manning, in a letter of 17 November (ibid., p. 66). The English government was thus aware of Spain's caution and weakness; this would have reassured them as to the feasibility of mounting a restricted naval campaign in 1656.
45. Bordeaux to Brienne, 30 September, PRO SP 31/3/98.
46. *Urkunden u. Achtenstuhe...*, vol. 7, pp. 728–30, quoted in Abbott, *Writings and Speeches*, vol. 4, pp. 43–5.
47. *Thurloe*, vol. 1, pp. 759–63. See also Thurloe's comments on the treaty in SP 103/12, f. 68. He was determined not to enter a closer league with France until the time was opportune.
48. Burnet, *History of my own Times*, pp. 131–2.
49. Longland to Thurloe, 18 December 1655, *Thurloe*, vol. 4, p. 295.
50. Giustinian to Senate, 29 November, *CSPV*, p. 145.
51. The French government had to order celebrations, Bordeaux to Brienne, 13 November 1655, PRO SP 31/3/98. See also the reports in *Thurloe*, vol. 4, p. 284. Intellectual opposition was evident in Boileau's *Ode* against a potential alliance (ed. Montgrédien, Paris, 1961).

8 1656 – England Delays an Offensive Alliance with France

1. For Mazarin's comments, see *Lettres de Cardinal Mazarin* (ed. Chéruel), vol. 8, p. 252. The revolt threatened by Marshal d'Hocquincourt, governor of Peronne, encouraged Mazarin to ratify the peace according to Sagredo's despatch of 3 December 1655; *CSPV 1655–6*, pp. 147–9.
2. Bordeaux to Brienne, 10 April 1655, PRO SP 31/3/99.
3. *Thurloe*, vol. 4, p. 121.
4. Sagredo, 14 January, *CSPV*, pp. 164–5.
5. Giustinian, Venetian ambassador in Rome, 15 January and 16 February, *CSPV*, pp. 166, 182.

6. According to Burnet, who was informed by Stouppe, the formal plan for a Protestant 'College' was intended 'to begin Cromwell's Kingship', i.e. the plan was probably drawn up in early 1657. See Burnet, *History of my own Times*, pp. 139–40. However, it is likely that the visit of Cromwell's spy, Dr Baily, to Rome was connected with this idea, at least in that he was to acquire information on the Catholic college, De Propagatione Fidei, as well as on papal attitudes to the King. This mission was known to Giustinian, Venetian ambassador in Paris, by 26 November 1655 (*CSPV*, p. 143). Its inception would tie in with Cromwell's interest in an Italian campaign in 1656, which he tried to press on Mazarin.

7. Thurloe to Pell, 21 February (OS), *Thurloe*, vol. 4, pp. 551–2.

8. For example, Cromwell's letters to Charles X in February and April 1656, Abbott, *Writings and Speeches*, vol. 4, pp. 94–5, 235–6.

9. Bordeaux to Mazarin, 10 April 1656, PRO SP 31/3/99. See also Giavarina's despatch of 10 March, *CSPV*, pp. 186–7.

10. Thurloe to Barrière, 8/18 March, *Thurloe*, vol. 4, p. 594.

11. Mazarin to Bordeaux, 26 April; Bordeaux to Mazarin, 8 May, PRO SP 31/3/99.

12. Bordeaux to Mazarin, 17 April, ibid. Apparently 'Fitts' had offered to double-cross Condé if France paid him enough.

13. Bordeaux to Mazarin, 24 April, ibid.

14. Bordeaux to Brienne, 18 April, ibid.

15. Giavarina, 17 March, *CSPV*, pp. 190–2.

16. Bordeaux to Brienne, 8 May, PRO SP 31/3/99.

17. *EHR*, XXI (1906), pp. 743–6.

18. Mazarin to Bordeaux, 26 April, PRO SP 31/3/99.

19. Bordeaux to Brienne, 15 May, ibid.

20. *CSPClar*, vol. 3, pp. 111–12.

21. Hyde to Clement, Royalist resident in Rome, 3/13 February, ibid., p. 93.

22. Clement to Hyde, 15 and 22 April, ibid., pp. 111 and 115.

23. Clarendon, *History of the Rebellion*, vol. 6, pp. 37, 47–9.

24. Bonnel to Thurloe, 27 July, *Thurloe*, vol, 5, pp. 221–2.

25. Lockhart to Thurloe, 8 June, ibid., pp. 53–4. Sagredo had noted Mazarin's opposition to an attack on Italy as early as 4 February (*CSPV*, p. 171).

26. Lockhart to Thurloe, 24 May, *Thurloe*, vol. 5, p. 21.

27. Lockhart to Thurloe, 10 July, ibid., pp. 172–3. See also Gardiner, *History of the Commonwealth and Protectorate*, vol. 4, pp. 243–4.

28. Lockhart to Thurloe, 26 July, *Thurloe*, vol. 5, pp. 217–18. Cromwell warned Count Bonde on 26 July/5 August that Lionne's success would cause 'unavoidable ruin' for the Protestants.

29. For example, report in BL Add. Mss 32093, f. 343.

30. Mazarin had initially refused to pay; Lockhart to Thurloe, 19 June, *Thurloe*, vol. 5, p. 100.

31. French Intelligence, 19 July, ibid., p. 198.

32. Lockhart to Thurloe, 20 July, ibid., p. 202.

33. Lockhart to Thurloe, 26 July, ibid., p. 217.

34. Lockhart to Thurloe, 8 August, ibid., pp. 282–3.
35. Lockhart to Thurloe, 12 August, ibid., p. 267.
36. *CSPClar*, vol. 3, p. 93.
37. For example, Charles and Hyde to de Vic, 5? November 1655, Hyde to de Vic, *c.* 17 November, *CSPClar*, vol. 3, pp. 62–3. For Cardenas's objections to this plan, see Ormonde to Hyde, 19 May 1656 (ibid., p. 191) and Talbot to Hyde, 31 July (ibid., p. 147). The ports were only opened in September 1656 after Blake had shown hopes of peace to be illusory, Hyde to Nicholas, 29 September, ibid., p. 176.
38. See Nieupoort to States-General, 15/25 February, BL Add. Mss 17677w, f. 229; and letters by Captains Thompson (1 January 1657, *CSPD 1657*, p. 6), and Pile (21 February, *CSPD 1655–6*, pp. 196–7).
39. Thurloe to Montague, 4/14 March; Carte, *Original Letters*, vol. 2, p. 87.
40. Ibid.
41. Examples of complaints about piracy: Pley, commander at Weymouth, to Admiralty Commissioners (from which quote is taken), 17 March (OS), *CSPD 1655–6*; Pley to Admiralty Commissioners, 7 and 12 April (OS), ibid., pp. 257 and 264; Captain Parker to Admiralty Commissioners, 8 April (OS), p. 257; Captain Pettock to Admiralty Commissioners, 8 April (OS), p. 259; Major Burton to Admiralty Commissioners, 14 April (OS), p. 257; Captain Hatsell to Admiralty Commissioners, 28 April, pp. 298–9.
42. Cromwell only supplemented the inadequate efforts of home-based ships with Montague's fleet in autumn 1657.
43. *CSPD 1655–6*, p. 293.
44. Ibid., p. 345.
45. Giavarina, 16 June, *CSPV*, pp. 230–2.
46. Montague, 20/30 April, *Thurloe*, vol. 5, p. 67. Cromwell accepted this argument and abandoned the planned attack, Cromwell to Blake and Montague, 8/18 June, ibid., pp. 101–2.
47. Cromwell to Blake and Montague, 28 April/8 May, ibid., p. 744.
48. Montague to Cromwell, 22 May/1 June, *Thurloe*, vol. 5, p. 69.
49. See below, n. 68.
50. Montague to Thurloe, 30 June/10 July, *Thurloe*, vol. 5, p. 171.
51. Cromwell to Blake and Montague, 28 August/7 September, ibid., p. 363.
52. Montague pointed out the advantages of a base in the Straits, Montague to Thurloe, 8/18 July 1656 (ibid., p. 195) and to Henry Cromwell, 10/20 February 1657 (*CSPD 1656–7*, p. 274). The Admiralty Commissioners approved the idea of an agreement with Tetuan in 1657 and recommended that Blake be sent out to negotiate and Nathaniel Luke be made consul, *CSPD 1656–7*, p. 274. Luke was sent with official instructions, SP 71/13, f. 103.
53. Montague to Thurloe, 20/30 September 1656, *Thurloe*, vol. 5, f. 103. Bordeaux reported that Cromwell told him the news of Potosi in a jubilant manner, Bordeaux to Brienne, 19 October, PRO SP 31/3/100. For the Spanish criticism, see Zane's despatch of 27 September, *CSPV*, p. 265.
54. For the encouraging effect of the news on Cromwell, see Bordeaux's

letter of 19 October to Brienne, PRO SP 31/3/100. The English now proceeded with new plans for an attack on Cuba (Bordeaux to Brienne, 26 October, ibid.) and an alliance with France, Denmark, Sweden and the Dutch (Bordeaux to Brienne, 2 November, ibid.) which showed their confidence now that naval strategy had been belatedly justified.

55. BL Add. Mss Ayscough 6125, ff. 34–60b. Cromwell made special mention of how the Royalists were now dependent on Catholic allies – the propaganda advantage which Thurloe had known would accrue from forcing the King and France apart.

56. For instances of MPs' complaints at commercial losses to trade and shipping in the Parliament of early 1659, see the speeches of Haselrig on 7 February (OS) and of Scot and Lloyd on 21 February (OS) in Burton's *Diary*, pp. 288, 394.

57. For the Portuguese Treaty of 10/20 July 1654, see BL Stowe Mss 192, ff. 1, 21.

58. See Giavarina's despatch of 12 May 1656 for John's reminder of the Church's power, *CSPV 1655–6*, pp. 213–15. Bordeaux's remarks on Cromwell's naïvety are in his despatch of 12 June, PRO SP 31/3/99.

59. John's letter was read in the Council on 14/24 September 1655, *CSPD 1655*, p. 334. The King refused a Protestant church to be erected in Lisbon; Maynard's letter in 'Public Intelligence' of 5–12 May 1656 (OS), Giavarina, 19 May (*CSPV*, pp. 216–18).

60. Bordeaux to Brienne, 22 May, PRO SP 31/3/99.

61. The Council's order to Meadowe of 19/29 February is in *CSPD 1655–6*, p. 190.

62. Ibid., p. 310: 5/15 May, 'Mr Secretary presents letters from Mr Meadowe, to be considered again tomorrow'. Cromwell ordered Blake and Montague to take action in a letter on 6/16 May, *Thurloe*, vol. 4, p. 769.

63. Thurloe to Henry Cromwell, 24 June 1656, ibid., vol. 5, p. 150. For Meadowe's refusal to leave, see Meadowe to Blake and Montague, 25 May/4 June, ibid., p. 59.

64. Meadowe to Blake and Montague, 25 May/4 June, ibid., p. 59.

65. Meadowe to Blake and Montague, 6/16 June, ibid., pp. 123–4.

66. Montague to Meadowe, 6/16 June, ibid.

67. Montague to Thurloe, 17/27 June, ibid., p. 126.

68. Meadowe, 6/16 June, as n. 65. Meadowe was granted lands to the value of £100 in compensation for his injury; *CSPD 1656–7*, pp. 224–5.

9 The French Alliance of March 1657

1. Bordeaux to Brienne, 4 August 1656, PRO SP 31/3/100.

2. *Clarke Papers*, vol. 3, p. 76. See also Giavarina's despatch of 8 December (*CSPV 1655–6*, p. 289) and his despatch of 23 February 1657 (*CSPV 1657–9*, p. 23).

3. See also Hyde to Mottet, Cardenas's secretary, 31 January 1657, *CSPClar*, vol. 3, p. 240.

4. Talbot to Hyde, *c.* 25 August 1656, ibid., p. 164.
5. This was acknowledged in Hyde's instructions to Bristol of 22 September 1656, ibid., p. 174. The Duke of Neuberg's activities are reported in Bordeaux to Mazarin, 28 September 1656, PRO SP 31/3/100. Bordeaux informed Brienne on the same date that Cromwell had informed Parliament of this threat (ibid.). The Duke had also sent a Jesuit priest to Rome in 1656 on Charles's behalf, see Clarendon, *History*, chapter 14, p. 121.
6. Talbot to Ormonde, 31 July, *CSPClar*, vol. 3, p. 151.
7. Lockhart to Thurloe, 17 September 1656, *Thurloe*, vol. 5, pp. 388–9.
8. As n. 7.
9. Bamfylde to Thurloe, 13 September, *Thurloe*, vol. 5, p. 436.
10. Lockhart to Thurloe, 11 September, ibid., pp. 368–9.
11. Bordeaux to Mazarin, 7 September and 4 December, Bordeaux to Brienne, 9 November, PRO SP 31/3/100. Lockhart himself believed that the restoration of Condé was the sole reason why Mazarin had given up hope of peace, not any goodwill towards England, Lockhart to Thurloe, 8 October, *Thurloe*, vol. 5, p. 450.
12. Bamfylde to Thurloe, 25 November, ibid., p. 563.
13. Dutch Intelligence, 18/28 July, ibid., p. 415.
14. Reported in Bennett's letter to Hyde of 13 July 1657, *CSPClar*, vol. 3, p. 324. De Haro in fact sent Cardenas's secretary to London to survey the situation, Bordeaux to Brienne, 4 January 1657, PRO SP 31/3/101.
15. This was according to Mazarin's informants in Brussels, Lockhart to Thurloe, 27 January 1657, *Thurloe*, vol. 6, p. 1.
16. Bristol to Hyde, 15 November 1656, *CSPClar*, vol. 3, p. 199; for Cardenas's secretary, see Bordeaux to Mazarin, 14 January 1657, PRO SP 31/3/100. Bristol informed Hyde that Caracena might be ready in three weeks, in his report of 26 November, *CSPClar*, vol. 3, p. 204.
17. Cromwell to Mazarin, 26 December 1656, Abbott, *Writings and Speeches*, vol. 4, pp. 368–9.
18. Bamfylde to Thurloe, 13 January 1657, *Thurloe*, vol. 5, pp. 753–4.
19. Lockhart to Thurloe, 7 February, ibid., vol. 6, p. 22.
20. Ibid.
21. Mazarin to Bordeaux, 7 March 1657 (PRO SP 31/3/101); Nani to Senate, 17/27 January, *CSPV 1657–9*, p. 10.
22. For Lockhart's mediation, see H.R. Rowen, *John de Witt*, p. 263.
23. Lockhart to Thurloe, 17 February, *Thurloe*, vol. 6, pp. 44–5.
24. For the terms of the treaty, see Guizot, *Cromwell*, vol. 2, pp. 481–6.
25. Lockhart to Thurloe, 25 March, *Thurloe*, vol. 6, p. 115.
26. Bamfylde to Thurloe, 15 April, ibid., pp. 175–6.
27. Secret Articles, 29 April/9 May, Abbott *Writings and Speeches*, vol. 4, pp. 915–19. As a result of this agreement, Cromwell warned Nieupoort that in future England would side with France against the Dutch in any conflict; Nieupoort to Ruysch, 18 May, *Thurloe*, vol. 6, p. 273.
28. Lockhart reported Mazarin's request for England to put Admiral Stokes at his disposal in his despatch to Thurloe of 17 March 1658, ibid., p. 854. Thurloe gave him the necessary permission, and Lockhart reported

the Cardinal's thanks on 21 April, ibid., p. 70. The Council of State issued orders to Stokes to sail to Marseilles and cooperate with Chevalier Paul's expedition on 31 May/10 June, ibid., p. 155.

29. Lockhart to Thurloe, 28 July, ibid., p. 251.
30. For example, Cromwell to William, Landgrave of Hesse-Cassel, March 1657, Masson, *Milton*, vol. 6, pp. 427–8.
31. *Thurloe*, vol. 2, pp. 441–2.
32. Bradshaw, consul in Hamburg and ambassador-designate to Russia, to Thurloe, 17 April 1657, ibid., vol. 6, p. 178. Also similar intelligence in an anonymous spy's report from Hamburg, dated the same, ibid., p. 179.
33. Nieupoort to States-General, 4/14 September 1657; *Brieven van Jan de Witt* (1724), vol. 2, p. 422.
34. Lockhart to Thurloe, 21 April, *CSPClar*, vol. 3, p. 275.
35. Cromwell met Schlezer on 14/24 May; see Schlezer's report to Kurfurst (in Berlin), *Urkunden u. Actenstuche*, vol. 7, pp. 766–8, quoted in Abbott, *Writings and Speeches*, vol. 6, pp. 319–20.
36. Bordeaux to Mazarin, 10 May; also in Bordeaux to Mazarin, 14 May, PRO SP 31/3/101.
37. Lockhart to Thurloe, 2 May, 28 May, *Thurloe*, vol. 6, pp. 220, 290.
38. Bamfylde to Thurloe, 30 May, ibid., p. 294.
39. Cromwell's meeting with Schlezer on 8/18 June is reported in Schlezer to Kurfurst, 19/29 June, *Urkunden u. Actenstuche*, vol. 3, pp. 773–5, quoted in Abbott, *Writings and Speeches*, vol. 4, pp. 554–5.
40. Eilenberg also tried to interest Cromwell in assisting the election of Charles Louis as Emperor. This may seem an odd choice of support for a near relation of Charles II, but the Elector's kinship with the Stuarts had always been a less potent force than his ambition; witness his dealings with the new Parliamentary leadership in 1641.
41. Thurloe to Jephson, 9/19 April 1658, *Thurloe*, vol. 7, p. 63.
42. For Frederick William's reply to Jephson see Jephson's letter to Thurloe of 1/11 May 1658, ibid., p. 108. For his later obstinacy, see Jephson to Thurloe, 21 June, ibid., p. 189.

10 England, France and Dunkirk, 1657–8

1. For example, Lockhart's letters of 8 August 1656 (*Thurloe*, vol. 5, pp. 252–3), 27 January 1657 (ibid., pp. 794–5), 7 February (ibid., vol. 6, p. 22), 11 February (ibid., pp. 55–7), and on the final agreement on 26 February (ibid., p. 63).
2. *DNB* on Sir John Reynolds, vol. 48, p. 47.
3. Bordeaux to Mazarin, 7 April, PRO SP 31/3/101.
4. Giavarina, 18 May, *CSPV 1657–9*, pp. 53–5.
5. Mazarin to Lockhart, 28 May, PRO SP 31/3/101. Bordeaux reported to Brienne on 2 June (ibid.) that he had informed Cromwell.
6. For a recent account, see Austin Woolrych, 'The Cromwellian Protectorate: A Military Dictatorship?', in *History*, LXXV (1990), pp. 207–31, particularly pp. 224–5.

7. Edmund Ludlow, *Memoirs*, vol. 2, p. 24.
8. Bordeaux to Brienne, 28 May, PRO SP 31/3/101.
9. Jennings (Antwerp) to Hyde, 23 May, *CSPClar*, vol. 3, p. 294.
10. For Cardenas's preference for Sexby to the King, see Bennet to Bristol, 13 May (ibid., p. 288) and Bennet to Bristol, 23 May (ibid., p. 293). Spain would do nothing without help from the United Provinces, presumably to counter the English fleet; Bennet to Hyde, 2 May ibid., p. 282. It was fortunate for England that Cromwell had not given in to mercantile pressure for a firmer policy on the Dutch.
11. Somer to Thurloe, 31 March, *Thurloe*, vol. 6, p. 133. See also Somer to Thurloe, 5 May, *CSPClar*, vol. 3, p. 283.
12. Bennet to Hyde, 23 May, ibid., p. 293.
13. See Firth, *Last Years*, vol. 2, p. 3 for a general summary, and Giavarina's despatch of 20 July (*CSPV 1657-9*, pp. 84-7). Lambert was joined in his opposition by Sydenham and Pickering, both known to be men of strong religious scruples, Bordeaux to Mazarin, 23 July, PRO SP 31/3/101. Sydenham threatened to resign along with Lambert (Bordeaux to Mazarin, 30 July, ibid.).
14. Giavarina, 25 May, *CSPV*, pp. 26-8.
15. Ibid., and also Giavarina's despatch of 8 June, pp. 61-3.
16. See Cromwell's orders to Blake and Montague of 28 August 1656, *Thurloe*, vol. 5, p. 363.
17. Giavarina, 6 July, *CSPV*, pp. 78-80.
18. Giavarina, 3 and 10 August, ibid., pp. 94-6. Blake had already indirectly aided Portugal by assisting Tetuan while they were preoccupied with Philip IV.
19. Giavarina, 20 July, ibid., pp. 84-7.
20. Bordeaux to Brienne, 16 July, PRO SP 31/3/101.
21. Bordeaux's account of Cromwell's sense of priorities is in his report to Brienne of 16 July, PRO SP 31/3/101.
22. Bordeaux to Brienne, 23 July, ibid.
23. Giavarina to Senate, 11/21 September, and 25 September/5 October, *CSPV*, pp. 101, 116. Mello's public entry to London is recorded in Giavarina's despatch of 4/14 September, ibid., p. 108.
24. Lockhart to Thurloe, 8 August, *Thurloe*, vol. 6, p. 426.
25. Lockhart to Thurloe, 8 August and 12 September, *Thurloe*, vol. 5, pp. 426, 495-6.
26. Lockhart to Thurloe, 7 September, ibid., vol. 6, pp. 487-9.
27. Thurloe to Lockhart, 17 August, Lockhart to Thurloe, 31 August, *Thurloe*, vol. 6, pp. 477, 490.
28. Cromwell to Lockhart, 31 August, ibid., p. 489.
29. Lockhart to Thurloe, 4/14 November 1657, PRO SP 31/3/101.
30. Guizot, *Cromwell*, vol. 2, p. 583; and Bordeaux to Brienne, 5 November, PRO SP 31/3/101.
31. Giavarina, 16 November *CSPV 1657-8*, p. 128.
32. Thurloe to Lockhart, 26 November, *Thurloe*, vol. 6, pp. 614-15.
33. Lockhart to Thurloe, 28 November, ibid., pp. 618-19.
34. Thurloe to Lockhart, 1 December, *CSPClar*, vol. 3, p. 526.
35. Lockhart to Thurloe, 11 December, *Thurloe*, vol. 6, pp. 624-5.

36. Thurloe to Henry Cromwell, 27 October (OS), ibid., p. 579.
37. Bennet to Hyde, 14 November, *CSPClar*, vol. 3, p. 381.
38. Giavarina, 8 March, 1658, *CSPV 1657-8*, pp. 171-2.
39. Giavarina, 8 and 15 March, 1658, ibid., pp. 171-2, 173-4. See also Anonymous to Hyde, 1 March, *CSPClar*, vol. 4, p. 17.
40. Giavarina, 8 March, *CSPV*, pp. 171-2.
41. For Cromwell's address to Parliament of 15/25 January 1658, see BL Add. Mss 6125, f. 82.
42. Ibid.
43. Ibid.
44. Giustinian, 8 January 1658, *CSPV*, pp. 150-1.
45. For the French protests at English treatment of Catholics in June 1657, see Giavarina's report of 22 June 1657, ibid., *1657-8*, pp. 72-5. For the protests in December, see Mazarin's letter to Bordeaux of 13 December, in Chéruel (ed.) *Lettres de Mazarin*, vol. 8, pp. 234-6.
46. *Thurloe*, vol. 6, pp. 610, 725.
47. Mazarin to Bordeaux, 13 December 1657.
48. Lockhart reported meeting 'Don Lewis' in his letter of 11 December, *Thurloe*, vol. 6, pp. 624-5. For Passerini, see Giavarina's reports of 25 January and 1 February, and Giustinian's of 5 February, *CSPV 1657-8*, pp. 155-6, 164-6.
49. For Goodson's report, see Rawlinson Mss 63, f. 210.
50. Hyde to O'Neale, 22 March; Bennet to Hyde, 15 May, *CSPClar*, vol. 4, pp. 24-5, 45.
51. The renewed treaty is recorded in PRO SP 108/55.
52. Giustinian, 9 April, *CSPV*, pp. 183-4.
53. Ibid. Giustinian did, however, approach the Spaniards who told him that they would accept a conference in the Pyrenees but not in Flanders, Giustinian, 6 May, ibid., p. 193.
54. Goodson to Thurloe, 4/14 May, *Thurloe*, vol. 7, p. 113.
55. Turenne's terms for Dunkirk; PRO SP 94/43, ff. 93-5.
56. Giavarina, 23 August, *CSPV*, pp. 234-5.
57. Lockhart promised to aid any English settlers whom Thurloe recommended, Lockhart to Thurloe, 3 July, *Thurloe*, vol. 7, p. 198. He also proposed a subscription to aid Flemish Protestants to settle there, Lockhart to Thurloe, 9 July, ibid., p. 216.
58. Boreel's remarks to Giustinian, as recorded in the latter's despatch of 14 July, *CSPV*, p. 223. Also see Giustinian's despatch of 16 June, in ibid., p. 212.
59. *Somers Tracts*, vol. 6, p. 331.
60. Cromwell to Louis XIV, c. 20/30 May, Abbott, *Writings and Speeches*, vol. 4, pp. 806-7.
61. Giustinian, 30 June, *CSPV*, p. 219.
62. Lockhart to Thurloe, 14/24 June, *Thurloe*, vol. 7, p. 174.
63. See J.H. Salmon, *Retz: Anatomy of a Conspirator*, pp. 308-9.
64. Ibid.
65. Lockhart to Thurloe, 3 July, *Thurloe*, vol. 7, pp. 197-8.
66. Ibid.
67. Lockhart to Thurloe, 6 July, ibid., p. 206.

68. For example, Donald Lupton's *Flanders: or an exact compendium of that fair, great, and fat country* (London, 1658).
69. Lockhart to Thurloe, 27 June, *Thurloe*, vol. 7, p. 178.
70. Lockhart to Thurloe, 6 July, as n. 65.
71. *Thurloe*, vol. 7, p. 198.
72. Ibid., p. 249.
73. Lockhart to Thurloe, 10 August, ibid., p. 303.
74. *Revenue Account of Dunkirk*, 1659, ibid., pp. 715–19. For the local peasants' poverty, see Lockhart's letter of 9 July, p. 215.
75. Lockhart to Thurloe, 9 July, *Thurloe*, vol. 7, p. 215.
76. *CSPD 1658–9*, p. 80.
77. Thurloe to Henry Cromwell, 27 July/6 August, *Thurloe*, vol. 7, p. 295.
78. Lockhart to Thurloe, 26 July, ibid., p. 279.
79. *Thurloe*, vol. 1, pp. 759–63.
80. Lockhart to Thurloe, 11 July, *Thurloe*, vol. 7, p. 223.
81. Quoted in Rowen, *John de Witt*, p. 72.

11 Cromwell and the Dutch, 1653–4

1. Thomas Gage, *The English–American His Travails: Or a New Survey of the West Indies*, pp. 1, 4.
2. S.R. Gardiner, *History of the Commonwealth and Protectorate*, vol. 2, pp. 324–9.
3. Ibid., pp. 169–70.
4. BL Add. Mss 27962.
5. Gardiner, *History of the Commonwealth and Protectorate*, vol. 2, pp. 177–9.
6. Ibid., p. 41.
7. *Thurloe*, vol. 1, p. 418.
8. Roger Lockyer, *Buckingham: The Life and Career of George Villiers, 1592–1628*, pp. 293, 357.
9. Gardiner, *History of the Commonwealth and Protectorate*, vol. 2, p. 288.
10. Quoted in ibid., pp. 287–8.
11. R.W. Stearns, *The Strenuous Puritan: A Life of Hugh Peter*, p. 189.
12. *Thurloe*, vol. 1, p. 239.
13. Stearns, *The Strenuous Puritan*, p. 391.
14. Quoted in A. Woolrych, *Commonwealth into Protectorate*, pp. 286–7.
15. Ibid.
16. *CSPD*, pp. 445, 451.
17. W.C. Abbott, *Letters and Speeches of Oliver Cromwell*, vol. 3, pp. 122–5.
18. *CSPD 1653*, pp. 362, 367, 370–2.
19. Gardiner, *History of the Commonwealth and Protectorate*, vol. 3, p. 41.
20. *Thurloe*, vol. 1, p. 370.
21. As n. 18.
22. *Thurloe*, vol. 1, p. 125.
23. Simancas Mss 2079: Consulta, 11/21 July 1653.
24. *Thurloe*, vol. 1, pp. 535, 538.
25. Ibid., p. 540.

26. *Verbael van Jan de Witt* (quoted by Abbott, *Writings and Speeches*), p. 171.
27. *Thurloe*, vol. 1, pp. 576, 597.
28. Abbott, *Letters and Speeches*, vol. 3, pp. 122–5.
29. Ibid.
30. Dutch Intelligence, 28 October/7 November 1653, quoted in *Thurloe*, vol. 1.
31. *Verbael van Jan de Witt*, p. 276.
32. Paulucci to Senate, 29 January/8 February 1654: *CSPV 1653–4*, pp. 179–80.
33. Paulucci to Senate, 14/24 January 1654, ibid., pp. 174–6.
34. Paulucci to Senate, 4/14 February 1654, ibid., pp. 182–3.
35. As n. 34.
36. *Thurloe*, vol. 2, pp. 74–5.
37. Ibid., pp. 177–8.
38. *CSPD 1654*, p. 79.
39. *Thurloe*, vol. 2, pp. 143, 154.
40. *CSPV*, p. 201.
41. Abbott, *Writings and Speeches*, vol. 3, p. 906.
42. Ibid., pp. 906–9; for Sir Thomas Vyner's appointment on 8/18 August to receive the money, Rawlinson Mss A328, ff. 125–7.
43. *Thurloe*, vol. 2, p. 235.
44. Ibid., pp. 238–9.
45. Ibid., p. 239.
46. Rawlinson Mss A 328, f. 27.
47. *Thurloe*, vol. 3, p. 359.
48. *Perfect Diurnal*, 15/25 May 1654, *Thurloe*, vol. 2, p. 299.
49. Ibid., pp. 365–70.
50. Ibid., pp. 477–8.
51. Cromwell to Estates of Zealand, 16/26 June 1654, BL Add. Mss 20291, f. 120; and again on 26 October/5 November 1654, Rawlinson Mss A261, ff. 20v–22.
52. BL Add. Mss 27962.
53. Sagredo to Senate, 9/19 June 1655, *CSPV 1655–6*, pp. 9–10.
54. PRO SP 103/46, Annex IIIg. Cromwell had complained to Beverning on 28 December/7 January 1653–4 of the King's 'grave injustices and insults'.
55. *Thurloe*, vol. 2, pp. 344, 404.
56. Abbott, *Writings and Speeches*, vol. 3, p. 370.
57. PRO SP 103/46.
58. The English government quietly dropped the matter. An East India Company ship en route to take it in 1659 seized St Helena instead.

12 The Uneasy Peace: England and the Dutch, 1654–8

1. *CSPV 1655–6*, pp. 99–101.
2. Abbott, *Writings and Letters*, vol. 3, pp. 434–43.
3. *Verbael van Jan de Witt*, pp. 482, 513.
4. Cromwell to the States-General, 12/22 September, 1655.

5. *Thurloe,* vol. 6, p. 271.
6. See Chapter 6 for Thompson's other activities supporting the Western Design. For Noell's proposals, see Colonial Office vol. 77, viii, nos. 44–5; and E.B. Sainsbury, *Court Minutes of the East India Company 1655–9,* pp. 122–6.
7. Dutch Intelligence, 5/15 January 1655, *Thurloe,* vol. 3, p. 80.
8. Richard Wylde's proposals for a 'national interest' in India with Portuguese cooperation; BL Sloane Mss 3271.
9. See Sainsbury, *Court Minutes.*
10. See Abbott, *Writings and Speeches,* vol. 4, p.
11. Penn, *Memorials,* vol. 2, pp. 28–9.
12. Paulucci to Senate, 5/15 May 1655, *CSPV 1655–6,* pp. 84–6.
13. *Brieven van Jan de Witt,* vol. 3, pp. 35–6.
14. Ibid.
15. Paulucci to Senate, 2/12 November 1655, *CSPV,* pp. 137–8.
16. See Chapter 14.
17. Cromwell to Nieupoort, 28 September/8 October 1655.
18. *Brieven van Jan de Witt,* vol. 3, pp. 145–6.
19. Bulstrode Whitelocke, *Memorials of English Affairs,* vol. 4, pp. 219–20.
20. *Thurloe,* vol. 4, p. 201.
21. Quirini to Senate, 9/19 January 1656, *CSPV,* p. 166.
22. Sagredo to Senate, 7/17 December 1655, ibid., pp. 154–5.
23. Giavarina to Senate, 28 February/10 March 1656, ibid., pp. 186–7.
24. See Chapter 14.
25. *Thurloe,* vol. 2, p. 459.
26. *Brieven van Jan de Witt,* vol. 3, p. 184; Quirini to Senate, 24 November/4 December 1655, *CSPV,* p. 104; Giavarina to Senate, 5/15 December 1656, ibid., pp. 292–3.
27. Nieupoort to the Council, 1/11 September and November 1654, PRO SP 84/160.
28. See Nieupoort's complaint of 9/19 December 1654 in ibid.
29. PRO SP 105/55, entry for 3/13 April 1655; and for Goffe, Lisle and Long's report on 30 March/9 April 1656 advising the ship's return, see SP 84/161, f. 140.
30. SP 84/160, f. 144.
31. Ibid., f. 152.
32. PRO SP 84/161, f. 189 – Strickland and Jones report on the *Oaken Tree.*
33. PRO SP 84/160, f. 247.
34. PRO SP 84/161, f. 103.
35. Ibid., f. 105.
36. Council Committee Book (PRO), entry for 30 November/10 December.
37. PRO SP 84/161, f. 123.
38. See Chapter 6.
39. As n. 37.
40. PRO SP 84/161, ff. 3, 10, 20, 42.
41. Council Order Book (PRO SP 25/75), entry for 4/14 July 1655.
42. Ibid., entry for 19/29 March 1655.
43. PRO SP 105/55; entry for 6/16 March 1656.

44. *Public Intelligencer*, 18–25 February 1656 (OS).
45. Council Committee Book (PRO), entry for 4/14 April 1656.
46. Ibid., entry for 10/20 April 1656.
47. *Brieven van Jan de Witt*, vol. 3, pp. 193–4.
48. *Thurloe*, vol. 5, p. 279.
49. *CSPClar*, vol. 3, p. 155.
50. *Thurloe*, vol. 5, p. 171.
51. Giavarina to Senate, 25 July/4 August 1656, *CSPV 1655–6*, pp. 247–9.
52. *Thurloe*, vol. 5, pp. 358–60.
53. Ibid., p. 361.
54. PRO SP 77/31.
55. Cromwell told Schlezer on 18/28 June that he was trying to lower the risk of war.
56. Carlbom, *Karl X*, pp. 97–8.
57. *Thurloe*, vol. 5, p. 590.
58. Ibid., p. 338.
59. Cromwell to the States-General, 21/31 August 1656, Abbott, *Writings and Speeches*, vol. 4, pp. 233–5.
60. H. Rowen, *John de Witt, Grand Pensionary of Holland.*
61. *Thurloe*, vol. 5, p. 537.
62. Ibid., p. 535.
63. *Brieven van Jan de Witt*, vol. 3, p. 323.
64. *Thurloe*, vol. 5, p. 73.
65. Quoted in Dutch Intelligence, *Thurloe*, vol. 5.
66. *Brieven van Jan de Witt*, vol. 3, p. 332.
67. Giavarina to Senate, 19/29 December 1656, *CSPV 1655–6*, p. 298.
68. Nani to Senate, 17/27 January 1657, and Giavarina to Senate, 2/12 March, *CSPV 1657–8*, pp. 10–11, 20–1; and see PRO SP 77/31, f. 403 on Gamarra's reception in Amsterdam in March 1657.
69. PRO SP 84/161, f. 18.
70. Giavarina to Senate, 2/12 January 1657, *CSPV*, pp. 3–6.
71. Giavarina to Senate, 5/15 December 1656 and 2/12 January 1657, *CSPV 1655–6*, p. 293 and *CSPV 1657–8*, pp. 3–6 as above.
72. *Thurloe*, vol. 6, pp. 190–1.
73. Ibid., pp. 149–50.
74. *CSPClar*, vol. 3, p. 270.
75. *Thurloe*, vol. 6, pp. 347–8.
76. PRO SP 84/161, f. 27.
77. Ibid., ff. 49, 51.
78. Schlezer to Kurfurst, 15/25 May 1656, *Urkunden u Actenstuche*, vol. 3, pp. 766–8.
79. *Thurloe*, vol. 6, pp. 347–8.
80. *Brieven van Jan de Witt*, vol. 3, pp. 286–7.
81. Giavarina to Senate, 24 July/3 August and 31 July/10 August 1657, *CSPV*, pp. 191–3, 194–6.
82. *Thurloe*, vol. 6, p. 559.
83. *Brieven van Jan de Witt*, vol. 3, pp. 398–9.
84. *Thurloe*, vol. 6, p. 477.

85. Ibid.
86. Ibid., p. 548.
87. Ibid., pp. 545–6.
88. Ibid., pp. 181–2.
89. Ibid., p. 609.
90. Ibid., p. 759.
91. *Thurloe*, vol. 7, pp. 31–2.
92. Ibid., pp. 790–1.
93. Meadowe's, *Narrative*, p. 62.
94. *Thurloe*, vol. 7, p. 113.
95. Ibid., p. 245.
96. Ibid., pp. 310–11.
97. Proceedings of Council of State, 10/20 and 12/22 November 1657, in PRO SP Interregnum I, pp. 264, 273.
98. Gamarra to de Haro, 15/25 January 1657 and Consulta, 5/15 May, Simancas Mss 2092. See also Jonathan Israel, *The Dutch Republic and the Hispanic World 1606–61*, chapter 7, section 2.
99. *Thurloe*, vol. 7, p. 49.
100. Downing, *Diary*, p. 97.
101. *Thurloe*, vol. 1, pp. 759–63 (the 'Memorandum').
102. Turenne to Beverweert, 23 June/3 July 1658 (*Algemeen Rijkarschief,* The Hague, Staten van Holland 1759, p. 217); De Witt to Beverweert, *c.* 19/29 July, ibid., p. 37; see also Rowen, *De Witt,* p. 332.
103. Sainsbury, *Court Minutes*, pp. 268–9.
104. *Thurloe*, vol. 7, p. 91.
105. Ibid., p. 293.
106. Ibid., p. 196.
107. Ibid., pp. 332–4.
108. *CSPD 1658*, pp. 7–9.
109. *Thurloe*, vol. 7, p. 253; Downing, *Diary*, p. 139.

13 Cromwell and the Baltic, 1654–6

1. See discussion in Chapter 1.
2. Michael Roberts, *Essays in Swedish History* (1953), pp. 358–84.
3. Cromwell's speech to Parliament of 25 January/4 February 1658; BL Add. Mss 6125, f. 82.
4. *Thurloe*, vol. 2, pp. 418–29.
5. Salwey was also considered for Constantinople.
6. Whitelocke, *Journal of the Swedish Embassy*, vol. 1, pp. 12–15.
7. PRO SP 108/516 (incomplete copy).
8. Cromwell to Charles X and the Duchy of Bremen, 27 October/6 November 1654; quoted in Abbott, *Writings and Speeches*, vol. 2.
9. *Thurloe*, vol. 2, p. 379.
10. For example, Henderson (agent in Cologne) to Thurloe, 2/12 February 1655; *CSPClar*, vol. 3, Pell, 8 April, Vaughan, *Cromwell*, vol. 1, p. 164.
11. *Thurloe*, vol. 2, p. 360.

12. Bodleian Library, Rawlinson Mss A261, ff. 19–19v.
13. Alexis' antagonism had been exaggerated but nevertheless existed. For rebuttal of some of the myths over this issue, see Loewenstein, 'Did Russia Intervene after the Execution of Charles I?', in *Bulletin of the Institute of Historical Research*, XIII (1940).
14. *Thurloe*, vol. 3, p. 173.
15. Ibid., p. 255. Jan Comenius' collection for Charles II among English residents in Poland is evidence that many of them were hostile, as were significant numbers among the communities in North German ports and Russia.
16. Ibid., p. 303; *CSPV 1655–6*, pp. 45–6.
17. *Brieven van Jan de Witt*, vol. 3, pp. 47, 92.
18. Carlbom, *Karl X*, pp. 16–18.
19. Cromwell flattered Coyet on occasion to make up for the lack of serious progress, usually with the inevitable Protestant propaganda. On 8/18 June, Coyet reported that Cromwell had called the two states 'the two pillars of Protestantism' who 'might hold Europe in subjection', BL Add. Mss 38100, f. 110v.
20. Quoted in Abbott, *Writings and Speeches*, vol. 3, p. 786.
21. *Brieven van Jan de Witt*, vol. 3, p. 92.
22. *Thurloe*, vol. 3, p. 618.
23. Ibid., p. 419.
24. *CSPD 1655*, pp. 201–2; Perfect Diurnal, 28 July (OS).
25. Bonde to Charles X, 23 August/2 September, Stockholm Transcripts quoted by S.R. Gardiner in *History of the Commonwealth and Protectorate*, vol. 4, p. 202.
26. BL Add. Mss 38100, f. 100; and *Thurloe*, vol. 3, p. 729.
27. BL Add. Mss 38100, f. 269v.
28. Ibid., ff. 189, 267.
29. *Urkunden u. Actenstuche*, vol. 7, pp. 713–4, quoted in Abbott, *Writings and Speeches*, vol. 4, p. 835.
30. *CSPD 1655*, pp. 315–17 and p. 325.
31. *Thurloe*, vol. 4, p. 92.
32. Kalling, *Bonde's Ambassadorship*, pp. 34–5; BL Add. Mss 38100, f. 52.
33. Whitelocke, *Memorials of English Affairs*, vol. 4, p. 221.
34. Ibid.
35. Quoted in H. Trevor-Roper, *Religion, the Reformation, and Social Change*.
36. Whitelocke, *Memorials of English Affairs*, pp. 221 et seq.
37. Whitelocke, *Diary*, p. 428.
38. Whitelocke, *Memorials of English Affairs*, vol. 4, p. 222.
39. Ibid.
40. Ibid.
41. Ibid., p. 223; *Diary*, p. 430.
42. Schlezer's report of 25 January/4 February, in *Urkunden u. Actenstuche*, vol. 7, p. 735.
43. Whitelocke, *Memorials*, vol. 4, pp. 223–4.
44. Ibid., *Diary*, p. 431.
45. Ibid., pp. 434–5.

46. Ibid., *Memorials*, vol. 4, p. 232.
47. Ibid., *Diary*, pp. 436–7.
48. As n. 45.
49. Carlbom, *Karl X*, pp. 90–4; BL Add. Mss 38100, f. 370v.
50. *Urkunden u. Actenstuche*, vol. 7, pp. 743–5.
51. Carlbom, *Karl X*, pp. 90–4.
52. Ibid., pp. 90–100.
53. *CSPD 1655*, p. 382.
54. As n. 52.
55. Gardiner, *History of the Commonwealth and Protectorate*, vol. 3, p. 119.

14 Cromwell and the Baltic, 1656–8

1. *CSPD 1655–6*, p. 41; Carlbom, *Karl X*, p. 112.
2. Carlbom, *Karl X*, pp. 112–17.
3. Ibid., p. 118.
4. Cromwell to Charles X, 21/31 August 1655, quoted in Abbott, *Writings and Speeches*, vol. 4.
5. *CSPD 1655*, pp. 50, 95, 115.
6. Ibid., p. 260; Whitelocke, *Diary*, pp. 446–7.
7. *Thurloe*, vol. 5, p. 413.
8. Giavarina, 10/20 October, *CSPV 1655–6*, p. 274.
9. As with the Dutch–Brandenburg Treaty, Cromwell showed no sign of joining other states' inter-Protestant alliances when they could be used against an important ally like Sweden.
10. Cromwell to Frederick III, 8/18 December 1656; Abbott, *Writings and Speeches*, vol. 4.
11. W. Michael, *Cromwell* (1907), vol. 2, pp. 168–9.
12. Ibid., vol. 2, pp. 223–4.
13. PRO SP 95/5/52.
14. *CSPD*, p. 304.
15. Ibid., p. 310.
16. *Thurloe*, vol. 6, p. 279.
17. *CSPD*, p. 291.
18. Ibid., pp. 304, 310.
19. The reform of the constitution and a dangerous Royalist plot including previously unknown malcontents were the most pressing problems – and directly affected the proposed ambassador as Thurloe's deputy.
20. Svenska riksradets protokoll, vol. 17, p. 52, quoted in Roberts, *Essays in Swedish History*, p. 188.
21. *Thurloe*, vol. 6, p. 294.
22. *Urkunden u. Actenstuche*, vol. 8, p. 765.
23. Ibid.
24. *Thurloe*, vol. 6, p. 220.
25. Ibid., vol. 1, pp. 759–63; *Somers Tracts*, vol. 6, p. 332.
26. *Thurloe*, vol. 6, p. 425.
27. Ibid., p. 361.

28. The commissioners were Judge-Advocate William Turner, Walter Walker and Richard Skynner.
29. *Thurloe*, vol. 6, p. 371.
30. Ibid., p. 353–4.
31. Vote of 28 June/8 July 1657.
32. As shown by his reaction to the Vaudois Massacre, see Chapter 6.
33. Giavarina, 7/17 August, *CSPV 1657–8*, pp. 98–9.
34. Quoted in Abbott, *Writings and Speeches*, vol. 4.
35. See Chapter 10 on the crisis in relations over Mardyke.
36. As n. 34.
37. Ibid., pp. 605–7.
38. Giavarina, 4/14 September, *CSPV 1657–8*, p. 103.
39. Carlbom, *Karl X*, pp. 345–9.
40. Carlbom, *Karl X*, pp. 345–9.
41. Ibid.
42. Bowman, *The Protestant Interest*, p. 58.
43. Abbott, *Writings and Speeches*, vol. 4, p. 649.
44. *Thurloe*, vol. 6, pp. 507–8.
45. See Chapter 10.
46. *Thurloe*, vol. 6, p. 533; *Brieven van Jan de Witt*, vol. 1, pp. 441–2.
47. *Thurloe*, vol. 6, p. 515.
48. *Public Intelligencer*, 26 October–2 November (OS).
49. *Thurloe*, vol. 6, pp. 566–7.
50. Ibid., pp. 573–5.
51. Michael, *Cromwell*, vol. 2, pp. 169–71.
52. *Thurloe*, vol. 6, pp. 545–6.
53. Ibid., p. 582.
54. Ibid., p. 727.
55. Ibid., p. 770–1.
56. *EHR*, VII, p. 727.
57. *Thurloe*, vol. 6, pp. 672–3.
58. BL Add. Mss 6125, f. 82.
59. *Thurloe*, vol. 6, pp. 797–801.
60. Ibid., pp. 864–8.
61. *Thurloe*, vol. 6, pp. 802–3.
62. P. Meadowe, *A Short Narrative of the principal actions in the Wars between England and Denmark*, p. 59.
63. *Thurloe*, vol. 6, pp. 766–7.
64. Meadowe, *Narrative*, p. 62.
65. *Thurloe*, vol. 7, p. 113.
66. Ibid., pp. 838–9.
67. Carlbom, *Karl X*, vol. 1, p. 289.
68. *Thurloe*, vol. 7, pp. 836–8.
69. Abbott makes this identification.
70. *EHR*, VII, pp. 734–5.
71. *Public Intelligencer*, 29 March–4/5 April (OS); *EHR*, VII, p. 737.
72. *Thurloe*, vol. 7, p. 150.
73. Cromwell's 'Instructions' to Meadowe, 9/19 April 1658, Abbott, *Writings and Speeches*, vol. 4.

74. *Thurloe*, vol. 7, p. 63.
75. *EHR*, VII, p. 728.

15 Cromwell and Russia, 1653–8

1.   H. Loewenstein, 'Did Russia Intervene after the Execution of Charles
     I?', in *BIHS*, XIII (1940).
2.   *Thurloe*, vol. 3, p. 171.
3.   Ibid.
4.   SP 25/121, entry for 26 May/5 June 1654.
5.   *Thurloe*, vol. 3, pp. 561–2.
6.   Ibid.
7.   Ibid.
8.   Ibid., p. 558.
9.   Ibid.
10. Ibid., p. 562.
11. Ibid., pp. 607–8.
12. Ibid., p. 173.
13. Ibid., pp. 255–7.
14. Ibid.
15. Ibid.
16. Prideaux to Thurloe, 17/27 March 1655, ibid., pp. 255–8. It may be
     significant that Miloslavsky, who unusually for Russian boyars had been
     abroad (on a diplomatic mission to Holland), was head of the chan-
     cellery administering foreign mercenaries (the *retarskoi prikaz*) who
     included Scots Royalist exiles.
17. Prideaux to Thurloe, 18/28 April, ibid., pp. 386–9.
18. Prideaux to Thurloe, 10/20 May, ibid., p. 426.
19. Prideaux to Thurloe, 2/12 July, ibid., p. 601.
20. Ibid., pp. 575–7.
21. As n. 19.
22. As n. 20.
23. Ibid., pp. 711–14.
24. See Chapter 8.
25. *Thurloe*, vol. 3, pp. 575–7.
26. Ibid., p. 601.
27. See Chapter 12.
28. For example, the dispute over the Hamburg merchants' election of
     Towneley as consul.
29. Bradshaw to Thurloe, 31 March/10 April 1657, *Thurloe*, vol. 5, p. 155.
30. Ibid., vol. 6, p. 155 (request for J. Dury).
31. Ibid., p. 278.
32. See Chapter 6.
33. *Thurloe*, vol. 6, p. 278.
34. Ibid., pp. 323–4.
35. Ibid., pp. 407–9, 439–40.
36. Bradshaw to Thurloe, 20/30 October, ibid.
37. Bradshaw to Thurloe, 1/11 November, ibid., p. 603.

38. Bradshaw to Thurloe, 27 November/6 December, ibid., pp. 635–6
     (Duke of Courland's advice). Bradshaw to Thurloe, 4/14 December,
     ibid., p. 651 (titles feared at fault). See also Bradshaw to Thurloe, 18/
     28 December, ibid., p. 607 and 5/15 January 1658, ibid., p. 731.
39. Bradshaw to Thurloe, 26 February/8 March 1658, ibid., pp. 826–7.

16 Cromwell, the City and Trade: Venice and the Turks

1.   BL Egerton Mss 2395, ff. 149–51.
2.   *CSPD 1655–6*, pp. 1–2, 98.
3.   Bernard Capp, *Cromwell's Navy*, pp. 79, 93.
4.   Gardiner, *History of the Commonwealth and Protectorate*, vol. 4, p. 150.
5.   Ibid., vol. i, p. 315.
6.   *Mercurius Politicus* E.826, 16, quoted in ibid., vol. 6, p. 149.
7.   Paulucci, 22 August 1654 (NS); *CSPV*, pp. 249–51.
8.   BL Add. Mss 9304, f. 99.
9.   BL Add. Mss 9304, f. 99.
10. Blake to Thurloe, 14/24 March 1655; *Thurloe*, vol. 3, p. 232.
11. Blake to Thurloe, 14/24 April, ibid., p. 390.
12. Dey to Blake, 7/17 April 1655, quoted in Gardiner, *History of the
     Commonwealth and Protectorate*, vol. 4, p. 157.
13. Boothouse's printed account in 1653, *A Brief Remonstrance of Several
     National Injuries perpetrated on the public Ministers and subjects of the
     Commonwealth by the Dey of Tunis*.
14. Longland to Thurloe, 8/18 June 1655, *Thurloe*, vol. 3, p. 526.
15. Giavarina to Senate, 8/18 May 1657, *CSPV 1657–9*, p. 55.
16. Giavarina to Senate, 29 May/8 June 1657, ibid., p. 67; and ditto, 26
     June/6 July, ibid., p. 79.
17. *CSPD 1657–8*, pp. 307–8.
18. Levant Company Court Book (PRO SP 105/151): entries for 15/25
     May and 23 May/2 June 1655.
19. *Merc. Fum.*, 27 June–4 July 1655 (OS).
20. Reported in Bendish's letter to the Levant Company, 5/15 June 1657,
     Levant Company Letter Book (PRO SP 105/112), p. 292.
21. Levant Company Court Book (PRO SP 105/151): election courts,
     January 1655, February 1656, February 1658.
22. Paulucci to Senate, 21/31 January 1654, *CSPV 1653–4*, pp. 177–8.
23. Paulucci to Senate, 28 July/7 August 1654, ibid., pp. 243–4.
24. Paulucci to Senate, 26 August/5 September 1654, ibid., pp. 255–6.
25. Paulucci to Senate, 19 February/1 March 1655, *CSPV 1655–6*, pp.
     24–6.
26. Giavarina to Senate, 29 August/8 September 1655, ibid., pp. 257–8.
27. Cromwell to Bendish, 19/29 October 1655, PRO SP 97/17, f. 131.
28. Giavarina to Senate, 22 August/1 September 1656, *CSPV 1655–6*, pp.
     290–2.
29. Giavarina to Senate, 29 November/8 December 1657, *CSPV 1657–8*,
     pp. 265–6.
30. Cromwell was reported to be 'much incensed'.

31. Abbott, *Writings and Speeches*, vol. 4, pp. 598–9.
32. As n. 29.
33. Thurloe requested Venice to include Galilee in a prisoner-exchange with the Turks in February 1657: Giavarina to Senate, 13/23 February 1657, *CSPV 1657–8*, pp. 18–19. The case was already over three years old, Galilee's father having petitioned the Council on 14/24 April 1654 (SP 25/75, Council Order Book) and heard that the Senate had issued orders to deal with it in 1654 (*CSPV 1653–4*, pp. 233–4).
34. *Thurloe*, vol. 5, p. 749.
35. Longland to Thurloe, 6/16 November 1657, ibid., vol. 4, pp. 607–8.

17 The Financial Aspects of Foreign Policy

1. As illustrated in the evidence of resistance to County Committees cited by John Morrill in *The Rebellion of the Provinces: Conservatives and Radicals in the English Civil War, 1630–50* (London: Allen & Unwin, 1976), pp. 125–30, 204–5.
2. 'Constitutionalism' was otherwise apparent in the search for precedents to justify current actions in Parliament – hence the interest of men like Sir Robert Bruce Cotton in pre-Norman legality.
3. See Ivan Roots, 'Swordsmen and Decimators: Oliver Cromwell's Major-Generals', in R.H. Parry (ed.), *The English Civil War and After* (London: Macmillan, 1970), pp. 59–77.
4. See Chapter 1.
5. BL Egerton Mss 2395, ff. 149–51.
6. Maurice Ashley, *Financial and Commercial Policy under the Cromwellian Protectorate*, passim.
7. Also, more privateers would have been available to take Spanish treasure in the West Indies in 1655–6.
8. Nicholas to Hyde, 21 March 1656, *CSPD 1655–6*, p. 276.
9. Chapter 10, n. 50.
10. BL Sloane Mss 3271.
11. BL Add. Mss 11411, ff. 11–12.
12. BL Egerton Mss 2395, ff. 87–8.
13. Ibid., f. 108.
14. Ibid., f. 110.
15. See Chapter 5.
16. BL Add. Mss 11411, f. 15.
17. E.B. Sainsbury (ed.), *Court Minutes of the East India Company*, p. v.
18. Maurice Thompson's petitions, 21 September 1654 (NS), PRO CO 77, vii, no. 80; 14 November (NS), ibid., no. 83; East India Company petitions, October 1654, ibid., no. 82; November 1654, ibid., no. 85.
19. Evidence of Thurloe's perceived importance in decision-making.
20. The importance of the Dutch was one reason for Cromwell to avoid antagonising them by supporting Noell and Thompson – especially after the outbreak of the Spanish War.
21. See the debates on policy in Chapters 3 and 4.
22. See Chapter 5, *Inadequacies of the Expedition*.

23. On 15 March (NS) 1658 Longland proposed hiring ships for trade under 'flags of convenience' – albeit partly to help the war effort by enquiring about the defences of Peru at Buenos Aires, *Thurloe*, vol. 6, p. 45.
24. See account in Burton's *Diary*, vol. 3.
25. As Cromwell had hoped in April 1654, *Clarke Papers*, vol. 3, pp. 203–6.
26. As n. 6.
27. BL Add. Mss 11411, f. 25.
28. PRO SP 28/334.
29. *Clarke Papers*, vol. 3, p. 61.
30. HMC *Reports*, vol. 5, p. 165.
31. Ashley, *Financial and Commercial Policy*, p. 69.
32. BL Add. Mss 2884 and 4156.
33. BL Add. Mss 2884.
34. See Chapter 8.
35. BL Egerton Mss 403.
36. See in particular the recent work of Roy Strong on Prince Henry's artistic patronage.
37. As n. 33.
38. As n. 32.
39. Estimate of 5 December 1659 (NS), in PRO E403/1757.
40. Bodleian Library, Carte Mss 74, f. 763 (Army cost); BL Rawlinson Mss A195, f. 241 (Navy cost).
41. BL Add. Mss 2884.
42. Bodleian Library, Carte Mss 74, ff. 63–5.
43. BL Add. Mss 22919, f. 11.

Bibliography

Manuscripts

Public Record Office, London
SP   18: State Papers Domestic
      65–77, 1654
      94–102, 1655
      123–31, 1656
      153–7, 1657
      179–83, 1658

SP   25: State Papers Domestic
      47–60, Council of State Order Books, December 1653 to March 1656
      75, Council of State Order Book 1654–6
      77, Council of State Order Book, March 1656 to September 1657
      78a, Council of State Order Book, July 1657 to September 1658
      121, Council of State Committee Book 1653–4
      122, Council of State Committee Book, 1655–6

SP   31/3: French Transcripts. Despatches of the French ambassadors in London and correspondence from Mazarin and his ministers.
      31/3/92, November 1653 to January 1654
      to 31/3/102, 1658

SP   31/12/43, correspondence of Cardenas with Madrid
SP   77/1, Algiers, 1595–1670
SP   71/22, Tripoli
SP   77/31, Flanders
SP   78/113, France 1650–7
SP   84/160, Holland, 1654–5
SP   84/161, Holland, 1655–6
SP   84/162, Holland, 1657–9
SP   94/43, Spain
SP   97/17, Turkey
SP   98/4, Tuscany
SP   103/46, Holland Treaties
SP   105/112, Levant Company Letter-Book, 1647–62
SP   105/151, Levant Company Court Book, 1648–60
SP   108/54, French Treaty, 1657
SP   108/55, French Treaty, 1658
SP   108/57, Portuguese Treaty Papers
SP   108/386, Portuguese Treaty Ratification
SP   108/516, Swedish Treaty
Colonial Office Papers 77:   East India Company Papers

British Library
Additional Manuscripts 2884, 4156, 6125, 11411, 35252, 298456, 32093
Egerton Manuscripts 2095, 2395
Lansdowne Manuscripts 745, 822
Stowe Manuscripts 185, 192
Thomason Manuscripts

Bodleian Library
Carte Manuscripts 74
Rawlinson Manuscripts A261
Tanner Manuscripts 52

Madrid: National Archives
Simancas Manuscripts.

Primary Sources

ABBOTT, W.C., *Writings and Speeches of Oliver Cromwell*, 4 vols (Cambridge: Cambridge University Press, 1937–47).
Brieven van Jan der Witt (Amsterdam, 1724).
BURTON, THOMAS, *Diary* (introduction by Ivan Roots) (reprint 1974).
BURNET, GILBERT, *History of my own Times*, ed. Osmund Airy (London, 1897).
Calendar of the Clarendon Papers Preserved in the Bodleian Library, 4 vols, ed. W.D. Macray (vols. 2 and 3) and C. Firth (vol. 4) (Oxford, 1882).
Calendar of State Papers Colonial 1574–1660, ed. W.D. Sainsbury (Longmans Green, 1860).
Calendar of State Papers Domestic Preserved in the State Paper Department of Her Majesty's Public Record Office, ed. Mary Everett Green: 1654 (1880), 1655 (1881), 1655–6 (1882), 1656–7 (1883), 1657–8 (1884), 1658–9 (1885).
Calendar of State Papers relating to English Affairs in the Archives of Venice . . . (Calendar of State Papers Venetian), ed. Allen B. Hindes: 1647–52 (1927), 1653–4 (1929), 1655–6 (1930), 1657–9 (1931).
CARLYLE, THOMAS, *Letters and Speeches of Oliver Cromwell with Elucidations by Thomas Carlyle*, ed. T.C. Lomas (3 vols, London, 1904).
CLARENDON, EDWARD HYDE, Earl of, *A History of the Rebellion and Civil Wars in England begun in 1641*, ed. W. Dunn Macray (Oxford: Clarendon Press, 6 vols, 1888).
The Clarke Papers, 4 vols, ed. C. Firth, Camden Society (London, 1891–1901).
EVELYN, JOHN, *Diary*, ed. E. de Beer (Oxford: Oxford University Press, 1959).
FIRTH, C. and RAIT, H. (eds), *Acts and Ordinances of the Interregnum 1642–60* (London, 3 vols, 1911).
GAGE, THOMAS, *The English–American His Travails by Sea and Land: or a New Survey of the West Indias*, ed. A. Newton (London: Routledge Press, 1928).

Harleian Miscellany, 10 vols, with additional notes by Thomas Park (London, 1808).

LUDLOW, EDMUND, *Memoirs*, ed. C. Firth, 2 vols (Oxford: Clarendon Press, 1894).

Marvell, Poems and Letters of Andrew, ed. H.M. Margoliouth, 3 vols (Oxford: Clarendon Press, 1971).

Mazarin, Lettres de Cardinal, ed. A. Chéruel (Paris: G. D'Avenel, 1890–4).

MEADOWE, PHILIP, *History of the Evangelical Churches of the Valleys of Piedmont and . . . the Late Bloody Massacre* (London, 1658).

MEADOWE, PHILIP, *A Short Narrative of the Principal Actions in the Wars between England and Denmark* (London, 1677).

PENN, GRANVILLE, *Memorials of the Professional Life and Times of Sir William Penn, 1644–70*, 2 vols (London: James Duncan, 1833).

Public Intelligencer newsletter.

SAINSBURY, E.B. (ed.), *Court Minutes of the East India Company, 1635–79*, 11 vols (Oxford, 1907–8).

SCOTT, W. (ed.), *Somers Tracts*, 13 vols (London, 1809–15).

STOUPPE, JEAN-BAPTISTE, *A Collection of Several Papers sent to His Highness Concerning the Bloody and Barbarous Massacres in Piedmont* (London, 1658).

Thurloe, State Papers of John, ed. Thomas Birch, 7 vols (London, 1742).

WHITELOCKE, BULSTRODE, *Diary*, ed. Ruth Spalding (1990).

WHITELOCKE, BULSTRODE, *Memorials of English Affairs from the Beginning of the Reign of Charles the First to the Happy Restoration of Charles the Second, 1682* (4 vols, 1853 edition).

WHITELOCKE, BULSTRODE, *Journal of the Swedish Embassy*, 2 vols (London, 1855).

Secondary Sources

ANDREWES, CHARLES M., *British Committees, Commissions and Councils of Trade and Navigation*, 3 vols (Baltimore, 1908).

ANDREWES, CHARLES M., *The Colonial Period of American History: The Settlements*, vol. 2 (New Haven, Conn.: Yale University Press, 1906).

ASHLEY, MAURICE, *Financial and Commercial Policy under the Cromwellian Protectorate* (London: Jonathan Cape, 1934).

ASHLEY, MAURICE, *Cromwell's Generals* (London: Jonathan Cape, 1954).

ASHLEY, MAURICE, *The Greatness of Oliver Cromwell* (London: Hodder & Stoughton, 1957).

AUBREY, PHILIP, *Mr Secretary Thurloe: Cromwell's Secretary of State 1652–60* (London: Athlone Press, 1990).

AYLMER, G.E., *The State's Servants: The Civil Service of the English Republic 1649–1660* (London: Routledge & Kegan Paul, 1961).

BOWMAN, J. *The Protestant Interest in Cromwell's Foreign Relations* (Heidelberg, 1900).

CAPP, BERNARD, *Cromwell's Navy: The Fleet and the English Revolution 1648–60* (Oxford: Clarendon Press, 1989).

CARLBOM, J.L., *Karl X Gustav, Fran Welchseln till Balt 1657. Taget over Balt och freden i Roskilde 1658* (Stockholm, 1910).

CORBETT, J., *England in the Mediterranean: A Study of the Rise and Influence of British Sea Power under the Stuarts, 1603–1714*, 2 vols (London: Longmans Green, 1904).

CUNDALL, F., *The Governors of Jamaica in the Seventeenth Century* (London, 1936).

DAWSON, W.H., *Cromwell's Understudy: The Life and Times of General John Lambert* (London: William Hodge, 1938).

FALLON, R. THOMAS, *Milton in Government* (Pittsburgh: University of Pennsylvania, 1993).

FIRTH, C.H., *The Last Years of the Protectorate*, 2 vols (London: Longmans, 1909).

FISHER, GODFREY, *Barbary Legend* (Oxford: Oxford University Press, 1957).

FRASER, ANTONIA, *Cromwell, our Chief of Men* (London: Weidenfeld & Nicolson, 1973).

GARDINER, S.R., *Cromwell's Place in History: Six Lectures delivered to the University of Oxford* (London: Longmans, 1898).

GARDINER, S.R,. *History of the Great Civil War*, 4 vols (London, Windrush Press repr, 1987).

GARDINER, S.R. *History of the Commonwealth and Protectorate, 1649–56*, 4 vols (London: Longmans Green, 1903).

GARDINER, S.R., *Oliver Cromwell* (London: Longmans Green, 1901).

GEYL, PIETER, *Orange and Stuart, 1641–72* (London: Weidenfeld & Nicolson, 1969).

GUIZOT, FRANÇOIS, *History of Oliver Cromwell and the English Civil War*, trans. A.R. Scoble (London, 1854).

HALEY, K.H.D., *The First Earl of Shaftesbury* (Oxford: Clarendon Press, 1968).

HARLOW, VINCENT, *History of Barbados, 1625–85* (Oxford: Oxford University Press, 1926).

HILL, CHRISTOPHER, *God's Englishman: Oliver Cromwell and the English Revolution* (London: Weidenfeld & Nicolson, 1970).

ISRAEL, JONATHAN, *The Dutch Republic and the Hispanic World, 1606–61* (Oxford: Oxford University Press, 1982).

JONES, C., NEWITT, S. and ROBERTS, S., *Politics and People in Revolutionary England: Essays in Honour of Ivan Roots* (Oxford: Basil Blackwell, 1986).

KALLING, P. *Riksradet Christer Bondes Ambassad Till England 1655* (Uppsala, 1851).

KNATCHEL, PHILIP A., *England and the Fronde* (New York: Cornell University Press, 1967).

KORR, CHARLES P.N., *Oliver Cromwell and the New Model Foreign Policy* (Berkeley: University of California Press, 1977).

LAMONT, WILLIAM M., *Godly Rule: Politics and Religion 1603–60* (London: Macmillan, 1969).

LOCKYER, ROGER, *Buckingham: The Life and Career of George Villiers 1592–1628* (London: Longmans, 1981).

MALTBY, WILLIAM S., *The Black Legend in England: The Development of Anti-Spanish Sentiment, 1558–1660* (Durham, NC: Duke University Press, 1978).

MASSON, D., *The Life of John Milton* (London, 1877).

MICHAEL, WOLFGANG, *Oliver Cromwell*, 2 vols (Berlin, 1907).

OLLARD, RICHARD, *Cromwell's Earl: A Life of Edward Mountagu 1st Earl of Sandwich* (London: HarperCollins, 1994).

PAUL, ROBERT, *The Lord Protector: Religion and Politics in the Life of Oliver Cromwell* (Lutterworth Press, 1955).

POWELL, J.R., *Robert Blake, General At Sea* (London: Collins, 1972).

ROBERTS, MICHAEL, *Essays in Swedish History* (London: Weidenfeld & Nicolson, 1953).

ROBERTS, MICHAEL, *Swedish Diplomats at Cromwell's Court* (London: Camden Society, 4th Series, 1988).

ROOTS IVAN, (ed.), *Cromwell: A Profile* (London: Macmillan, 1973).

ROUTLEDGE, F.J., *England and the Treaty of the Pyrenees 1659* (London, 1953).

ROWE, VIOLET, *Sir Henry Vane the Younger: A Study in Political and Administrative History* (London: Athlone Press, 1970).

ROWEN, H.R., *John de Witt, Grand Pensionary of Holland, 1625–72* (Princeton: Princeton University Press, 1978).

RUIGH, ROBERT E., *The Parliament of 1624: Politics and Foreign Policy* (Cambridge, Mass.: Harvard University Press, 1971).

SALMON, J.H., *Retz: Anatomy of a Conspirator* (London: Weidenfeld & Nicolson, 1969).

SHARPE, KEVIN, *The Personal Rule of Charles I* (New Haven: Yale University Press, 1992).

SHERWOOD, ROY, *The Court of Oliver Cromwell* (London: Croom Helm, 1977).

SPALDING, RUTH, *The Improbable Puritan: A Life of Bulstrode Whitelocke, 1605–75* (London: Faber & Faber, 1975).

STEARNS, R.W. *The Strenuous Puritan: A Life of Hugh Peter* (Urbana Illinois: Illinois University Press, 1954).

SYMMONS, CHARLES, *Life of Milton* (London, 1806).

TOMLINSON H., (ed.), *Before the English Civil War* (London: Macmillan, 1983).

TREVOR-ROPER, HUGH, *Religion, the Reformation, and Social Change* (Oxford: Clarendon Press, 1956).

TURNBULL, G.H., *Dury, Hartlib, and Comenius: Gleanings from Hartlib's Papers* (Liverpool: University Press of Liverpool; London: Hodder & Stoughton, 1947).

UNDERDOWN, DAVID, *Royalist Conspiracy in England 1649–60* (New Haven, Conn.: Yale University Press, 1960).

VAUGHAN, R., *The Protectorate of Oliver Cromwell* (London, 1839).

WEBSTER, CHARLES, *The Great Instauration: Science, Medicine and Social Reform 1626–60* (London: Duckworth, 1975).

WILLIAMSON, J.A., *The Caribbee Islands Under the Proprietory Patents* (Oxford: Oxford University Press, 1926).

WILSON, C.H., *Profit and Power: England and the Dutch Wars* (London: Weldenfeld & Nicolson, 1955).

WOOLRYCH, AUSTIN, *Commonwealth to Protectorate* (Oxford: Clarendon Press, 1982).

WORDEN, BLAIR, *The Rump Parliament, 1649–1653* (Cambridge: Cambridge University Press, 1977).

Articles

BEER, GEORGE L., 'Cromwell's Policy in its Economic Aspects', *Political Science Quarterly*, XVI (1901), pp. 582–611.

FIRTH, C.H., 'Cromwell and the Insurrection of 1655', *English Historical Review (EHR)*, III (1898), pp. 313–50.

FIRTH, C.H., 'Cromwell's Instructions to Lockhart, 1656', *English Historical Review*, XXI (1906), pp. 742–6.

FIRTH, C.H., 'Royalist and Cromwellian Armies in Flanders, 1651–61', *Transactions of the Royal Historical Society (TRHS)*, XVII (1903), pp. 69–110.

GAUNT, P., 'The Single Person's Confidants and Dependants: Oliver Cromwell and his Protectoral Councillors', *Historical Journal*, XXXII (1989), pp. 537–60.

KEEN, B., 'The Black Legend Revisited', *Hispanic American Review*, XLIX (1969), pp. 703–19.

KUPPERMANN, K., 'Errand to the Indies: Puritan Colonization from Providence Island through the Western Design', *William and Mary Quarterly*, XLV (1988), pp. 70–99.

LOEWENSTEIN, H., 'Did Russia Intervene after the Execution of Charles I?', *Bulletin of the Institute of Historical Research (BIHS)*, XIII (1940).

LOOMIE, A.J., 'Alonso de Cardenas and the Long Parliament 1640–8', *English Historical Review*, VII (1902), pp. 289–307.

PRESTWICH, MENNA, 'Diplomacy and Trade under the Protectorate', *Journal of Modern History* (1950), pp. 103–21.

STRONG, F., 'Causes of Cromwell's West Indies Expedition', in *American Historical Review*, IV (1898–9), pp. 228–45.

SWAINE, S.R., 'The English Acquisition and Loss of Dunkirk', *Transactions of the Royal Historical Society*, I (1884), pp. 69–110.

VENNING, TIMOTHY, 'Cromwell's Foreign Policy and the Western Design', *Cromwelliana* (1994), pp. 41–52.

WOOLRYCH, AUSTIN, 'The Cromwellian Protectorate: A Military Dictatorship?', *History*, LXXV (1990), pp. 207–31.

Index

301